Leadership and Decision-Making Skills Vol. 2

TECH 3013

Rogers State University

create.mheducation.com

ISBN-13: 9781308104362

ISBN-10: 1308104367

Contents

Focus on the Followers

Part

3

Focus on the Followers

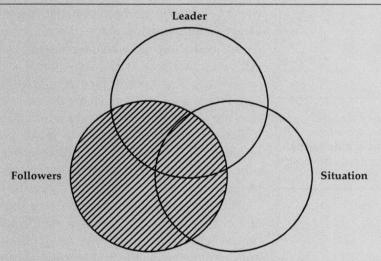

We began Part 2 with the notion that the individual leader is the most critical element of leadership. We begin Part 3 by qualifying that sentiment. Although the importance of a good leader cannot be denied, followers play an equally important, if often overlooked, role in the success of any group or organization. There can be no leaders without followers, but most research to date has focused on leadership. Researchers have only recently given serious consideration to the topics of followers and followership.

This research has revealed several interesting questions and findings. First, virtually everyone is a follower at some point in his or her life. And perhaps more importantly, anyone occupying a position of authority plays a followership role at times: first-line supervisors report to midlevel managers, midlevel managers report to vice presidents, vice presidents report to CEOs, and CEOs report to boards of directors. Because the same people play both leadership and followership roles, it is hardly surprising that the values, bases of power, personality traits, mental abilities, and behaviors used to describe effective leaders can also be used to describe effective followers. Followers vary in all the same ways that leaders vary.

Second, there are times when situational demands require that individuals in formal followership roles step into leadership roles. For example, a sergeant may take over a platoon when her lieutenant is wounded in battle, a volunteer may take over a community group when the leader moves away, a software engineer may be asked to lead a project because of unique programming skills, or team members can be asked to make decisions about team goals, work priorities, meeting schedules, and the like. That being the case, followers who are perceived to be the most effective are most likely to be asked to take the lead when opportunities arise. So understanding what constitutes effective followership and exhibiting those behaviors can help improve a person's promotion opportunities. Effective followership plays such an important role in the development of future leadership skills that freshman at all the U.S. service academies (the Air Force, Army, Navy, Coast Guard, and Merchant Marine Academies) spend their first year in formal follower roles. Following the path set by the service academies, perhaps the most effective people in any organization are those who are equally adept at playing *both* leadership and followership roles. Many people make great leaders but ultimately fail because of their inability to follow orders or get along with peers. And other people are great at following orders but cause teams to fail because of their reluctance to step into leadership roles.

Better followership often begets better leadership.
Barbara Kellerman, Harvard University

Third, it is important to remember the vital role followers play in societal change and organizational performance. The Civil Rights and more recent Tea Party movements are good examples of what happens when angry followers decide to do something to change the status quo. And this is precisely why totalitarian societies, such as North Korea, Myanmar, or Iran, tightly control the amount and type of information flowing through their countries. Organizational leaders should treat followers as important assets because they are the people creating the products, taking orders, serving customers, and collecting payments. Research has consistently shown that more engaged employees are happier, more productive, and more likely to stay with organizations than those who are disengaged.[1] Moreover, ethical followers can help leaders avoid making questionable decisions, and high-performing followers often motivate leaders to raise their own levels of performance.[2,3] Wars are usually won by armies with the best soldiers, teams with the best athletes usually win the most games, and companies with the best employees usually outperform their competitors—so it is to a leader's benefit to choose the best followers.[4]

Fourth, although asking why anyone would want to be a leader is an interesting question, perhaps a more interesting question is asking why anyone would want to be a follower. Being a leader clearly has some advantages, but why would anyone freely choose to be a subordinate to someone else? Why would you be a follower? Evolutionary psychology hypothesizes that people follow because the benefits of doing so outweigh the costs of going it alone or fighting to become the leader of a group.[5] Thousands of years ago most people lived in small, nomadic groups, and these groups offered individuals more protection, resources for securing food, and mating opportunities than they would have had on their own. The groups with the best leaders and followers were more likely to survive, and those poorly led or consisting of bad followers were more likely to starve. Followers who were happy with the costs and benefits of membership stayed with the group; those who were not either left to join other groups or battled for the top spots. Evolutionary psychology also rightly points out that leaders and followers can often have different goals and agendas. In the workplace, leaders may be making decisions to maximize financial performance, whereas followers may be acting to improve job security. Therefore, leaders adopting an evolutionary psychology approach to followership must do all they can to align followers' goals with those of the organization and ensure that the benefits people accrue outweigh the costs of working for the leader; followers will either mutiny or leave if goals are misaligned or inequities are perceived.

However, social psychology tells us that something other than cost–benefit analyses may be happening when people choose to play followership roles. In some situations people seem too willing to abdicate responsibility and follow orders, even when it is morally offensive to do so. The famous Milgram experiments of the 1950s demonstrated that people would follow orders, even to the point of hurting others, if told to do so by someone they perceived to be in a position of authority. You would think the infamy of the Milgram research would subsequently inoculate people from following morally offensive or unethical orders, but a recent replication of the Milgram experiments showed that approximately 75 percent of both men and women will follow the orders of complete strangers who they believe occupy some position of authority.[6] Sadly, the genocides of Bosnia, Rwanda, Darfur, and Syria may be real examples of the Milgram effect. For leadership practitioners, this research shows that merely occupying positions of authority grants leaders a certain amount of influence over the actions of their followers. Leaders need to use this influence wisely.

Social psychology also tells us that identification with leaders and trust are two other reasons why people choose to follow. Much of the research in Chapter 14 concerning charismatic and transformational leadership shows that a leader's personal magnetism can draw in followers and convince them to take action. This effect can be so strong as to cause followers to give their lives for a cause. The terrorist attacks of September 11, 2001; the Mumbai, Bali, and London Tube bombings; the attempted bombing of a Delta airlines flight in December 2009; and suicide bomber attacks in Iraq and Afghanistan are examples of the personal magnetism of Osama bin Laden and the Al-Qaeda cause. Although most people do not have the personal magnetism of an Osama bin Laden or a Martin Luther King, those who do need to decide whether they will use their personal magnetism for good or evil.

Trust is a common factor in these hypotheses of cost–benefit analysis, compliance with authority, or willing identification with leaders. It is unlikely that people will follow leaders they do not trust.[3] It can be hard to rebuild trust once it has been broken, and followers' reactions to lost trust typically include disengagement, leaving, or seeking revenge on their leaders. Many acts of poor customer service, organizational delinquency, and workplace violence can be directly attributed to disgruntled followers,[7] and the economic downturn put considerable strain on trust between leaders and followers. Many leaders, particularly in the financial services industry, seemed happy to wreck the global economy and lay off thousands of employees while collecting multimillion-dollar compensation packages. Given the lack of trust between leaders and followers in many organizations these days, we have to wonder what will happen to the best and brightest followers once jobs become more readily available. Because of the importance of trust in team and organizational performance, leaders need to do all they can to maintain strong, trusting relationships with followers.

The final question or finding of the followership research concerns follower frameworks. Over the past 40 years or so researchers such as Hollander,[3] Zaleznik,[8] Kelley,[9] Chaleff,[10] Kellerman,[11] Adair,[12] McCroskey and colleagues,[13] Potter and Rosenbach,[14] and Curphy[15] have developed various models for describing different types of followers. These models are intended to provide leaders with additional insight into what motivates followers and how to improve individual and team performance. The frameworks developed by these researchers usually describe three to six different followers types and have more similarities than differences; for illustration a more detailed description of two of these models follows.

The Potter and Rosenbach Followership Model

Potter and Rosenbach[14] believe follower inputs are vital to team performance because followers are closest to the action and often have the best solutions to problems. Their model is based on two independent dimensions, which include follower performance levels and the strength of leader–follower relationships. The performance initiative dimension is concerned with the extent to which an individual follower can do his or her job, works effectively with other members of the team, embraces change, and views himself or herself as an important asset in team performance. Followers receiving higher scores on this dimension are competent, get along well with others, support leaders' change initiatives, and take care of themselves; those with lower scores do not have the skills needed to perform their jobs, do not get along with others, and actively resist change. The relationship initiative dimension is concerned with the degree to which followers act to improve their working relationships with their leaders. Followers receiving higher scores on this dimension are loyal and identify with their leaders' vision of the future but will raise objections and negotiate differences when need be; those with lower scores are disloyal, will not raise objectives even when it would be beneficial to do so, and pursue their own agendas even when they are misaligned with those of their boss.

Because the performance and relationship initiatives are independent dimensions, they can be placed on vertical and horizontal axes and used to describe four different types of followers. As shown in the diagram, the different types of followers include subordinates, contributors, politicians, and partners. Subordinates are followers in the more traditional sense; they do what they are told, follow the rules, are low to medium performers, and do not have particularly good relationships with their leaders. These individuals often rise in more bureaucratic, hierarchical organizations because they tend to remain with organizations for long periods, stay out of trouble, and do not make waves.

Potter and Rosenbach Followership Model

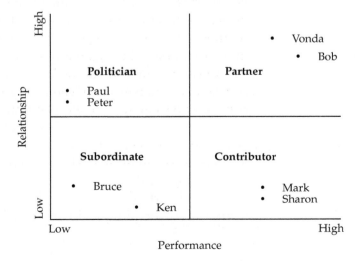

Contributors are different in that they are hard workers and often are motivated to be subject matter experts in their organizations. Although these individuals can be great researchers, programmers, or accountants, they have no interest in interpersonal dynamics or building stronger relationships with their leaders. They rarely seek out their leaders' perspectives, generally wait for direction, and work best in jobs where they can be left alone to do their thing.

Politicians are an interesting group: these individuals put much more emphasis on getting along well with their boss than getting things done. They are loyal and sensitive to interpersonal dynamics, and as such can give leaders good insights into other team members. There appear to be two types of politicians—some delight in playing the game and are good in positions that require lots of interaction with others. They often confuse activity with productivity, can be administratively challenged, and can often be found in sales or public relations because they are good at talking to people and closing deals. The other type of politician tends to be manipulative, selfish, and have unhealthy needs to be the center of attention. These people play games, start rumors, get little done but take credit for others' work, and jockey to been seen as indispensable to their leaders. Leaders who fall under this type of politician's spell often have teams with poor morale and performance.

Partners are individuals who are committed to high performance and building good relationships with their leaders. Partners take the time to understand their leaders' perspectives and buy into their vision for the team. Because they are strongly motivated to make an impact, partners work closely with their leaders to identify issues and work out solutions. Unlike politicians, partners are much more likely to raise uncomfortable issues and hold leaders accountable for decisions.

Several aspects of the Potter and Rosenbach followership model are worthy of additional comment. First, the situation plays an important role in determining followership types. Some individuals may be partners in one software firm but subordinates in another firm or may move from contributor to subordinate when working for a new boss. Organizational culture, the demands of the position, available resources, other team members, and the leader all affect followership types. Second, although it is natural for leaders to think partners make the best followers, Potter and Rosenbach maintain that all four types of followers can play valuable roles in organizations. Nonetheless, if leaders want to surround themselves with partners, they need to create team climates that encourage effective followership. To do this, leaders must clearly spell out their performance and relationship expectations for followers. Leaders also need to role model partner behavior for their followers when given opportunities to do so, seek followers' input on issues and decisions, and do debriefings on projects to demonstrate effective followership and build trust. If leaders take all these actions and team members choose to remain subordinates, contributors, or politicians, then leaders may want to consider replacing these individuals with those who have the potential to become partners.

Third, the Potter and Rosenbach followership model is useful in that it helps leaders understand their own followership type, the different kinds of followers, what kind of followers they currently have, and what they can do to create effective followership. As depicted in the figure, leaders often find followership scatter plots helpful in determining how to best motivate and lead members of their teams.

However, this model has two potential drawbacks. First, the model puts much of the onus of effective followership on followers. It is up to followers to identify with their leaders, buy into their leaders' vision, raise objections, and perform at a high level. But it is difficult for followers to take these actions if their leaders have not articulated a compelling vision of the future, encouraged constructive feedback, or provided the resources needed for followers to perform at high levels. Here we see that leaders and followers play equally important roles in effective followership.

This leads us to the second drawback of the model. As we will discuss in more detail in Chapter 15, it may be that more than half the people occupying positions of authority are unable to build teams or get results through others. That being the case, what happens to followership when the leader is incompetent, unethical, or evil? The Potter and Rosenbach model states that the situation plays an important role in effective followership, but it may not take into account the role that ineffective leadership plays in followership. The next model, however, considers the role incompetent leadership plays on followership.

The Curphy and Roellig Followership Model

The Curphy and Roellig followership model[15] builds on some of the earlier followership research of Hollander,[3] Kelley,[9] Chaleff,[10] and Kellerman[11] and is similar to the Potter and Rosenbach model in that it also consists of two independent dimensions and four followership types. The two dimensions of the Curphy and Roellig model are critical thinking and engagement. Critical thinking is concerned with a follower's ability to challenge the status quo, ask good questions, detect problems, and develop solutions. High scorers on critical thinking are constantly

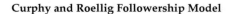

Curphy and Roellig Followership Model

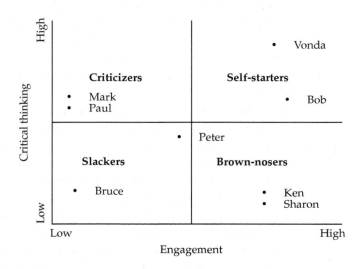

identifying ways to improve productivity or efficiency, drive sales, reduce costs, and so forth; those with lower scores believe it is the role of management to identify and solve problems.

Engagement is concerned with the level of effort people put forth at work. High scorers are optimistic and hardworking, put in long hours when needed, are enthusiastic about being part of the team, and are driven to achieve results; low scorers are lazy and disengaged and would rather be doing anything but the task at hand.

Like the Potter and Rosenbach followership model, the Curphy and Roellig model can be used to assess current followership types. Self-starters, such as Bob and Vonda in the figure, are individuals who are passionate about the team and will exert considerable effort to make it successful. They are also constantly thinking of ways to improve team performance as they raise issues, develop solutions, and enthusiastically carry out change initiatives.[16] When encountering problems, self-starters are apt to resolve issues and then tell their leaders what they did rather than waiting to be told what to do. This followership type also helps to improve their leaders' performance because they will voice opinions prior to and provide constructive feedback after bad decisions.[17]

Self-starters are a significant component of high-performing teams and are by far the most effective followership type. Leaders who want to have these followers should keep in mind the underlying psychological driver of this type and the behaviors they need to exhibit if they want to encourage self-starters. In terms of the underlying psychological driver, leaders need to understand that self-starters fundamentally lack patience. They do not suffer fools gladly and expect their leaders to promptly clear obstacles and acquire the resources needed to succeed. Leaders who consistently make bad decisions, dither, or fail to quickly secure needed resources or follow through on commitments are not apt to have self-starters on their teams. It is important for leaders wanting to encourage self-starters to articulate a clear vision and goals for their teams because this type operates by seeking forgiveness rather than permission. If self-starters do not know where the team is going, they may make decisions and take actions that are counterproductive. And self-starters whose decisions get overruled too many times are likely to disengage and become criticizers or slackers. In addition to making sure they understand the team's vision and goals, leaders also need to provide self-starters with needed resources, interesting and challenging work, plenty of latitude and regular performance feedback, recognition for strong performance, and promotion opportunities.[18] The bottom line is that self-starters can be highly rewarding but challenging team members, and leaders need to bring their best game to work if they want to successfully manage these followers.

Brown-nosers, such as Ken and Sharon in the figure, share the strong work ethic but lack the critical thinking skills of self-starters. Brown-nosers are earnest, dutiful, conscientious, and loyal employees who will do whatever their leaders ask them to do. They never point out problems, raise objections, or make any waves, and they do whatever they can to please their bosses. Brown-nosers constantly check in with their leaders and operate by seeking permission rather than forgiveness. It is not surprising that many leaders surround themselves with brown-nosers—these individuals are sources of constant flattery and tell everyone how lucky they are to be working for such great bosses. It may also not be surprising that brown-nosers often go quite far in organizations, particularly those not having good performance metrics. Organizations lacking clear goals and measures of performance often make personnel decisions on the basis of politics, and brown-nosers work hard to have no enemies (they can never tell who their next boss will be) and as such play politics well.

Because brown-nosers will not bring up bad news, put everything in a positive light, never raise objections to bad decisions, and are reluctant to make decisions, teams and organizations consisting of high percentages of brown-nosers are highly dependent on their leaders to be successful. Leaders can do several things to convert brown-nosers into self-starters, however, and perhaps the first step is to understand that fear of failure is the underlying psychological issue driving brown-noser behavior. Often brown-nosers have all the experience and technical expertise needed to resolve issues, but they do not want to get caught making "dumb mistakes" and lack the self-confidence needed to raise objections or make decisions. Therefore, leaders wanting to convert brown-nosers need to focus their coaching efforts on boosting self-confidence rather than the technical expertise of these individuals. Whenever brown-nosers come forward with problems, leaders need to ask them how they think these problems should be resolved; putting the onus of problem resolution back on this type boosts both their critical thinking skills and their self-confidence. Whenever practical, leaders need to support the solutions offered, provide reassurance, resist stepping in when solutions are not working out as planned, and periodically ask these individuals what they are learning by implementing their own solutions. Brown-nosers will have made the transition to self-starters when they openly point out both the advantages and disadvantages of various solutions to problems leaders are facing.

Bruce and Peter in the figure are slackers—they do not exert much effort toward work and believe they are entitled to a paycheck for just showing up and that it is management's job to solve problems. Slackers are clever at avoiding work and are stealth employees: they often disappear for hours on end, make it a practice to look busy but get little done, have many excuses for not getting projects accomplished, and spend more time devising ways to avoid completing tasks then they would just getting them done. Slackers are content to spend entire days surfing the Internet, shopping online, chatting with co-workers, or taking breaks rather than being productive at work. Nonetheless, slackers want to stay off their boss's radar screens, so they often do just enough to stay out of trouble but never more than their peers.

Transforming slackers into self-starters can be challenging because leaders need to improve both the engagement and critical thinking skills of these individuals. Many leaders mistakenly believe slackers have no motivation; but it turns out that slackers have plenty of motivation that is directed toward activity unrelated to work. This type of follower can spend countless hours on videogames, riding motorcycles, fishing, side businesses, or other hobbies, and if you ask them about their hobbies, their passion shows. Slackers work to live rather than live to work and tend to see work as a means of paying for their other pursuits. Thus the underlying psychological driver for slackers is motivation for work; leaders need to find ways to get these individuals focused on and exerting considerably more effort toward job activities. One way to improve work motivation is to assign tasks that are more in line with these followers' hobbies. For example, assigning research projects to followers who enjoy surfing the Internet might be a way to improve work motivation.

Improving job fit is another way to improve motivation for work. Many times followers lack motivation because they are in the wrong jobs, and assigning them to other positions within teams or organizations that are a better fit with the things they are interested in can improve both the engagement and critical thinking skills of these individuals.

At the end of the day the work still has to get done, and many times the leader does not have the flexibility to assign preferred tasks or new jobs to these individuals (or would not want to reward them for substandard efforts). In this case leaders need to set unambiguous objectives and provide constant feedback on work performance, and then gradually increase performance standards and ask for more input on solutions to problems. Because slackers dislike attention, telling these individuals they have a choice of either performing at higher levels or becoming the focus of their leaders' undivided attention can help improve their work motivation and productivity. Leaders should have no doubt, however, that converting slackers to self-starters is difficult and time-consuming. It may be easier to replace slackers with individuals who have the potential to become self-starters then spend time on these conversion efforts.

The last of the four types, criticizers, are followers who are disengaged from work yet possess strong critical thinking skills. But rather than directing their problem identification and resolution skills toward work-related issues, criticizers are instead motivated to find fault in anything their leaders or organizations do. Criticizers make it a point of telling coworkers what their leaders are doing wrong, how any change efforts are doomed to failure, how bad their organizations are compared to competitors, and how management shoots down any suggestions for improvement.[19] Criticizers are the most dangerous of the four types because they believe it is their personal mission to create converts. They are often the first to greet new employees and "tell them how things really work around here." And because misery loves company, they tend to hang out with other criticizers. Effectively managing teams and organizations with criticizers can be among the most difficult challenges leaders face.

Because they are motivated to create converts, criticizers are like an organizational cancer. And like many cancers, criticizers respond best to aggressive treatments. Leaders need to understand that the need for recognition is the key psychological driver underlying criticizer behavior. At one time criticizers were self-starters who got their recognition needs satisfied through their work accomplishments. But for some reason they were not awarded a promotion they felt they deserved, an organizational restructuring took away some of their prestige and authority, or they worked for a boss who felt threatened by their problem-solving skills.

Criticizers act out because they crave recognition, and leaders can begin the reconversion to self-starters by finding opportunities to publicly recognize these individuals. As stated earlier, criticizers are good at pointing out how decisions or change initiatives are doomed to failure. When criticizers openly raise objections, leaders need to thank them for their inputs and then ask how they think these issues should be resolved. Most criticizers may initially resist offering solutions because they have drawers full of solutions that were ignored in the past and may be reluctant to share their problem-solving expertise in public. Leaders need to break through this resistance and may need to press criticizers for help. And once criticizers offer solutions that leaders can live with, leaders need to adopt these solutions and publicly thank criticizers for their efforts. Repeating this pattern of soliciting solutions, adopting suggestions, and publicly recognizing criticizers for their efforts will go a long way toward converting this group into self-starters. If leaders make repeated attempts to engage criticizers but they fail to respond, termination is a viable option for this type. Because of criticizers' need to create similar-minded co-workers, leaders who do not aggressively deal with these individuals may eventually find themselves leading teams made up of nothing but criticizers. In these situations it may be the leaders who are asked to look for another job rather than the one or two criticizers they failed to deal with properly.

Like the Potter and Rosenbach followership model, the Curphy and Roellig followership model has several aspects that are worth additional comment. First, the model can help leaders assess follower types and determine the best ways to motivate direct reports. Second, leaders need to understand that followership types are not static; they change depending on the situation. The following diagram depicts how a person's followership type changed as she switched jobs, inherited different bosses, was given different responsibilities, and so on. This particular individual started her professional career as a brown-noser, moved up to become a self-starter, spent some time as a criticizer, and is now a slacker. When asked why their followership type changed over time, most people say their immediate boss was the biggest factor in these changes. Thus leaders have a direct impact on effective followership—either by selecting direct reports with self-starter potential or developing direct reports into self-starters.

Third, it is not unusual for followers to start careers or new jobs as brown-nosers. New employees need time to learn the job before they feel comfortable making suggestions for improvement. The question for leaders is whether they take deliberate action to convert brown-nosers into self-starters. Fourth, organizations having decent selection processes are more likely to hire brown-nosers and self-starters than criticizers and slackers. Additional research has shown the longer people stay in organizations, the

Curphy and Roellig Followership Journey Line

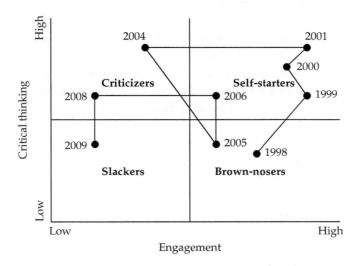

more likely they will be criticizers. Over time people learn how to develop critical thinking skills about their functional expertise. It is usually only a matter of time before these finely honed critical thinking skills are trained on leaders, teams, and organizations.[20,21] It only takes a few bad apples to disrupt a team, so leaders need to aggressively deal with slackers and criticizers if they want to build high performing teams. At the other extreme, teams and organizations populated with criticizers and slackers need to take a hard look at their leadership. The criticizer and slacker followership types may be ways that direct reports cope with clueless bosses.[22]

Fifth, because people in positions of authority also play followership roles, they need to realize how their own followership type affects how they lead others. For example, leaders who are self-starters are likely to set high expectations, reward others for taking initiative, and give top performers plenty of latitude and needed resources. Leaders who are brown-nosers will squelch objections and demand that direct reports constantly check in. They will also expect their employees to do what they are told and not make waves. Leaders who are slackers are laissez-faire leaders who are disengaged from work, are unresponsive to followers' requests, and lead teams that get little accomplished. Leaders who are criticizers will complain not only about their organizations but also about their employees. As such, these leaders tend to manage by exception and find fault in everything their followers do.

We started Part 3 by stating that followers play an important role in team and organizational performance. We hope that some of the main

330   Part Three   *Focus on the Followers*

research findings and questions about followership described in this section will prompt readers to give more thought to effective followership. The next two chapters will explore the topic of followers in considerably more detail. Individual followers differ in all the ways that individual leaders differ, but different things happen when groups of followers have to work together to get things done. Leaders wanting to build winning teams need to be aware of the role of employee motivation, engagement, and satisfaction and group dynamics play in team performance.

Chapter 9

Motivation, Satisfaction, and Performance

Introduction

Polls estimate that if companies could get 3.7 percent more work out of each employee, the equivalent of 18 more minutes of work for each eight-hour shift, the gross domestic product in the U.S. would swell by $355 billion, twice the total GDP of Greece.
The Gallup Organization

Hardly a competent workman can be found in a large establishment who does not devote a considerable amount of his time to studying just how slow he can work and still convince his employer that he is going at a good pace.
Frederick W. Taylor, industrial engineer

Why do followers join some teams but not others? How do you get followers to exhibit enough of the critical behaviors needed for the team to succeed? And why are some leaders capable of getting followers to go above and beyond the call of duty? The ability to motivate others is a fundamental leadership skill and has strong connections to building cohesive, goal-oriented teams and getting results through others. The importance of follower motivation is suggested in findings that most people believe they could give as much as 15 percent or 20 percent more effort at work than they now do with no one, including their own bosses, recognizing any difference. Perhaps even more startling, these workers also believed they could give 15 percent or 20 percent *less* effort with no one noticing any difference. Moreover, variation in work output varies significantly across leaders and followers. The top 15 percent of workers in any particular job may produce 20 to 50 percent more output than the average worker, depending on the complexity of the job. Put another way, the best computer programmers or salesclerks might write up to 50 percent more programs or process 50 percent more customer orders.[1,2] Might better methods of motivating workers lead to higher productivity from *all* workers? Is motivating an individual follower different than motivating a group of followers? Are more motivated workers happier or more satisfied workers? Does money increase productivity and satisfaction, or can leaders do other things to increase the motivation and satisfaction levels of their followers? For example, the U.S. Army pays over $1 billion in retention bonuses each year.[3] Is this money well spent?

Creating highly motivated and satisfied followers depends mostly on understanding others. Therefore, whereas motivation is an essential part of leadership, it is appropriate to include it in this part of the book, which focuses on followers. As an overview, this chapter will address three key areas. First, we will examine the links among leadership, motivation, satisfaction, and performance—four closely related concepts. Second, we will review some major theories and research about motivation and satisfaction. Last, and perhaps most important, we will discuss what leaders can do to enhance the motivation and satisfaction of their followers if they implement these different theories.

Defining Motivation, Satisfaction, and Performance

Motivation, satisfaction, and performance seem clearly related. For example, Colin Powell was the U.S. Army Chief of Staff during the first Gulf War and Secretary of State during the second Gulf War. Powell probably could have pursued a number of different vocations but was *motivated* to complete ROTC as an undergraduate and join the U.S. Army. He was also motivated to put in extra time, energy, and effort in his various positions while in the U.S. Army and was judged or rated by his superiors as being an exceptional performer. His outstanding *performance* as an officer was crucial to his promotion as the head of the Joint Chiefs of Staff during the Reagan and George H. W. Bush administrations and his later appointment as Secretary of State. We could also infer that he was happy or *satisfied* with military life because he was a career officer in the U.S. Army. Figure 9.1 provides an overview of the general relationships among leadership, motivation, satisfaction, and performance. As we can see, some leadership behaviors, such as building relationships or consideration (Chapter 7), result in more satisfied followers. Satisfied followers are more likely to remain with the company and engage in activities that help others at work (organizational citizenship behaviors). Other leadership behaviors, such as setting goals, planning, providing feedback, and rewarding good performance (initiating structure from Chapter 7), appear to more directly influence followers to exert higher levels of effort toward the accomplishment of group goals. Research has shown that these follower behaviors result in higher levels of customer satisfaction and loyalty, which in turn lead to better team performance in retail, sales, or restaurant settings.[4–18] And individuals and teams with higher performance levels often achieve more rewards, which further increase follower satisfaction and performance.[19,20] Thus the leader's ability to motivate followers is vitally important to both the morale and performance of the work group. However, the leader's use of motivational techniques is not the only factor affecting group performance. Selecting the right people for the team, correctly using power and influence tactics, being seen as ethical and credible, possessing the right personality traits and high levels of intelligence, acquiring the necessary resources, and developing follower

FIGURE 9.1
Relationships among Leadership, Job Satisfaction, and Performance

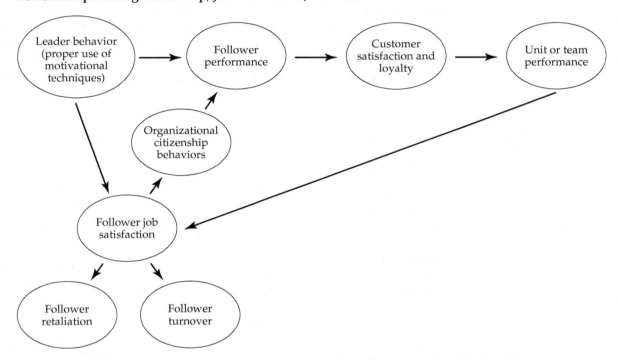

Sources: M. A. Huselid, "The Impact of Human Resource Management Practices on Turnover, Productivity, and Corporate Financial Performance," *Academy of Management Journal* 38, no. 4 (1995), pp. 635–72; T. Butorac, *Recruitment and Retention: The Keys to Profitability at Carlson Companies,* presentation given at Personnel Decisions International, Minneapolis, MN, June 11, 2001; D. J. Koys, "The Effects of Employee Satisfaction, Organizational Citizenship Behavior, and Turnover on Organizational Effectiveness: A Unit-Level, Longitudinal Study," *Personnel Psychology* 54, no. 1 (2001), pp. 101–14; J. Husserl, "Allied's Organizational Life Cycle," *Management Education & Development* 24, no. 3 (1998), p. 8; Sirota Consulting, *Establishing the Linkages between Employee Attitudes, Customer Attitudes, and Bottom-Line Results* (Chicago, IL: Author, 1998); D. S. Pugh, J. Dietz, J. W. Wiley, and S. M. Brooks, "Driving Service Effectiveness through Employee–Customer Linkages," *Academy of Management Executive* 16, no. 4 (2002), pp. 73–84; B. Schneider, P. J. Hanges, D. B. Smith, and A. N. Salvaggio, "Which Comes First: Employee Attitudes or Organizational, Financial and Market Performance?" *Journal of Applied Psychology* 88, no. 5 (2003), pp. 836–51.

skills are other leadership factors affecting a group's ability to accomplish its goals.

Most people probably think of motivation as dealing with choices about what we do and how much effort we put into doing it. Most researchers define **motivation** as anything that provides *direction, intensity,* and *persistence* to behavior.[21-23] Thus motivation comes into play whenever someone chooses an activity or task to engage in, puts forth a certain level of effort toward this activity, and persists with this effort for some time. Like personality traits and types, motivation is not directly observable; it must be inferred from behavior. We would infer that one person is highly motivated to do well in school if she spent a lot of time studying for exams. She could choose to spend her time and energy on socializing, intramurals, or volunteer work, but because she is spending time outlining readings and

You have brains in your head. You have feet in your shoes. You can steer yourself in any direction you choose.

Dr. Seuss

reviewing class notes, we say she is motivated to do well in school. At work, if one person regularly assembles twice as many iPads as any other person in his work group—assuming all have the same abilities, skills, and resources—then we likely would say this first person is more motivated than the others. We use the concept of motivation to explain differences we see among people in the energy and direction of their behavior. Thus the energy and effort Ang Lee expended creating *Life of Pi* or the governments of Iran and North Korea spend developing their nuclear capabilities would be examples of the direction, intensity, and persistence components of motivation.

Performance, on the other hand, concerns behaviors directed toward the organization's mission or goals or the products and services resulting from those behaviors. At work or school we can choose to perform a wide variety of behaviors, but performance would include only those behaviors related to the production of goods or services or obtaining good grades. Performance differs from **effectiveness,** which generally involves making judgments about the adequacy of behavior with respect to certain criteria such as work group or organizational goals. Ang Lee spent several years creating the movie *Life of Pi.* The behaviors he exhibited in getting the film made constitute performance; the revenues generated and Academy Awards won by the movie indicate his effectiveness as a movie director. However, performance is affected by a variety of factors. Intelligence, skill, and the availability of key resources can affect a follower's behavior in accomplishing organizational goals (that is, performance) independently of that person's level of motivation. *Thus an adequate level of motivation may be a necessary but insufficient condition of effective performance.*

Job satisfaction is not how *hard* one works or how *well* one works, but rather how much one *likes* a specific kind of job or work activity. Job satisfaction deals with one's attitudes or feelings about the job itself, pay, promotion or educational opportunities, supervision, co-workers, workload, and so on.[11,24,25] Various polls over the past half-century have consistently shown that a majority of men and women report liking their jobs.[26–30] Research has also shown that people who are more satisfied with their jobs are more likely to engage in **organizational citizenship behaviors**— behaviors not directly related to one's job but helpful to others at work. Organizational citizenship behaviors create a more supportive workplace. Examples might include volunteering to help another employee with a task or project or filling in for another employee when asked. Happier workers tend to be more helpful workers.[31–37]

Although people generally like the work they do, several events have caused a downturn in job satisfaction levels among employees in the United States over the past decade. From roughly 2002 to 2007 the United States enjoyed strong economic growth, and companies rapidly expanded the products and services they provided. Because it took time to hire and train employees to meet increased demand, those already employed

A company is always perfectly designed to produce what it is producing. If it has quality problems, cost problems, or productivity problems, then the behaviors associated with these outcomes are being reinforced. This is not conjecture. This is the cold, hard reality of human behavior.

Anonymous

There is one virtue to the 35-hour workweek. It is one of the few French ideals that we don't need to worry about copyrighting. Nobody else wants it.

Nicolas Sarkozy, former prime minister of France

had to cope with larger workloads. This period also saw a tremendous amount of consolidation (companies buying one another) and reorganization (restructuring functions, processes, and personnel) to better meet increased demand. Change was an overarching theme from 2002 to 2007, and leaders and followers were constantly devising new ways to deliver products and services to customers. This continuing cycle of consolidation, reorganization, and change made it difficult for employees to develop any loyalty for their organizations—they never knew if their work unit was going to be sold or merged with another work unit. This period, perhaps more than most, broke the implicit contract between employers and employees. Before 2002 many employees felt if they worked hard they could spend their entire careers at a single company. But after all the acquisitions, downsizings, and restructurings many employees developed more of a mercenary attitude toward employers. If they worked for a company that did not treat them well, had a bad boss, or did not get the pay or promotions they felt they deserved, they would find a position with another employer. And with the economy enjoying strong growth, there were plenty of opportunities for people to find other employment.

Although people were working longer hours and coping with more change than ever before, most people found 2002 to 2007 to be a cakewalk compared to what they experienced during the economic recession of 2008 to 2010. The global recession caused companies to freeze hiring and training programs and lay off record numbers of employees. The unemployment rate in the United States increased from 5 to over 10 percent, and many people went months or even years without finding meaningful work. Those lucky enough to remain employed wound up doing more than they did before with fewer resources and lower pay. Employees generally felt lucky to have a job and were not apt to complain (for fear of losing their jobs), but many were frustrated with their employers. This increased workload and sense of frustration cut job satisfaction to record lows, and a big question was whether the best and brightest employees were leaving for other opportunities once the economy started picking up.[38] Companies can ill afford to lose their best people just when their fortunes are improving, so many have implemented programs to retain their high-potential talent.[39,40]

Today many leaders face the dual challenges of having to achieve increasingly difficult team goals while having fewer followers available to do the work. The best leaders and organizations understand that one way to meet these challenges is to recruit, develop, and retain top leadership and technical talent. Savvy companies that spend considerably more time and effort attracting, developing, and retaining the best people often report superior financial results.[9,11,39–46] For example, many of the organizations appearing in *Fortune* magazine's "The 100 Best Companies to Work For" also do well when compared to the S&P 500 Index. *The best leaders may be those who can motivate workers to perform at a high level while maintaining an equally high level of job satisfaction.* See Highlight 9.1 for a discussion of productivity and job satisfaction.

People who have jobs, rather than careers, worry about work–life balance because they are unable to have fun at work.

Tomas Chamorro-Premuzic, consultant

Productivity and Satisfaction across the Globe

HIGHLIGHT 9.1

The global recession has caused American and European businesses to downsize considerably, but many have been able to maintain customer satisfaction and revenue levels with fewer employees. In terms of the number of hours worked, the average U.S. employee works 137 hours per year more than the typical Japanese employee, 260 hours more per year compared to the average British employee, and 499 hours more than the average French employee. In other words, over a 40-year work career, U.S. employees will work the equivalent of 10 more years than the average French employee. The work ethic of the French has been mocked by outsiders for years and is seen as a significant barrier to the country's ability to compete in the global marketplace. American companies are noted for having some of the highest productivity in the world, but might there also be a downside to these high productivity levels? Research has shown that some of the risks associated with longer workweeks include job dissatisfaction, poorer physical and mental health, and distressed family and social relationships. But other research by Chamorro-Premuzic shows that workaholics have higher social status, high achievers live longer, and the ten most workaholic nations produce most of the world's gross domestic product. Chamorro-Premuzic argues that many employees have become self-indulgent, pampered, and so enthralled with the pursuit of well-being that they have forgotten the value of hard work and achievement. He believes the pursuit of work–life balance is a myth perpetrated by positive psychologists and self-help gurus trying to make people feel good about their failures and inability to achieve things. People who put in long hours and hate their jobs are likely to suffer all the negative effects identified earlier. Those who are engaged, have fun at work, and view their current positions as part of a career path versus a job do not suffer these ill effects and end up being much more successful.

Do you think that workers today are not as motivated or achievement oriented as those in the past? Is there such a thing as work–life balance? Is working longer hours a good or bad thing?

Sources: J. M. Brett and L. K. Stroh, "Working 61 Plus Hours a Week: Why Do Managers Do It?" *Journal of Applied Psychology* 88, no. 1 (2003), pp. 67–78; "Schumpeter: Overstretched" *The Economist*, May 22, 2010, p. 72; "Schumpeter: The French Way of Work" *The Economist*, November 19, 2011, p. 71; H. Schachter, "Get Over It: There Is No Work–Life Balance, Just Work," *The Globe and Mail*, February 28, 2013; http://blogs.hbr.org/cs/2013/02/embrace_work-life_imbalan.html; http://news.yahoo.com/s/ap/20100105/ap_on_bi_ge/us_unhappy_workers.

Having now defined motivation, performance, and job satisfaction, we can explore their relationships a bit further. We have already noted how motivation does not always ensure good performance. If followers lack the necessary skills or resources to accomplish a group task, then trying to motivate them more could be unproductive and even frustrating.[47,48] For example, no high school basketball team is likely to defeat the Los Angeles Lakers, however motivated the players may be. The players on the high school team simply lack the abilities and skills of the Lakers players. Higher motivation will usually affect performance only if followers already have the abilities, skills, and resources to get the job done. Motivating others is an important part of leadership, but not all of it; pep talks and rewards are not always enough.

Ping Fu

PROFILES IN LEADERSHIP 9.1

Ping Fu is the Chinese-born cofounder and CEO of Geomagic, a company that provides 3D imaging used in engineering, art, archeology, metrology, and biomechanical product design. Started in 1997, Geomagic's technology is used in the creation of customized prosthetic limbs, and if you wore braces growing up they may have been designed with the help of Geomagic technology.

Ping Fu's journey to becoming a corporate CEO is far from typical. She grew up in Shanghai in the home of two well-educated parents. At the age of eight she was listed as a "black" citizen—someone who had to atone for the greed and corruption committed by her parents and ancestors when Mao's cultural revolution swept the country. She spent the next years separated from her parents, working 14 hour days in a factory, foraging for scraps, and tending to her little sister between shifts. When the Cultural Revolution ended she enrolled in school and eventually wrote her dissertation on China's one-child policy, where she found that the government's use of brutal enforcement

techniques was causing shockingly high rates of infanticide. Her dissertation was leaked to the press, and its wide publication was a major embarrassment to the Chinese government. In 1984 China quietly deported Ping Fu to the United States.

Ping Fu learned English and computer programming while working as a babysitter, maid, and waitress. She eventually landed a job with the National Center for Supercomputing Applications (NCSA) where she worked on earthquake prediction modeling and 3D imaging. In 1997 she made a New Year's resolution to "create something of value" and left the NCSA to start up Geomagic. In early 2013 she sold the company to 3D Systems, a 3D printing company, for $55 million.

What theory or theories of motivation best explain Ping Fu's journey to CEO?

Sources: P. Fu. *Bend, Not Break* (New York: Penguin Group, 2012); "An Executive Memoir: The World Is 3D," *The Economist,* January 12, 2013, p. 72; M. Kirkpatrick, "The Art of Resilience," *The Wall Street Journal,* January 9, 2013, p. A11.

Always bear in mind that your resolution to succeed is more important than any other one thing.

Abraham Lincoln, U.S. president

The relationships between motivation and job satisfaction are more straightforward; in fact many theories of motivation are also theories of job satisfaction. The implicit link between satisfaction and motivation is that satisfaction increases when people accomplish a task, particularly when the task requires a lot of effort. It might also seem logical that *performance* must be higher among more satisfied workers, but this is not always so.[12,17,24,49,50] Although satisfaction and performance are correlated, happy workers are not always the most productive ones; nor are unhappy or dissatisfied workers always the poorest performers. It is possible, for example, for poorly performing workers to be fairly satisfied with their jobs (maybe because they are paid well but do not have to work hard). It is also possible for dissatisfied workers to be relatively high performers (they may have a strong work ethic, have no other employment options, or be trying to improve the chances of getting out of their current job). Despite the intuitive appeal of believing that satisfied workers usually perform better, satisfaction has only an indirect effect on performance. Nevertheless, having both satisfied *and* high-performing followers is a goal leaders should usually strive to achieve. One example of a high performer is featured in Profiles in Leadership 9.1.

Understanding and Influencing Follower Motivation

What do leaders do to motivate followers to accomplish group goals? Are all leaders and followers motivated the same way? Is there a universal theory of motivation? In other words, did Osama bin Laden and General David Petraeus, one time commander of U.S. forces in Afghanistan, use the same or different techniques to motivate their followers? As described in Highlight 9.2, organizations spend billions on motivating employees; but do these interventions actually improve job satisfaction, retention, and performance? Research can answer these questions, and few topics of human behavior have been the subject of so much attention as that of motivation. So much has been written about motivation that a comprehensive review of the subject is beyond the scope of this book. We will, however, survey several major approaches to understanding follower motivation, as well as

Organizations Spend Billions on Motivational Programs for Employees, and All They Get Are Burned Feet

HIGHLIGHT 9.2

Organizations are constantly looking for quick fixes for their performance and effectiveness problems. The barriers to team or organizational performance often include a lack of resources and skills, unclear goals, poor performance or accountability standards, or incompetent leadership. But rather than adopting methods to directly address these issues, many organizations instead have employees listen to motivational speakers or engage in whitewater rafting, bungee jumping, or firewalking events. The motivational speaking circuit includes former professional athletes, astronauts, fighter pilots, and military generals, successful and failed business leaders, politicians, psychologists, and consultants. Motivational speaking engagements can be lucrative—one of the authors worked with a speaker who gave one speech in Las Vegas at lunch and the same speech that evening in Minneapolis and made $150,000 for the day. The author also has worked with a group of ex-fighter pilots who do half-day "Business Is Combat" seminars for $30,000 to $75,000.

Companies think nothing of spending like this to motivate employees. For example, the software consulting firm EMC has spent $625,000 to have 5,000 employees walk over burning coals. But do expensive speakers and extreme activities actually improve organizational performance? Unfortunately exhaustive research has shown virtually no link between motivational spending and company revenues, profitability, or market share. Perhaps the biggest problem is that employees may find it difficult to see the link between walking over a bed of hot coals or participating in a Business Is Combat mission planning event and making another 20 sales calls every week. The problem is that these events do not address the root cause of many organizational woes but instead covertly shift the burden to "underperforming" employees. Other than bankrolling the motivation industry, these programs have another effect: nine U.S. Air Force recruiters had to go to the emergency room after they received second- and third-degree burns on their feet after one of these motivational programs.

Sources: D. Jones, "Firms Spend Billions to Fire Up Workers—With Little Luck," *USA Today,* May 10, 2001, pp. 1–2A; P. G. Chronis, "9 Burn Feet in National Guard Recruiters' Fire Walk," *Denver Post,* December 28, 1998, pp. 1A, 17A; G. J. Curphy and R. T. Hogan, "Managerial Incompetence: Is There a Dead Skunk on the Table?" working paper, 2004; G. J. Curphy, M. J. Benson, A. Baldrica, and R. T. Hogan, *Managerial Incompetence,* unpublished manuscript, 2007.

address the implications of these approaches for follower satisfaction and performance. These motivational theories and approaches give leaders a number of suggestions to get followers to engage in and persist with different behaviors. However, some motivational theories are particularly useful in certain situations but not as applicable in others. Just as a carpenter can build better wooden structures or furniture by having a larger set of tools, so can leaders solve a greater number of motivational problems among followers by becoming familiar with different motivational theories and approaches. People who have only hammers in their toolkits are likely to see every problem as a nail needing hammering, and it is not unusual for less effective leaders to call on a limited number of approaches to any motivational problem. *Leaders who know about different motivational theories are more likely to choose the right theory for a particular follower and situation, and often have higher-performing and more satisfied employees as a result.*

Most performance problems can be attributed to unclear expectations, skill deficits, resource/equipment shortages, or a lack of motivation. Of these underlying causes, leaders seem to have the most difficulty in recognizing and rectifying motivation problems. An example might help to illustrate this point. A major airline was having serious problems with the customer service of its flight attendants. Passenger complaints were on the rise, and airplane loading (the average number of people per flight) was decreasing. The perceived lack of customer service was beginning to cost the airline market share and revenues; to fix the problem it decided to have all 10,000 flight attendants go through a two-day customer service training program. Unfortunately passenger complaints only got worse after the training. A thorough investigation of the underlying cause of the problem revealed that flight attendants knew what they were supposed to do, had all the skills necessary to perform the behaviors, and usually had the resources and equipment necessary to serve customers. The root cause was a lack of motivation to go the extra mile for customers. When asked what they found to be the most motivating aspect of being a flight attendant, most stated "time off." In other words, the flight attendants were most motivated when they were *not* at work. (Because of work schedules, flight attendants typically get two weeks off per month.) Given that a strong union represented the flight attendants, how would you go about solving this dilemma? The next section will give you some ideas on how to resolve this and other motivation problems that you may face as a leader.

As stated earlier, leaders can use many different theories and approaches to motivate followers. In this section we will discuss the key aspects of five popular and useful approaches to understanding motivation in work or leadership contexts. Some may wonder why these motivational approaches were included and others excluded from this section, and sound arguments could be made for changing the motivational approaches described. Our intention is to provide a broad view of different

The truth of the matter is that you always know the right thing to do. The hard part is doing it.
Norman Schwarzkopf, U.S. Army

TABLE 9.1
Five Motivational Approaches

Theory or Approach	Major Themes of Characteristics
Maslow's hierarchy of needs	Satisfy needs to change behavior
Achievement orientation	Possess certain personality traits
Goal setting	Set goals to change behavior
Operant approach	Change rewards and punishments to change behavior
Empowerment	Give people autonomy and latitude to increase their motivation for work

Your job is to figure out what you have to do in order to do what you want to do.

Jim Earley, consultant

motivational approaches and not be so comprehensive as to overwhelm readers. The five theories and approaches are listed in Table 9.1. For illustrative purposes we will also discuss how leadership practitioners could apply these approaches to motivate two fictitious followers, Julie and Ling Ling. Julie is a 21-year-old ski lift operator in Banff, Alberta, Canada. Her primary job is to ensure that people get on and off her ski lift safely. She also does periodic equipment safety checks and maintains the lift lines and associated areas. Julie works from 8:30 a.m. to 5:00 p.m. five days a week, is paid a salary, and has a pass that allows her to ski for free whenever she is off work. Ling Ling is a 35-year-old real estate agent in Hong Kong. She works for an agency that locates and rents apartments for people on one- to three-year business assignments for various multinational companies. She works many evenings and weekends showing apartments, and she is paid a salary plus a commission for every apartment she rents. How the five approaches could be used to motivate Julie and Ling Ling will be discussed periodically throughout this section.

Maslow's Hierarchy of Needs: How Does Context Affect Motivation?

One way to get followers to engage in and persist with the behaviors needed to accomplish group goals is to appeal to their needs. **Needs** refer to internal states of tension or arousal, or uncomfortable states of deficiency people are motivated to change. Hunger would be a good example of a need: people are motivated to eat when they get hungry. Other needs might include the need to live in a safe and secure place, to belong to a group with common interests or social ties, or to do interesting and challenging work. If these needs were not being met, people would choose to engage in and persist with certain behaviors until they were satisfied. According to this motivational approach, leadership practitioners can get followers to engage in and persist with certain behaviors by correctly identifying and appeasing their needs.

According to Maslow, people are motivated by five basic types of needs.[51] These include the need to survive physiologically, the need for security, the need for affiliation with other people (that is, belongingness),

FIGURE 9.2
Maslow's Hierarchy
of Needs

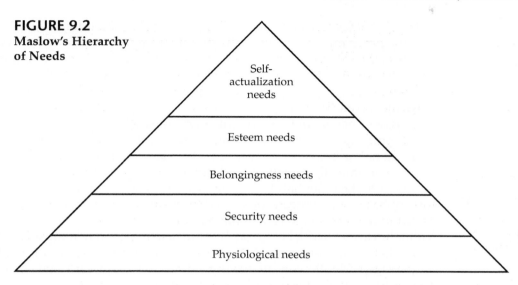

the need for self-esteem, and the need for self-actualization. Maslow's conceptualization of needs is usually represented by a triangle with the five levels of needs arranged in a **hierarchy of needs** (see Figure 9.2). According to Maslow, any person's behavior can be understood primarily as the effort directed to satisfy a particular level of need in the hierarchy. Which level happens to be motivating a person's behavior at any time depends on whether lower needs in the hierarchy have been satisfied. According to Maslow, lower-level needs must be satisfied before the next-higher level becomes salient in motivating behavior.

Maslow believed higher-level needs like those for self-esteem or self-actualization would not become salient (even when unfulfilled) until lower needs were satisfied. Thus a practical implication of his theory is that leaders can motivate follower behavior only by taking account of a follower's or team's position on the needs hierarchy. Applying Maslow's hierarchy to Julie, it might be inefficient to try to motivate our ski lift operator by appealing to how much pride she could take in a job well done (that is, to her self-esteem) if she was underdressed for weather conditions. If her boss wanted Julie to do more, she should first make sure that Julie's physiological needs were met, that she worked and lived in a secure place, and that she had ample opportunities to socialize with other employees. Only after these lower needs had been met should the boss try to increase Julie's self-esteem. Thus if leadership practitioners want to use Maslow's hierarchy of needs to motivate employees to work harder, they need to determine where their followers are on the needs hierarchy and ensure that all lower-order needs are satisfied before appealing to their followers' self-esteem or self-actualization needs. Leadership practitioners should watch for mismatches between their motivational efforts and followers' *lowest* (on the hierarchy) unsatisfied needs.

How could you determine the needs of flight attendants, and what kind of program would you implement to improve customer service? Although Maslow's theory provides some useful ideas on how to improve customer service, it has several limitations. For one thing, the theory does not make specific predictions about what an individual will do to satisfy a particular need.[21,52] For example, if Ling Ling was trying to get her belongingness needs met, she might exert considerable effort to establish new friendships at work, try to make friends outside work, or join several professional or business associations. This lack of specificity and predictive power limits the practical applicability of Maslow's theory in real-life settings. On the other hand, awareness of the general nature of the various sorts of basic human needs described in this theory seems fundamentally useful to leaders. Leaders will have a difficult time getting followers to maintain various work behaviors by emphasizing good relationships with co-workers or appealing to their sense of pride if the job pays only minimum wage and followers are having a difficult time making ends meet. A person may be reluctant to volunteer for a self-actualizing opportunity in support of a political campaign if such participation may risk that person's financial security. Perhaps the greatest insight provided by this theory is that leadership practitioners may need to address some basic, fundamental areas before their attempts to get followers and teams to expend more effort on work-related behaviors will be successful.

Along these lines, it may be interesting to look at how Maslow's hierarchy of needs could be applied to U.S. and European workers over the past 10 years. One could argue that during the economic growth years many workers were putting in long hours but operating at the esteem and self-actualization levels. However, during the U.S. and European recessions those who remained employed switched their focus to meeting their security needs. These individuals were working longer hours than ever before, but this was to ensure they had a job versus making a meaningful contribution or being fulfilled. And many of those who were not gainfully employed may have spent much of their time just trying to get food on the table (physiological needs). As the economy in these two regions recovers, it will be interesting to see if leaders will be able to convince followers that their lower-level needs will be met and get them to shift their focus to self-esteem and self-actualization needs.

Achievement Orientation: How Does Personality Affect Motivation?

Is it possible that some people are naturally more motivated or have "more fire in the belly" than others? Do some people automatically put forth a higher level of effort toward group goals simply because they are hardwired this way? Unlike Maslow's theory, which claims all people share some fundamental needs, this approach to motivation is simple. To improve group performance, leaders should select only followers who

Some players you pat their butts, other players you kick their butts, and some players you leave alone.

Pete Rose

The best job goes to the person who can get it done without passing the buck or coming back with excuses.

Napoleon Hill, author

Employability: Finding and Keeping a Job

HIGHLIGHT 9.3

Employability can be defined as the ability to gain and keep a job, and with high unemployment rates in the United States and Europe this has become an important political topic. Youth unemployment rates in some European countries exceed 25 percent, and 40 percent of the unemployed in the United States have not had jobs in over two years. Situational, follower, and leader factors all play a role in who gets hired, can keep a job, or get fired, and it is worth describing these factors in more detail.

Clearly situational factors play a pervasive role in employability. When the economy is booming jobs are plentiful, but they are few and far between during recessions. Even during growing economies some may lose their jobs because of mergers, restructurings, or bankruptcies. Although economic conditions determine how many jobs are available, follower and leader factors play important roles in who fills these positions. Research shows that leaders are looking for followers who can get the job done (they have relevant experience, often gained through internships, or enough IQ to get up to speed quickly on the position) and possess good interpersonal skills. Intelligence alone is not enough, as height and personal appearance have been found to have just as much bearing on hiring decisions as GPA. Primping and preening apparently have as much impact as studying hard when it comes to many leaders' hiring decisions.

Leader biases also come into play when evaluating the performance of followers after they get hired. It turns out that office politics can play a bigger role in performance evaluations than objective performance results. Research has shown that performance review ratings for salespeople can be more highly correlated with completing paperwork and other administrative tasks than the dollar amounts actually sold. With many jobs lacking more objective performance measures, leader bias may play a pervasive role in performance review ratings. Those who get along with others, do not make any enemies, and flatter their bosses may rise higher in organizations than those who produce actual results.

What role do you think leader biases play in determining who gets hired or promoted into state or federal government, military, human resources, or IT positions? Has bias or favoritism played a role in your being selected for an activity or athletic team? Did this bias work for or against you? What is more important for career success: intelligence, experience, personality, motivation, or appearance?

Sources: R. Hogan, T. Chamorro-Premuzic, and R. B. Kaiser, "Employability and Career Success: Bridging the Gap between Theory and Reality," *Industrial and Organizational Psychology: Perspectives on Science and Practice* 1, no. 6 (2013), pp. 3–16; R. Hogan, "High Potentials Who Fail," in *Who Can Get and Keep a Job? Understanding Employability*, R. Hogan (chair). Symposium presented at the 26th Annual Conference of the Society of Industrial and Organizational Psychology, Chicago, IL, 2011. T. Chamorro-Premuzic, "Hidden Genius, Wasted Talent: Intelligence, Entrepreneurship, and Unemployability," in *Who Can Get and Keep a Job? Understanding Employability*, R. Hogan (chair). Symposium presented at the 26th Annual Conference of the Society of Industrial and Organizational Psychology, Chicago, IL, 2011. G. Curphy, "What We Know about Employability," in *Who Can Get and Keep a Job? Understanding Employability*, R. Hogan (chair). Symposium presented at the 26th Annual Conference of the Society of Industrial and Organizational Psychology, Chicago, IL, 2011. L. Kwoh, "'Rank and Yank' Retains Loyal Fans," *The Wall Street Journal*, January 31, 2012, p. B6.

both possess the right skills and have a higher level of a personality trait called achievement orientation. (See Highlight 9.3.)

Atkinson has proposed that an individual's tendency to exert effort toward task accomplishment depends partly on the strength of his or her motivation to achieve success, or as Atkinson called it, **achievement orientation**.[21,53] McClelland further developed Atkinson's ideas and said that individuals with a strong achievement orientation (or in McClelland's terms, a strong *need for achievement*) strive to accomplish socially acceptable endeavors and activities. These individuals also prefer tasks that provide immediate and ample feedback and are moderately difficult (that is, tasks that require a considerable amount of effort but are accomplishable). Additionally, individuals with a strong need to achieve feel satisfied when they successfully solve work problems or accomplish job tasks. Individuals with a relatively low need to achieve generally prefer easier tasks and do not feel satisfied by solving problems or accomplishing assigned tasks. McClelland maintained that differences in achievement orientation are a primary reason why people differ in the levels of effort they exert to accomplish assignments, objectives, or goals. Thus achievement orientation is a bit like "fire in the belly"; people with more achievement orientation are likely to set higher personal and work goals and are more likely to expend the effort needed to accomplish them. People with low levels of achievement motivation tend to set lower personal and work goals and are less likely to accomplish them.[54]

Achievement orientation is also a component of the Five Factor Model or OCEAN model of personality dimension of conscientiousness (see Chapter 6). Conscientiousness has been found to be positively related to performance across virtually all jobs as well as predict success in school, in the military, in blue-collar and retail workers, and in management positions. All things being equal, people with higher levels of achievement orientation are likely to do better in school, pursue postgraduate degrees, get promoted more quickly, and get paid higher salaries and bonuses than their lower-scoring counterparts.[46,55–64]

Given that individuals with higher achievement orientation scores set high personal goals and put in the time and effort necessary to achieve them, it is hardly surprising that achievement orientation is often a key success factor for people who advance to the highest levels of the organization. For example, achievement orientation appears to be a common success factor underlying the careers of Ping Fu, Mark Roellig, James Mwangi, and Richard Branson (Profiles in Leadership 9.1 to 9.4, respectively). Although achievement orientation is often associated with higher performance, high achievers can become demoralized when facing unclear or impossible tasks. Working with elite Army Ranger units, Britt found that these units almost always performed at high levels and were often successful. But when given unclear missions with few resources and impossible timelines, these same units could self-destruct quickly. In these situations the units felt they were being set up to fail, and fail they did. This phenomenon is clearly depicted in the movie *Black Hawk Down*, where Army Ranger units were sent to Mogadishu, Somalia, to capture a Somalian warlord. The important lesson here is that leaders need to give high achievers clear goals and the resources they need to succeed.[65] (See Highlight 9.4.)

What Really Motivates Workers?

HIGHLIGHT 9.4

Which of the following items do you think best motivates workers?

A. Recognition

B. Incentives

C. Interpersonal support

D. Support for making progress

E. Clear goals

If you are like 600 managers who were asked this question in 2010, you would choose A. Recognition for good work. However, if we look over daily diaries of hundreds of employees over a multiyear period, the answer seems to be D. Support for making progress. Employees reported striving to do their best and having the strongest positive emotions on days when they felt they were making headway in their work assignments or got support to overcome obstacles. Emotions and drive were lowest on those days when they felt they were spinning their wheels

or encountered roadblocks. These research results indicate that leaders can best motivate followers and teams by providing meaningful goals, resources, and encouragement; being decisive; and minimizing irrelevant demands. Leaders can also help motivate followers by rolling up their sleeves and pitching in and not exerting time pressure so intense that even minor glitches are perceived as major crises.

The good news is that many of the things leaders can to do motivate followers are under their direct control. It is also worth noting that this research reported that recognition helps to improve motivation, but only if people feel they are making progress toward individual or team goals. How does making progress toward goals relate to Maslow's hierarchy of needs or to people with low or high levels of achievement orientation?

Source: T. M. Amabile and S. J. Kramer, "What Really Motivates Workers?" *Harvard Business Review*, January–February 2010, pp. 44–45.

How could a leader apply this knowledge of achievement orientation to improve the performance of Julie, Ling Ling, and the flight attendants? Perhaps the first step would be to ensure that the hiring process selected individuals with higher levels of achievement orientation. Assuming they had higher scores, we would expect Ling Ling to work with her boss to set aggressive goals for renting apartments and then work as many nights and weekends as were needed to achieve them. We might also expect Ling Ling to obtain her MBA from Hong Kong University over the next few years. Julie could also be expected to set high personal and work goals, but she may find that her job limits her ability to pursue these goals. Unlike Ling Ling, who can control the number of nights and weekends she works, Julie has no control over the number of people who ride on her lift. The job itself may limit Julie's ability to fulfill her high level of achievement orientation. As a result, she may pursue other activities, such as becoming an expert skier, joining the ski patrol, doing ski racing, looking for additional responsibilities or opportunities for advancement, or finding another job where she has the opportunity to achieve and get rewarded for her efforts. Because Julie would set and work toward high personal goals, a good boss would work closely with Julie to find work-related ways to capitalize on her achievement orientation. Thus achievement

346   Part Three   *Focus on the Followers*

Capacity is its own motivation.
David Campbell, Center for Creative Leadership

A good goal is like strenuous exercise—it makes you stretch.
Mary Kay Ashe, CEO

orientation may be a dual-edged sword. Leadership practitioners may be able to hire a group of highly motivated followers, but they also need to set clear expectations, provide opportunities for followers to set and achieve work-related goals, and provide feedback on progress toward goals. Otherwise followers may find different ways to fulfill their high levels of achievement orientation.

Applying the achievement orientation approach to the flight attendant situation or to U.S. workers from 2002 to 2009 leads to some interesting thoughts. Perhaps the airline did not screen for conscientiousness when hiring flight attendants and does not have enough people with high scores to deliver good customer service. Or the company could have hired only people with high conscientiousness scores but not set any measurable goals, repeatedly ignored requests for better equipment, failed to back up staff when they were challenged by "bad" travelers, or not given any recognition for jobs well done. In this case the flight attendants could feel that they have been set up for failure. With respect to people working in the United States from 2002 to 2009, those with the highest levels of achievement orientation were most likely to get promoted during the economic boom and stay with their companies during the recession. However, because many companies went under or eliminated entire work units or functions, some achievement-oriented types found themselves out of jobs. Because work is so important to people with high levels of achievement orientation, some of these individuals probably found work elsewhere. Others may have been devastated by their job loss and remain bitter about being set up for failure.

Goal Setting: How Do Clear Performance Targets Affect Motivation?

One of the most familiar and easiest formal systems of motivation to use with followers is **goal setting.** From the leader's perspective, this involves setting clear performance targets and then helping followers create systematic plans to achieve them. According to Locke and Latham, goals are the most powerful determinants of task behaviors. Goals direct attention, mobilize effort, help people develop strategies for achievement, and help people continue exerting effort until the goals are reached. This leads, in turn, to even higher goals.[66–69]

Goal-setting theory has been rated #1 in importance among 73 management theories by organizational behavior scholars.
Ed Locke, University of Maryland

Locke and Latham reported that nearly 400 studies involving hundreds of tasks across 40,000 individuals, groups, and organizations in eight different countries have provided consistent support for several aspects of goal setting. First, this research showed goals that were both *specific* and *difficult* resulted in consistently higher effort and performance when contrasted to "do your best" goals. Second, *goal commitment* is critical. Merely having goals is not enough. Although follower participation in setting goals is one way to increase commitment, goals set either by leaders unilaterally or through participation with followers can lead to necessary levels of commitment. Commitment to assigned goals was often as high

Mark Roellig

PROFILES IN LEADERSHIP 9.2

Mark Roellig is currently the executive vice president and general counsel of MassMutual Financial Group. Growing up in Michigan, Mark attended the University of Michigan to obtain an undergraduate degree in mathematics in three years. He went on to earn his law degree at George Washington University and an MBA degree from the University of Washington. Mark started his professional career as an attorney practicing civil litigation at two law firms in Seattle before joining Pacific Northwestern Bell Telephone Company in 1983. He spent the next 17 years working in the law division of the company as it transformed from Pacific Northwestern Bell to US West to Qwest Communications. During this time Mark rapidly moved through the ranks and eventually became the executive vice president of public policy, human resources, and law for US West. In this role Mark managed a group of over 1,000 employees and an annual budget of $250,000,000.

After US West was acquired by Qwest, Mark spent some time as the general counsel for Storage Technology Corporation and Fisher Scientific International before moving into his current role in 2005. MassMutual Financial Group is a financial services company that has over $450,000,000,000 in assets under management and is ranked as a *Fortune* 100 firm. Mark is currently responsible for the law, public policy, and corporate services divisions and manages a team of 500 employees and a $160,000,000 annual budget. Having been the top lawyer and board secretary for four *Fortune* 500 companies, Mark has learned a number of valuable lessons about leadership and management over the years. Some of these key lessons include developing strategic plans that support and advance the business objectives, surrounding oneself with top talent, setting clear goals to support plans, using metrics to track progress, rewarding top performers, building teams, and creating performance-based cultures. Some of Mark's accomplishments since joining MassMutual include the following:

- A 57 percent reduction in outside counsel costs.
- A 27 percent reduction in total legal costs.
- An 18 percent reduction in dispute resolution costs.
- A 15 percent increase in customer satisfaction ratings.
- Consistently receiving some of the best employee satisfaction scores across the company.

Mark obsesses over talent and spends a considerable amount of time hiring top lawyers and then putting them in various training programs and rotational assignments to help them develop needed legal and leadership skills. Over the years a number of his direct reports have gone on to be general counsels or top lawyers in a number of other firms, and because of his unique combination of skills Mark is constantly asked to lead projects and functions outside the legal area, as well as provide advice on complex business, public policy, board of director, and personnel issues.

How would you use Maslow's hierarchy of needs, achievement orientation, goal setting, and the operant approach to describe Mark Roellig's career? Which motivational approaches best describe his leadership philosophy?

Sources: http://boston.citybizlist.com/lstg/lstgDetail.aspx?id-4030; M. Roellig, *Summary of 2009 Law Division Activities,* presentation given to the MassMutual Audit Committee on April 13, 2010, in Springfield, MA.

as commitment to goals followers helped to set, provided the leader was perceived to have legitimate authority, expressed confidence in followers, and provided clear standards for performance. Third, followers exerted the greatest effort when goals were accompanied by *feedback*; followers getting goals or feedback alone generally exerted less effort. (See Highlight 9.5 for a practical application of goal-setting theory.)

The Balanced Scorecard

HIGHLIGHT 9.5

A practical method for implementing goal setting in organizations involves the creation of balanced scorecards. Kaplan and Norton argue that most of the measures typically used to assess organizational performance are too limited in scope. For example, many organizations set goals and periodically review their financial performance, but these indicators suffer from time lags (it may take a month or longer before the financial results of specific organizational activities are available) and say little about other key organizational performance indicators, such as customer satisfaction, employee turnover, and operational performance. To get around these problems, Kaplan and Norton advocate creating a set of goals and metrics for customers, employees, internal operations, and finance. Customer and employee goals and metrics make up leading indicators because problems with customer satisfaction and employee turnover often result in subpar operational and financial performance.

Curphy has developed balanced scorecards for rural Minnesota hospitals and school districts. For example, hospitals begin this process with a comprehensive review of their market demographics, customer trends, financial performance, internal operations (pharmacy, surgical use, infection rates, radiology and lab use, and so on), and staffing and facility data. Key community and health care leaders then create a new five-year vision for the hospital and set strategic priorities in the customer, financial, internal operations, and workforce and facilities categories. These priorities are refined further to create clear, measurable goals with readily available metrics to track monthly progress. These balanced scorecard goals are used to drive specific department goals and track hospital performance and have been very effective in helping all hospital employees understand how their efforts contribute to the hospital's overall performance. In several cases hospital performance has dramatically improved as a result of these balanced scorecard efforts. A partial example of a typical balanced scorecard for one of these rural hospitals is as follows:

- **Customer:** Improve patient satisfaction ratings from 74 to 86 percent by 1 January 2015.
- **Customer:** Increase the number of live births from 12 to 20 per month by 1 January 2015.
- **Financial:** Reduce average accounts payable from 84 to 53 days by 1 January 2015.
- **Financial:** Increase operating margins from 2 to 6 percent by 1 January 2015.
- **Internal operations:** Increase orthopedic surgeries from 4 to 8 per day by 1 March 2015.
- **Internal operations:** Reduce patient infection rates from 1 to .5 percent by 1 March 2015.
- **Workforce:** Reduce days needed to hire nurses from 62 to 22 days by 1 March 2015.
- **Workforce:** Reduce employee turnover rates from 27 to 12 percent by 1 March 2015.

A monthly balanced scorecard report is included in all employee pay statements and is a key topic of discussion in hospital and department staff meetings. Staff members review goal progress and regularly devise strategies for achieving department and hospital goals. A nice thing about the balanced scorecard is that it helps employees be proactive and gives them permission to win. In too many organizations employees work hard but never see how their results contribute to team or organizational performance. Adopting balanced scorecards is a way to get around these problems.

Sources: G. J. Curphy, *The Blandin Education Leadership Program* (Grand Rapids, MN: The Blandin Foundation, 2004); R. S. Kaplan and D. P. Norton, "The Balanced Scorecard: Measures That Drive Performance," *Harvard Business Review,* January–February 1992, pp. 71–79; R. S. Kaplan and D. P. Norton, *The Balanced Scorecard* (Boston, MA: Harvard Business School Press, 1996); R. S. Kaplan and D. P. Norton, *The Strategy Focused Organization* (Boston, MA: Harvard Business School Press, 2001); G. Curphy and R Hogan, *The Rocket Model: Practical Advice for Building High Performing Teams* (Tulsa, OK: Hogan Press, 2012).

Several other aspects of goal setting are also worth noting. First, goals can be set for any aspect of performance, be it reducing costs, improving the quality of services and products, increasing voter registration, or winning a league championship. Nevertheless, leaders need to ensure that they do not set conflicting goals because followers can exert only so much effort over a given time.[70] Second, determining just how challenging to make goals creates a bit of a dilemma for leaders. Successfully completed goals give followers a sense of job satisfaction, and easy goals are more likely to be completed than difficult goals. However, easily attainable goals result in lower levels of effort (and performance) than do more difficult goals. Research suggests that leaders might motivate followers most effectively by setting moderately difficult goals, recognizing partial goal accomplishment, and making use of a continuous improvement philosophy by making goals incrementally more difficult.[71–76]

A leader's implicit and explicit expectations about goal accomplishment can also affect the performance of followers and teams. Research by Dov Eden and his associates in Israel has provided consistent support for the Pygmalion and Golem effects.[77,78] The **Pygmalion effect** occurs when leaders articulate high expectations for followers; in many cases these expectations alone will lead to higher-performing followers and teams. Unfortunately the **Golem effect** is also true—leaders who have little faith in their followers' ability to accomplish a goal are rarely disappointed. Thus a leader's expectations for a follower or team have a good chance of becoming a self-fulfilling prophecy (Chapter 2). These results indicate that leaders wanting to improve individual or team performance should set high but achievable goals and express confidence and support that the followers can get the job done.[79,80]

How could leadership practitioners apply goal setting to Julie and Ling Ling to increase their motivation levels? Given the research findings just described, Julie and Ling Ling's bosses should work with these two followers to set specific and moderately difficult goals, express confidence that they can achieve their goals, and provide regular feedback on goal progress. Julie and her boss could look at Julie's past performance or other lift operators' performance as a baseline, and then set specific and measurable goals for the number of hours worked, the number of people who fall off the lift during a shift, customer satisfaction survey ratings from skiers, the length of lift lines, or the number of complaints from customers. Similarly, Ling Ling and her boss could look at some real estate baseline measures and set goals for the number of apartments rented for the year, the total monetary value of these rentals, the time it takes to close a lease and complete the necessary paperwork, customer complaints, and sales expenses. Note that both Ling Ling and Julie's bosses would need to take care that they do not set conflicting goals. For example, if Julie had a goal only for the number of people who fell off the lift, she might be likely to run the lift slowly, resulting in long lift lines and numerous customer

350   Part Three   *Focus on the Followers*

If you can't measure it, then you can't manage it.

Peter Drucker, leadership researcher

complaints. In a similar vein, bosses need to ensure that individual goals do not conflict with team or organizational goals. Ling Ling's boss would need to make sure that Ling Ling's goals did not interfere with those of the other real estate agents in the firm. If Ling Ling's goals did not specify territorial limits, she might rent properties in other agents' territories, which might cause a high level of interoffice conflict. Both bosses should also take care to set measurable goals; that way they could give Julie and Ling Ling the feedback they need to stay on track.

Goal setting could also help the airline company motivate flight attendants to provide better service to customers. Airline executives may believe customer satisfaction is critically important for keeping planes full, but they may not have set a specific goal for or devised a good way to measure customer satisfaction on individual flights. Customer service may improve only when the airline sets a clear customer satisfaction goal, makes feedback against the goal readily available, and holds flight attendants accountable for improved customer satisfaction results. Likewise, goal setting was also very prevalent for U.S. workers from 2002 to 2010. The first five years of this period saw a steady increase in market share, revenues, new product, profitability, and similar goals set each year, but the economic recession resulted in most if not all corporate goals being scaled back to where they were five years earlier. For example, a company with a $500,000,000 revenue goal in 2003 and steady growth may have had a $700,000,000 revenue goal by 2007. With the recession this revenue goal may have been scaled back to $500,000,000 in 2008. Although many key organizational goals were scaled back during the 2008 to 2010 recession, most leaders had significantly fewer people to get the goals accomplished. In many cases those who remained found that they needed to get much more work done with many fewer people. Those who were laid off often set goals for finding new jobs and the activities they would engage in to make this happen. Because goal setting is such a widely used and powerful motivational technique, more about this topic can be found in Chapter 11.

You get what you reinforce, but you do not necessarily get what you pay for.

Fred Luthans, University of Nebraska, and Alexander Stajkovic, University of California, Irvine

The Operant Approach: How Do Rewards and Punishment Affect Motivation?

One popular way to change the direction, intensity, or persistence of behavior is through rewards and punishments. It will help at the outset of this discussion of the **operant approach** to define several terms. A **reward** is any consequence that *increases* the likelihood that a particular behavior will be repeated. For example, if Julie gets a cash award for a suggestion to improve customer service at the ski resort, she will be more likely to forward additional suggestions. **Punishment** is the administration of an aversive stimulus or the withdrawal of something desirable, each of which *decreases* the likelihood that a particular behavior will be repeated.[81] Thus if Ling Ling loses her bonus for not getting her paperwork in on time, she will be less likely to do so again in the future. Both rewards and punishments

James Mwangi

PROFILES IN LEADERSHIP 9.3

One of the factors limiting economic growth in Africa is poor infrastructure. Much of Africa lacks the roads, train lines, electrical grids, and Internet access needed to move goods and services from place to place. One of these infrastructure limitations is banking. Many African nations operate on a cash basis and do not have the financial service systems needed to make deposits, transfer money, or take out loans.

In 1994 the Equity Building Society, a bank in rural Kenya that provided financial services to the poor, was on the verge of bankruptcy. Bad management, an economic downturn, and a number of bad loans had brought the bank to the brink of failure. The Board of Directors turned to James Mwangi for help, and he started the bank's transformation by converting loan owners to shareholders. This gave those holding loans an equity stake in the bank's future, and the number of bad loans eventually shrank to less than 1.5 percent of the total shillings loaned. Mwangi also changed the focus of the bank from providing home mortgages to issuing microloans to poor farmers and shopkeepers. Farmers could take out loans as small as 500 shillings (about $9.00) and use this money for seed, fertilizer, tools, and cell phones. Under Mwangi's leadership the Equity Building Society returned to solvency and expanded across Kenya. In 2000 the bank reported a net profit of 33.6 million shillings that had grown to over 12 billion shillings by the end of 2012.

Do you think Maslow's hierarchy of needs, achievement orientation, goal setting, the operant approach, or empowerment best explain the success of the Equity Building Society?

Source: "Kenya's Biggest Bank: The Cult of Equity," *The Economist*, December 8, 2012, p. 76.

can be administered in a contingent or noncontingent manner. **Contingent** rewards or punishments are administered as *consequences of a particular behavior.* Examples might include giving Julie a medal immediately after she wins a skiing race or giving Ling Ling a bonus check for exceeding her sales quota. **Noncontingent** rewards and punishments are not associated with particular behaviors. Monthly paychecks might be examples if both Julie and Ling Ling receive the same amount of base pay every month whatever their actual effort or output. Finally, behaviors that are not rewarded may eventually be eliminated through the process of **extinction.**

When properly implemented, there is ample evidence to show that the operant approach can be an effective way to improve follower motivation and performance.[82–90] Some of this research has also shown that rewards work better than punishments, particularly if administered in a contingent manner.[83,85,88,91–94] When comparing the relative impact of different types of rewards, Stajkovic and Luthans reported that incentive pay targeted at specific follower behaviors was the most effective, followed by social recognition and performance feedback, for improving follower performance in credit card processing centers.[85] Although some may argue otherwise, the research clearly shows that leaders who properly design and implement contingent reward systems do indeed increase follower productivity and performance. See Highlight 9.6 for more information about incentive systems.

Professional Athlete and Executive Salary Demands

HIGHLIGHT 9.6

General managers are responsible for the overall performance of their professional sports teams. They help select players and coaches; negotiate media, player, coach, and stadium contracts; keep team morale at a high level; and take action to ensure the team wins the championship and makes money. One of the most difficult issues general managers deal with is negotiating contracts with players. Players look at their own pay and performance and compare them to those of other athletes in the league. If they feel their compensation is not consistent with that of other players, they usually ask to be traded or for a new contract to be negotiated. These comparisons have led to the $100 million–plus salaries now commanded by star players in basketball, football, and baseball. But what happens to team morale, the win–loss record, and financial performance when one or two players make substantially more money than the rest of the team? Research on professional baseball teams over an eight-year period indicated that teams with high pay dispersion levels (large gaps between the highest-and lowest-paid starting players) did less well financially and were less likely to win division championships. Researchers surmised that this drop in team performance was due to the high levels of pay dispersion, which eroded team performance and increased inequity for other players on the team. The trick for general managers seems to be to find enough financial rewards to induce higher levels of performance but not create inequity situations for the rest of the team.

The effects of pay inequity that are readily apparent with professional athletes' pay also hold true for top executives. Many boards of directors worry that if they do not pay their CEOs and top executives at least on par with those in other companies, they run the risk of executive turnover. But executives who negotiate large signing bonuses and big annual pay packages don't necessarily achieve better results than their lower-paid counterparts. Far too many executives tout the benefits of pay for performance but appear much more concerned with their own pay than their company's performance. For example, the compensation for the average United States worker rose at a 0.3 percent annual rate from 1980 to 2004, yet the average CEO's compensation grew at a rate of 8.5 percent annually. CEOs promised an average of 11.5 percent annual earnings growth over this period but actually only achieved 6 percent growth, which was slightly less than the annual percentage growth rate for the overall economy from 1980 to 2004. Despite the fact that the average CEO performed no better than the overall economy, in 1980 the average CEO made 42 times as much as the average worker, and by 2004 this had increased to 280 times the average worker's salary. The top executives in Japanese companies currently make 20 to 30 times more than the average employee, and one has to wonder if companies with high pay dispersions achieve the same suboptimal results as do professional athletic teams with high pay dispersions. With workers putting in longer hours for less pay and the people on top getting fat paychecks and bonuses irrespective of results, is it any wonder that workers are less satisfied and engaged?

Sources: M. Bloom, "The Performance Effects of Pay Dispersions on Individuals and Organizations," *Academy of Management Journal* 42, no. 1 (1999), pp. 25–40; J. Lublin, "Boards Tie CEO Pay More Tightly to Performance," *The Wall Street Journal,* February 21, 2006, pp. A1 and A14; L. A. Bebchuk and J. M. Fried, "Pay without Performance: Overview of the Issues," *The Academy of Management Perspectives* 20, no. 1 (2006), pp. 5–24; J. Bogle, "Reflections on CEO Compensation," *The Academy of Management Perspectives* 22, no. 2 (2008), pp. 21–25.

How can a leader design and implement an operant system for improving followers' motivation and performance levels? Using operant principles properly to improve followers' motivation and performance requires several steps. First, *leadership practitioners need to clearly specify what behaviors are important.* This means that Julie's and Ling Ling's leaders will need to specify what they want them to do, how often they should do it, and the level of performance required. Second, *leadership practitioners need to determine if those behaviors are currently being punished, rewarded, or ignored.* Believe it or not, sometimes followers are actually rewarded for behaviors that leaders are trying to extinguish, and punished for behaviors that leaders want to increase. For example, Julie may get considerable positive attention from peers by talking back to her leader or for violating the ski resort dress code. Similarly, Ling Ling may be overly competitive and get promoted ahead of her peers (such as by renting apartments in her peers' territories), even when her boss extols the need for cooperation and teamwork. And leaders sometimes just ignore the behaviors they would like to see strengthened. An example here would be if Julie's boss consistently failed to provide rewards when Julie worked hard to achieve impressive safety and customer service ratings (see Highlight 9.7).

How am I supposed to feed my family on only $14 million a year?
Latrell Sprewell, professional basketball player

Third, *leadership practitioners need to find out what followers actually find rewarding and punishing.* Leaders should *not* make the mistake of assuming that all followers will find the same things to be rewarding or punishing. One follower's punishment may be another follower's reward. For example, Ling Ling may dislike public attention and actually exert less effort after being publicly recognized, yet some of her peers may find public attention rewarding. Fourth, *leadership practitioners need to be wary of creating perceptions of inequity when administering individually tailored rewards.* A peer may feel that she got the same results as Ling Ling, yet she received a smaller bonus check for the quarter. Leaders can minimize inequities by being clear and consistent with rewards and punishments. Fifth, *leadership practitioners should not limit themselves to administering organizationally sanctioned rewards and punishments.* Often leaders are limited in the amount of money they can give followers for good performance. However, research has shown that social recognition and performance feedback significantly improved productivity in followers, and these rewards do not cost any money.[84,85] Using ingenuity, leaders can often come up with an array of potential rewards and punishments that are effective and inexpensive and do not violate organizational norms or policies. Julie might find driving the snow cat to be enjoyable, and her boss could use this reward to maintain or increase Julie's motivation levels for operating the ski lift. Finally, because the administration of noncontingent consequences has relatively little impact, *leadership practitioners should administer rewards and punishments in a contingent manner whenever possible.* Highlight 9.7 provides examples of the unintended consequences of implementing an operant approach to boost organizational performance.

The Folly of Rewarding A While Hoping for B

HIGHLIGHT 9.7

Steven Kerr has written a compelling article detailing how many of the reward systems found in government, sports, universities, businesses, medicine, and politics often compel people to act in a manner contrary to that intended. For example, voters want politicians to provide the specifics of their programs or platform, yet politicians often get punished for doing so. Some constituency is bound to be hurt or offended whenever the specifics of a program are revealed, which in turn will cost the politician votes. If a politician keeps overall goals vague, more voters are likely to agree with the politician and vote for him or her in the next election. Businesses, like universities and politicians, often use inappropriate reward systems. According to Kerr, the following are some of the more common management reward follies:

We hope for . . .	But we often reward . . .
Long-term growth	Quarterly earnings
Teamwork	Individual effort
Commitment to total quality	Shipping on schedule, even with defects
Reporting honest news	Reporting good news, whether it is true or not

Kerr states that managers who complain about unmotivated workers should consider the possibility that their current reward system is incongruent with the performance they desire. And nowhere is this lack of congruence between what companies want and what they reward more visible than with executive compensation. Boards often have to front millions of dollars to new CEOs to get them to join the company, and then often must provide stock options and other forms of compensation to retain these individuals even though they consistently fail to hit their numbers. Many corporations talk a good game when it comes to pay for performance, but their actions indicate they are more likely to reward tenure while hoping for improved performance.

Sources: S. Kerr, "On the Folly of Rewarding A, While Hoping for B," *Academy of Management Executive* 9, no. 1 (1995), pp. 7–14; S. Kerr, "Establishing Organizational Goals and Rewards," *Academy of Management Executive* 18, no. 4 (2004), pp. 122–23; S. D. Levitt and S. J. Dubner, *Freakonomics* (New York: HarperCollins Publishers, 2005); L. Bebchuck and J. Fried, *Pay without Performance* (Boston, MA: Harvard University Press, 2004); L. Bebchuck and J. Fried, "Pay without Performance: Overview of the Issues," *The Academy of Management Perspectives* 20, no. 1 (2006), pp. 5–24; P. Dvorak, "Limits on Executive Pay: Easy to Set, Hard to Keep," *The Wall Street Journal*, April 9, 2007, pp. B1 and B5; J. S. Lublin, "Boards Tie CEO Pay More Tightly to Performance," *The Wall Street Journal*, February 21, 2006, pp. A1 and A4.

The operant approach can also be used to improve customer service for flight attendants. Using the tenets described earlier, the airline would need to specify which customer satisfaction behaviors were important, determine if those behaviors were being reinforced or punished, determine what attendants found to be rewarding, and administer valued rewards whenever attendants demonstrated good customer service behaviors.

The operant approach to motivation was alive and well in the United States from 2002 to 2012 and continues to be a popular motivational technique in many companies today. Most organizations tout a "pay for performance" culture and pay bonuses or commissions for results obtained. This can most clearly be seen in sales positions, where salespeople are paid a percentage of the total dollars they sell. Needless to say, salespeople experienced a large drop in compensation when customers stopped buying products and services during the 2008 to 2010 recession, despite exhibiting all the behaviors needed to retain customers or get new business in the door. This example points out a shortcoming of the operant technique, which is that situational factors can overwhelm the effectiveness of a reward program. Sometimes people can get big bonuses or commissions without working hard because they are selling a hot product or the economy is experiencing a boom. Other times they may do all the right things but nobody wants to buy their products because of factors beyond their control (such as selling pickup trucks when gasoline is $4.00 per gallon). (See Highlight 9.8.)

The Culture of Praise

HIGHLIGHT 9.8

There is no doubt that the generation of people entering the workforce these days has had more positive reinforcement while growing up than any previous generation. As children these individuals got positive strokes in the form of rewards, ribbons, plaques, and certificates for just showing up to athletic events or school activities. For example, one of this book's authors went to a school assembly for one of his children and watched teachers pass out awards to all 300 students in the elementary school. Some of the awards were for student achievement or citizenship, but many were for "completing your homework for three days in a row" and "having a nice smile." Thirty years ago it was difficult to earn an athletic letter in one or two sports, but some of today's athletic jackets have 20 to 30 awards and letters. This culture of praise was intended to boost self-esteem and better prepare students for life after high school, but as described in Highlight 9.7, the use of unconditional praise has had some unintended implications that organizations must deal with.

One implication is that people now entering the workforce are much more likely to be self-centered, "narcissistic praise junkies" than the people they are working for. Because of the constant positive reinforcement they received when growing up, a much higher percentage of people in this generation think they are special and should get rewarded for anything and everything they do. Organizations, recognizing this need in their youngest employees, are taking some extraordinary steps to boost the self-esteem of (and retain) these individuals. For example, Lands' End and Bank of America teach managers how to compliment employees using e-mail, prize packages, and public displays of appreciation. The Scooter Store has a "celebration assistant" whose job is to throw 25 pounds of confetti and pass out 100 to 500 helium balloons to employees each week. The Container Store estimates that one of its 4,000 employees is rewarded every 20 seconds.

But what is the impact of these praise and recognition programs? Company officials argue they would see high levels of turnover without these programs. But if this younger generation gets constant recognition just for meeting minimum standards, what happens when they get promoted into supervisory positions? The short-term consequence may be improved retention of young employees, but the long-term consequence may be leaders who are unable to deal with difficult business or personnel issues.

Source: J. Zaslow, "The Most Praised Generation Goes to Work," *The Wall Street Journal*, April 20, 2007, pp. W1 and W7.

Empowerment: How Does Decision-Making Latitude Affect Motivation?

Empowerment is the final approach to motivation that will be discussed in this chapter. In general, people seem to fall into one of two camps with respect to empowerment. Some people believe empowerment is about delegation and accountability; it is a top-down process in which senior leaders articulate a vision and specific goals and hold followers responsible for achieving them. Others believe empowerment is more of a bottom-up approach that focuses on intelligent risk taking, growth, change, trust, and ownership; followers act as entrepreneurs and owners who question rules and make intelligent decisions. Leaders tolerate mistakes and encourage cooperative behavior in this approach to empowerment.[95–99] Needless to say, these two conceptualizations of empowerment have very different implications for leaders and followers. And it is precisely this conceptual confusion that has caused empowerment programs to fail in many organizations.[95] Because of the conceptual confusion surrounding empowerment, companies such as Motorola will not use this term to describe programs that push decision making to lower organizational levels. These companies would rather coin their own terms to describe these programs, thus avoiding the confusion surrounding empowerment.

We define empowerment as having two key components. For leaders to truly empower employees, they must delegate leadership and decision making down to the lowest level possible. Employees are often the closest to the problem and have the most information, and as such can often make the best decisions. A classic example was the UPS employee who ordered an extra 737 aircraft to haul parcels that had been forgotten in the last-minute Christmas rush. This decision was clearly beyond the employee's level of authority, but UPS praised his initiative for seeing the problem and making the right decision. The second component of empowerment, and the one most often overlooked, is equipping followers with the resources, knowledge, and skills necessary to make good decisions. Often companies adopt an empowerment program and push decision making down to the employee level, but employees have no experience in creating business plans, submitting budgets, dealing with other departments within the company, or directly dealing with customers or vendors. Not surprisingly, ill-equipped employees can make poor, uninformed decisions, and managers in turn are likely to believe that empowerment was not all it was cracked up to be. The same happens with downsizing as employees are asked to take on additional responsibilities but are given little training or support. Such "forced" empowerment may lead to some short-term stock gains but tends to be disastrous in the long run. Thus empowerment has both delegation and developmental components; delegation without development is often perceived as abandonment, and development without delegation can often be

Hemmed in by rules and treated as unimportant, people get even.
Rosabeth Moss Kanter, Harvard University

perceived as micromanagement. Leaders wishing to empower followers must determine what followers are capable of doing, enhance and broaden these capabilities, and give followers commensurate increases in authority and accountability.

The psychological components of empowerment can be examined at both macro and micro levels. Three macro psychological components underlie empowerment: motivation, learning, and stress. As a concept, empowerment has been around since at least the 1920s, and the vast majority of companies that have implemented empowerment programs have done so to increase employee motivation and, in turn, productivity. As a motivational technique empowerment has a mixed record; often empowered workers are more productive than unempowered workers, but at times this may not be the case. When empowerment does not increase productivity, senior leaders may tend to see empowerment through rose-colored glasses. They hear about the benefits an empowerment program is having in another company but do not consider the time, effort, and changes needed to create a truly empowered workforce. Relatedly, many empowerment programs are poorly implemented—the program is announced with great fanfare, but little real guidance, training, or support is provided, and managers are quick to pull the plug on the program as soon as followers start making poor decisions. Adopting an effective empowerment program takes training, trust, and time; but companies most likely to implement an empowerment program (as a panacea for their poor financial situation) often lack these three attributes.[100,101] In addition, worker productivity and job dissatisfaction in the United States and Europe are at an all-time high. Many companies are dealing with high levels of employee burnout, and adding responsibilities to overfilled plates is likely to be counterproductive. As reported by Xie and Johns, some empowerment programs create positions that are just too big for a person to handle effectively, and job burnout is usually the result.[102]

Although the motivational benefits of empowerment are sometimes not realized, the learning and stress reduction benefits of empowerment are more clear-cut. Given that properly designed and implemented empowerment programs include a strong developmental component, a key benefit to these programs is that they help employees learn more about their jobs, company, and industry. These knowledge and skill gains increase the intellectual capital of the company and can be a competitive advantage in moving ahead. In addition to the learning benefits, well-designed empowerment programs can help reduce burnout. People can tolerate high levels of stress when they have a high level of control. Given that many employees are putting in longer hours than ever before and work demands are at an all-time high, empowerment can help followers gain some control over their lives and better cope with stress. Although an empowered worker may have the same high work demands as an unempowered worker, the

Power and Empowerment

HIGHLIGHT 9.9

A famous Lord Acton quote is "Power corrupts," which essentially means that the more power one has the more likely one is to break laws, rules, and societal norms. Leadership researcher Rosabeth Moss Kanter has an interesting variation of this quote that relates to the concept of empowerment. According to Kanter, powerlessness also corrupts. In other words, if workers are given only a small amount of power, they will jealously guard whatever power they have. Employees with little power do not show their unhappiness by voicing their opinions but instead flex their muscles by demanding tribute before responding to requests. They rigidly adhere to the policies governing their position and ensure there are no exceptions to anyone following their rules. Customers are told to submit all required forms, get signed permissions from other entities, and follow bureaucratic procedures to the letter if they want anything done, and it will take requesters months to see tangible results. Because speed is an essential component of execution, powerlessness can paralyze companies needing to quickly build products, process orders, submit invoices, receive payments, service customers, or hire and train new employees.

A good example of how powerlessness can impact a company's public reputation comes from the airline industry. One particular airline had a policy stating three bags could be checked for free but passengers would be charged $200 for each bag over the limit. A group of soldiers were flying home after a one-year deployment in Afghanistan and had checked four bags, which they were authorized to do according to their military orders. The gate agents insisted company policy took precedence over military orders and charged each of the soldiers $200 for the additional bags. Unable to get the issue resolved with the gate agents, two of the solders recorded the incident and posted the videos on YouTube, which soon went viral. The airline endured a major public relations fiasco before quickly apologizing and reimbursing the soldiers.

What motivational approaches would best describe the gate agents? In what ways could the airline industry empower gate agents to better service passengers?

Sources: R. Moss Kanter, "Powerlessness Corrupts," *Harvard Business Review*, July–August 2010, p. 36; http://www.businessweek.com/management/when-scorecards-and-metrics-kill-employee-engagement-07122011.html.

empowered worker will have more choices in how and when to accomplish these demands and as such will suffer from less stress. Giving workers more control over their work demands can reduce turnover and in turn improve the company's bottom line. (See Highlight 9.9.)

There are also four micro components of empowerment. These components can be used to determine whether employees are empowered or unempowered, and include self-determination, meaning, competence, and influence.[95,96,103] Empowered employees have a sense of self-determination; they can make choices about what they do, how they do it, and when they need to get it done. Empowered employees also have a strong sense of meaning; they believe what they do is important to them and to the company's success. Empowered employees have a high level of competence: they know what they are doing and are confident they can get the job done. Finally, empowered employees have an impact on others and believe that they can influence their teams or work units and that

FIGURE 9.3
The Empowerment Continuum

Empowered Employees ←――――→ **Unempowered Employees**

- Self-determined.
- Sense of meaning.
- High competence.
- High influence.

- Other-determined.
- Not sure if what they do is important.
- Low competence.
- Low influence.

co-workers and leaders will listen to their ideas. In summary, empowered employees have latitude to make decisions, are comfortable making these decisions, believe what they do is important, and are seen as influential members of their team. Unempowered employees may have little latitude to make decisions, may feel ill equipped and may not want to make decisions, and may have little impact on their work unit, even if they have good ideas. Most employees probably fall somewhere between the two extremes of the empowerment continuum, depicted in Figure 9.3.

Empowerment and the operant approach make an important point that is often overlooked by other theories of motivation: by changing the situation, leaders can enhance followers' motivation, performance, and satisfaction. Unfortunately many leaders naively assume it is easier to change an *individual* than it is to change the *situation,* but this is often not the case. The situation is not always fixed, and followers are not the only variable in the performance equation. Leaders can often see positive changes in followers' motivation levels by restructuring work processes and procedures, which in turn can increase their latitude to make decisions and add more meaning to work. Tying these changes to a well-designed and well-implemented reward system can further increase motivation. However, leaders are likely to encounter some resistance whenever they change the processes, procedures, and rewards for work, even if these changes are for the better. Doing things the old way is relatively easy—followers know the expectations for performance and usually have developed the skills needed to achieve results. Followers often find that doing things a new way can be frustrating because expectations may be unclear and they may not have the requisite skills. Leaders can help followers work through this initial resistance to new processes and procedures by showing support, providing training and coaching on new skills, and capitalizing on opportunities to reward progress. If the processes, procedures, and rewards are properly designed and administered, then in many cases followers will successfully work through their resistance and, over time, wonder how they ever got work done using the old systems. The successful transition to new work processes and procedures will rest squarely on the shoulders of leaders. How could you use empowerment to improve the performance of Julie or Ling-Ling or the customer service levels of flight attendants? What information would you need to gather, how would you implement the program, and what would be the potential pitfalls of your program? And what do you think happened to empowerment as North American and European companies went through the economic recession of 2008 to 2012?

Motivation Summary

Some people believe it is virtually impossible to motivate anyone, and leaders can do little to influence people's decisions regarding the direction, intensity, and persistence of their behavior. Clearly there is a lot followers bring to the motivational equation, but we feel that a leader's actions can and do affect followers' motivation levels. If leaders did not affect followers' motivation levels, it would not matter whom one worked for—any results obtained would be solely due to followers' efforts. But as you will read in Chapter 15, whom one works for matters a lot. We hope that after reading this chapter you will have a better understanding of how follower characteristics (needs and achievement orientation), leader actions (goal setting), and situational factors (contingent rewards and empowerment) affect how you and your followers are motivated (and demotivated). Moreover, you should be able to start recognizing situations where some theories provide better insights about problems in motivation levels than others. For example, if we go back to the survival situation described in Chapter 1, we can see that Maslow's hierarchy of needs provides better explanations for the behavior of the survivors than empowerment or the operant approach. On the other hand, if we think about the reasons we might not be doing well in a particular class, we may see that we have not set specific goals for our grades or that the rewards for doing well are not clear. Or if we are working in a bureaucratic organization, we may see few consequences for either substandard or superior performance; thus there is little reason to exert extra effort. Perhaps the best strategy for leaders is to be flexible in the types of interventions they consider to affect follower motivation. That will require, of course, familiarity with the strengths and weaknesses of the different theories and approaches presented here.

Similarly, we need to consider how the five motivational approaches can be used with both individuals and teams. Much of this section focused on applying the five approaches to individuals, but the techniques can also be used to motivate teams of followers. For example, leaders can set team goals and provide team rewards for achieving them. Leaders can also hire team members who have high levels of achievement orientation and then provide everyone on the team with the decision-making latitude and skills needed to adequately perform their jobs. Leaders can also assess where their teams are currently at on the hierarchy of needs and take actions to ensure that lower-order needs are satisfied. Again, having a good understanding of the five motivational approaches will help leaders determine which ones will be most effective in getting teams to change behavior and exert extra energy and effort.

One of the most important tools for motivating followers has not been fully addressed in this chapter. As described in Chapter 14, charismatic or transformational leadership is often associated with extraordinarily high levels of follower motivation, yet none of the theories described in this chapter can adequately explain how these leaders get their followers to do more than they thought possible. Perhaps this is due to the fact that the theories in this chapter take a rational or logical approach to motivation, yet transformational leadership uses emotion as the fuel to drive followers' heightened motivational levels. Just as our needs, thoughts, personality traits, and rewards can motivate us to do something different, so can our emotions drive us to engage in and persist with particular activities. A good example here may be political campaigns. Do people volunteer to work for these campaigns because of some underlying need or personal goals, or because they feel they will be rewarded by helping out? Although these are potential reasons for some followers, the emotions generated by political campaigns, particularly where the two leading candidates represent different value systems, often seem to provide a better explanation for the large amount of time and effort people contribute. Leadership practitioners should not overlook the interplay between emotions and motivation, and the better able they are to address and capitalize on emotions when introducing change, the more successful they are likely to be.

A final point concerns the relationship between motivation and performance. Many leadership practitioners equate the two, but as we pointed out earlier in this chapter, they are not the same concepts. Getting followers to put in more time, energy, and effort on certain behaviors will not help the team to be more successful if they are the wrong behaviors to begin with. Similarly, followers may not know how and when to exhibit behaviors associated with performance. Leadership practitioners must clearly identify the behaviors related to performance, coach and train their followers in how and when to exhibit these behaviors, and then use one or more of the theories described in this chapter to get followers to exhibit and persist with the behaviors associated with higher performance levels.

Understanding and Influencing Follower Satisfaction

As stated earlier, job satisfaction concerns one's attitudes about work, and there are several practical reasons why job satisfaction is an important concept for leaders to think about. Research has shown that satisfied workers are more likely to continue working for an organization.[22,104–109] Satisfied workers are also more likely to engage in organizational citizenship behaviors that go beyond job descriptions and role requirements and help reduce the workload or stress of others in the organization. Dissatisfied workers are more likely to be adversarial in their relations with

TABLE 9.2 Why People Leave or Stay with Organizations

Why Do People Leave Organizations?	Why Do People Stay with Organizations?
Limited recognition and praise	Promises of long-term employment
Compensation	Exciting work and challenge
Limited authority	Fair pay
Poor organizational culture	Encourages fun, collegial relationships
Repetitive work	Supportive management

Sources: B. Kaye and S. Jordan-Evans, *Love 'Em or Lose 'Em: Getting Good People to Stay* (4th ed.) (San Francisco: Berrett-Koehler, 2008), www.sigmaassessmentsystems.com; Pace Communication, *Hemispheres Magazine*, November 1994, p. 155; "Keeping Workers Happy," *USA Today*, February 10, 1998, p. 1B.

Seventy to ninety percent of the decisions not to repeat purchases of anything are not about product or price. They are about dimensions of service.

Barry Gibbons, Burger King

Too many highly trained, committed professionals return again and again to the methodology that employee engagement programs are what 'WE might do to make THEM feel invested in US.' They are an HR brand-loyalty marketing program, really.

Mark Kille, human resources consultant

leadership (filing grievances, for example) and engage in diverse counterproductive behaviors.[110–118] Dissatisfaction is a key reason why people leave organizations, and many of the reasons people are satisfied or dissatisfied with work are within the leader's control (see Table 9.2).[105–107,118]

Although the total costs of dissatisfaction are difficult to measure, the direct costs of replacing a first-line supervisor or an executive can range from $5,000 to $400,000 per hire, depending on recruiting, relocation, and training fees, and these costs do not include those associated with the productivity lost as a result of unfilled positions.[119] Other indirect costs include the loss of customers. A survey of major corporations showed that 49 percent switched to another vendor because of poor customer service.[120] Employees are probably not going to provide world-class service if they are unhappy with their job, boss, or company. The inability to retain customers directly affects revenues and makes investors think twice about buying stock in a company. Relatedly, Schellenbarger reported that 35 percent of investor decisions are driven by nonfinancial factors. Number 5 on a list of 39 factors investors weighed before buying stock was the company's ability to attract and retain talent. These findings imply that a company's stock price is driven not only by market share and profitability, but also by service and bench strength considerations. Thus employee satisfaction (or dissatisfaction) can have a major impact on the organization's bottom line.[121] (See Highlight 9.10.)

Of these outcomes, perhaps employee turnover has the most immediate impact on leadership practitioners. It would be hard for Julie's or Ling Ling's bosses to achieve results if, respectively, ski resort or real estate personnel were constantly having to be replaced and the leader was spending an inordinate amount of time recruiting, hiring, and training replacements. Although some level of **functional turnover** is healthy for an organization (some followers are retiring, did not fit into the organization, or were substandard performers), dysfunctional turnover is not. **Dysfunctional turnover** occurs when the "best and brightest" in an organization become dissatisfied and leave. Dysfunctional turnover is most likely to occur when downsizing is the response to organizational decline

Improving Safety on Offshore Oil Platforms

HIGHLIGHT 9.10

One of the most dangerous jobs in the world is that of an offshore oil rig employee. These employees often work 12- to 16-hour days for two- to four-week shifts operating heavy equipment in confined spaces. Not only is the work long and hard, but many employees face additional dangers from high seas, cold weather, icebergs, hurricanes, and well blowouts. Because of these conditions and the nature of work, many energy companies are concerned with safety. But what can well managers do to create safe oil platforms? It turns out that using a combination of several motivational techniques may be the best way to reduce oil platform accidents.

To reduce accidents, well managers must first set clear goals and performance expectations for safety. If employees believe only production is important to well managers, they will do what they think is right to boost productivity and will pay little attention to safety issues. So managers must set the tone for safety by setting safety goals and constantly reminding employees of safety issues. Second, they must hire employees who are motivated to perform safe work behaviors. Well managers should use personality inventories to hire employees with higher conscientiousness scores because they tend to be risk averse and much more rule abiding than those with lower conscientiousness scores. Third, well managers must ensure that their compensation systems recognize and reward safe behaviors. If the compensation system rewards only productivity, employees will do what they need to in order to maximize their rewards. The same is true if the compensation system rewards both productivity *and* safety. Using this three-pronged approach will not eliminate all oil rig accidents, but it will go a long way toward reducing accident rates.

It appears that BP did not use these proven techniques to improve safety at the Deepwater Horizon oil rig in the Gulf of Mexico. Much of the evidence to date shows that instead BP emphasized productivity and cost cutting. BP used a cheaper (and less safe) well head design, and there were questions whether the equipment used would operate safely at a depth of 5,000 feet. There were ample warnings that the cementing process used to prevent blowouts was not working, and the company did not have good backup plans to deal with blowouts and spills occurring at these depths. The end result was an explosion on the Deepwater Horizon oil rig that killed 11 people and the biggest oil spill in U.S. history. It will take years for the Gulf of Mexico to recover from this environmental disaster, and BP will spend over $23,000,000,000 to cover cleanup and compensation costs.

Unfortunately BP has had a long history of poor safety and environmental performance. In 2005, 15 people were killed and 170 injured in a massive explosion at its Texas City refinery; since then BP refineries have accounted for 760 "egregious, willful" safety violations. These violations are administered when companies demonstrate an intentional disregard of the law or show indifference to employee safety and health. For comparison, other U.S. energy firms had a total of 19 such violations over the same period. What would you do to create an environmentally aware and safety-friendly culture at BP?

Source: R. Gregory, R. T. Hogan, and G. J. Curphy, "Risk-Taking in the Energy Industry," *Well Connected* 5, no. 6 (June 2003), pp. 5–7; http://online.wsj.com/article/SB12599149005978193.html; http://abcnews.go.com/WN/bps-dismal-safety-record/story?id=10763042; http://www.guardian.co.uk/environment/2010/jul/01/bp-deepwater-horizon-oil-spill.

(increased costs or decreased revenues, market share, or profitability). In these situations, dysfunctional turnover may have several devastating effects. First, those individuals in the best position to turn the company around are no longer there. Second, those who remain are even less capable of successfully dealing with the additional workload associated with the downsizings. Compounding this problem is that training budgets also tend to be slashed during downsizings. Third, organizations that downsize have a difficult time recruiting people with the skills needed to turn the company around. Competent candidates avoid applying for jobs within the organization because of uncertain job security, and the less competent managers remaining with the company may decide not to hire anyone who could potentially replace them. Because leaders can play an important role in followers' satisfaction levels, and because followers' satisfaction levels can have a substantial impact on various organizational outcomes, it is worth going into this topic in greater detail (see Highlight 9.11).[104,105,108,122–124]

Employee Motivation, Satisfaction, and Engagement

HIGHLIGHT 9.11

Engagement has been a hot topic over the past 10 years and many companies have spent millions implementing employee engagement programs. But what is employee engagement, is it different from employee motivation and satisfaction, how is it measured, does it matter, and can it be improved? It can be fairly difficult to answer these questions, as employee engagement is defined, measured, and implemented differently across organizations. Some of the common themes that run through the many definitions of engagement seem to be heightened employee emotional levels and more focused energy directed toward work activities. Engaged employees are believed to be more committed to team and company success, to put forth more effort, and to put in the hours necessary to get the job done; disengaged employees don't care about company success and are more interested in collecting paychecks than in completing assigned tasks. This definition of engagement—choosing to act, increased effort levels, and persistence through task completion—is not much different than the definition of motivation found at the beginning of this chapter.

Surveys are typically used to measure employee engagement levels. These surveys are administered every year or two to all the employees in an organization and the results are analyzed to determine what percentage of people are actively engaged,

engaged, disengaged, or actively disengaged. Geographic regions, industry, economic conditions, job types, and engagement definitions all affect the percentage of employees falling into each of these four categories, and companies report that anywhere between 19 to 67 percent of their employees are actively engaged. For example, after 20 years of economic malaise some studies report that Japan has the lowest employee engagement in Asia; others state that engagement in Latin America is among the highest in the world but has dropped precipitously in North America and Europe in 2012. The use of common surveys has allowed companies to benchmark themselves over time, against their competitors, or with companies of similar sizes, in the same geographic regions, and the like.

One of the reasons that the study of employee engagement has become so popular over the last few years is the engagement–shareholder value chain, where it is believed that employee engagement drives higher customer service, customer loyalty, sales, profitability, and share price. Explained another way, companies with higher percentages of actively engaged and engaged employees should ultimately generate higher shareholder returns. Consulting firms that sell employee engagement surveys and improvement programs certainly believe this to be the case and offer statistical data to support the engagement–shareholder value chain, but the facts don't always line up with the marketing hype. It is generally true that companies with higher employee engagement report better business results, but it is uncertain from these findings whether engagement drives performance or performance drives engagement. It could be that employees working for companies with killer apps, great products, or superior business models are made to feel more engaged rather than employee engagement driving improved results. In addition, employee engagement surveys measure feelings and attitudes, whereas organizations are more interested in actions, behaviors, and productivity. The links between emotions and actions may not be direct, as many professional athletes may not have strong loyalties to their teams but perform at high levels, and employees may be emotionally invested in their jobs, but equipment limitations or family circumstances impact their ability to perform.

How people are managed can impact employee engagement levels, so many companies have adopted leadership development and employee engagement programs to improve employee engagement. Some of these programs seem to be based more on the opinions of self-help gurus rather than on solid research. For example, some engagement consultants advocate letting employees work from home, offering regular recognition, or taking employees out to dinner on a regular basis. Although there is nothing inherently wrong with doing any of these things, research shows that these programs can be detrimental to teamwork and employee engagement if employees spend limited time working together or if the leader is boring or incompetent. Best Buy and Yahoo! discontinued their work-at-home programs because managers thought these programs focused employees more on "me" than on "we."

But perhaps the biggest problem with many employee engagement programs is that they seem to be adult versions of the culture of praise described in Highlight 9.8 and they make leaders solely responsible for follower engagement levels. Situational factors are rarely acknowledged, yet the economy, failing businesses, and family circumstances can affect follower engagement. Follower factors also play a role, as employees can choose whether or not to engage. Some may be more motivated to collect paychecks or to make life miserable for others than to engage in work activities. Firing these individuals may be the best thing leaders can do to improve overall engagement levels, but this would be viewed as a setback or a failure of leadership by many engagement advocates.

Do you think employee engagement is important? Is it any different than motivation and satisfaction? What would you do as a leader if you wanted to improve the engagement levels of your followers?

Sources: K. B. Paul and C. L. Johnson, "Engagement at 3M: A Case Study," in *The Executive Guide to Integrated Talent Management,* eds. K. Oakes and P. Galagan (Alexandria, VA: American Society for Training and Development Press, 2011); M. Buckingham and C. Coffman, *First, Break All The Rules* (New York: Simon & Schuster, 1999); J. W. Carlson, "Worker Flexibility Gets a Time-Out," *The Minneapolis Star Tribune,* March 7, 2013, p. A11; Aon Hewitt, *Trends in Global Employee Engagement* (Chicago: Author, 2011); G. Curphy, "Followership: An Overlooked Component in Organizational Success," Presentation given at the ASTD-Lake Superior Chapter Monthly Conference, Duluth, MN, March, 2013; http://www.tlnt.com/2012/11/26/employee-engagement-heres-why-its-a-problem-worldwide/; http://www.forbes.com/sites/kevinkruse/2012/06/22/employee-engagement-what-and-why/; http://www.bersin.com/blog/post/TheBusinessOfTalent/; http://www.chartvcourse.com/enav-172-html/; http://www.ere.net/2012/02/23/what's-wrong-with-employee-engagement-the-top-20-potential-problems/.

Global, Facet, and Life Satisfaction

There are different ways to look at a person's attitudes about work, but researchers usually collect these data using some type of job satisfaction survey.[107,122,123,125,126] Such surveys are usually sent to all employees, the responses are collected and tabulated, and the results are disseminated

TABLE 9.3
Typical Items on a Satisfaction Questionnaire

1. Overall, I am satisfied with my job.
2. I feel the workload is about equal for everyone in the organization.
3. My supervisor handles conflict well.
4. My pay and benefits are comparable to those in other organizations.
5. There is a real future for people in this organization if they apply themselves.
6. Exceptional performance is rewarded in this organization.
7. We have a good health care plan in this organization.
8. In general, I am satisfied with my life and where it is going.

These items are often rated on a scale ranging from *strongly disagree* (1) to *strongly agree* (5).

throughout the organization. Table 9.3 presents examples of three different types of items typically found on a job satisfaction survey. Item 1 is a **global satisfaction** item, which assesses the overall degree to which employees are satisfied with their organization and their job. Items 2 through 7 are **facet satisfaction** items, which assess the degree to which employees are satisfied with different aspects of work, such as pay, benefits, promotion policies, working hours and conditions, and the like. People may be relatively satisfied overall but still dissatisfied with certain aspects of work. For example, from 2001 to 2011 job security was a primary factor driving employee satisfaction, and the economic downturn in 2008 to 2010 only heightened this concern. A recent study by the Society of Human Resources Management indicated that the opportunity to use skills and abilities, compensation, job security, communication, and relationships with immediate supervisors were the biggest drivers of overall job satisfaction.[127] A study of junior officers in the U.S. Army revealed that overall satisfaction had been in decline and a higher percentage of officers were choosing to leave the army. The two primary reasons for this high level of dysfunctional turnover seemed to be dissatisfaction with immediate supervisors and top leadership. Many junior officers reported that they were tired of working for career-obsessed supervisors who had a strong tendency to micromanage and would just as soon throw them under a bus if it would advance their career.[128–130] This decline in global satisfaction is not limited to the U.S. Army: the same phenomenon is happening in many American and European companies today. Much of this decline can be attributed to higher follower expectations, greater follower access to information through technology, economic downturns, organizational downsizings, and incompetent bosses.

Leadership practitioners should be aware of several other important findings regarding global and facet satisfaction. The first finding is that people generally tend to be happy with their vocation or occupation. They may not like the pay, benefits, or their boss, but they seem to be satisfied with what they do for a living. The second finding pertains to the **hierarchy effect:** in general, people with longer tenure or in higher positions tend to have higher global and facet satisfaction ratings than those newer to or lower in the organization.[131] Because people higher in the organization are happier at work, they may not understand or appreciate why people at lower levels are less satisfied. From below, leaders at the top can appear naive and out of touch. From above, the complaints about morale, pay, or resources are often perceived as whining. One of this book's authors once worked with a utilities company that had downsized and was suffering from all the ill effects associated with high levels of dysfunctional turnover. Unfortunately the executive vice president responsible for attracting and retaining talent and making the company "an employer of choice" stated that he had no idea why employees were complaining and that things would be a lot better if they just quit whining. Because the executive did not understand or appreciate the sources of employee complaints, the programs to improve employee morale completely missed the mark, and the high levels of dysfunctional turnover continued. The hierarchy effect also implies that it will take a considerable amount of top leaders' focus and energy to increase the satisfaction levels of nonmanagement employees—lip service alone is never enough. See Highlight 9.12 for examples of companies who do not seem to take employee satisfaction very seriously.

Compensation is another facet of job satisfaction that can have important implications for leadership practitioners. As you might expect, the hierarchy effect can be seen in pay: a survey of 3 million employees reported that 71 percent of senior management, 58 percent of middle management, and only 46 percent of nonmanagers rate their pay as "very good." Of nonmanagers, 33 percent rate their pay as "so-so" and 20 percent rate their pay as "very poor."[132] Given the wage gap between males and females, a disproportionate number of females can probably be found in these less satisfied groups. Many of these females may be the highest performers in their positions; therefore, this wage discrepancy, in combination with relatively small annual pay increases over the past few years, may contribute to disproportionately high levels of dysfunctional turnover among females.

People who are happier with their jobs also tend to have higher life satisfaction ratings. **Life satisfaction** concerns one's attitudes about life in general, and Item 8 in Table 9.3 is an example of a typical life satisfaction question. Because leaders are often some of the most influential people in their followers' lives, they should never underestimate the impact they have on their followers' overall well-being.

Job satisfaction surveys are used extensively in both public and private institutions. Organizations using these instruments typically administer them every one or two years to assess workers' attitudes about different aspects of work, changes in policies or work procedures, or other initiatives. Such survey results are most useful when they can be compared with those from some **reference group.** The organization's past results can be used as one kind of reference group—are people's ratings of pay,

Would life on a slave ship be much better if the galley master first asked the rowers to help write a mission statement? What employers need to come to terms with is the economic, cultural, and societal benefits of being loyal to their employees. If they don't, eventually their abuses will bite them on the ass.

Daniel Levine, author

Leaders are often the only people surprised by employee satisfaction results. In reality, employees have been talking about the issues identified in these surveys for quite some time.

Dianne Nilsen, business executive

The Wall of Shame: The Ten Worst Companies to Work For in America

HIGHLIGHT 9.12

Most people want to work in companies where they feel valued, have good job security, and get paid a fair wage. Many organizations work hard to fulfill these needs and those that do are often seen as some of the best companies to work for in America. But other companies seem to treat employees as widgets in production lines and put little value on employee satisfaction or engagement. In the past it was hard to know how organizations treated their employees, but the advent of satisfaction and engagement surveys, the Internet, and social media has made this much easier. *Forbes* magazine publishes top companies to work for lists based on employee surveys, and the *Indeed*, *Glassdoor*, and *TheJobCrowd* websites allow current and former employees to provide anonymous ratings and comments about employers. There appears to be ample interest in getting unvarnished views of employers, as *Glassdoor* has 14 million registered users and indeed gets over 85 million visits a month.

Although the worst-companies-to-work-for list varies from year to year, it takes a considerable amount of time for a company to move from the bottom of the list. Put another way, the worst companies to work for have been that way for some time and will likely remain that way in the future. Although situational factors can affect employee ratings, more often than not top and middle management get all the credit for creating employee-unfriendly work environments. Some of the worst companies to work for in 2012 were as follows:

10. GameStop. Employees felt this video game company put sales over customer service, and the company made *Consumer Reports* annual "naughty list" in 2011 for poor customer service.

9. Rite Aid. Employees at this drugstore chain believed management did not know what they were doing and forced people to work overtime and on holidays.

8. Hewlett-Packard. Employees were frustrated that this computer giant had seen more upper management turmoil than any other large company in the United States.

7. Robert-Half International. Employers at this temporary staffing agency said the company's focus on "activity metrics" and "growth expectations" over "team morale" created a toxic working environment.

6. Sears. Aging infrastructure, antiquated systems, low pay, and poor benefits got in the way of employees providing good customer service.

5. OfficeMax. Micromanagement and poor pay were the leading reasons why employees chose to leave this office supply company.

4. Hertz. Employees routinely complained about top management being out of touch, low hourly pay, and menial jobs.

3. RadioShack. Reviewers did not like this retail company's complicated commission structure and long hours. Like GameStop, RadioShack also made *Consumer Reports'* list for bad customer service.

2. Dillard's. Dislike for the CEO and the sales incentive program were the biggest frustrations with this retail department store chain.

1. Dish Network. Many reviewers disliked the long hours, mandatory overtime, lack of flexibility, and no holiday work schedules. Caleb Hannan at *Yahoo! Finance* labeled Dish Network as the "meanest company to work for" in 2013.

What theories of motivation or satisfaction would best explain the reasons that people choose to leave the worst companies to work for? What theories would best explain why people choose to remain with these companies? How would these companies stack up to the worst companies to work for in Western Europe or China?

Sources: "Job-Review Sites: Honesty Unvarnished," *The Economist,* December 8, 2012, p. 68; http://finance.yahoo.com/news/dish-network-meanest-company-america-194008712.html?page-1; http://247wallst.com/2012/08/10/americas-worst-companies-to-work-for/2/.

FIGURE 9.4
Results of a Facet Satisfaction Survey

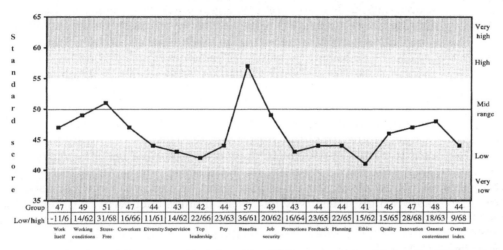

Group	47	49	51	47	44	43	42	44	57	49	43	44	44	41	46	47	48	44
Low/high	-11/6	14/62	31/68	16/66	11/61	14/62	22/66	23/63	36/61	20/62	16/64	23/65	22/65	15/62	15/65	28/68	18/63	9/68
	Work itself	Working conditions	Stress-Free	Coworkers	Diversity	Supervision	Top leadership	Pay	Benefits	Job security	Promotions	Feedback	Planning	Ethics	Quality	Innovation	General contentment	Overall index

Source: D. P. Campbell and S. Hyne, *Manual for the Revised Campbell Organizational Survey* (Minneapolis, MN: National Computing Systems, 1995).

promotion, or overall satisfaction rising or falling over time? Job satisfaction ratings from similar organizations can be another reference group—are satisfaction ratings of leadership and working conditions higher or lower than those in similar organizations?

Figure 9.4 shows the facet and global satisfaction results for approximately 80 employees working at a medium-sized airport in the western United States. Employees completing the survey included the director of aviation and his supervisory staff ($n = 11$), the operations department ($n = 6$), the airfield maintenance department ($n = 15$), the communications department ($n = 6$), the airport facilities staff ($n = 12$), the administration department ($n = 10$), and the custodial staff ($n = 20$). The airport is owned by the city and has seen tremendous growth since the opening of its new terminal; in fact, less than two years later aircraft loads exceeded the capacity of the new terminal. Unfortunately staffing had remained the same since the opening, and the resulting workload and stress were thought to be adversely affecting morale and job satisfaction. Because of these concerns, the director of aviation decided to use a job satisfaction survey to pinpoint problem areas and develop action plans to resolve them.

Scores above 50 on Figure 9.4 are areas of satisfaction; scores below 50 are areas of dissatisfaction when compared to national norms. Here we see that airport employees are very satisfied with their benefits, are fairly satisfied with the work itself, but are dissatisfied with top leadership, ethics, supervision, feedback, promotion opportunities, and the like. All airport employees got to review these results, and each department discussed the factors underlying the survey results and developed and implemented action plans to address problem areas. Top leadership, in this case the director of aviation, was seen as the biggest source of dissatisfaction by all departments. The director was a genuinely nice person and meant well, but he never articulated his vision for the airport, never explained how employees' actions were related to this mission, failed to set goals for each department, did not provide feedback, never clarified roles or areas of responsibilities for his staff, delegated action items to whomever he happened to see in the hall, often changed his mind about key decisions, and failed to keep his staff informed of airline tenant or city council decisions. When confronted with this information, the director placed the blame on the rapid growth of the airport and the lack of staffing support from the city (the fundamental attribution error from Chapter 2). The city manager then gave the director six months to substantially improve employee satisfaction levels. The director did not take the problem seriously; so, not surprisingly, the survey results six months later were no different for top leadership. The director was subsequently removed from his position because of his failure to improve the morale at the airport.

It is rarely enough to merely administer surveys. Leaders must also be willing to take action on the basis of survey results or risk losing credibility and actually increasing job dissatisfaction. Upon receiving the results of these surveys, leaders with bad results may feel tempted to not share any results with their followers, but this is almost always a mistake. Although the results may not be flattering, the rumors are likely to be much worse than the results themselves. Also, followers will be less willing to fill out subsequent satisfaction surveys if they see denial of the results and little change to the workplace. Furthermore, leaders feeling defensive about such results and tempted to hide them should remember that the bad results may surprise no one but themselves; therefore, what's to hide? On a practical level, leaders should never assess employees' attitudes about work unless they are willing to share the results and take action.

The question: If you had to describe your office environment as a type of television show, what would it be? The responses: "Survivor," 38 percent; soap opera, 27 percent; medical emergency, 18 percent; courtroom drama, 10 percent; science fiction, 7 percent.
Andrea Nierenberg, New York University

Three Theories of Job Satisfaction

As shown in Table 9.4, all five of the theories of motivation described earlier in this chapter provide insight into followers' levels of job satisfaction too. For example, it would be difficult for Julie to be satisfied with her job if she was consistently underdressed for weather conditions or for Ling Ling to be satisfied if her goals were unclear, she was not given feedback, or she failed to be rewarded for good performance. Nonetheless, several other theories offer even better explanations for job satisfaction, including affectivity, Herzberg's two-factor theory, and organizational justice.

Affectivity: Is the Cup Half Empty or Half Full?

Affectivity refers to one's tendency to react to stimuli in a consistent emotional manner. People with a disposition for **negative affectivity** consistently react to changes, events, or situations in a negative manner. They

TABLE 9.4
Eight Theories of Satisfaction

Theory or Approach	How Leaders Can Improve Job Satisfaction
Maslow's hierarchy of needs	Helping ensure people's needs are satisfied
Achievement orientation	Securing needed resources, clearing obstacles, and allowing people to work on activities that matter to them
Goal setting	Setting high goals and helping people to accomplish them
Operant approach	Administering rewards
Empowerment	Giving people needed training and more decision-making authority
Affectivity	Hiring happier people
Herzberg's two-factor theory	Giving people more meaningful work
Organizational justice	Treating people fairly

tend to be unhappy with themselves and their lives, and are more likely to focus on the downside or disadvantages of a situation. People with a disposition for **positive affectivity** consistently react to changes, events, or situations in a positive manner. They are happy with their lives and tend to take an upbeat, optimistic approach when faced with new situations. People with a positive affective disposition tend to see a cup as half full; people with a negative affective disposition are more likely to describe a glass as half empty. These two groups of individuals are thought to attend to, process, and recall information differently, and these differences affect both job satisfaction and satisfaction with life itself. Researchers have found that negative affectivity is related to job dissatisfaction, and positive affectivity to job satisfaction. Of course such results are not surprising—we all know individuals who never seem happy whatever their circumstances, and others who seem to maintain a positive outlook even in the most adverse circumstances.[133-136] (See Highlight 9.13.)

These findings suggest that leadership initiatives may have little impact on a person's job satisfaction if her affective disposition is either extremely positive or negative. For example, if Ling Ling has a negative affective disposition, she may remain dissatisfied with her pay, working conditions, and so forth *no matter what her leader does.* This is consistent with the findings of a study of identical twins reared apart and together, which discovered that affectivity has a strong genetic component.[134,137] Given that leaders can do little to change followers' genetic makeup, these findings highlight the importance of using good selection procedures when hiring employees. Trying to increase followers' job satisfaction is a reasonable goal, but some followers may be hard to please.

From a leader's perspective, affectivity can have several implications in the workplace. First, a leader's own affectivity can strongly influence followers' morale or satisfaction levels. Say you worked for a leader with

Some people are next to impossible to please.
Anonymous

The Happiest Occupations, States, and Countries

HIGHLIGHT 9.13

Polls show that job and life satisfaction vary considerably by occupation, state, and even the country in which one lives. And although the United States is the richest nation in the world, it ranked only 16th in life satisfaction. Life satisfaction surveys of 130,000+ people reveal the following (listed in order):

Happiest occupations: business owners, professionals, managers/executives, and farming/forestry

Least happy occupations: transportation, services, installation, and construction

Happiest states: Utah, Hawaii, Wyoming, Colorado, and Minnesota

Least happy states: West Virginia, Kentucky, Mississippi, Ohio, and Arkansas

Happiest countries: Denmark, Finland, the Netherlands, and New Zealand

Least happy countries: Zimbabwe, Ukraine, Armenia, and Russia

Sources: http://new.yahoo.com/s/livescience/20100701/sc_livescience/isrichestnationbutnothappiest; http://livescience.com/culture/091110-fifty-happy-states.html; http://finance.yahoo.com/news/Happy-business-owners-changes-apf-1598303505.html?x=0$.v=1; http://abcnews.go.com/Business/Economy/story?id=7585729&page=1; http://thehappinessshow.com/HappiestCountries.htm.

negative affectivity. Chances are he or she would always find fault in your work and constantly complain about organizational policies, resources, and so on. The opposite might be true if you worked for someone with positive affectivity. Second, leading a high percentage of followers having either positive or negative affectivity would likely result in very different leadership experiences. The positive group may be much more tolerant and willing to put up with organizational changes; the negative group would likely find fault in any change the leader made. Increasing job satisfaction through affectivity means hiring those with positive affectivity. However, few, if any, selection systems address this important workplace variable. Because negative affectivity may not be assessed or even apparent until a follower has been on the job for a while, perhaps the best advice for leadership practitioners is that some followers may have a permanent chip on their shoulders, and there may be little you can do to change it.

Herzberg's Two-Factor Theory: Does Meaningful Work Make People Happy?

If you don't want people to have Mickey Mouse attitudes, then don't give them Mickey Mouse work.
Frederick Herzberg,
researcher

Herzberg developed the **two-factor theory** from a series of interviews he conducted with accountants and engineers. Specifically, he asked what satisfied them about their work and found that their answers usually could be sorted into five consistent categories. Furthermore, rather than assuming that what dissatisfied people was always just the opposite of what satisfied them, he also specifically asked what *dissatisfied* people about their jobs. Surprisingly, the list of satisfiers and dissatisfiers represented entirely different aspects of work.

TABLE 9.5
Motivators and Hygiene Factors of the Two-Factor Theory

Source: Adapted from F. Herzberg, *Work and the Nature of Men* (Cleveland, OH: World Publishing, 1966).

Hygiene Factors	Motivators
Supervision	Achievement
Working conditions	Recognition
Co-workers	The work itself
Pay	Responsibility
Policies/procedures	Advancement and growth
Job security	

Herzberg labeled the factors that led to *satisfaction* at work **motivators,** and he labeled the factors that led to *dissatisfaction* at work **hygiene factors.** The most common motivators and hygiene factors are listed in Table 9.5. According to the two-factor theory, efforts directed toward improving hygiene factors will not increase followers' motivation or satisfaction. No matter how much leaders improve working conditions, pay, or sick leave policies, for example, followers *will not* exert additional effort or persist longer at a task. For example, followers will probably be no more satisfied to do a dull and boring job if they are merely given pleasant office furniture. On the other hand, followers may be asked to work in conditions so poor as to create dissatisfaction, which can distract them from constructive work.[138–140] (See Highlight 9.14.)

Given limited resources on the leader's part, the key to increasing followers' satisfaction levels according to this two-factor theory is to just adequately satisfy the hygiene factors while maximizing the motivators for a particular job. It is important for working conditions to be adequate, but it is even more important (for enhancing motivation and satisfaction) to provide plenty of recognition, responsibility, and possibilities for advancement (see Figure 9.5). Although giving followers meaningful work and then recognizing them for their achievement seem straightforward enough, these techniques are underutilized by leaders.[40,45,140] In other words, Herzberg argues that leaders would be better off restructuring work to make it more meaningful and significant than giving out shirts with company logos or decreasing medical copays.

The two-factor theory offers leaders ideas about how to bolster followers' satisfaction, but it has received little empirical support beyond Herzberg's own results. Perhaps it is not an accurate explanation for job satisfaction despite its apparent grounding in data. We present it here partly because it has become such a well-known approach to work motivation and job satisfaction that this chapter would appear incomplete if we ignored it. One problem with two-factor theory, however, seems to lie in the original data on which it was based. Herzberg developed his theory after interviewing only accountants and engineers—two groups who are hardly representative of workers in other lines of work or activity.

374   Part Three   *Focus on the Followers*

Role Ambiguity, Role Conflict, and Job Satisfaction

HIGHLIGHT 9.14

The eight theories of job satisfaction provide useful frameworks for understanding why people may or may not be happy at work. But two other key causes of job dissatisfaction do not fit neatly into one of these frameworks. The first has to do with **role ambiguity,** which occurs whenever leaders or followers are unclear about what they need to do and how they should do it. Many people come to work to succeed, but too many leaders set followers up for failure by not providing them with the direction, training, or resources they need to be successful. In these situations followers may exert a high level of effort, but they often are not working on the right things and as a result get little accomplished. This sense of frustration quickly turns to dissatisfaction and eventually causes people to look for someplace else to work. An example here is an executive vice president of human resources who left a position early in his career after he had been on the job for only two weeks. During those first two weeks he had never seen his boss, did not have a desk, and did not even have a phone. The irony was that he was working for a major Canadian phone company.

Role conflict occurs when leaders and followers are given incompatible goals to accomplish. For example, leaders may be told that their goals are to boost output while reducing headcount. It will be difficult to achieve both goals unless the leader is given some new process, technology, or product that significantly increases worker productivity. When given seemingly incompatible goals. leaders often focus their efforts on accomplishing some goals to the exclusion of others. This may have been the case with BP's Deepwater Horizon oil rig disaster, where managers were told to drill for oil safely and in an environmentally friendly manner while reducing costs and boosting production. The managers on the rig seemed to focus on production and cost reduction goals, and the end result was the death of 11 workers and an unprecedented environmental disaster.

Although role conflict is a source of dissatisfaction, people need to realize that a key challenge for leaders is to successfully achieve seemingly incompatible goals. If the team has only a productivity goal, many leaders are likely to be successful in helping their team to accomplish this goal. If the team has productivity and profitability goals, fewer leaders are likely to be successful. And if the team has productivity, profitability, safety, quality, and customer satisfaction goals, an even smaller subset of leaders will be successful in all of these areas. The fact is that most teams and organizations have more than one goal, and effective leaders are able to get their teams to successfully accomplish all assigned goals. Hiring achievement-oriented team members, setting clear goals, regularly measuring and reporting on goal progress, clearing obstacles, obtaining needed resources, and providing contingent rewards will go a long way toward the successful accomplishment of multiple goals and improved employee satisfaction.

Sources: G. J. Curphy and R. Hogan, *The Rocket Model: Practical Advice for Building High Performing Teams* (Tulsa, OK: Hogan Press, 2012); "Building High Performing Teams," presentation given at the Minnesota Professionals for Psychology Applied to Work, Minneapolis, MN, February 2013; G. J. Curphy, *Applying the Rocket Model to Virtual Teams,* unpublished manuscript, 2013; G. J. Curphy and M. Roellig, *Followership,* unpublished manuscript, 2010.

FIGURE 9.5
Herzberg's Two-Factor Theory

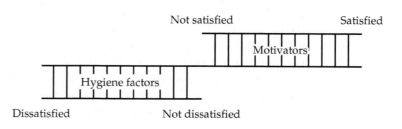

Furthermore, his subjects typically attributed job satisfaction to *their* skill or effort, yet blamed their dissatisfaction on circumstances beyond their control. This sounds suspiciously like the fundamental attribution error described earlier in this book. Despite such limitations, the two-factor theory has provided useful insight into what followers find satisfying and dissatisfying about work.

Organizational Justice: Does Fairness Matter?

Organizational justice is based on the premise that people who are treated unfairly are less productive, satisfied, and committed to their organizations. Moreover, these individuals are also likely to initiate collective action and engage in various counterproductive work behaviors.[141] According to Trevino, organizational justice is made up of three related components. **Interactional justice** reflects the degree to which people are given information about different reward procedures and are treated with dignity and respect. **Distributive justice** concerns followers' perceptions of whether the level of reward or punishment is commensurate with an individual's performance or infraction. Dissatisfaction occurs when followers believe someone has received too little or too much reward or punishment. Perceptions of **procedural justice** involve the process by which rewards or punishments are administered. If someone is to be punished, followers will be more satisfied if the person being punished has been given adequate warnings and has had the opportunity to explain his or her actions, and if the punishment has been administered in a timely and consistent manner.[142] Research has shown that these different components of organizational justice are related to satisfaction with the leader, pay, promotion, the job itself, organizational citizenship behaviors, and counterproductive work behaviors (in instances where perceived injustice was taking place).[31,143–150]

So what should leaders do to improve follower satisfaction and reduce turnover using organizational justice theory? The underlying principle for organizational justice is fairness; going back to our earlier characters, do Ling Ling or Julie feel that the process in which rewards or punishments are administered is fair? Are the potential rewards commensurate with performance? Do Julie and Ling Ling believe the reward system is unbiased? What would the flight attendants say about whether they were treated with dignity and respect, whether rewards were commensurate with performance, or whether rewards were administered fairly? How about the survivors and those who were laid off during the economic recession of 2008 to 2010? Leaders who want to improve job satisfaction using this approach need to ensure that followers answer yes to these three questions; if not, leaders need to change the reward and punishment system if they want to improve job satisfaction using organizational justice theory. Brockner notes that fairness in the workplace makes intuitive

True patriotism hates injustice in its own land more than anywhere else.

Clarence Darrow, attorney

Business opportunities are like buses, there's always another one coming.

Richard Branson, industrialist

Richard Branson

PROFILES IN LEADERSHIP 9.4

Richard Branson is the chairman of Virgin Industries, which owns such companies as Virgin Airlines, Virgin Records, Virgin Galactic, Virgin Fuels, Virgin Media, Virgin Comics, and Virgin Health Care. An entrepreneur since the age of 16, Branson had his first business success publishing *Student* magazine in 1966. From there he started Virgin Records, which at the time was an audio record mail order business. In 1972 he owned a chain of record stores, Virgin Records, and installed a recording studio. At the time the studio was used by a number of top bands, including Mike Oldfield, the Sex Pistols, and Culture Club.

In the 1980s Branson ventured into the airline industry with the launch of Virgin Atlantic Airways. He expanded his airline holdings to include Virgin Express, a low-cost European carrier, and Virgin Blue, an Asia-Pacific carrier. In 2004 he partnered with Paul Allen and Burt Rutan to launch Virgin Galactic, a space tourism company. His Virgin Fuels business was launched to find more environmentally friendly fuels for automobiles and airplanes.

Having a long history of creating successful companies, selling them, and then using the proceeds to fund other business ventures, Branson sold Virgin Records to EMI for approximately $750,000,000 and sold Virgin Mobile for $1,500,000,000. Virgin Industries currently employs 50,000 people in 30 countries and generates $23,000,000,000 in annual revenues. With a personal net worth of over $4,000,000,000, Branson has turned his attention to more humanitarian causes. Working with the likes of Nelson Mandela, Jimmy Carter, Desmond Tutu, and Bono, Branson is looking to develop peaceful resolutions to long-standing conflicts. He is an active promoter of using entrepreneurship to solve environmental problems. What motivational approach would best describe Richard Branson?

Sources: http://www.solarnavigator.net/sponsorship/richard_branson.htm; http://renewableenergyaccess.com/rea/news/story?id=46071; http://groovygecko.net/anon.groovy/clients/akqa/projectamber/press/The_Elders-Press_Release.pdf; http://www.ft.com/cms/s/0/7f5dd8f32-bfa0-11dc-8052-0000779fd2ac.html; http://virgin.com/richard-branson/autobiography/; http://www.hoovers.com/company/Virgin_Group_Ltd/crjkji-1.html.

sense but is woefully lacking in many organizations. Too many managers play favorites, avoid rather than directly deal with uncomfortable situations, or for legal reasons cannot reveal how certain issues were handled.[36] These instances of perceived unfairness are often the underlying causes of job dissatisfaction in many organizations.

Summary

This chapter has reviewed research concerning motivation, satisfaction, and performance. Motivation was defined as anything that provides direction, intensity, and persistence to behavior. Although motivation is an important aspect of performance, performance and motivation are not the same thing. Performance is a broader concept than motivation; abilities, skills, group norms, and the availability of resources can all affect followers' levels of performance. Job satisfaction is a set of attitudes that people have about work. Although many people are generally satisfied with their jobs, they often have varying levels of satisfaction with different aspects of their jobs, such as pay, working conditions, supervisors, or co-workers.

Many of the approaches to understanding motivation have distinct implications for increasing performance and satisfaction. Therefore, several different theories of motivation were reviewed in this chapter. Maslow's hierarchy of needs assumes that people are motivated to satisfy a universal set of needs. Achievement orientation views motivation as a personality trait and assumes some people are hardwired to be more motivated than others. Goal setting examines motivation from a cognitive perspective. This approach assumes that people make rational, conscious choices about the direction, intensity, and persistence of their behaviors, and generally engage in behaviors that maximize payoffs and minimize costs. The last two theories, empowerment and operant approach, examine motivation from a situational perspective. Leadership practitioners likely will be more effective if they learn to recognize situations where various approaches, or the insights particular to them, may be differentially useful.

Several other theories seem to be more useful for explaining followers' attitudes about work. Some research suggests that individuals vary in the characteristic tenor of their affectivity; some people generally have positive attitudes about work and life whereas others are generally unhappy about work and life. Such differences have a genetic component and may limit the extent to which initiatives by leaders will change follower satisfaction. Leaders may be able to increase satisfaction levels by giving followers more meaningful work and by treating them fairly. Followers (and leaders) are more likely to have positive attitudes about work if they believe that what they do is important and that the reward and disciplinary systems are fair and just.

Key Terms

motivation, *333*
performance, *334*
effectiveness, *334*
job satisfaction, *334*
organizational
    citizenship
    behaviors, *334*
needs, *340*
hierarchy of
    needs, *341*
achievement
    orientation, *343*
goal setting, *346*
Pygmalion effect, *349*
Golem effect, *349*
operant approach, *350*

reward, *350*
punishment, *350*
contingent, *351*
noncontingent, *351*
extinction, *351*
empowerment, *356*
functional
    turnover, *362*
dysfunctional
    turnover, *362*
global
    satisfaction, *366*
facet satisfaction, *366*
hierarchy effect, *366*
life satisfaction, *367*
reference group, *367*

negative
    affectivity, *370*
positive
    affectivity, *371*
two-factor theory, *372*
motivators, *373*
hygiene factors, *373*
role ambiguity, *374*
role conflict, *374*
organizational
    justice, *375*
interactional
    justice, *375*
distributive
    justice, *375*
procedural justice, *375*

Questions

1. Why do you think there are so many different theories or approaches to understanding motivation? Shouldn't it be possible to determine which one is best and just use it? Why or why not?

2. Many good leaders are thought of as good motivators. How would you rate Barack Obama, Rachel Maddow, Meg Whitman, or Rush Limbaugh in terms of their ability to motivate others?

3. What is your own view of what motivates people to work hard and perform well?

4. Do you know of any examples where reward systems are inconsistent with desired behavior? How are personal values related to rewards?

5. What do you find personally satisfying or dissatisfying at work or school? For those things you find dissatisfying, how could you make them more satisfying? What theory of job satisfaction best explains your actions?

Activities

1. Earlier in this chapter you were asked how five motivation approaches could be used to improve the customer service levels of flight attendants. Break into five groups, and have each group discuss how they would design and implement a motivation program using one of these approaches. Each group should then give a 15-minute presentation on their findings. The presentation should include the approach they used, how they would collect any needed additional data, the program design, program implementation, potential barriers to the program, and their evaluation of the effectiveness of their program.

2. Identify two companies you would like to work for and check out their *Indeed* or *Glassdoor* reviews. Would you want to work for these companies? Why or why not?

3. Interview someone in a leadership position who has been through a merger or a downsizing and determine their level of satisfaction before and after these events.

4. People often leave bosses, not organizations. Interview people with 10 to 20 years of work experience and ask them to list the reasons they have left jobs. How many people left because of bad bosses? How did the reasons for leaving relate to the motivation and satisfaction approaches described in this chapter?

5. How would motivating a group of volunteers for a community project differ from motivating a group of employees in a for-profit business or a platoon of soldiers?

Minicase

Initech versus the Coffee Bean

Consider Peter Gibbons, an employee of the fictional Initech Corporation from the movie *Office Space*. Peter has been asked to meet with efficiency experts (Bob and Bob) to discuss his work environment. One of the Bobs is curious about Peter's tendency toward underperformance and confronts him about his lack of attention to office policies and procedures. It seems Peter has been turning in his TPS reports late and without the company-mandated cover sheet:

Peter: You see, Bob, it's not that I'm lazy, it's that I just don't care.

Bob: Don't? Don't care?

Peter: It's a problem of motivation, all right? Now if I work my butt off and Initech ships a few extra units, I don't see another dime, so where's the motivation? And here's another thing, I have eight different bosses right now.

Bob: Eight?

Peter: Eight, Bob. So that means when I make a mistake, I have eight different people coming by to tell me about it. That's my only real motivation, not to be hassled, that and the fear of losing my job. But you know, Bob, that will only make someone work just hard enough not to get fired.

The environment at Initech is an all too familiar one to many office workers. It is an environment in which success is directly proportional to how busy you look, where questioning authority is taboo, and where meticulous attention to paperwork is the only way to get promoted.

Contrast Initech to The Coffee Bean—a chain of gourmet coffee shops. In an effort to boost employee morale and increase productivity, the management team at The Coffee Bean decided to pursue the FISH philosophy. FISH is a management training program that stresses fun in the workplace. It espouses four principles:

Play—"Work that is made fun gets done."

Make Their Day—"When you make someone's day through a small act of kindness or unforgettable engagement, you can turn even routine encounters into special memories."

Be There—"Being there is a great way to practice wholeheartedness and fight burnout."

Choose Your Attitude—"When you learn you have the power to choose your response to what life brings, you can look for the best and find opportunities you never imagined possible."

Stores in The Coffee Bean chain were encouraged to use these principles to make the stores a fun place for employees and customers. The stores have created theme days where employees dress up for themes (NFL day, basketball day, pajama day)—and then give discounts to customers who dress the same. There are also trivia games in which customers who can answer trivia questions get discounts on their coffee purchases. Nancy Feilen, a Coffee Bean store manager, explains, "We tried to come up with something that would help strike up a conversation with guests and engage fun in the stores for team members and guests." In other stores, customers play Coffee Craps. If a customer rolls a 7 or an 11, he gets a free drink. Some stores have used Fear Factor Fridays: if the store sells a certain number of drinks, one of the baristas will agree to some act—in one case a barista ate a cricket.

The results? One store increased the average check by 12 percent in six months; turnover has decreased significantly—general managers typically left after 22 months with the chain but now stay an average of 31 months; and the turnover rate for hourly employees dropped to 69 percent from more than 200 percent over a three-year period.

So where would you rather work?

1. How would you gauge Peter's achievement orientation? What are some of the needs not being met for Peter Gibbons at Initech? What changes might improve Peter's motivation?
2. Would you judge the leaders at Initech as more likely to invoke the Pygmalion or the Golem effect? What about the environment at The Coffee Bean—Pygmalion or Golem effect?
3. Why has The Coffee Bean seen such a significant reduction in its turnover?

Sources: http://www.findarticles.com/p/articles/mi_m3190/is_2_38/ai_112248126; http://www.imdb.com/title/tt0151804/quotes; http://www.charthouse.com/home.asp; http://www.gazettenet.com/business/02242003/3706.htm.

Part End Notes

1. G. Anders, "Management Leaders Turn Attention to Followers," *The Wall Street Journal*, January 24, 2007, p. B3.
2. S. Jones, "The Lost Art of Following," *The Minneapolis Star Tribune*, October 7, 2007, p. AA1–AA5.
3. E. Hollander, *Inclusive Leadership* (New York: Routledge/Taylor and Francis, 2008).
4. B. Shamir, "From Passive Recipients to Active Coproducers: Followers Role in the Leadership Process," in *Follower-Centered Perspectives on Leadership: A Tribute to the Memory of James R. Meindl*, eds. B. Shamir, R. Pillai, M. C. Bligh, M. Uhl-Bien (Greenwich, CT: Inform.Age, 2007).
5. M. Van Vugt, R. Hogan, and R. B. Kaiser, "Leadership, Followership, and Evolution: Some Lessons from the Past," *American Psychologist* 63, no. 3, pp. 182–96.

Chapter 9   *Motivation, Satisfaction, and Performance*   **381**

6. J. M. Burger, "Replicating Milgram: Would People Still Obey Today?" *American Psychologist* 64, no. 1, pp. 1–11.

7. P. Bordia, S. L. D. Restubog, and R. L. Tang, "When Employees Strike Back: Investigating Mediating Mechanisms between Psychological Contract Breach and Workplace Deviance," *Journal of Applied Psychology* 93, no. 5 (2008), pp. 1104–17.

8. A. Zaleznik, "The Dynamics of Subordinacy," *Harvard Business Review*, May–June 1965, pp. 119–131.

9. R. E. Kelley, *The Power of Followership: How to Create Leaders People Want to Follow, and Followers Who Led Themselves* (New York: Doubleday, 1982).

10. I. Chaleff, *The Courageous Follower* (3rd ed.) (San Francisco: Berrett-Koehler, 2009).

11. B. Kellerman, "What Every Leader Needs to Know about Followers," *Harvard Business Review*, December 2007, pp. 84–91.

12. R. Adair, "Developing Great Leaders, One Follower at a Time," in *The Art of Followership: How Great Followers Create Great Leaders and Organizations*, eds. R. E. Riggio, I. Chaleff, and J. Lipman-Blumen (San Francisco: Jossey-Bass, 2008), pp. 137–53.

13. J. C. McCroskey, V. P. Richmond, A. D. Johnson, and H. T. Smith, "Organizational Orientations Theory and Measurement: Development of Measures and Preliminary Investigations," *Communication Quarterly* 52 (2004), pp. 1–14.

14. E. H. Potter III and W. E. Rosenbach, "Followers as Partners: Ready When the Time Comes," in *Military Leadership*, 6th ed. (Boulder, CO: Westview Press, 2009).

15. G. J. Curphy and M. E. Roellig, *Followership*, unpublished manuscript (North Oaks, MN: Author, 2010).

16. U. K. Bindl, S. K. Parker, P. Totterdell, and G. Hagger-Johnson, "Fuel of the Self-Starter: How Mood Relates to Proactive Goal Regulation," *Journal of Applied Psychology* 97, no. 1 (2012), pp. 134–50.

17. E. R. Burris, "The Risks and Rewards of Speaking Up: Managerial Responses to Employee Voice," *Academy of Management Journal* 55, no. 4 (2012), pp. 851–75.

18. D. Mercer, *Follow to Lead: The 7 Principles of Being a Good Follower* (Mustang, OK: Tate Publishing, 2011).

19. E. Holm and J. S. Lublin, "Loose Lips Trip up Good Hands Executive," *The Wall Street Journal*, August 1, 2011, pp. C1, C3.

20. A. L. Blanchard, J. Welbourne, D. Gilmore, and A. Bullock, "Followership Styles and Employee Attachment to the Organization," *The Psychologist-Manager Journal* 12, no. 2 (2009), pp. 111–31.

21. D. Brooks, "The Follower Problem," *The New York Times: The Opinion Page*, June 11, 2012, http://www.nytimes.com/2012/06/12/opinion/brooks-the-follower-problem.html?

22. R. Sutton, "How a Few Bad Apples Ruin Everything," *The Wall Street Journal*, October 23, 2011, http://online.wsj.com/article_email/

Chapter End Notes

1. J. E. Hunter, F. L. Schmidt, and M. K. Judiesch, "Individual Differences in Output Variability as a Function of Job Complexity," *Journal of Applied Psychology* 74 (1990), pp. 28–42.

2. E. Matson and L. Prusak, "The Performance Variability Dilemma," *MIT Sloan Management Review* 45, no. 1 (2003), pp. 38–44.

3. Associated Press, "Democrats Hit Troop Extensions," April 12, 2007, http://www.military.com/NewsContent.

4. M. A. Huselid, "The Impact of Human Resource Practices on Turnover, Productivity, and Corporate Financial Performance," *Academy of Management Journal* 38, no. 4 (1995), pp. 635–72.

5. Sirota Consulting, *Establishing the Linkages between Employee Attitudes, Customer Attitudes, and Bottom-Line Results* (Chicago: Author, 1998).

6. D. J. Koys, "The Effects of Employee Satisfaction, Organizational Citizenship Behavior, and Turnover on Organizational Effectiveness: A Unit-Level, Longitudinal Study," *Personnel Psychology* 54, no. 1 (2001), pp. 101–14.

7. S. D. Pugh, J. Dietz, J. W. Wiley, and S. M. Brooks, "Driving Service Effectiveness through Employee–Customer Linkages," *Academy of Management Executive* 16, no. 4 (2002), pp. 73–81.

8. B. A. S. Koene, A. L. W. Vogelaar, and J. L. Soeters, "Leadership Effects on Organizational Climate and Financial Performance: Local Leadership Effect in Chain Organizations," *The Leadership Quarterly* 13, no. 3 (2002), pp. 193–216.

9. G. A. Gelade and M. Ivery, "The Impact of Human Resource Management and Work Climate on Organizational Performance," *Personnel Psychology* 56, no. 2 (2003), pp. 383–404.

10. J. Z. Carr, A. M. Schmidt, J. K. Ford, and R. P. DeShon, "Climate Perceptions Matter: A Meta-analytic Path Analysis Relating Molar Climate, Cognitive and Affective States, and Individual Level Work Outcomes," *Journal of Applied Psychology* 89, no. 4 (2004), pp. 605–19.

11. I. Smithey-Fulmer, B. Gerhart, and K. S. Scott, "Are the 100 Best Better? An Empirical Investigation of the Relationship between Being a 'Great Place to Work' and Firm Performance," *Personnel Psychology* 56, no. 4 (2003), pp. 965–93.

12. D. B. McFarlin, "Hard Day's Work: A Boon for Performance but a Bane for Satisfaction?" *Academy of Management Perspectives* 20, no. 4 (2006), pp. 115–16.

13. S. A. Hewlett and C. Buck Luce, "Extreme Jobs: The Dangerous Allure of the 70-Hour Work Week," *Harvard Business Review,* December 2006, pp. 48–49.

14. J. C. Rode, M. L. Arthaud-Day, C. H. Mooney, J. P. Near, T. T. Baldwin, W. H. Bommer, and R. S. Rubin, "Life Satisfaction and Student Performance," *Academy of Management Learning & Education* 4, no. 4 (2005), pp. 421–33.

15. J. D. Shaw, N. Gupta, and J. E. Delery, "Alternative Conceptualizations of the Relationship between Voluntary Turnover and Organizational Performance," *Academy of Management Journal* 48, no. 5 (2005), pp. 50–68.

16. K. Birdi, C. Clegg, M. Patterson, A. Robinson, C. B. Stride, T. D. Wall, and S. J. Wood, "The Impact of Human Resources and Operations Management Practices on Company Productivity," *Personnel Psychology* 61, no. 3 (2008), pp. 467–502.

17. A. G. Walker, J. W. Smither, and D. A. Waldman, "A Longitudinal Examination of Concommitant Changes in Team Leadership and Customer Satisfaction," *Personnel Psychology* 61, no. 3 (2008), pp. 547–78.

18. R. B. Kaiser, R. T. Hogan, and S. B. Craig, "Leadership and the Fate of Organizations," *American Psychologist* 63, no. 2 (2008), pp. 96–110.

19. C. Kiewitz, "Happy Employees and Firm Performance: Have We Been Putting the Cart before the Horse?" *Academy of Management Executive* 18, no. 2 (2004), pp. 127–29.

20. B. Schneider, P. J. Hanges, D. B. Smith, and A. N. Salvaggio, "Which Comes First: Employee Attitudes or Organizational Financial and Market Performance?" *Journal of Applied Psychology* 88, no. 5 (2003), pp. 836–51.

21. R. Kanfer, "Motivation Theory in Industrial and Organizational Psychology," in *Handbook of Industrial and Organizational Psychology*, vol. 1, eds. M. D. Dunnette and L. M. Hough (Palo Alto, CA: Consulting Psychologists Press, 1990), pp. 75–170.

22. E. A. Locke and G. P. Latham, "What Should We Do about Motivation Theory? Six Recommendations for the Twenty-First Century," *Academy of Management Review* 29, no. 3 (2004), pp. 388–403.

23. R. M. Steers, R. T. Mowday, and D. L. Shapiro, "The Future of Work Motivation Theory," *Academy of Management Review* 29, no. 3 (2004), pp. 379–87.

24. F. E. Saal and P. A. Knight, *Industrial Organizational Psychology: Science and Practice* (Belmont, CA: Brooks/Cole, 1988).

25. T. A. Judge, C. J. Thoresen, J. E. Bono, and G. K. Patton, "The Job Satisfaction–Job Performance Relationship: A Qualitative and Quantitative Review," *Psychological Bulletin* 127 (2001), pp. 376–407.

26. D. P. Campbell and S. Hyne, *Manual for the Revised Campbell Organizational Survey* (Minneapolis, MN: National Computer Systems, 1995).

27. Health, Education, and Welfare Task Force, *Work in America* (Cambridge, MA: MIT Press, 1973).

28. R. Hoppock, *Job Satisfaction* (New York: Harper, 1935).

29. F. J. Smith, K. D. Scott, and C. L. Hulin, "Trends in Job-Related Attitudes in Managerial and Professional Employees," *Academy of Management Journal* 20 (1977), pp. 454–60.

30. G. L. Staines and R. P. Quinn, "American Workers Evaluate the Quality of Their Jobs," *Monthly Labor Review* 102, no. 1 (1979), pp. 3–12.

31. J. A. Colquitt, B. A. Scott, J. B. Rodell, D. M. Long, C. P. Zapata, D. E. Conlon, and M. J. Wesson, "Justice at the Millennium, a Decade Later: A Meta-Analytic Test of Social Exchange and Affect-Based Perspectives," *Journal of Applied Psychology* 98, no. 2 (2013), pp. 199–36.

32. R. Cropanzano, D. E. Rupp, and Z. S. Byrne, "The Relationship of Emotional Exhaustion to Work Attitudes, Job Performance, and Organizational Citizenship Behaviors," *Journal of Applied Psychology* 88, no. 1 (2003), pp. 160–69.

33. R. Ilies, B. A. Scott, and T. A. Judge, "The Interactive Effects of Personality Traits and Experienced States on the Intraindividual Patterns of Citizenship Behavior," *Academy of Management Journal* 49, no. 3 (2006), pp. 561–75.

34. B. R. Dineen, R. J. Lewicki, and E. C. Tomlinson, "Supervisory Guidance and Behavioral Integrity: Relationships with Employee Citizenship and Deviant Behavior," *Journal of Applied Psychology* 91, no. 3 (2006), pp. 622–35.

35. L. Y. Sun, S. Aryee, and K. S. Law, "High Performance Human Resource Practices, Citizenship Behavior, and Organizational Performance: A Relational Perspective," *Academy of Management Journal* 50, no. 3 (2007), pp. 558–77.

36. J. Brockner, "Why It's So Hard to Be Fair," *Harvard Business Review,* March 2006, p. 122–30.

37. D. S. Whitman, D. L. Van Rooy, and C. Viswesvaran, "Satisfaction, Citizenship Behaviors, and Performance in Work Units: A Meta-Analysis of Collective Construct Relations," *Personnel Psychology* 63, no. 1 (2010), pp. 41–81.

38. http://news.yahoo.com/s/ap/20100105/ap/_on_bi_ge/us_unhappy_workers.

39. "Schumpeter: Overstretched," *The Economist,* May 22, 2010, p. 72.

40. K. B. Paul and C. L. Johnson, "Engagement at 3M: A Case Study," in *The Executive Guide to Integrated Talent Management,* eds. K. Oakes and P. Galahan (Alexandria, VA: ASTD Press, 2011), pp. 133–46.

41. D. Ulrich, "Integrated Talent Management," in *The Executive Guide to Integrated Talent Management,* eds. K. Oakes and P. Galahan (Alexandria, VA: ASTD Press, 2011), pp. 189–12.

42. R. Charan, S. Drotter, and J. Noel, *The Leadership Pipeline: How to Build the Leadership-Powered Company* (San Francisco: Jossey-Bass, 2001).

43. B. N. Pfau, and S. A. Cohen, "Aligning Human Capital Practices and Employee Behavior with Shareholder Value," *Consulting Psychology Journal* 55, no. 3 (2003), pp. 169–78.

44. M. A. Huselid, R. W. Beatty, and B. E. Becker, "'A Players' or 'A Positions'? The Strategic Logic of Workforce Management," *Harvard Business Review,* December 2005, pp. 110–21.

45. G. J. Curphy and M. Roellig, "Followership," working paper, 2010.

46. R. T. Hogan, *Personality and the Fate of Organizations* (Mahwah, NJ: Lawrence Erlbaum Associates, 2007).

47. J. P. Campbell, "The Cutting Edge of Leadership: An Overview," in *Leadership: The Cutting Edge,* eds. J. G. Hunt and L. L. Larson (Carbondale: Southern Illinois University Press, 1977).

48. J. P. Campbell, "Training Design for Performance Improvement," in *Productivity in Organizations: New Perspectives from Industrial and Organizational Psychology,* eds. J. P. Campbell, R. J. Campbell, and Associates (San Francisco: Jossey-Bass, 1988), pp. 177–216.

49. M. T. Iaffaldano and P. M. Muchinsky, "Job Satisfaction and Job Performance: A Meta-analysis," *Psychological Bulletin* 97 (1985), pp. 251–73.

50. E. A. Locke and G. P. Latham, "Work Motivation and Satisfaction: Light at the End of the Tunnel," *Psychological Science* 1 (1990), pp. 240–46.

51. A. H. Maslow, *Motivation and Personality* (New York: Harper & Row, 1954).

52. E. L. Betz, "Two Tests of Maslow's Theory of Need Fulfillment," *Journal of Vocational Behavior* 24 (1984), pp. 204–20.

53. J. W. Atkinson, "Motivational Determinants of Risk Taking Behavior," *Psychological Review* 64 (1957), pp. 359–72.

54. D. C. McClelland, *Power: The Inner Experience* (New York: Irvington, 1975).

55. M. R. Barrick and M. K. Mount, "The Big Five Personality Dimensions and Job Performance: A Meta-analysis," *Personal Psychology* 44 (1991), pp. 1–26.

56. T. A. Judge and R. Ilies, "Relationship of Personality to Performance Motivation: A Meta-analytic Review," *Journal of Applied Psychology* 87, no. 4 (2002), pp. 797–807.

57. R. Hogan, T. Chamorro-Premuzic, and R. B. Kaiser, "Employability and Career Success: Bridging the Gap Between Theory and Reality," *Industrial and Organizational Psychology: Perspectives on Science and Practice* 1, no. 6 (2013), pp. 3–16.

58. G. J. Curphy and K. D. Osten, "Technical Manual for the Leadership Development Survey," *Technical Report No. 93-14* (Colorado Springs, CO: U.S. Air Force Academy, 1993).

59. T. A. Judge and J. D. Kanmeyer-Mueller, "On the Value of Aiming High: The Causes and Consequences of Ambition," *Journal of Applied Psychology* 97, no. 4 (2012), pp. 758–75.

60. R. T. Hogan and J. Hogan, *Manual for the Hogan Personality Inventory* (Tulsa, OK: Hogan Assessment Systems, 1992).

61. D. L. Nilsen, Using Self and Observers' Rating of Personality to Predict Leadership Performance, unpublished doctoral dissertation, University of Minnesota, 1995.

62. S. A. Hewlett, "Executive Women and the Myth of Having It All," *Harvard Business Review*, April 2002, pp. 66–67.

63. G. J. Curphy, *Hogan Assessment Systems Certification Workshop Training Manuals* (Tulsa, OK: Hogan Assessment Systems, 2003).

64. R. Gregory, R. T. Hogan, and G. J. Curphy, "Risk-Taking in the Energy Industry," *Well Connected* 5, no. 6 (June 2003), pp. 5–7.

65. T. W. Britt, "Black Hawk Down at Work," *Harvard Business Review*, January 2003, pp. 16–17.

66. E. A. Locke and G. P. Latham, "Building a Practically Useful Theory of Goal Setting and Task Motivation: A 35-Year Odyssey," *American Psychologist* 57, no. 9 (2002), pp. 705–18.

67. E. A. Locke, "Goal Setting Theory and Its Applications to the World of Business," *Academy of Management Executive* 18, no. 4 (2004), pp. 124–25.

68. G. P. Latham, "The Motivational Benefits of Goal Setting," *Academy of Management Executive* 18, no. 4 (2004), pp. 126–29.

69. E. A. Locke and G. P. Latham, "Has Goal Setting Gone Wild, or Have Its Attackers Abandoned Good Scholarship?" *Academy of Management Perspectives* 23, no. 1 (2009), pp. 17–23.

70. L. D. Ordonez, M. E. Schweitzer, A. D. Galinsky, and M. H. Bazerman, "Goals Gone Wild: The Systematic Side Effects of Overprescribing Goal Setting," *Academy of Management Perspectives* 23, no. 1 (2009), pp. 6–16.

71. S. Kerr and S. Landauer, "Using Stretch Goals to Promote Organizational Effectiveness and Personal Growth: General Electric and Goldman Sachs," *Academy of Management Executive* 18, no. 4 (2004), pp. 139–43.

72. Y. Fried and L. Haynes Slowik, "Enriching Goal-Setting Theory with Time: An Integrated Approach," *Academy of Management Review* 29, no. 3 (2004), pp. 404–22.

73. E. A. Locke, "Linking Goals to Monetary Incentives," *Academy of Management Executive* 18, no. 4 (2004), pp. 130–33.

74. S. B. Sitkin, K. E. See, C. C. Miller, M. W. Lawless, and A. M. Carton, "The Paradox of Stretch Goals: Organizations in Pursuit of the Seemingly Impossible," *Academy of Management Review* 36, no. 3 (2011), pp. 544–66.

75. M. Imai, *Kaizen: The Key to Japan's Competitive Success* (New York: Random House, 1986).

76. D. D. Van Fleet, T. O. Peterson, and E. W. Van Fleet, "Closing the Performance Feedback Gap with Expert Systems," *Academy of Management Executive* 19, no. 3 (2005), pp. 35–42.

77. O. B. Davidson and D. Eden, "Remedial Self-Fulfilling Prophecy: Two Field Experiments to Prevent Golem Effects among Disadvantaged Women," *Journal of Applied Psychology* 83, no. 3 (2000), pp. 386–98.

78. D. Eden, D. Geller, A. Gewirtz, R. Gordon-Terner, I. Inbar, M. Liberman, Y. Pass, I. Salomon-Segev, and M. Shalit, "Implanting Pygmalion Leadership Style through Workshop Training: Seven Field Experiments," *Leadership Quarterly* 11, no. 2 (2000), pp. 171–210.

79. S. S. White and E. A. Locke, "Problems with the Pygmalion Effect and Some Proposed Solutions," *Leadership Quarterly* 11, no. 3 (2000), pp. 389–416.

80. D. B. McNatt, "Ancient Pygmalion Joins Contemporary Management: A Meta-analysis of the Result," *Journal of Applied Psychology* 83, no. 2 (2000), pp. 314–21.

81. R. D. Arvey and J. M. Ivancevich, "Punishment in Organizations: A Review, Propositions, and Research Suggestions," *Academy of Management Review* 5 (1980), pp. 123–32.

82. G. J. Curphy, "What We Really Know about Leadership (But Seem Unwilling to Implement)," presentation given at the Minnesota Professionals for Psychology Applied to Work, Minneapolis, MN, January 2004.

83. L. S. Anderson, *The Cream of the Corp* (Hastings, MN: Anderson Performance Improvement Company, 2003).

84. S. E. Markham, K. D. Scott, and G. H. McKee, "Recognizing Good Attendance: A Longitudinal Quasi-Experimental Field Study," *Personnel Psychology* 55, no. 3 (2002), pp. 639–60.

85. A. D. Stajkovic and F. Luthans, "Differential Effects of Incentive Motivators on Performance," *Academy of Management Journal* 44, no. 3 (2001), pp. 580–90.

86. F. Luthans and A. D. Stajkovic, "Reinforce for Performance: The Need to Go beyond Pay and Even Rewards," *Academy of Management Executive* 13, no. 2 (1999), pp. 49–57.

87. M. Bloom and G. T. Milkovich, "Relationships among Risk, Incentive Pay, and Organizational Performance," *Academy of Management Journal* 41, no. 3 (1998), pp. 283–97.

88. G. D. Jenkins, A. Mitra, N. Gupta, and J. D. Shaw, "Are Financial Incentives Related to Performance? A Meta-analytic Review of Empirical Research," *Journal of Applied Psychology* 83, no. 5 (1998), pp. 777–87.

89. J. L. Komacki, S. Zlotnick, and M. Jensen, "Development of an Operant-Based Taxonomy and Observational Index on Supervisory Behavior," *Journal of Applied Psychology* 71 (1986), pp. 260–69.

90. R. D. Pritchard, J. Hollenback, and P. J. DeLeo, "The Effects of Continuous and Partial Schedules of Reinforcement of Effort, Performance, and Satisfaction," *Organizational Behavior and Human Performance* 16 (1976), pp. 205–30.

91. F. Luthans and R. Kreitner, *Organizational Behavior Modification and Beyond: An Operant and Social Learning Approach* (Glenview, IL: Scott Foresman, 1985).

92. P. M. Podsakoff and W. D. Todor, "Relationships between Leader Reward and Punishment Behavior and Group Process and Productivity," *Journal of Management* 11 (1985), pp. 55–73.

93. P. M. Podsakoff, W. D. Todor, and R. Skov, "Effects of Leader Contingent and Noncontingent Reward and Punishment Behaviors on Subordinate Performance and Satisfaction," *Academy of Management Journal* 25 (1982), pp. 810–25.

94. R. D. Arvey, G. A. Davis, and S. M. Nelson, "Use of Discipline in an Organization: A Field Study," *Journal of Applied Psychology* 69 (1984), pp. 448–60.

95. R. E. Quinn and G. M. Spreitzer, "The Road to Empowerment: Seven Questions Every Leader Should Consider," *Organizational Dynamics*, Autumn 1997, pp. 37–49.

96. S. H. Wagner, C. P. Parker, and N. D. Christiansen, "Employees That Think and Act Like Owners: Effects of Ownership Beliefs and Behaviors on Organizational Effectiveness," *Personnel Psychology* 56, no. 4 (2003), pp. 847–71.

97. A. Srivastava, K. M. Bartol, and E. A. Locke, "Empowering Leadership in Management Teams: Effects on Knowledge Sharing, Efficacy, and Performance," *Academy of Management Journal* 49, no. 6 (2006), pp. 1239–51.

98. S. E. Seibert, S. R. Silver, and W. A. Randolph, "Taking Empowerment to the Next Level: A Multiple-Level Model of Empowerment, Performance, and Satisfaction," *Academy of Management Journal* 47, no. 3 (2004), pp. 332–49.

99. M. Ahearne, J. Mathis, and A. Rapp, "To Empower or Not Empower Your Sales Force? An Empirical Examination of the Influence of Leadership Empowerment Behavior on Customer Satisfaction and Performance," *Journal of Applied Psychology* 90, no. 5 (2005), pp. 945–55.

100. J. Combs, Y. Liu, A. Hall, and D. Ketchen, "How Much Do High Performance Work Practices Matter? A Meta-analysis of Their Effects on Organizational Performance," *Personnel Psychology* 59 (2006), pp. 502–28.

101. L. R. Offermann, "Leading and Empowering Diverse Followers," in *The Balance of Leadership and Followership*, eds. E. P. Hollander and L. R. Offermann, Kellogg Leadership Studies Project (College Park: University of Maryland Press, 1997), pp. 31–46.

102. J. L. Xie and G. Johns, "Job Scope and Stress: Can Job Scope Be Too High?" *Academy of Management Journal* 38, no. 5 (1995), pp. 1288–1309.

103. G. M. Spreitzer, "Psychological Empowerment in the Workplace: Dimensions, Measurement, and Validation," *Academy of Management Journal* 38, no. 5 (1995), pp. 1442–65.

104. J. C. McElroy, P. C. Morrow, and S. N. Rude, "Turnover and Organizational Performance: A Comparative Analysis of the Effects of Voluntary, Involuntary, and Reduction-in-Force Turnover," *Journal of Applied Psychology* 86, no. 6 (2001), pp. 1294–99.

105. J. A. Krug, "Why Do They Keep Leaving?" *Harvard Business Review*, February 2003, pp. 14–15.

106. A. Hewitt, *Trends in Global Employee Engagement*, (Chicago: Author, 2011).

107. G. Curphy, "How You Lead Those You Perceive as Uncommitted? Start by Looking in the Mirror," *Journal of Character and Leadership Integration*, Winter, (2011).

108. D. Rigby, "Look before You Lay Off," *Harvard Business Review*, April 2002, pp. 20–21.

109. D. S. Levine, *Disgruntled: The Darker Side of the World of Work* (New York: Berkley Boulevard Books, 1998).

110. B. E. Litzky, K. E. Eddleston, and D. L. Kidder, "The Good, The Bad, and the Misguided: How Managers Inadvertently Encourage Deviant Behaviors," *Academy of Management Perspectives* 20, no. 1 (2006), pp. 91–103.

111. D. W. Organ and K. Ryan, "A Meta-analytic Review of Attitudinal and Dispositional Predictors of Organizational Citizenship Behavior," *Personnel Psychology* 48 (1995), pp. 775–802.

112. L. A. Bettencourt, K. P. Gwinner, and M. L. Meuter, "A Comparison of Attitude, Personality, and Knowledge Predictors of Service-Oriented Organizational Citizenship Behaviors," *Journal of Applied Psychology* 86, no. 1 (2001), pp. 29–41.

113. R. C. Mayer and M. B. Gavin, "Trust in Management and Performance: Who Minds the Shop While Employees Watch the Boss?" *Academy of Management Journal* 48, no. 5 (2005), pp. 874–88.

114. B. J. Tepper, M. K. Duffy, C. A. Henle, L. Schurer Lambert, "Procedural Injustice, Victim Precipitation, and Abusive Supervision," *Personnel Psychology* 59 (2006), pp. 101–23.

115. G. Strauss, "Workers Hone the Fine Art of Revenge: Acts of Violence, Harassment toward Boss on Rise in Corporate World," *Denver Post*, August 24, 1998, p. 6E.

116. A. E. Colbert, M. K. Mount, J. K. Harter, L. A. Witt, and M. R. Barrick, "Interactive Effects of Personality and Perceptions of the Work Situation on Workplace Deviance," *Journal of Applied Psychology* 89, no. 4 (2004), pp. 599–609.

117. B. Marcus and H. Schuler, "Antecedents of Counterproductive Behavior at Work: A General Perspective," *Journal of Applied Psychology* 89, no. 1 (2004), pp. 647–60.

118. R. P. Tett and J. P. Meyer, "Job Satisfaction, Organizational Commitment, Turnover Intention, and Turnover: Path Analyses Based on Meta-analytic Findings," *Personnel Psychology* 46 (1993), pp. 259–93.

119. G. J. Curphy, "In-Depth Assessments, 360-Degree Feedback, and Development: Key Research Results and Recommended Next Steps," presentation at the Annual Conference for HR Managers at US West Communications, Denver, CO, January 1998.

120. T. Peters, *The Circle of Innovation: You Can't Shrink Your Way to Greatness* (New York: Random House, 1997).

121. S. Schellenbarger, "Investors Seem Attracted to Firms with Happy Employees," *The Wall Street Journal,* March 19, 1997, p. I2.

122. A. G. Bedeian and A. A. Armenakis, "The Cesspool Syndrome: How Dreck Floats to the Top of Declining Organizations," *Academy of Management Executive* 12, no. 1 (1998), pp. 58–63.

123. P. W. Hom and A. J. Kinicki, "Towards a Greater Understanding of How Dissatisfaction Drives Employee Turnover," *Academy of Management Journal* 44, no. 5 (2001), pp. 975–87.

124. P. W. Hom, L. Roberson, and A. D. Ellis, "Challenging Conventional Wisdom about Who Quits: Revelations from Corporate America," *Journal of Applied Psychology* 93, no. 1 (2008), pp. 1–34.

125. D. P. Campbell, G. J. Curphy, and T. Tuggle, *360 Degree Feedback Instruments: Beyond Theory,* workshop presented at the 10th Annual Conference of the Society for Industrial and Organizational Psychology, Orlando, FL, May 1995.

126. P. Morrel-Samuels, "Getting the Truth into Workplace Surveys," *Harvard Business Review,* February 2002, pp. 111–20.

127. http://www.kellyglobal.net/eprise/main/web/us/mykelly/en/careertips_jan13_jobsecurity

128. http://www.strategicstudiesinstitute.army.mil/pubs/summary.cfm?q=912.

129. Associated Press, "Military Pay Soars," April 11, 2007, http://military.com/NewsContent.

130. http://www.armytimes.com/news/2007/09/army_bonuses_070910w/.

131. D. P. Campbell and S. Hyne, *Manual for the Revised Campbell Organizational Survey* (Minneapolis, MN: National Computer Systems, 1995).

132. C. Kleiman, "Survey: Job Satisfaction Can Be Costly to Employers," *Denver Post,* June 22, 1997, p. J–4.

133. T. A. Judge and R. Ilies, "Relationship of Personality to Performance Motivation: A Meta-analytic Review," *Journal of Applied Psychology* 87, no. 4 (2002), pp. 797–807.

134. R. Ilies and T. A. Judge, "On the Heritability of Job Satisfaction: The Mediating Role of Personality," *Journal of Applied Psychology* 88, no. 4 (2003), pp. 750–59.

135. S. Anchor, "Positive Intelligence: Three Ways Individuals Can Cultivate Their Own Sense of Well-Being and Set Themselves Up to Succeed," *Harvard Business Review*, January–February 2012, pp. 100–2.

136. G. Morse, "The Science Behind the Smile: An Interview with Daniel Gilbert," *Harvard Business Review,* January-February 2012, pp. 85-90.

137. R. D. Arvey, T. J. Bouchard Jr., N. L. Segal, and L. M. Abraham, "Job Satisfaction: Environmental and Genetic Components," *Journal of Applied Psychology* 74 (1989), pp. 187–92.

138. F. Herzberg, "The Motivation-Hygiene Concept and Problems of Manpower," *Personnel Administrator* 27 (1964), pp. 3–7.

139. F. Herzberg, *Work and the Nature of Man* (Cleveland, OH: World Publishing, 1966).

140. F. Herzberg, "One More Time: How Do You Motivate Employees?" *Harvard Business Review*, January 2003, pp. 87–96.

141. B. H. Sheppard, R. J. Lewicki, and J. W. Minton, *Organizational Justice: The Search for Fairness in the Workplace* (New York: Lexington Books, 1972).

142. L. K. Trevino, "The Social Effects of Punishment in Organizations: A Justice Perspective," *Academy of Management Review* 17 (1992), pp. 647–76.

143. P. A. Siegel, C. Post, J. Brockner, A. Y. Fishman, and C. Garden, "The Moderating Influence of Procedural Fairness on the Relationship between Work–Life Conflict and Organizational Commitment," *Journal of Applied Psychology* 90, no. 1 (2005), pp. 13–24.

144. J. A. Colquitt, "On the Dimensionality of Organizational Justice: A Construct Validation of a Measure," *Journal of Applied Psychology* 86, no. 2 (2001), pp. 386–400.

145. J. A. Colquitt, D. E. Conlon, M. J. Wesson, C. O. L. H. Porter, and K. Y. Ng, "Justice at the Millennium: A Meta-analytic Review of 25 Years of Organizational Justice Research," *Journal of Applied Psychology* 86, no. 2 (2001), pp. 425–45.

146. M. L. Ambrose and R. Cropanzano, "A Longitudinal Analysis of Organizational Fairness: An Examination of Reactions to Tenure and Promotion Decisions," *Journal of Applied Psychology* 88, no. 2 (2003), pp. 266–75.

147. B. J. Tepper and E. C. Taylor, "Relationships among Supervisors' and Subordinates' Procedural Justice Perceptions and Organizational Citizenship Behaviors," *Academy of Management Journal* 46, no. 1 (2003), pp. 97–105.

148. T. Simons and Q. Roberson "Why Managers Should Care about Fairness: The Effects of Aggregate Justice Perceptions on Organizational Outcomes," *Journal of Applied Psychology* 88, no. 3 (2003), pp. 432–43.

149. E. C. Hollensbe, S. Khazanchi, and S. S. Masterson, "How Do I Assess If My Supervisor and Organization Are Fair: Identifying the Rules Underlying Entity-Based Justice Perceptions," *Academy of Management Journal* 51, no. 6 (2008), pp. 1099–116.

150. B. C. Holtz and C. M. Harold, "Fair Today, Fair Tomorrow? A Longitudinal Investigation of Overall Justice Perceptions," *Journal of Applied Psychology* 94, no. 5 (2009), pp. 1185–99.

Chapter 10

Groups, Teams, and Their Leadership

Introduction

April 20, 2013; Loveland Pass, Colorado. The daily avalanche bulletin was straightforward and ominous: there was a serious risk of hard slab avalanches on north-facing slopes, triggered near the tree line. Two days earlier, a snowboarder triggered the same type of large, fast-moving, destructive slide near the tree line on a north-facing slope near Vail Pass. And the six men reading these bulletins were hardly backcountry novices. They were among the most experienced members of a larger group of people gathered to raise money for the Colorado Avalanche Information Center. Their backgrounds were impressive from a technical perspective: a professional mountain guide and educator; an expert skier and avalanche safety advocate; an avid backcountry snowboarder; a snowboarder and geologic engineer; a professional snowboard sales representative; and an expert snowboarder and manager of a snowboard shop.

Yet after reading the bulletins and discussing them, the group packed their equipment, including avalanche safety gear, and proceeded to climb onto a known hard-slab north-facing slope at the tree line. At approximately 10:15 a.m., this group of men triggered a massive slide that was approximately two football fields wide and four football fields long in the Sheep Creek drainage area—an area known by all six of the men to be prone to the very kind of avalanche these experts had just discussed. All six were buried in the 60 mile per hour onslaught of heavy snow; only one survived.

How could six experts make such a tragic mistake? As we are learning, it had little to do with their individual expertise or equipment. As avalanche researcher Ian McCammon reports in his seminal study, it is more likely that they fell victim to group and social factors.[1] The snowboarders were members of a group and apparently knew more about the technical aspects of avalanches than they did about the powerful potential dangers of groups and teams.

Yet at the other extreme, groups and teams can deliver the most outstanding results imaginable as has been demonstrated by the U.S. Navy SEALs. And in our increasingly complex world, groups and teams can accomplish feats impossible for lone individuals to achieve. Learning about how to capture the best aspects of groups and teams while avoiding the pitfalls is something a leader in today's world must know. Knowledge about groups and teams does not replace all you have learned thus far about individuals—it builds upon that knowledge.

Certainly, leaders need to understand some things about themselves. Their skills, abilities, values, motives, and desires are important considerations in determining their leadership style and preferences. Leaders also need to understand, as much as possible, the same characteristics of their followers. But if you could know characteristics of both yourself and each of your followers, that would still not be enough. This is because groups and teams are different than solely the skills, abilities, values, and motives of those who compose them. Groups and teams have their own special characteristics.

Although much of the leadership literature today is about the individual who fills the leadership role, a survey of 35 texts about organizational behavior found that, in each one, the chapter about leadership is in the section about group behavior.[2] This should not be terribly surprising because groups (even as small as two people) are essential if leaders are to affect anything beyond their own behavior. What may be surprising is that the concept of groups is sometimes omitted entirely from books about leadership. The **group perspective** looks at how different group characteristics can affect relationships both with the leader and among the followers.

We are born for cooperation, as are the feet, the hands, the eyelids, and the upper and lower jaws.
Marcus Aurelius

With *teams* and *teamwork* being current buzzwords, it is worth clarifying the difference between groups and teams, although this difference is mostly one of degree. We will begin the chapter with that clarification. The larger distinction, as just noted, is between the characteristics of groups and the characteristics of individuals. We will spend the first half of the chapter discussing some factors that are unique to groups. Given the high interest in organizational teamwork, the latter portion of this chapter will present a model developed to help leaders design, diagnose, and leverage high-impact factors to create the conditions that foster team effectiveness. This chapter will conclude with a section about virtual teams, which are becoming ever more present, if not popular.

Individuals versus Groups versus Teams

As noted previously, there is a significant difference between individual work and group work. But what is the difference between group work and teamwork?

You will learn, in the next section of this chapter, that two identifying characteristics of groups are mutual interaction and reciprocal influence. Members of teams also have mutual interaction and reciprocal influence, but we generally distinguish teams from groups in four other ways. First, team members usually have a stronger sense of identification among themselves than group members do. Often both team members and outsiders can readily identify who is and who is not on the team (athletic uniforms are one obvious example); identifying members of a group may be more difficult. Second, teams have common goals or tasks; these may range from developing a new product to winning an athletic league championship. Group members, on the other hand, may not have the same degree of consensus about goals that team members do. Group members may belong to the group for a variety of personal reasons, and these may clash with the group's stated objectives. (This phenomenon probably happens with teams, too, although perhaps not to the same extent.)

When it comes to anything that's social, whether it's your family, your school, your community, your business or your country, winning is a team sport.

Bill Clinton

Third, task interdependence typically is greater with teams than with groups. For example, basketball players usually are unable to take a shot unless other team members set picks or pass the ball to them (see Profiles in Leadership 10.1 about Phil Jackson). On the other hand, group members often can contribute to goal accomplishment by working independently; the successful completion of their assigned tasks may not be contingent on other group members. Of course task interdependence can vary greatly even across teams. Among athletic teams, for example, softball, football, soccer, and hockey teams have a high level of task interdependence, whereas swimming, cross-country, and track teams have substantially lower levels of task interdependence.

Phil Jackson

PROFILES IN LEADERSHIP 10.1

In Part 2 of this book, which discussed individual leadership characteristics, it was fairly easy to come up with a leader who typified the particular aspect of leadership we were illustrating. This is not quite so easy for teams. If you consider Ginnett's definition of leadership ("The leader's job is to create the conditions for the team to be successful"), the real team leader might be behind the scenes or, in this case, not even on the court.

Phil Jackson is a basketball coach, but not just any coach. Jackson was the coach of champion Michael Jordan and ultimately of the championship Chicago Bulls. Certainly basketball is a team sport; and as Michael Jordan and other Bulls found out,

having arguably the best player in the sport does not necessarily translate to the best team in the game. In many of the years when Jordan won the individual scoring championship, the Bulls didn't win the championship. Jackson's job as head coach was to transform spectacular individual players into a spectacular team.

Perhaps the best way to get a sense of this challenge and the teamwork Jackson built to win the championship is to extract a few lines from his book *Sacred Hoops*:

The most important part of the (coach's) job takes place on the practice floor, not during the game. After a certain point you have to trust the players

continued

continued

to translate into action what they've learned in practice. Using a comprehensive system of basketball makes it easier for me to detach myself in that way. Once the players have mastered the system, a powerful group intelligence emerges that is greater than the coach's ideas or those of any individual on the team. When a team reaches that state, the coach can step back and let the game itself "motivate" the players. You don't have to give them any "win one for the Gipper" pep talks, you just have to turn them loose and let them immerse themselves in the action. . . .

The sign of a great player was not how much *he* scored, but how much he lifted his teammate's performance. . . .

You can't beat a good defensive team with one man. It's got to be a team effort. . . .

It took a long time for Michael to realize he couldn't do it all by himself. Slowly, however, as the team began to master the nuances of the system, he learned that he could trust his teammates to come through in the clutch. It was the beginning of his transformation from a gifted solo artist into a selfless team player. . . .

What appealed to me about the system was that it empowered everybody on the team by making them more involved in the offense, and demanded that they put their individual needs second to those of the group. This is the struggle every leader faces: how to get members of the team who are driven by the quest for individual glory to give themselves over wholeheartedly to the group effort.

Source: P. Jackson and H. Delehanty, *Sacred Hoops: Spiritual Lessons of a Hardwood Warrior* (New York: Hyperion, 1995).

Fourth, team members often have more differentiated and specialized roles than do group members. Group members often play a variety of roles within the group; however, team members often play a single, or primary, role on a team. Finally, it is important to bear in mind that the distinctions we have been highlighting probably reflect only matters of degree. We might consider teams to be highly specialized groups.

The Nature of Groups

Perhaps we should begin by defining what a **group** is. A group can be thought of as "two or more persons who are interacting with one another in such a manner that each person influences and is influenced by each other person."[3] Three aspects of this definition are particularly important to the study of leadership. First, this definition incorporates the concept of reciprocal influence between leaders and followers—an idea considerably different from the one-way influence implicit in the dictionary's definition of followers. Second, group members interact and influence each other. Thus people waiting at a bus stop would not constitute a group because there generally is neither interaction nor influence between the various individuals. On the other hand, eight people meeting to plan a school bond election would constitute a group because there probably would be a high level of mutual interaction among the attendees. Third, the definition does not constrain individuals to only one group. Almost everyone belongs to a number of different groups; an individual could be a member of various service, production, sports, religious, parent, and volunteer groups simultaneously.

Although people belong to many groups, just as they do to many organizations, groups and organizations are not the same thing (groups, of course, can exist within organizations). Organizations can be so large that most members do not know most of the other people in the organization. In such cases there is relatively little intermember interaction and reciprocal influence. Similarly, organizations typically are just too large and impersonal to have much effect on anyone's feelings, whereas groups are small and immediate enough to affect both feelings and self-image. People often tend to identify more with the groups they belong to than with the organizations they belong to; they are more psychologically invested in their groups. Also, certain important psychological needs (like social contact) are better satisfied by groups than by organizations.

Perhaps an example will clarify the distinction between groups and organizations. Consider a church so large that it may fairly be described as an organization—so large that multiple services must be offered on Sunday mornings, dozens of different study classes are offered each week, and there are numerous different choirs and musical ensembles. In such a large church, the members could hardly be said to interact with or influence each other except on an occasional basis. Such size often presents both advantages and disadvantages to the membership. On one hand, it makes possible a rich diversity of activities; on the other hand, its size can make the church itself (the overall organization) seem relatively impersonal. It may be difficult to identify with a large organization other than in name only ("I belong to First Presbyterian Church"). In such cases many people identify more with particular groups within the church than with the church itself; it may be easier to *feel* a part of some smaller group such as the high school choir or a weekly study group.

Although groups play a pervasive role in society, in general people spend little time thinking about the factors that affect group processes and intragroup relationships. Therefore, the rest of this section will describe some group characteristics that can affect both leaders and followers. Much of the research on groups goes well beyond the scope of this chapter (see Gibbard, Hartman, & Mann, 1974; Shaw, 1981; Hackman, 1990), but six concepts are so basic to the group perspective that they deserve our attention.[3,4,43] These six concepts are group size, stages of group development, roles, norms, communication, and cohesion. Five of them will be addressed in the following sections. The sixth, communication, permeates them all.

Group Size

The size of any group has implications for both leaders and followers. First, leader emergence is partly a function of group size. The greater number of people in a large versus a small group will affect the probability that any individual is likely to emerge as leader. Second, as groups become larger, **cliques** are more likely to develop.[5] Cliques are subgroups of individuals who often share the same goals, values, and expectations. Because cliques generally wield more influence than individual members, they are likely to exert considerable influence—positively or negatively—on the larger group. Leaders need to identify and deal with cliques within their groups; many intragroup conflicts are the results of cliques having different values, goals, and expectations.

Third, group size also can affect a leader's behavioral style. Leaders with a large **span of control** tend to be more directive, spend less time with individual subordinates, and use more impersonal approaches when influencing followers. Leaders with a small span of control tend to display more consideration and use more personal approaches when influencing followers.[6–9] Fourth, group size also affects group effectiveness. Although some researchers have suggested the optimal number of workers for any task is between five and seven,[10,11] it probably is wise to avoid such a simple generalization. The answer to the question of appropriate group size seems to be "just big enough to get the job done." Obviously the larger the group, the more likely it is that it will involve differentiated skills, values, perceptions, and abilities among its members. Also, more "people power" will certainly be available to do the work as group size increases.

There are, however, limits to the benefits of size. Consider the question, "If it takes 1 person two minutes to dig a one-cubic-foot hole, how long will it take 20 people to dig the same size hole?" Actually, it probably will take the larger group considerably *longer*, especially if they all participate at the same time. Beyond the purely physical limitations of certain tasks, there may be decreasing returns (on a per capita basis) as group size increases. This is true even when the efforts of all group members are combined on what is called an **additive task.** An additive task is one where the group's output simply involves the combination of individual outputs.[12] Such a case may be illustrated by the number of individuals needed to push a stalled truck from an intersection. One individual probably would not be enough—maybe not even two or three. At some point, though, as group size increases in this additive task, there will be enough combined force to move the truck. However, as the group size increases beyond that needed to move the truck, the individual contribution of each member will appear to decrease. Steiner[13] suggested this may be due to

A committee is an animal with four back legs.
Jean le Carre

process loss resulting from factors such as some members not pushing in the right direction. Process losses can be thought of as the inefficiencies created by more and more people working together.

Group size can affect group effectiveness in a number of other ways. As group size increases, the diminishing returns of larger work groups may be due to **social loafing,**[14] which is the phenomenon of reduced effort by people when they are not individually accountable for their work. Experiments across different sorts of tasks have tended to demonstrate greater effort when every individual's work is monitored than when many individuals' outputs are anonymously pooled into a collective product. Recent evidence, however, suggests the process may be considerably more complicated than initially thought.[15] The performance decrement may be affected more by the level of task complexity or the reward structure (cooperative versus competitive) than by outcome attribution.

Sometimes working in the presence of others may actually increase effort or productivity through a phenomenon called **social facilitation.** Social facilitation was first documented in classic experiments at the Hawthorne plant of the Western Electric Company (see Highlight 10.1). However, social facilitation is not limited to research situations. It refers to any time people increase their level of work due to the presence of others. Typically this occurs when the presence of others increases individual accountability for work, in contrast to other occasions when being in a group reinforces individual anonymity and social loafing.[16]

Developmental Stages of Groups

Just as children go through different stages of development, so do groups. Tuckman's[17] review of over 60 studies involving leaderless training, experimental, or therapeutic groups revealed that groups generally went through four distinct stages of development. The first stage, **forming,** was characterized by polite conversation, the gathering of superficial information about fellow members, and low trust. The group's rejection of emerging potential leaders with negative characteristics also took place during the forming stage. The second stage, **storming,** usually was marked by intragroup conflict, heightened emotional levels, and status differentiation as remaining contenders struggled to build alliances and fulfill the group's leadership role. The clear emergence of a leader and the development of group norms and cohesiveness were the key indicators of the **norming** stage of group development. Finally, groups reached the **performing** stage when group members played functional, interdependent roles that were focused on the performance of group tasks.

The four stages of group development identified by Tuckman[18] are important for several reasons. First, people are in many more leaderless groups than they may realize. For example, many sports teams, committees, work groups, and clubs start out as leaderless teams. Team or club captains or committee spokespersons are likely to be the emergent

Social Facilitation and the Hawthorne Effect

HIGHLIGHT 10.1

Social facilitation was first documented in experiments conducted at the Hawthorne plant of the Western Electric Company during the late 1920s and early 1930s. These classic studies were originally designed to evaluate the impact of different work environments.[19,20] Among other things, researchers varied the levels of illumination in areas where workers were assembling electrical components and found that production increased when lighting was increased. When lighting was subse-quently decreased, however, production again increased. Faced with these confusing data, the researchers turned their attention from physical aspects of the work environment to its social aspects. As it turns out, one reason workers' production increased was simply because someone else (in this case the researchers) had paid attention to them. The term *Hawthorne effect* is still used today to describe an artificial change in behavior due merely to the fact that a person or group is being studied.

> *If you start yelling and becoming obtrusive and beboppin' around, you give the impression of insecurity, and that becomes infectious. It bleeds down into the actors, and they become nervous; then it bleeds down into the crew, and they become nervous, and you don't get much accomplished that way. You have to set a tone and just demand a certain amount of tranquility.*
>
> **Clint Eastwood on being a film director**

leaders from their respective groups. On a larger scale, perhaps even many elected officials initially began their political careers as the emergent leaders of their cliques or groups, and were then able to convince the majority of the remaining members in their constituencies of their viability as candidates.

Another reason it is important to understand stages of group development is the potential relationships between leadership behaviors and group cohesiveness and productivity. Some experts have maintained that leaders need to focus on consideration or group maintenance behaviors during the norming stage to improve group cohesiveness, and on task behaviors during the performing stage to improve group productivity.[21,22] They also have suggested that leaders who reverse these behaviors during the norming and performing stages tend to have less cohesive and less productive groups. Thus being able to recognize stages of group development may enhance the likelihood that one will emerge as a leader as well as increase the cohesiveness and productivity of the group being led.

Tuckman's model is widely known if for no other reason than the fact that its components rhyme with each other; but it is not without criticism. Recall that the subjects for Tuckman's research were training, experimental, or therapy groups. None of these particularly represent teams forming to do work in an organizational context. For example, Ginnett observed many surgical teams and never once saw them engage in storming behaviors as they formed. You wouldn't want to be the patient if there was a formation argument between the surgeon, the anesthesiologist, and the scrub nurse about who was going to get to use the scalpel today.

Gersick[23] proposed a better model for teams in organizational settings. In studying **project teams,** she found that teams don't necessarily jump right in and get to work. Rather, they spend most of the first half of the team's life muddling through various ideas and strategies. Then, about midway into the project, the team seems to experience the equivalent of a midlife crisis where there is a flurry of activity and a reexamination of the strategy to see if it will allow them to complete their work. Gersick labeled this process **punctuated equilibrium,** which is obviously quite different from Tuckman's four-stage model.

Group Roles

Group roles are the sets of expected behaviors associated with particular jobs or positions. Most people have multiple roles stemming from the various groups with which they are associated. In addition, it is not uncommon for someone to occupy numerous roles within the same group as situations change. Ginnett[24] found that members of airline crews have varying roles over the course of a day. Although some behaviors were universally associated with certain roles, effective team members on these airline crews generally were more flexible in changing their behavior as other role demands changed. For example, whereas the captain of an airplane is responsible for its overall operation and decision making during a flight, flight attendants often take over responsibility for planning and carrying out the crew's social activities in the evening (when the flight is over). One captain in the study, however, continued to make *all* the crew's decisions, including their evening social plans; he was inflexible with regard to the role of decision maker. Not coincidentally, he was seen as a less effective leader—even during the actual flights—than more flexible captains.

Some roles, like positions on athletic teams, have meaning only in relatively specific contexts. Generally speaking, for example, a person plays only a lineman's role during football games (admittedly, at many schools being an intercollegiate athlete is a role that extends to aspects of student life outside sports). Other roles are more general in nature, including certain common ones that play a part in making any group work—or not work—well. Highlight 10.4 on page 401 presents a vivid example of how powerful roles can be as determinants of behavior.

In Chapter 8 leader behavior was characterized initially in terms of two broad functions. One deals with getting the task done (**task role**) and the other with supporting relationships within the work group (**relationship role**). Similarly, roles in groups can be categorized in terms of task and relationship functions (see Highlight 10.2). Many of the roles in Highlight 10.2 are appropriate for followers, not just the official group leader; all of these different roles are part of the leadership process and all contribute to a group's overall effectiveness. Moreover, the distinction between task and relationship roles is somewhat arbitrary. It is sensible enough when looking at the short-term impact of any given behavior, but in another sense relationship roles are task roles. After all, task-oriented behavior may be adequate for accomplishing short-term objectives, but an appropriately

Task and Relationship Roles in Groups

HIGHLIGHT 10.2

TASK ROLES

Initiating: Defining the problem, suggesting activities, assigning tasks.

Information seeking: Asking questions, seeking relevant data or views.

Information sharing: Providing data, offering opinions.

Summarizing: Reviewing and integrating others' points, checking for common understanding and readiness for action.

Evaluating: Assessing validity of assumptions, quality of information, reasonableness of recommendations.

Guiding: Keeping group on track.

RELATIONSHIP ROLES

Harmonizing: Resolving interpersonal conflicts, reducing tension.

Encouraging: Supporting and praising others, showing appreciation for others' contributions, being warm and friendly.

Gatekeeping: Assuring even participation by all group members, making sure that everyone has a chance to be heard and that no individual dominates.

Source: Adapted from K. D. Benne and P. Sheats, "Functional Roles of Group Members," *Journal of Social Issues* 4 (1948), pp. 41–49.

cohesive and supportive group increases the potential for long-term effectiveness at future tasks as well as present tasks. Although the roles in Highlight 10.2 generally contribute to a group's overall effectiveness, several types of problems can occur with group roles and can impede group performance. One type of role problem concerns the **dysfunctional roles,** listed in Highlight 10.3. The common denominator among these roles is how the person's behavior serves primarily selfish or egocentric purposes rather than group purposes.

Another role problem is **role conflict.** Role conflict involves receiving contradictory messages about expected behavior and can in turn adversely affect a person's emotional well-being and performance.[25]

Dysfunctional Roles

HIGHLIGHT 10.3

Dominating: Monopolizing group time, forcing views on others.

Blocking: Stubbornly obstructing and impeding group work, persistent negativism.

Attacking: Belittling others, creating a hostile or intimidating environment.

Distracting: Engaging in irrelevant behaviors, distracting others' attention.

Source: Adapted from K. D. Benne and P. Sheats, "Functional Roles of Group Members," *Journal of Social Issues* 4 (1948), pp. 41–49.

The Stanford Prison Experiment

HIGHLIGHT 10.4

A fascinating demonstration of the power of roles occurred when social psychologist Philip Zimbardo and his colleagues[26] created a simulated prison environment at Stanford University. From a larger group of volunteers, two dozen male college students were randomly assigned to be either "prisoners" or "guards." The simulation was quite realistic, with actual cells constructed in the basement of one of the university buildings. The guards wore uniforms and carried nightsticks and whistles; their eyes were covered by sunglasses. The prisoners were "arrested" at their homes by police cars replete with blazing sirens. They were handcuffed, frisked, blindfolded, and brought to the "jail." They were fingerprinted, given prisoner outfits, and assigned numbers by which they would henceforth be addressed.

It did not take long for the students' normal behavior to be overcome by the roles they were playing. The guards became more and more abusive with their power. They held prisoners accountable for strict adherence to arbitrary rules of prison life (which the guards themselves created) and seemed to enjoy punishing them for even minor infractions. They increasingly seemed to think of the prisoners—truly just other college students—as bad people. The

emotional stress on the prisoners became profound, and just six days into the two-week schedule the experiment was halted. This unexpected outcome occurred because participants' roles had become their reality. They were not just students role-playing guards and prisoners; to a disconcerting degree they became guards and prisoners.

What should people conclude from the Stanford prison study? At an abstract level, the study dramatically points out how behavior is partly determined by social role. Additionally, it is clear how just being in the role of leader, especially to the extent that it is attended by tangible and symbolic manifestations of power, can affect how leaders think and act toward followers. Still another lesson people might draw involves remembering that the volunteers all had many different roles in life than those assigned to them in the study, though being a guard or a prisoner was certainly the salient one for this period. Whereas everyone has many roles, the salience of one or another often depends on the situation, and a person's behavior changes as his or her role changes in a group.

Source: P. Zimbardo, C. Haney, W. Banks, and D. Jaffe, "The Mind Is a Formidable Jailer: A Pirandellian Prison," *New York Times Magazine,* April 8, 1973, pp. 38–60.

Role conflict can occur in several different ways. Perhaps most common is receiving inconsistent signals about expected behavior from the same person. When the same person sends mixed signals, it is called **intrasender role conflict** ("I need this report back in five minutes, and it had better be perfect"). **Intersender role conflict** occurs when someone receives inconsistent signals from several others about expected behavior. Still another kind of role conflict is based on inconsistencies between different roles a person may have. Professional and family demands, for example, often create role conflicts. **Interrole conflict** occurs when someone is unable to perform all of his roles as well as he would like. A final type occurs when role expectations violate a person's values. This is known as **person–role conflict.** An example of person–role conflict might occur if a store manager encourages a salesperson to mislead customers about the quality of the store's products when this behavior is inconsistent with the salesperson's values and beliefs.

A different sort of role problem is called **role ambiguity.** In role conflict, one receives clear messages about expectations, but the messages are not all congruent. With role ambiguity, the problem is lack of clarity about exactly what the expectations are.[27,28] There may have been no role expectations established at all, or they may not have been clearly communicated. A person is experiencing role ambiguity if she wonders, "What am I supposed to be doing?" It is important for leaders to be able to minimize the degree to which dysfunctional roles, role conflict, and role ambiguity occur in their groups because these problems have been found to have a negative impact on organizational commitment, job involvement, absenteeism, and satisfaction with co-workers and supervisors.[29]

Group Norms

Norms are the informal rules groups adopt to regulate and regularize group members' behaviors. Although norms are only infrequently written down (see Highlight 10.5) or openly discussed, they nonetheless often have a powerful and consistent influence on behavior.[30] That is because most people are good at reading the social cues that inform them about

Putting It In Writing[31]

Rick Reilly

HIGHLIGHT 10.5

Why are sports' unwritten rules unwritten? Get a Xerox machine under these puppies and have a copy on everybody's desk in the morning.

After we gave up a touchdown in our first Touch Football/Pulled Groinathon of the year, the guys on the other team sneered and said, "Suckers walk."

"Says who?" asked our left tackle, Cementhead.

"It's an unwritten rule," explained the other side's captain. "Oh, yeah?" said Cementhead. "Show me where." Which is exactly my point. Why are sports' unwritten rules unwritten? Get a Xerox machine under these puppies and have a copy on everybody's desk in the morning.

The coach always sits in the first row on the team bus. If he is out sick or dead, the seat remains empty.

Apologize for a point won on a net cord.

Take two or three pitches if your pitcher just made the second out of the inning.

Never, ever put your finger in someone else's bowling ball.

The starting goalie is always the first player on the ice.

If a line judge makes a bad call in your favor, purposely double-fault the next point.

A manager never drinks at the same bar as his players.

Never knock in the tying run in the ninth inning of an exhibition game. Far better to lose than go extra innings in spring training.

No NBA player attempting a layup in the fourth quarter of a tight game should go unfouled.

In a losing clubhouse you must act as if there has been a death in the family.

Hand the manager the ball when he comes to the mound to take you out.

Never shoot the puck into the net after a whistle blows.

Do not talk to or sit near a pitcher with a no-hitter going. And never bunt to break one up.

A first base coach never stands in the first base coaching box.

Never blow your nose before a fight. (It makes the eyes swell easier later on.)

Stand as far away as possible from a skeet shooter with a perfect score going.

Never walk on a player's putting line, including the two feet on the other side of the cup.

Always clear the inside lane for faster runners.

Never stand behind the pool table pocket your opponent is shooting for.

Never let the interviewee hold the mike.

A catcher may complain to the ump all he wants about balls and strikes, as long as he doesn't turn around and do it face-to-face.

Never hit the quarterback during practice.

Never start the 100 meters in a decathlon into a wind. Trade false starts until the breeze is favorable.

When a soccer player is hurt, the opponents must kick the ball out of play.

Except for Rocky Marciano, the challenger always enters the ring first—and always will.

Throw a handful of salt into the air before your sumo wrestling match begins.

It's true: Suckers walk.

The bus may be delayed by superstars only.

When the coach finally wraps up a long meeting with "Any questions?" nobody better ask one.

Rookies shag balls, whether they are millionaires or not.

Never shoot high on the goalie during warm-ups.

The back nine is always pressed.

You must admit it when you hit a forehand on the second bounce.

On the playground, offense calls the fouls.

Never write down the score of a bowler who is on a run of strikes.

Never admit you trapped the ball while trying to make a catch.

No overhead smashes at women in mixed doubles.

The caddie of the last player to putt plants the flag.

NBA refs will take some trash from head coaches but not a word from an assistant.

Never steal with a five-run lead after the seventh inning.

You must alter your course to help a boat in distress.

Boxers never blink during a ref's prefight instructions.

When a receiver drops a pass, go back to him on the next play.

Card games are played in the back of the plane.

Scrubs stand during NBA timeouts.

Winners buy.

Got it, Cementhead?

existing norms. For example, most people easily discern the dress code in any work environment without needing written guidance. People also are apt to notice when a norm is violated, even though they may have been unable to articulate the norm before its violation was apparent. For example, most students have expectations (norms) about creating extra work for other students. Imagine the reaction if a student in some class complained that not enough reading was being assigned for each lesson or that the minimum length requirements for the term paper needed to be substantially raised.

Norms do not govern all behaviors—just those a group feels are important. Norms are more likely to be seen as important and are more apt to be enforced if they (1) facilitate group survival; (2) simplify, or make more predictable, what behavior is expected of group members; (3) help the group avoid embarrassing interpersonal problems; or (4) express the central values of the group and clarify what is distinctive about the group's identity.[32]

The norms that group members value, such as those just listed, are essentially inward looking. They help the team take care of itself and avoid embarrassing situations caused by inappropriate member behaviors. Hackman[33] recommends that the leader has a responsibility to focus the team outwardly to enhance performance. Specifically, he suggests two core norms be created to enhance performance:

1. Group members should actively scan the environment for opportunities that would require a change in operating strategy to capitalize upon them.
2. The team should identify the few behaviors that team members must always do and those they should never do to conform to the organization's objectives.

By actively implementing these two norms, the team is forced to examine not only its organizational context but the much larger industry and environmental shells in which it operates. One irony about norms is that an outsider to a group often is able to learn more about norms than an insider. An outsider, not necessarily subject to the norms herself, is more apt to notice them. In fact, the more "foreign" an observer is, the more likely it is the norms will be perceived. If a man is accustomed to wearing a tie to work, he is less likely to notice that men in another organization also wear ties to work, but is *more* likely to note that the men in a third organization typically wear sweaters or sweatshirts around the office.

Group Cohesion

Group cohesion is the glue that keeps a group together. It is the sum of the forces that attract members to a group, provide resistance to leaving it, and motivate them to be active in it. Highly cohesive groups interact with and influence each other more than less cohesive groups do. Furthermore, a highly cohesive group may have lower absenteeism and lower turnover than a less cohesive group, and low absenteeism and turnover often contribute to higher group performance; higher performance can, in turn, contribute to even higher cohesion, thus resulting in an increasingly positive spiral.

However, greater cohesiveness does not always lead to higher performance. A highly cohesive but unskilled team is still an unskilled team, and such teams will often lose to a less cohesive but more skilled one.

Finding good players is easy. Getting them to play as a team is another story.

Casey Stengel

Additionally, a highly cohesive group may sometimes develop goals that are contrary to the larger organization's goals. For example, members of a highly cohesive research team at a particular college committed themselves to working on a problem that seemed inherently interesting to them. Their nearly zealous commitment to the project, however, effectively kept them from asking, or even allowing others to ask, if the research aligned itself well with the college's stated objectives. Their narrow and basic research effort deviated significantly from the college's expressed commitment to emphasize applied research. As a result, the college lost some substantial outside financial support.

Other problems also can occur in highly cohesive groups. Researchers[34,35] have found that some groups can become so cohesive they erect what amount to fences or boundaries between themselves and others. Such **overbounding** can block the use of outside resources that could make them more effective. Competitive product development teams can become so overbounded (often rationalized by security concerns or inordinate fears of "idea thieves") that they will not ask for help from willing and able staff within their own organizations.

One example of this problem was the failed mission to rescue U.S. embassy personnel held hostage in Iran during the Carter presidency. The rescue itself was a complicated mission involving many different U.S. military forces. Some of these forces included sea-based helicopters. The helicopters and their crews were carried on regular naval vessels, though most sailors on the vessels knew nothing of the secret mission. Senior personnel were so concerned that some sailor might leak information, and thus compromise the mission's secrecy, that maintenance crews aboard the ships were not directed to perform increased levels of maintenance on the helicopters immediately before the critical mission. Even if a helicopter was scheduled for significant maintenance within the next 50 hours of flight time (which would be exceeded in the rescue mission), crews were not told to perform the maintenance. According to knowledgeable sources, this practice affected the performance of at least one of the failed helicopters, and thus the overall mission.

Janis[36] discovered still another disadvantage of highly cohesive groups. He found that people in a highly cohesive group often become more concerned with striving for unanimity than objectively appraising different courses of action. Janis labeled this phenomenon **groupthink** and believed it accounted for a number of historic fiascoes, including Pearl Harbor and the Bay of Pigs invasion. It may have played a role in the *Challenger* disaster, and it also occurs in other cohesive groups ranging from business meetings to air crews, and from therapy groups to school boards.

What is groupthink? Cohesive groups tend to evolve strong informal norms to preserve friendly internal relations. Preserving a comfortable, harmonious group environment becomes a hidden agenda that tends to

Symptoms of Groupthink

HIGHLIGHT 10.6

An illusion of invulnerability, which leads to unwarranted optimism and excessive risk taking by the group.

Unquestioned assumption of the group's morality and therefore an absence of reflection on the ethical consequences of group action.

Collective rationalization to discount negative information or warnings.

Stereotypes of the opposition as evil, weak, or stupid.

Self-censorship by group members from expressing ideas that deviate from the group consensus due to doubts about their validity or importance.

An illusion of unanimity such that greater consensus is perceived than really exists.

Direct pressure on dissenting members, which reinforces the norm that disagreement represents disloyalty to the group.

Mindguards who protect the group from adverse information.

Source: Adapted from I. L. Janis, *Groupthink,* 2nd ed. (Boston: Houghton Mifflin, 1982).

suppress dissent, conflict, and critical thinking. Unwise decisions may result when concurrence seeking among members overrides their willingness to express or tolerate deviant points of view and think critically. Janis[37] identified a number of symptoms of groupthink, which can be found in Highlight 10.6.

A policy-making or decision-making group displaying most of the symptoms in Highlight 10.6 runs a big risk of being ineffective. It may do a poor job of clarifying objectives, searching for relevant information, evaluating alternatives, assessing risks, and anticipating the need for contingency plans. Janis[38] offered the following suggestions as ways of reducing groupthink and thus of improving the quality of a group's input to policies or decisions. First, leaders should encourage all group members to take on the role of critical evaluator. Everyone in the group needs to appreciate the importance of airing doubts and objections. This includes the leader's willingness to listen to criticisms of his or her own ideas. Second, leaders should create a climate of open inquiry through their own impartiality and objectivity. At the outset, leaders should refrain from stating personal preferences or expectations that may bias group discussion. Third, the risk of groupthink can be reduced if independent groups are established to make recommendations on the same issue. Fourth, at least one member of the group should be assigned the role of devil's advocate—an assignment that should rotate from meeting to meeting. Groupthink may have been one of the social factors that played a part in the avalanche tragedy described at the beginning of this chapter.

One final problem with highly cohesive groups may be what Shephard[39] has called **ollieism.** Ollieism, a variation of groupthink, occurs when illegal actions are taken by overly zealous and loyal subordinates who believe that what they are doing will please their leaders. It derives its name from the actions of Lieutenant Colonel Oliver North, who among other things admitted he lied to the U.S. Congress about his actions while working on the White House staff during the Iran–Contra affair. Shephard cited the slaying of Thomas à Becket by four of Henry II's knights and the Watergate break-in as other prime examples of ollieism. Ollieism differs from groupthink in that the subordinates' illegal actions usually occur without the explicit knowledge or consent of the leader. Nevertheless, Shephard pointed out that, although the examples cited of ollieism were not officially sanctioned, the responsibility for them still falls squarely on the leader. It is the leader's responsibility to create an ethical climate within the group, and leaders who create highly cohesive yet unethical groups must bear the responsibility for the group's actions.

After reading about the uncertain relationships between group cohesion and performance, and the problems with overbounding, groupthink, and ollieism, you might think cohesiveness should be avoided. Nothing, however, could be further from the truth. First, problems with overly cohesive groups occur relatively infrequently, and in general leaders will be better off thinking of ways to create and maintain highly cohesive teams than not developing these teams out of concern for potential groupthink or overbounding situations. Second, perhaps the biggest argument for developing cohesive groups is to consider the alternative— groups with little or no cohesiveness. In the latter groups, followers would generally be dissatisfied with each other and the leader, commitment to accomplishing group and organizational goals may be reduced, intragroup communication may occur less frequently, and interdependent task performance may suffer.[40] Because of the problems associated with groups having low cohesiveness, leadership practitioners need to realize that developing functionally cohesive work groups is a goal they all should strive for.

In summary, the group perspective provides a complementary level of analysis to the individual perspective presented earlier in this chapter. A follower's behavior may be due to his or her values, traits, or experience (the individual perspective), or this behavior may be due to the followers' roles, the group norms, the group's stage of development, or the group's level of cohesiveness (the group perspective). Thus the group perspective can also provide both leaders and followers with a number of explanations for why individuals in groups behave in certain ways. Moreover, the six group characteristics just described can give leaders and followers ideas about factors that may be affecting their ability to influence other group members and how to improve their level of influence in the group.

Teams

With so much attention devoted to teams and teamwork in today's organizations, it is appropriate to spend a fair amount of time examining teams and the factors that impact their effectiveness. After considering some differential measures of team effectiveness, we will look at a comprehensive model of team leadership.

Effective Team Characteristics and Team Building

Teams definitely vary in their effectiveness. Virtually identical teams can be dramatically different in terms of success or failure (see Highlight 10.7). We must ask, therefore, what makes one team successful and another unsuccessful. Although this is an area only recently studied, exploratory work at the Center for Creative Leadership has tentatively identified several key characteristics for effective team performance (see Highlight 10.8 for a historical perspective on teamwork from the Golden Age of Pirates).

The Center for Creative Leadership's research with teams indicated that successful and unsuccessful teams could be differentiated on the basis of eight key characteristics, the first six of which are primarily concerned with task accomplishment.[41] First, effective teams had a *clear mission* and *high performance standards*. Everyone on the team knew what the team was trying to achieve and how well he or she had to perform in order to achieve the team's mission. Second, leaders of successful teams

He that would be a leader must be a bridge.
Welsh proverb

Examples of Effective and Ineffective Teams

HIGHLIGHT 10.7

Most people can readily think of a number of examples of ineffective and effective teamwork. Consider the relative effectiveness of the teams depicted in the following two true stories:

Ineffective teamwork: After an airline flight crew failed to get a "nose gear down and locked" indicator light to come on while making a landing approach into Miami, all three crew members became involved in trying to change the burned-out indicator bulb in the cockpit. Nobody was flying the airplane, and none of them were monitoring the flight of the L-1011 as it descended into the Everglades and crashed.

Effective teamwork: The crew of a DC-10, having lost all capability to control the airplane through flight controls as a result of an engine explosion, realized they needed all the help they could get. Captain Al Haynes discovered that another experienced captain was traveling in the passenger cabin and invited him to come up to the cabin to help the regular crew out. Miraculously, their combined abilities enabled the crew—using techniques developed on the spot—to control the plane to within a few feet of the ground. Even though there were fatalities, over 180 people survived a nearly hopeless situation.

Teamwork from the Golden Age of Pirates

HIGHLIGHT 10.8

Thanks to Walt Disney Studios and their multiple versions of *Pirates of the Caribbean*, we all know about pirates and their life on the high seas. They were a ruthless band of ne're-do-wells who, without a pirate captain that virtually kidnapped them from a bar, would probably have been otherwise completely unemployed. Once aboard ship, they and their 15 or so compatriots were harshly dealt with by an autocratic and dictatorial captain and his assistant. Violation of arbitrary rules would doom the poor sailor to walk the plank to a watery grave. When they did stumble upon a potential target of opportunity, they would try to outflank it and then, under a steady barrage of cannon fire, descend upon the other ship, usually sending it to the bottom of the ocean. The pirate crew, populated by men with severed arms and pegs for legs, would be forced to bury their treasure on some island and hope to recover it later.

There is one problem with our Walt Disney view of pirates—almost none of it is true with the possible exception of the "ruthless" part. These big-screen images of pirates appear to be either a compilation of characters from novels such as Robert Louis Stevenson's *Treasure Island*[i] or made up entirely from a screenwriter's imagination. Owing in large part to a magnificent traveling exhibit by the National Geographic Society,[ii] we now know a great deal more about what pirate life was really like. Combining these findings and artifacts with an authentic book on pirates,[iii] we get a very different picture and one that is surprisingly a lot closer to high-performance teamwork than you might expect.

Before describing the real life of pirates during the Golden Age (approximately 1650–1730 in the Caribbean), it is important to understand that this is neither the sole period of piracy nor its sole geographic location. Pirates are known to have existed thousands of years ago, even before the emergence of the Egyptian civilization.[iv] Northern Europe had both Saxon and Viking pirates and the Islamic pirates of the Barbary Coast victimized the Mediterranean. There were pirates in the South China Sea in the 18th and 19th centuries. Even today, the Somali pirates are hunted by multinational flotillas. But here we are focusing our view on the Golden Age of Pirates and their exploits in the Caribbean and Atlantic Coast of the United States.

Piracy in the Golden Age had an unusual birthplace. According to Captain Johnson, "privateers are the nursery for pirates." Privateers are private individuals or, in this case, ships, sanctioned and authorized by governments by a *letter of marque* to attack foreign shipping during wartime. Both the Spanish and the English governments had used them extensively to augment their navies. And so did the Americans. During the Revolutionary war, the Continental navy had only 64 ships, but there were at least 700 privateers. In fact, these privateers brought such devastation on English commerce that the English merchants pressured King George to give up the fight in America. Even George Washington acknowledged that there would have been no victory in the American Revolution without privateers. This tradition was so prevalent that it is included in Article 1, Section 8 of the U.S. Constitution: "The Congress shall have Power to . . . grant Letters of Marque and Reprisal, and make Rules concerning Captures on Land and Water. . . ." But when the wars ended, piracy tended to replace privateering in the Caribbean.

If we now look at what we actually know about the pirates of the Golden Age, and use as our lens the upcoming perspective on organizational shells by Hackman and Ginnett for start-up of high-performance teams, we get an interesting highlight on teamwork.

Task

The task of pirates was indeed one that required a team. Rather than a random act of spontaneity, the overtaking of a target ship was a well-planned-out

continued

continued

and orchestrated event. In fact, the pirate ship was uniquely selected for this capability. Ships like the *Whydah* were highly sought after by pirates. Until its capture by pirate leader Sam Bellamy, the *Whydah* had been a slaver. As we will see in the next section on composition, this was critical to its mission as a pirate ship. But for now, suffice it to say that the pirate team was most often not a band of 10 to 20 scraggly men but more likely an overwhelming large boarding party of up to 160 heavily armed troops. If at all possible, they never approached their target with cannons blazing in an attempt to sink their adversary. Their common task was to "liberate" the booty, not to sink it to the bottom of the sea. Because slave ships had to move their "human cargo" rapidly across the ocean, they were among the fastest vessels on the sea, thus ideal for the pirate mission. A typical pirate attack involved overtaking the target vessel as rapidly as possible, and upon nearing it, raising the pirate flag to let the victims know they were about to be overwhelmed. In the highly coordinated boarding activity commanded by the pirate quartermaster (more about the quartermaster later), not only were pirates interested in the booty but also possibly in the ship and any able-bodied members of the captured crew who could augment their own resources. Crews attacked with speed, skill, and urgency, functioning as tight, cohesive units. Laziness, incompetence, disloyalty, and cowardice were never tolerated since those traits endangered everyone. The tactics were well known at the time: surrender and the life of the crew (minus the officers) would be spared. Any resistance at all would mean that the entire crew was murdered.

The reward structure associated with this task was interesting as well. The booty was divided among the pirates in a predetermined fashion. Although the captain and quartermaster received a larger portion than a working crew member, it was not disproportionate by today's executive compensation standards. A captain and quartermaster might receive two to three times what the other members received. This will make more sense when we look at the authority dynamics.

Composition

As mentioned, the pirate crew was large—in fact, too large to be considered a high-performance team today. A team of 160 now makes no sense. But that number really should be regarded as the pirate organization because the crew was subdivided into much smaller teams with specific tasks and objectives. Given that a pirate organization had up to 160 members, the slave ship was ideally suited to sustain them. Slave ships were perfect prizes for pirates: easy to maneuver, unusually fast, armed to the hilt—and provisioned with large galleys designed to feed the slave cargo and thus suitable for the large pirate crew.

Contrary to the movie version of pirate conscription, where it was often the government vessels that conscripted their crews, paying them little to nothing and generally abusing them, positions on a pirate vessel were much sought after. When word got around that a pirate captain was looking to fill or augment a crew, volunteers abounded. According to Captain Johnson,[v] when a captain announced that his ship was "going on the account," every tavern, brothel, and alleyway buzzed with anticipation. One could not just volunteer and hope to be selected. A potential pirate crew member had to demonstrate competence at a particular required skill, be it carpenter, sail maker, rigger, cook, musician, or doctor. And all had to be fighters.

Finally, Hollywood versions are fond of characterizing pirates as a "motley crew." Crews included ordinary seamen, free black men, political dissidents, escaped slaves, indentured servants, Africans freed from slave ships taken at sea, Native Americans, and runaway plantation workers, speaking many languages and hailing from many nations. Today, we might describe such a collection of team members not as "motley" but, in our more politically correct moments, as "appropriately diverse."

Norms

All groups have norms but they are seldom written down. The pirates were better at this than many teams today. Not only did they write them down, but each potential crew member had to sign

"The Articles" before they could become a member. It is also reported that members signed along the right and left margins, not at the bottom, signifying that no man was greater than the rules as a whole, but all agreed to them. One set of Articles has survived and is presented here:[vi]

Pirate Code of Conduct
Bartholomew Roberts Shipboard Articles 1721

- ARTICLE I - Every man shall have an equal vote in affairs of moment. He shall have an equal title to the fresh provisions or strong liquors at any time seized, and shall use them at pleasure unless a scarcity may make it necessary for the common good that a retrenchment may be voted.
- ARTICLE II - Every man shall be called fairly in turn by the list on board of prizes, because over and above their proper share, they are allowed a shift of clothes. But if they defraud the company to the value of even one dollar in plate, jewels or money, they shall be marooned. If any man rob another he shall have his nose and ears slit, and be put ashore where he shall be sure to encounter hardships.
- ARTICLE III - None shall game for money either with dice or cards.
- ARTICLE IV - The lights and candles should be put out at eight at night, and if any of the crew desire to drink after that hour they shall sit upon the open deck without lights.
- ARTICLE V - Each man shall keep his piece, cutlass and pistols at all times clean and ready for action.
- ARTICLE VI - No boy or woman to be allowed amongst them. If any man shall be found seducing any of the latter sex and carrying her to sea in disguise he shall suffer death.
- ARTICLE VII - He that shall desert the ship or his quarters in time of battle shall be punished by death or marooning.
- ARTICLE VIII - None shall strike another on board the ship, but every man's quarrel shall be ended on shore by sword or pistol in this manner. At the word of command from the quartermaster, each man being previously placed back to back, shall

turn and fire immediately. If any man do not, the quartermaster shall knock the piece out of his hand. If both miss their aim they shall take to their cutlasses, and he that draweth first blood shall be declared the victor.
- ARTICLE IX - No man shall talk of breaking up their way of living till each has a share of I,000. Every man who shall become a cripple or lose a limb in the service shall have 800 pieces of eight from the common stock and for lesser hurts proportionately.
- ARTICLE X - The captain and the quartermaster shall each receive two shares of a prize, the master gunner and boatswain, one and one half shares, all other officers one and one quarter, and private gentlemen of fortune one share each.
- ARTICLE XI - The musicians shall have rest on the Sabbath Day only by right. On all other days by favour only.

Three points stand out. First, nothing is mentioned about wayward pirates walking the plank; however, violating the rules (norms) was cause for literally being kicked off the team. Secondly, Article IX is clearly one of the earliest forms of disability compensation. If a pirate became disabled as a result of doing his job, he would receive up to 800 pieces of eight or roughly 10 years compensation. Finally, the crew was governed in a remarkably democratic style, which leads directly to our final factor in describing high-performance teams, the use of authority.

Authority

Authority on a pirate ship was drawn from the Articles. Not only were the decisions and rewards shared reasonably equally by all members of the crew, but the officers (the captain and the quartermaster) were elected positions. While the captain dictated orders in battle and the quartermaster led the raiding parties, many other onboard decisions were made by a majority vote, often by a show of hands. Captains were elected by a show of hands and could be removed by the same method. Incompetence by elected leaders was simply not tolerated. One crew went through a total of

continued

412   Part Three   *Focus on the Followers*

continued

13 captains in two months; infamous Captains Morgan, Kidd, and Blackbeard at one time or another were all voted out of office.[vii] The quartermaster walked an even tighter line because he had to serve both the captain as his second in command and the crew, who had elected him. Thus the notion of the all-powerful captain and quartermaster who mercilessly inflicted pain on their crews is apparently far from the truth.

It appears that the men (and a few women) who were the pirates from the Golden Age of Piracy practiced many of the behaviors that we would expect of high-performance teams today. While condoning neither their objectives nor motives, perhaps it is most instructive to consider that high-performance teamwork is not something we have just invented in the 21st century. Apparently, teamwork has been around for quite some time—not out of fancy or the fad of the month—but out of necessity for accomplishing complex tasks.

Notes

i. R. L Stevenson, *Treasure Island* (London: Cassell and Company, Limited, 1883).
ii. *Real Pirates: The Untold Story of the* Whydah *from Slave Ship to Pirate.* An exhibit of the National Geographic Society.
iii. Captain Charles Johnson, *A General History of the Robberies and Murders of the Most Notorious Pyrates* (Britain: Rivington, 1774).
iv. D. Pickering, *Pirates* (London: HarperCollins Publishers, 2006).
v. It is interesting that no one knows who Captain Charles Johnson actually was. Most seem to agree that this was a pseudonym, but the author's true identity remains a mystery. Some have argued that the true author was Daniel Defoe, more famous for his novel *Robinson Crusoe*.
vi. http://www.elizabethan-era.org.uk/pirate-code-conduct.htm
vii. Pickering, *Pirates*.

often *took stock* of their equipment, training facilities and opportunities, and outside resources available to help the team. Leaders of effective teams spent a considerable amount of time *assessing the technical skills* of the team members. After taking stock of available resources and skills, good leaders would work to *secure resources and equipment* necessary for team effectiveness. Moreover, leaders of effective teams would spend a considerable amount of time *planning* and *organizing* to make optimal use of available resources, to select new members with needed technical skills, or to improve needed technical skills of existing members.

The last two characteristics of effective teams were concerned with the group maintenance or interpersonal aspects of teams. Hallam and Campbell's[42] research indicated that *high levels of communication* were often associated with effective teams. These authors believed this level of communication helped team members to stay focused on the mission and to take better advantage of the skills, knowledge, and resources available to the team. High levels of communication also helped to *minimize interpersonal conflicts* on the team, which often drained energy needed for team success and effectiveness. The characteristics of effective teams identified in this research provide leadership practitioners with a number of ideas about how they may be able to increase the effectiveness of their work units or teams.

A different avenue to group and team effectiveness has been to use a normative approach. One example of this technique is described in *Groups That Work (and Those That Don't)*.[43] Ginnett[44,45] has developed an expanded model focusing specifically on team leadership, which we will examine in more detail later in this chapter. For now, our concern is with one of the three major leadership functions in Ginnett's model that focuses on team design. The model suggests four components of design of the team itself that help the team get off to a good start, whatever its task. This is important because it is not uncommon to find that a team's failure can be traced to its being set up inappropriately from the beginning. If a team is to work effectively, the following four variables need to be in place:

1. *Task:* Does the team know what its task is? Is the task reasonably unambiguous and consistent with the mission of the team? Does the team have a meaningful piece of work, sufficient autonomy to perform it, and access to knowledge of its results?

2. *Boundaries:* Is the collective membership of the team appropriate for the task to be performed? Are there too few or too many members? Do the members collectively have sufficient knowledge and skills to perform the work? In addition to task skills, does the team have sufficient maturity and interpersonal skills to be able to work together and resolve conflicts? Is there an appropriate amount of diversity on the team? That is, are members different enough that they have varied perspectives and experiences, and yet similar enough to be able to communicate and relate to one another?

3. *Norms:* Does the team share an appropriate set of norms for working as a team? Norms can be acquired by the team in three ways: (a) they can be imported from the organization existing outside the team, (b) they can be instituted and reinforced by the leader or leaders of the team, or (c) they can be developed by the team itself as the situation demands. If the team is to have a strategy that works over time, it must ensure that conflicting norms do not confuse team members. It also needs to regularly scan and review prevailing norms to ensure that they support overall objectives.

4. *Authority:* Has the leader established a climate where her authority can be used in a flexible rather than a rigid manner? Has she, at one end of the authority continuum, established sufficient competence to allow the group to comply when conditions demand (such as in emergencies)? Has she also established a climate such that any member of the team feels empowered to provide expert assistance when appropriate? Do team members feel comfortable in questioning the leader on decisions where there are no clear right answers? In short, have conditions been created where authority can shift to appropriately match the demands of the situation?

FIGURE 10.1
Organizational Shells

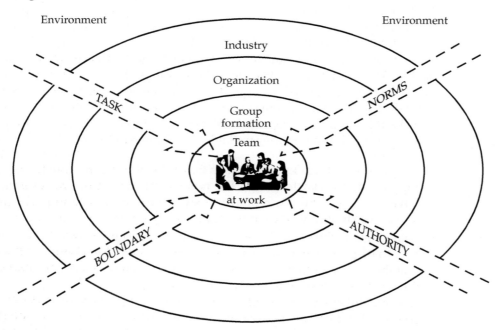

Many of these team design components may be imported from preexisting conditions in the organization within which the team is forming, from the industry in which the organization operates, or even from the environment in which the industry exists. To help team leaders consider these various levels, Hackman and Ginnett[46,47] developed the concept of **organizational shells** (see Figure 10.1). Notice that the four critical factors for team design (task, boundary, norms, and authority) are necessary for the group to work effectively. In some cases, all the information about one of these critical factors may be input from the industry or organizational shell level. Here the leader need do little else but affirm that condition. In other cases, there may be too little (or even inappropriate) input from the organizational level to allow the team to work effectively. Here the leader needs to modify the factors for team design. Ideally this is done during the formation process—the final shell before the team actually begins work.

These ideas may require a new way of thinking about the relationship between a leader and followers. In many organizational settings, leaders are assigned. Sometimes, however, the people who create conditions for improved group effectiveness are not the designated leaders at all; they may emerge from the ranks of followers. This model has been used to differentiate between effective and ineffective "self-managing work groups"—teams where the followers and leaders were the same people.

Moreover, because the model is prescriptive, it suggests what ineffective work groups can do to be successful. That same purpose underlies the following model as well.

Team Leadership Model

Because we have emphasized that leadership is a group or team function and have suggested that one measure of leadership effectiveness may be whether the team achieves its objectives, it is reasonable to examine a model specifically designed to help teams perform more effectively: the **Team Leadership Model**, or **TLM**[48–50] (shortened from earlier versions that called it the Team Effectiveness Leadership Model). Another way to think of this model is as a mechanism to first identify what a team needs to be effective, and then to point the leader either toward the roadblocks that are hindering the team or toward ways to make the team even more effective than it already is. This approach is similar to McGrath's[51] description of leadership, which suggested that the leader's main job is to determine the team's needs and then take care of them. This approach also will require us to think about leadership not as a function of the leader and his or her characteristics but as a function of the team. As the title of the model suggests, team effectiveness is the underlying driver.

We have mentioned this model of group or team effectiveness briefly before, but now we will explore it in greater detail. The original model for examining the "engine of a group" was developed by Richard Hackman and has been the basis for much research on groups and teams over the last 30 years.[52] The model presented here includes major modifications by Ginnett and is an example of a leadership model that has been developed primarily using field research. While there have been controlled experimental studies validating portions of the model,[53] the principal development and validation have been completed using actual high-performance teams operating in their own situational context. Examples of the teams studied in this process include commercial and military air crews in actual line flying operations, surgical teams in operating suites, executive teams, product development and manufacturing teams, combat teams, fire department teams, and teams preparing the space shuttle for launch. A complete illustration of the model will be shown later. Because of its complexity, it is easier to understand by starting with a few simpler illustrations.

At the most basic level, this model (see Figure 10.2) resembles a systems theory approach with inputs at the base (individual, team, and organizational factors), processes or throughputs in the center (what the team actually does to convert inputs to outputs and what we can tell about the team by actually observing team members at work), and outputs at the top (how well the team did in accomplishing its objectives, ideally a high-performance team). It is often helpful to think of these components as parts of a metaphorical iceberg. While almost everyone can see the outputs of the team (the portion of the iceberg above the waterline), and some can

The leaders who work most effectively, it seems to me, never say 'I'. And that's not because they have trained themselves not to say 'I'. They don't think 'I'. They think 'we'; they think 'team'. They understand their job to be to make the team function. They accept responsibility and don't sidestep it, but 'we' gets the credit. . . . This is what creates trust, what enables you to get the task done."

Peter F. Drucker

416   Part Three   *Focus on the Followers*

FIGURE 10.2
An Iceberg Metaphor for Systems Theory Applied to Teams

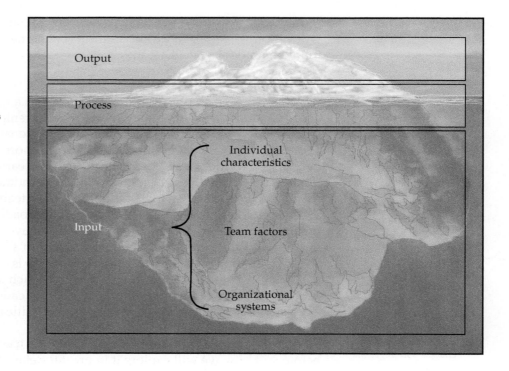

see the processes, most of the inputs are in the organizational background (or underwater in the iceberg metaphor). But anyone who has seen an iceberg recognizes that most of its mass is the part that is underwater—and this part supports the part that is visible. So it is with the leadership work in teams. Much of the leadership work is done in the background, and many of the components may be developed before the team is constituted. As we will see, the leader's job is to create the conditions for the team to be effective, and much of that work is done at the input level.

As helpful as the iceberg is as a metaphor, an iceberg is unwieldy and a little messy in a classroom. Therefore, the TLM will be presented from here on as a four-sided pyramid or for those more geometrically gifted, a square pyramid. We will examine each of the major systems theory stages (input, process, output) as they apply to the TLM. However, we will proceed through the model in reverse order—looking at outputs first, then the process stage, and then inputs.

Outputs

What do we mean by outputs? Quite simply, **outputs** (see Figure 10.3) are the results of the team's work. For example, a football team scores 24 points. A production team produces 24 valves in a day. A tank crew hits 24 targets on an artillery range. Such raw data, however, are insufficient for assessing team effectiveness.

FIGURE 10.3
Basic TLM Outputs: Outcomes of High-Performance Teams

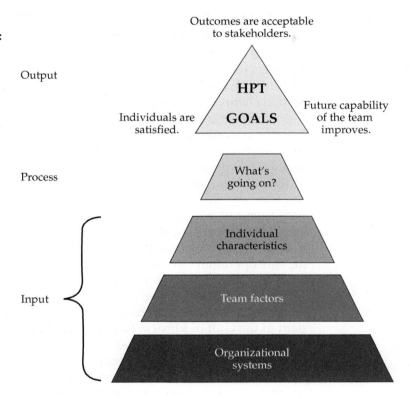

How do we know if a team's output is good? How do we know if a team is effective? Even though it was possible for the three teams just mentioned to measure some aspect of their work, these measurements are not helpful in determining their effectiveness, either in an absolute sense or in a relative sense. For comparison and research purposes, it is desirable to have some measures of team effectiveness that can be applied across teams and tasks. Hackman[54] argued that a group is effective if (1) the team's productive output (goods, services, decisions) meets the standards of quantity, quality, and timeliness of the people who use it; (2) the group process that occurs while the group is performing its task enhances the ability of the members to work as members of a team (either the one they were on or any new teams they may be assigned to) in the future; and (3) the group experience enhances the growth and personal well-being of the individuals who compose the team.

Process

It should be obvious why leaders should be concerned with the outputs listed in the preceding section. After all, if a team does not "produce" (output), it cannot be considered effective. But what is process? And why should a leader care about it? Actually, there are several reasons why a leader might want to pay attention to the team's process—how the team goes about its work. Some teams may have such a limited number of products that the leader can ill afford to wait until the product is delivered to assess its acceptability to the client. For example, a team whose task is to build one (and only one) satellite to be launched into orbit will have no second chances. There may be no opportunity to correct any problem once the satellite is launched (or, as was the case with the flawed Hubble Space Telescope, correction can be made only at great expense). Therefore, it may be desirable for the leader of such a team to assess the team's work while it is working rather than after the satellite is launched. Other kinds of teams have such high standards for routine work that there simply are not enough critical indicators in the end product to determine effectiveness from outcome measures. As an example of this situation, a team operating a nuclear power plant is surrounded by so many technical backup systems that it may be difficult to determine team effectiveness by looking at "safe operation" as a measurement criterion. But we have evidence that not all teams in nuclear power plants operate equally well (Chernobyl and Three Mile Island are two examples). There is evidence that poor teamwork was a contributing cause in the 2010 BP Deepwater Horizon accident in the Gulf of Mexico. It would seem helpful to be able to assess real teams "in process" rather than learn about team problems only after disastrous outcomes. Even leaders of noncritical teams might like to be able to routinely monitor their teams for evidence of effective or ineffective processes. So how teams go about their work can provide useful information to the leader.

Because process assessment is so important, let us focus for a moment on the block containing the four process measures of effectiveness in Figure 10.4. These four **process measures** of effectiveness provide criteria by which we can examine how teams work. If a team is to perform effectively, it must (1) work hard enough, (2) have sufficient knowledge and skills within the team to perform the task, (3) have an appropriate strategy to accomplish its work (or ways to approach the task at hand), and (4) have constructive and positive group dynamics among its members. The phrase *group dynamics* refers to interactions among team members, including such aspects as how they communicate with others, express feelings toward each other, and deal with conflict with each other, to name but a few characteristics. Assessing and improving group process is no trivial matter, as has been documented extensively in a comprehensive view of group process and its assessment by Wheelan.[55]

What should the leader do if she discovers a problem with one of these four process measures? Paradoxically, the answer is not to focus her attention on that process per se. While the four process measures are fairly good diagnostic measures for a team's ultimate effectiveness, they are unfortunately not particularly good leverage points for fixing the problem. An analogy from medicine would be a doctor who diagnoses the symptoms of an infection (a fever) but who then treats the symptoms rather

FIGURE 10.4
TLM Process Variables: Diagnose the Team Using the Process Variables

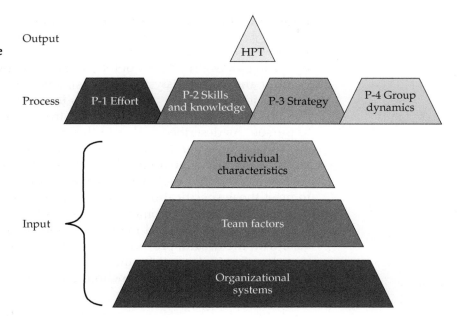

than attacking the true underlying cause (a nail in the patient's foot). Similarly at the team level, rather than trying to correct a lack of effort being applied to the task at hand (perhaps a motivation problem), the team leader would be better advised to discover the underlying problem and fix that than to assume that a motivational speech to the team will do the job. This is not to imply that teams cannot benefit from process help. It merely suggests that the leader should ensure that there are no design problems (at the input level) that should be fixed first.

Inputs

> *Individual commitment to a group effort—that is what makes a team work, a company work, a society work, a civilization work."*
>
> **Vince Lombardi**

In a manufacturing plant, **inputs** are the raw materials that are processed into products for sale. Similarly in team situations, inputs are what is available for teams as they go about their work. However, an important difference between an industrial plant and a team is that for a plant, the inputs are physical resources. Often for team design, we are considering psychological factors. Levels of inputs range from the individual level to the environmental level. Some of these inputs provide little opportunity for the leader to have an influence—they are merely givens. Leaders are often put in charge of teams with little or no control over the environment, the industry, or even the organizational conditions. However, the leader can directly influence other inputs to create the conditions for effective teamwork.

Figure 10.2 shows the multiple levels in the input stage of the model. Note that in addition to the four team variables earlier (task, composition, norms, and authority), there are input factors at the individual and organizational levels as well and that these levels both surround and affect the team design level.

Leadership Prescriptions of the Model

Creation

Following McGrath's[56] view of the leader's role (the leader's main job is to identify and help satisfy team needs), and Ginnett's definition that the leader's job is to create the conditions for the team to be successful, it is possible to use the TLM to identify constructive approaches for the leader to pursue. As described earlier in this chapter, what leaders do depends on where a team is in its development. Ideally we should build a team as we build a house or an automobile. We should start with a concept, create a design, engineer it to do what we want it to do, and then manufacture it to meet those specifications. The TLM provides the same linear flow for design of a team. The somewhat broader version of the TLM model is shown in Figure 10.5, and the leader should, as just noted, begin at the base with the dream, proceed through all the design variables, and then pay attention to the development needs of the team. In this way she can implement the three critical functions for team leadership: **dream, design,** and **development.**

FIGURE 10.5
Three Functions of TLM Leadership

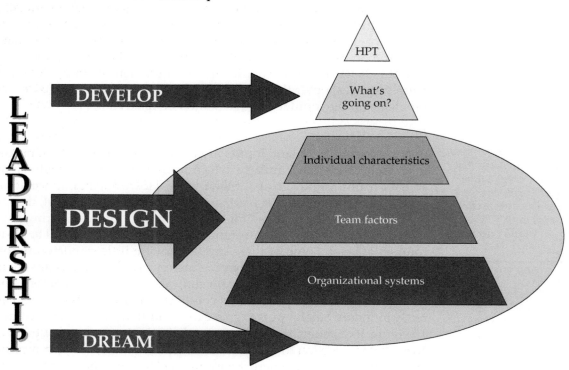

Dream

Obviously the team needs to have a clear vision. In their book *The Wisdom of Teams*[57] Katzenbach and Smith suggested that this may be the most important single step in teamwork. If the team has a challenging and demanding goal, teamwork may be necessary to accomplish the task. In highly effective work teams, the leader ensures that the team has a clear vision of where they are going. The communication of a vision frequently involves metaphorical language so that team members actually "paint their own pictures" of where the team is headed.

Design

If you've ever watched a great coach, you might have marveled at his or her calm demeanor while the game is being played. Perhaps one of the biggest reasons for this composure is that coaches realize most of their work is done by the time the game starts. They have recruited the right players, they have trained and equipped them, they have designed a strategy for their opponents, and they have instilled in the team the appropriate attitudes and values. In short, they have already done the design work. The importance of the design function of leadership cannot be overstated. Whether in the start-up of a team or in the midstream assignment of leaders, designing the team is critical. Unfortunately this is also often the most frequently omitted step in the culture of many traditional organizations.

Managers have long been trained to detect deviations and correct them. But what if the deviations are not detectable until the output stage? At their best, managers often detect deviations at the process stage and attempt to fix them "right where they are seen." Far too often, little time or attention is focused at the organizational, team, and individual input levels. Senior-level leaders may resist changing the organizational systems for a number of reasons, including having a vested interest in maintaining the status quo (whatever it is, it has at least let them rise to their current position). And while individual team leaders may have little control over the organizational context and systems, they can always make an impact in their own team's design at both the individual and team levels.

Development

If the leader finds that the team has a clear sense of direction and vision, and the input variables at the individual, organizational, and team levels are contributing positively to team effectiveness (that is, the design portion of the leader's job has been taken care of), then she can turn her attention to the development level. Development is the ongoing work done with the team at the process level to continue to find ways to improve an already well-designed team. Given our individualistic culture, we have identified many teams in organizations that are apparently well designed and supported at the individual input level, but that have had no training or experience in the concept of teamwork. There are times when effective teamwork is based on very different concepts than effective individual work. For example, for a team to do well, the individuals composing the team must sometimes not maximize their individual effort. Referred to as *subsystem nonoptimization,* this concept is at first not intuitively obvious to many newly assigned team members. Nevertheless, consider the example of a high school football team that has an extremely fast running back and some good (but considerably slower) blocking linemen as members of the offense. Often team members are told they all need to do their absolute best if the team is going to do well. If our running back does his absolute best on a sweep around the end, he will run as fast as he can. By doing so, he will leave his blocking linemen behind. The team is not likely to gain much yardage on such a play, and the linemen and the running back, who have done their individual best, are apt to learn an important experiential lesson about teamwork. Most important, after several such disastrous plays, all the team members may be inclined to demonstrate poor team process (lower effort, poor strategy, poor use of knowledge, and poor group dynamics represented by intrateam strife). If we assume that all the input stage variables are satisfactorily in place, ongoing coaching may now be appropriate. The coach would get better results if he worked out a better coordination plan between the running back and the linemen. In this case, the fast running back needs to slow down (not perform maximally) to give the slower but excellent blockers a chance to do their work. After they have been given a chance to contribute to the play, the running back will have a much better chance to excel individually, and so will the team as a whole.

As straightforward as this seems, few leaders get the opportunity to build a team from the ground up. More often a leader is placed into a team that already exists, has most, if not all, of its members assigned, and is in a preexisting organizational context that might not be team friendly. Although this situation is more difficult, all is not lost. The TLM also provides a method for diagnosis and identification of key **leverage points** for on-the-fly change.

Diagnosis and Leverage Points

Let us assume that you, as a new leader, have been placed in charge of a poorly performing existing team. After a few days of observation, you have discovered that its members are just not working hard. They seem to be uninterested in the task, frequently wandering off or not even showing up for scheduled teamwork. By focusing on the process level of the TLM, we would diagnose this at the process level as a problem of effort. (The core or "engine" of the TLM is shown in Figure 10.6, which, as noted earlier, can be thought of as a four-sided pyramid.) Note that preceding the term *effort* at the process level is the label "P-1" and that all variables on this side of the pyramid have a "1" designation as well. Rather than just encouraging the team members to work harder (or threatening them), we should first look at the input level to see if there is

FIGURE 10.6
Team Leadership Model

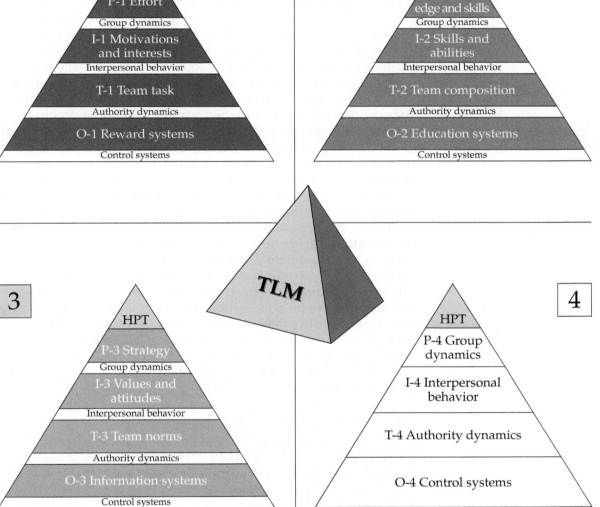

some underlying problem. But you do not need to examine all 12 input variables (or, said another way, you do not need to spin the pyramid around to worry about each of the four faces). Because we have already diagnosed a P-1 level process problem, the TLM is designed to focus your attention on the key leverage points to target change for the specific problem identified in diagnosis. Each face of the pyramid shows the input variables at the individual, team, and organizational levels that most impact the process variable that we might diagnose. The factors on the "1" side of the pyramid are referred to as the leverage points for impacting P-1 effort. (See the "1" face of the pyramid in Figure 10.6.) The individual level (I-1) suggests that we look at the interests and motivations of the individual team members. These are referred to as **individual factors** in the model. If we have built a team to perform a mechanical assembly task, but the individuals assigned have little or no interest in mechanical work and instead prefer the performing arts, they may have little interest in contributing much effort to the team task. Here, using instruments such as the Campbell Interest and Skills Survey to select personnel may help our team's effort level from an individual perspective.[58]

While it may seem tempting to move to the team-level inputs next, remember that this model emphasizes how teams are influenced by both individual and organizational-level inputs. Therefore, we will look at the **organizational level** next. At the organizational level (O-1), the model suggests that we should examine the reward system that may be impacting the team. If the individuals have no incentive provided by the organization for putting forth effort, they might not be inclined to work hard. Similarly, the reward system may be structured to reward only individual performance. Such a reward structure would be inconsistent with designs for a team task, where interdependence and cooperation among members are often underlying premises. If a professional basketball organization rewards players based only on individual points scored, with no bonuses for team performance (games won or making the playoffs), you can expect little passing, setting picks for teammates, and so on.

Both the individual and organizational-level variables contribute to the team's ability to perform the task. But there can also be problems at the **team design** level. Here (T-1) a poorly designed task is hypothesized to be unmotivating. If a job is meaningless, lacks sufficient autonomy, or provides no knowledge of results, we would not expect to see followers putting forth much effort.

In review, we just walked through an example of how to use the TLM model. We found key leverage points at various levels of the input stage that affect how the team works (team process). In the example cited, we diagnosed a process-level problem with effort (P-1), so we examined the 1-level variables at the individual, organizational, and team levels as the most likely location for finding input-stage problems. By the way, the concept of leverage point does not imply that only factors at the corresponding "numbers" should be considered. For example, a team's effort might be affected by an oppressive and authoritarian leader. As we will discuss next, this foundation-level variable can have a tremendous impact on the other variables. Indeed, so powerful is this component that we should examine the process measure of group dynamics (P-4) and its corresponding leverage points in more detail. Consider the following two examples:

Surgical team: A surgical team composed of highly experienced members is involved in a surgical procedure that each member has participated in numerous times before. During one portion of the procedure, the surgeon asks for a particular instrument. The scrub nurse looks across the table at the assistant with a questioning gaze and then hands the surgeon the instrument he requested. Recognizing that the instrument he has been handed (and asked for) is not correct for the current procedure, he throws it down on the table and curses at the scrub nurse. All members of the surgical team take a half-step back from the table and all casual conversation stops. No one offers any further voluntary assistance to the surgeon.

Commercial airline crew: A commercial airline crew is making a routine approach into an uncrowded airport on a clear day. The captain is flying and has declared a visual approach. His final approach to the runway is not good, which greatly complicates the plane's landing, and the landing is poor. After taxiing to the gate, the captain and his entire crew debrief (discuss) the poor approach, and the team members talk about what they could do individually and collectively to help the captain avoid or improve a poor approach in the future. The captain thanks the members for their help and encourages them to consider how they could implement their suggestions in other situations.

Obviously the group dynamics are very different in these two cases. In the first example, the surgeon's behavior, coupled with his status, created a condition inappropriate for effective teamwork. The airline captain in the second example, even though not performing the task well, created a team environment where the team was much more likely to perform well in the future. In both of these cases, we would have observed unusual (one negative and one positive) group dynamics while the team was at work. These are examples of the group dynamics at the P-4 level.

Again returning to the model for determining points of leverage, we would check the I-4 variable at the individual level to determine if the team members involved had adequate interpersonal skills to interact appropriately. At the organizational level, the O-4 variable would suggest we check organizational components to determine if any organizational control systems inhibit or overly structure the way in which the team can make decisions or control its own fate. Such factors may include organizational design or organizational structure limitations (such as functional hierarchies or "silos"), or it may be a rigid computerized control system that specifies every minute detail of the tasks not only for the team as a whole but for all the individuals composing the team. These excessive controls at the organizational level can inhibit effective teamwork. Finally, at the team design level, the T-4 variable would have us examine authority dynamics created between the leader and the followers. Authority dynamics describe the various ways the team members, including the leader, relate and respond to authority. It is at the team level that the followers have opportunities to relate directly with the team's authority figure, the team leader. The intricacies of how these various authority dynamics can play themselves out in a team's life are more complex than is warranted for this chapter; suffice it to say that authority relationships range from autocratic to laissez-faire. (For a more detailed explanation of this concept, see Ginnett.)[59] But even without further description, it should be no surprise that the varied group dynamics observed in the previous two examples were leveraged by the leaders' different use of authority.

It would be simple if leaders could identify and specify in advance the ideal type of authority for themselves and their teams, and then work toward that objective. However, teams seldom can operate effectively under one fixed type of authority over time. The leader might prefer to use his or her favorite style, and the followers might also have an inherent preference for one type of authority or another; but if the team is to be effective, the authority dynamics they are operating with should complement the demands of the situation. Situations change over time, and so should the authority dynamics of the team. This idea is similar to a point made earlier in this book—that effective leaders tend to use all five sources of leader power.

In research on the behavior of leaders in forming their teams, Ginnett[60] found that highly effective leaders used a variety of authority dynamics in the first few minutes of a team's life. At one point in the first meeting of the team, the leader would behave directively, which enabled him to establish his competence and hence his legitimate authority. At another time, the same leader would actively seek participation from each member of the team. By modeling a range of authority behaviors in the early stages of team life, effective leaders laid the groundwork for continuing expectations of shifting authority as the situational demands changed.

Concluding Thoughts about the Team Leadership Model

Not all components of the TLM have been discussed here because of its complexity. For example, we have not discussed **material resources.** Even if a team is well designed, has superior organizational systems supporting its work, and has access to superior-quality ongoing development, without adequate physical resources it is not likely to do well on the output level. Also note that background shells (discussed earlier in this chapter) representing the industry and the environment have not been included in this simplified depiction of the TLM. Although the team leader may have little opportunity to influence these shells, they will certainly have an impact on the team.

Further, several feedback loops (not shown in the pyramid depictions of the TLM) provide information to various levels of the organization. Usually information is available to the organization as a whole (either formally or informally) about which teams are doing well and which are struggling. Whether leaders have access to this information is largely a function of whether they have created or stifled a safe climate. Feedback at the individual level can influence the perceived efficacy of the individual members of the team,[61,62] while the overall potency of the team is impacted even for tasks that the team has yet to attempt.[63]

Finally, let us reinforce a limitation noted earlier. For ease of use and guidance, this model has been presented as if it were a machine (for example, if P-2 breaks, check I-2, O-2, and T-2). As with other models of leadership or other human systems, however, nothing is that simple. Obviously other variables affect teams and team effectiveness. There are also complex interactions between the variables described in this model. But we have considerable evidence that the model can be useful for understanding teams,[64] and, in light of the relationship between teams and leadership, we are now using it as an underlying framework in courses to help leaders more effectively lead their teams. While we have more than 20 years of experience using the TLM to help teams and team leaders, it is certainly not the only team model available. The "Rocket Model" will also be discussed in the next chapter.

The secret is to work less as individuals and more as a team. As a coach, I play not my eleven best, but my best eleven.

Knute Rockne

"Well, I guess I did it again, guys? Missed a field goal in the final seconds. But hey, we're a team, right? Right, guys? Guys?"

It has been shown that leaders can influence team effectiveness by (1) ensuring that the team has a clear sense of purpose and performance expectations; (2) designing or redesigning input-stage variables at the individual, organizational, and team design levels; and (3) improving team performance through ongoing coaching at various stages, but particularly while the team is actually performing its task. These midcourse corrections should not only improve the team outcomes but also help to avoid many of the team-generated problems that can cause suboptimal team performance.[65] Whether the leader gets the luxury of creation or is thrust into the leadership of an existing team, the TLM has been shown to be a useful tool in guiding leader behavior. It also is handy if you believe that a leader's job is to create the conditions for a team to be effective.

Let us integrate the variables from this model into our leader–follower–situation framework (see Figure 10.7). Clearly there are variables of importance in each of the three arenas. However, in this model leader

FIGURE 10.7
Factors from the Team Leadership Model and the Interactional Framework

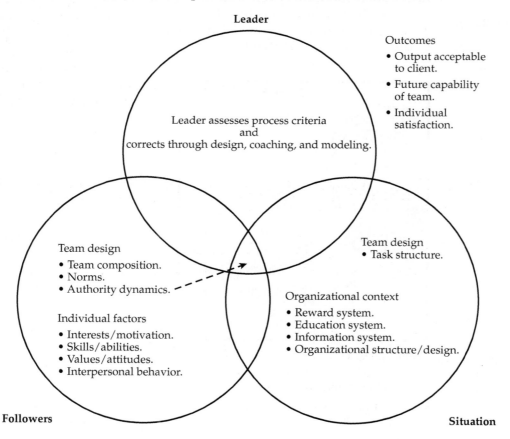

characteristics play a lesser role because the leader's job is to work on what is not being provided for the team so it can perform its task. The focus thus has shifted from the leader to the followers and to the situation.

Virtual Teams

Just as teams and teamwork have become essential to the accomplishment of work in organizations, so will be an understanding of teams that are not in a single location. With the movement toward the global market-place and the resultant globalization of organizations, it is appropriate to briefly consider the difficulties and recommended solutions for leading **geographically dispersed teams (GDTs).** There is considerable discussion about the labeling of such teams,[66] but for simplicity we will call them **virtual teams** here.

The marketplace for many firms is now the globe (see Highlight 10.9). Western corporations are recognizing that growth and development opportunities are often much greater in Russia and other nations of the former Soviet Union, China, Latin America, and Africa than they are in the markets of North America and Europe. But this realization brings new challenges for leading teams that are not only dispersed geographically but are often culturally different as well. Fortunately, information and communication technology offers some new opportunities, if not solutions, for these problems.[67] But is the mere opportunity to communicate electronically sufficient to ensure teamwork? Apparently not. (See Highlight 10.10.)

What Is the "Global Population" of Your Classroom?

HIGHLIGHT 10.9
The authors of this book attended a training session conducted by a major corporation intended for its newly appointed executives. One session was devoted to demonstrating the need for a global perspective in today's environment. To illustrate the key point, the instructor divided the room into unequal groups representing the geographical distribution of the world's population and had each group stand up in turn. As each group stood, she told them the proportion of the global population they represented. The proportions she used are provided here.

You might try this in your classroom—it makes the point dramatically.

Australia and New Zealand	2%
North America	5%
Former Soviet Union	5%
Latin America	7%
Western/Eastern Europe	10%
Africa	12%
Asia	56%

Leading Virtual Teams: 10 Principles

HIGHLIGHT 10.10

Terence Brake is the president of TMA-Americas and specializes in globalization. He suggests the following guidance for leaders of virtual teams:

Virtual when used in relation to teamwork is an unfortunate term. It implies there is almost teamwork, but not quite. *Virtual* has associations with *nearly, close to,* and *bordering on.* As one wit said, "If you want virtual results, create a virtual team." Alternatively, it is a fortunate term if taken to imply that greater efforts are needed to achieve real teamwork in virtual teams. What principles can help you do this?

1. *Be proactive.* We often talk of "virtual" teams (VTs) as if they were all of a kind, but each one has its unique challenges. Some have a high level of cultural diversity. Others are more homogeneous. Some use one primary technology for collaboration, while others use a diverse mix. Some are short-lived, targeted on solving an immediate problem. Others are longer-term and strategic. Some cross time zones, and others none. By understanding the most likely challenges to occur, you can take proactive measures and increase team confidence. Confidence is a building block of virtual team performance.

2. *Focus on relationships before tasks.* Early on, team communications should have a significant "getting to know you" component. They should also demonstrate enthusiasm and optimism. Members need to feel valued for who they are, not just what they do. They need to feel engaged and connected. Trust is usually built early on virtual teams, or not at all. Some observers talk of the "virtual paradox"—virtual teams being highly dependent on trust, but not operating under conditions supportive of trust building. Trust is often built on perceived similarities, but distance makes this process difficult. Chances for misunderstanding are also increased. Goodwill and engagement will solve most problems. Isolation and alienation create problems. Connect, and then collaborate.

3. *Seek clarity and focus early on.* Invest up-front time in clarifying the team's purpose and roles and responsibilities. There is enough uncertainty when working at a distance; it doesn't need to be added to by ambiguity and confusion. Clear purpose and accountabilities support cohesion. Translate purpose and overall accountabilities into specific objectives and tasks so that everyone knows what is expected, by whom, and by when. Virtual teams are highly susceptible to "focus drift" and fragmentation, so keep reminding the team of purpose, objectives, and so on.

4. *Create a sense of order and predictability.* In a world wanting us to embrace chaos, "order" and "predictability" might appear unfashionable. But they are critical to the success of virtual teams. Uncertainty creates anxiety, fear, and withdrawal. The result is a demotivated and unproductive team. Use common team tools, templates, and processes; have predetermined times for communicating together; check in with team members regularly without trying to micromanage; be accessible and an anchor point for the team. Shared expectations are psychological threads connecting separate minds.

5. *Be a cool-headed, objective problem solver.* Problems on virtual teams can appear larger than they actually are; people feeling isolated can lose perspective. Small issues, quickly resolved when working face-to-face, often fester and spread paranoia and distrust. You should establish yourself as someone who is totally fair; you don't play favorites, and you don't overburden some at the expense of others. You also need to be pragmatic. When there is a problem, you keep calm, you engage the team in finding practical solutions, and you communicate often. Panic is a virus that breeds exceptionally well in silent, isolated spaces.

6. *Develop shared operating agreements.* To reduce threats of uncertainty and ambiguity,

common methods and processes—operating agreements—need to be established quickly. These agreements provide the team with shared mental models for working together. Typically, operating agreements need to be created in areas such as planning, decision making, communicating, and coordination. A team charter acts as a common reference point and can help orient new team members. Take time during team "meetings" to review how well the operating agreements are working.

7. *Give team members personal attention.* Just as you would on a face-to-face team, allocate time to "meet" with individuals. Find out how he or she is feeling about things. Give each person an opportunity to share personal successes, challenges, needs, and wants. It can be difficult to do this in team "meetings" where the emphasis is on shared tasks and problem solving. Empathize with that person who is on the road, working at home, or in a remote office. Listening, caring, sympathizing, recognizing—they cost little, but benefit everyone.

8. *Respect the challenges of the virtual environment.* I once lived on a boat, and I soon learned to respect the power of nature—the winds, tides, swells, rain, ice, and drought. I had to pay very close attention to these elements or they could sink me, swamp me, or ground me. There is always the temptation to carry over habits from one environment (land, face-to-face teamwork) into another (river, working at a distance). We must recognize the differences and adapt. Listening, empathizing, communi-

cating, coordinating, engaging, energizing, and enabling all need to be enhanced.

9. *Recognize the limits of available technologies.* Unless you really have to, don't try and do everything via a virtual team. Sometimes teams are working on projects so complex that no matter how much video- or teleconferencing time they have, it will not be enough. Sometimes it pays dividends to bring people together for a few days. Never assume that because you have been designated a "virtual" team, you must always work in that mode. Focus on cost/benefit over the life of the project. Technology is a tool, and all tools are good for some tasks and not others.

10. *Stay people-focused.* Distance can make faceless abstractions of us all. Never lose sight of the fact that your virtual team members are people, with all that that entails—needs for belonging, meaning, accomplishment, and recognition; feelings of frustration, anger, excitement, boredom, and alienation; political pressures and personal pressures. Think about those features of your physical workplace that enable teams to work well together, such as formal meeting rooms, informal spaces, and the coffee area, and see what you can do to humanize your virtual workplace—team pictures and bios, bulletin boards, chat areas.

Applying these virtual team leadership principles will help you avoid *almost* and *close to* teamwork. Virtual teamwork is only going to increase, so many of us need to re-skill ourselves for leading at a distance.

Researchers at the Conference Board[68] have reported that five major areas must change for global teams to work. The five listed were senior management leadership, innovative use of communication technology, adoption of an organization design that enhances global operations, the prevalence of trust among team members, and the ability to capture the strengths of diverse cultures, languages, and people.

Armstrong and Cole[69] did in-depth studies of virtual teams and have reported three conclusions that should be considered by leaders of these teams. First, the distance between members of a virtual team is multidimensional. "Distance" includes not just geographical distance but also organizational distance (different group or department cultures), temporal distance (different time zones), and differences in national culture. Second, the impact of such distances on the performance of a distributed work group is not directly proportional to objective measures of distance. In fact, Armstrong and Cole suggested that a new measure of distance between group members that reflects the degree of group cohesion and identity—a measure of psychological distance between members—would predict group performance better than geographical distance. Finally, differences in the effects of distance on work groups are due at least partially to two intervening variables: (1) integrating practices *within* a virtual team, and (2) integrating practices *between* a virtual team and its larger host organization.

With increasing numbers of virtual teams, we are beginning to see evidence that these teams, when designed and constructed properly, might be even more effective than in-place teams. In a study of successful "far-flung teams,"[70] three rules emerged that enhanced the teams' performance. First, the leaders needed to not only select for diversity but then exploit that diversity for the team's benefit. Second, technology needed to simulate reality. For example, e-mail was a poor way for a team to communicate because it either focused on one-on-one communications (as opposed to team-level) or drowned people in paperwork if everyone was copied. Surprisingly, the researchers didn't think much of videoconferencing. What seemed to work best was a specifically designed "virtual work space." This included not only a team Web space with a home page prominently displaying the team's mission but also pages for people, purpose, and a meeting center, among other features. Other teams have found wikis essential to keep global teams up to date.[71] Third, leaders must be particularly diligent to hold virtual teams together. Face-to-face teams can confront forces that splinter the groups, but such forces can be accentuated in virtual teams. Leaders of successful virtual teams overcommunicated, pushed for the adoption of a common language, and merged work practices. One particularly successful tactic was to have team members work in ad hoc pairs for a week or two so they would get to know each other better. This also seemed to discourage the formation of cliques. And, as described for the TLM earlier, the leaders spent a great deal of time working in the organizational background to ensure that team members were allotted sufficient time to work on the virtual project.

Finally, a number of frameworks under development can help leaders work with virtual teams, and these frameworks may provide specific useful factors. However, in our admittedly limited exposure to virtual teams in a pure research sense, a number of our clients have reported that the TLM has been quite useful in considering process problems and in suggesting appropriate leverage points for intervention. One thing is clear: virtual teams require more leadership, not less.

On the Horizon

Two emerging themes from the literature are worth noting as we move forward in leading groups and teams. In December 2012, the Society of Industrial and Organizational Psychology devoted half their journal to **collective leadership** approaches. In their lead article,[72] the authors suggest an overview of five approaches to collective leadership: team leadership, network leadership, shared leadership, complexity leadership, and collective leadership. The authors of this article then present varying amounts of science and applications for the differing labels they have provided. Team leadership appears to be the most studied and applied while other categories are, at this time, purely theoretical with virtually no empirical research. While this label (collective leadership) is relatively new, the concept is not. In the first edition of this textbook, published in 1990, we noted that leadership is fundamentally a group phenomenon, just as we have in this chapter. Whether or not this "collective leadership label catches on remains to be seen."

Another new concept seems more appealing. Labeled **clusters**, these are intact teams that are self-managed. Aron provides the following description of the cluster:

> Clusters are a radical alternative to our traditional notion of teams. They are formed outside a company context, but are hired and paid by companies as a unit, as a permanent part of the company. They manage, govern and develop themselves; define their own working practices and tools; and share out remuneration. Technology trends and tools like "the cloud," and collaboration suites, are evolving to make this more and more workable. The business or agency treats the cluster as an atomic unit of resource and it hires, fires and positions the cluster as a unit. Likewise, each cluster appears as such a unit in the business's organization chart. Clusters plug together like Lego bricks to achieve the business's goals.[73]

This approach sounds very similar to the way the U.S. government employs the Navy SEALs. The SEALS are an intact team that trains together and manages themselves as a unit. When called upon, they are "hired" as a unit and perform as a unit. That business is considering such a concept makes sense because traditional methods of forming and developing a team within an organization, only to disband that team when the project is completed, inevitably results in value loss.

Summary

The group perspective showed that followers' behaviors can be the result of factors somewhat independent of the individual characteristics of followers. Group factors that can affect followers' behaviors include group size, stages of group development, roles, norms, and cohesion. Leadership practitioners should use these concepts to better understand followers' behaviors. Leaders should also use a team perspective for understanding follower behavior and group performance. Leadership practitioners need to bear in mind how a team's sense of identity, common goals or tasks, level of task interdependence, and differentiated roles affect functional and dysfunctional follower behavior. Additionally, because effective teams have several readily identifiable characteristics, leadership practitioners may want to use the suggestions provided by Hackman,[74] Ginnett,[75] or Hallam and Campbell[76] to develop more effective teams.

The Team Leadership Model posited that team effectiveness can best be understood in terms of inputs, processes, and outcomes. The input level consists of the individual characteristics of the followers; the design of the team itself; and various organizational systems that create the context in which the teams will operate. The process level concerns how teams behave while going about their tasks, and the output level concerns whether customers and clients are satisfied with the team's product, whether the team improves and develops as a performing unit, and whether followers are satisfied to be members of the team. By identifying certain process problems in teams, leaders can use the model to diagnose appropriate leverage points for action at the individual, team design, or organizational levels, or for ongoing development at the process level. Leaders concerned with teamwork in organizational settings have found this framework useful in helping them conceptualize factors affecting team effectiveness and identifying targets for change. Last, we mentioned the emerging concepts of collective leadership and clusters.

Key Terms

group perspective, 392
group, 394
cliques, 396
span of control, 396
additive task, 396
process loss, 397
social loafing, 397
social facilitation, 397
forming, 397
storming, 397
norming, 397
performing, 397
project teams, 398
punctuated
    equilibrium, 399
group roles, 399
task role, 399
relationship role, 399
dysfunctional
    roles, 400

role conflict, 400
intrasender role
    conflict, 401
intersender role
    conflict, 401
interrole conflict, 401
person–role
    conflict, 401
role ambiguity, 402
norms, 402
group cohesion, 404
overbounding, 405
groupthink, 405
ollieism, 407
organizational
    shells, 414
Team Leadership
    Model (TLM), 415
outputs, 416

process measures, 418
inputs, 419
dream, 420
design, 420
development, 420
leverage point, 422
individual factors, 424
organizational
    level, 424
team design, 424
material resources, 426
geographically
    dispersed teams
    (GDTs), 429
virtual teams, 429
collective
    leadership, 433
clusters, 433

Questions

1. How do the tenets of Ginnett's Team Leadership Model compare with the components of team performance described earlier?
2. Not all group norms are positive or constructive from the leader's perspective. If a group holds counterproductive norms, what should the leader do?
3. On the basis of what you know about global cultures, would people from the United States, Japan, or Chile be more comfortable with a group or team-based approach to work?

Activity

NASA Exercise—Lost on the Moon

Your spaceship has crash-landed on the dark side of the moon and you are scheduled to rendezvous with the mother ship, which is 200 miles away on the lighted side of the moon. The crash has ruined the ship and destroyed all the equipment except for the 15 items listed here. Your crew's survival depends on reaching the mother ship, so you must choose the most critical items available to take on the 200-mile trip. Your task is to rank-order the 15 items in the order of their importance for your survival. Place a "1" beside the most important item, a "2" beside the second most important item, and so on until you have ranked all 15 items.

_____ Box of matches
_____ Food concentrate
_____ 50 feet of nylon rope
_____ Parachute silk
_____ Solar-powered portable heating unit
_____ Two .45 caliber pistols
_____ One case of dehydrated milk
_____ Two 100-pound tanks of oxygen
_____ Stellar map
_____ Self-inflating life raft
_____ Magnetic compass
_____ Five gallons of water
_____ Signal flares
_____ First-aid kit with hypodermic syringes
_____ Solar-powered FM transmitter/receiver

Your instructor has the "NASA Expert" answers and the instructions for completing the exercise.

Minicase

Integrating Teams at Hernandez & Associates

Marco Hernandez is president of Hernandez & Associates Inc., a full-service advertising agency with clients across North America. The company provides a variety of marketing services to support its diverse group of clients. Whether called on to generate a strategic plan, create interactive Web sites, or put together a full-blown media campaign, the team at Hernandez & Associates prides itself on creative solutions to its clients' marketing challenges.

The firm was founded in 1990 with an emphasis in the real estate industry. It quickly expanded its client base to include health care, as well as food and consumer products. Like many small firms, the company grew quickly in the "high-flying" 1990s, but its administrative costs to obtain and serve businesses also skyrocketed. And, as with many businesses, the agency's business was greatly affected by the terrorist attacks of September 11, 2001, and the economic downturn that followed. Clients' shrinking budgets forced them to scale back their business with Hernandez & Associates, and staff cutbacks meant that clients needed more marketing support services as opposed to full-scale campaigns.

Hernandez & Associates now faced a challenge—to adapt its business to focus on what the clients were asking for. Specifically, clients, with their reduced staffs, were looking for help responding to their customers' requests and looking for ways to make the most of their limited marketing budgets. Its small, cohesive staff of 20 employees needed to make some fast changes.

As president of Hernandez & Associates, Marco Hernandez knew his team was up for the challenge. He had worked hard to create an environment to support a successful team—he recruited people who had solid agency experience, and he consistently communicated the firm's mission to his team. He made sure the team had all the resources it needed to succeed and constantly took stock of these resources. He had built his team as he built his business and knew the group would respond to his leadership. But where to start? Getting the team to understand that growth depended on a shift in how it served its clients was not difficult—each of the employees of the small firm had enough contact with the clients that they knew client needs were changing. But making significant changes to the status quo at Hernandez & Associates would be difficult. Group roles had to change—creative folks had to think about how to increase a client's phone inquiries and Web site visits; account people needed a better understanding of the client's desire for more agency leadership. And everyone needed a better sense of the costs involved. The company as a whole required a more integrated approach to serving clients if they hoped to survive. Marco needed a plan.

1. Like many leaders, Marco has a team in place and does not have the luxury of building a new team to adapt to the changing business environment his firm now faces. Use the TLM to help Marco diagnose the problems faced by the firm and identify leverage points for change.
   a. Consider the major functions of the TLM—input, process, and output. Where do most of the firm's challenges fall?
   b. What are the team's goals for outputs?
2. Identify potential resources for Marco and his team in implementing a strategy to change the way they do business at Hernandez & Associates.

End Notes

1. McCammon, "Evidence of Heuristic Traps in Recreational Avalanche Accidents." Paper presented at the International Snow Science Workshop, Penticton, British Columbia, September 30–October 4, 2002.
2. R. C. Ginnett, "Effectiveness Begins Early: The Leadership Role in the Formation of Intra-Organizational Task Groups," unpublished manuscript, 1992.
3. G. S. Gibbard, J. J. Hartman, and D. Mann, *Analysis of Groups: Contribution to the Theory, Research, and Practice* (San Francisco: Jossey-Bass, 1974).
4. M. Shaw, *Group Dynamics: The Psychology of Small Group Dynamics*, 3rd ed. (New York: McGraw-Hill, 1981).
5. G. A. Yukl, *Leadership in Organizations*, 1st ed. (Englewood Cliffs, NJ: Prentice Hall, 1981).
6. I. J. Badin, "Some Moderator Influences on Relationships between Consideration, Initiating Structure, and Organizational Criteria," *Journal of Applied Psychology* 59 (1974), pp. 380–82.
7. B. E. Goodstadt and D. Kipnis, "Situational Influences on the Use of Power," *Journal of Applied Psychology* 54 (1970), pp. 201–07.
8. D. Kipnis, S. M. Schmidt, and I. Wilkinson, "Intraorganizational Influence Tactics: Explorations in Getting One's Way," *Journal of Applied Psychology* 65 (1980), pp. 440–52.
9. J. G. Udell, "An Empirical Test of Hypotheses Relating to Span of Control," *Administrative Science Quarterly* 12 (1967), pp. 420–39.
10. B. M. Bass, *Leadership, Psychology, and Organizational Behavior* (New York: Harper, 1960).
11. B. P. Indik, "Organizational Size and Member Participation: Some Empirical Tests of Alternative Explanations," *Human Relations* 18 (1965), pp. 339–50.
12. I. D. Steiner, *Group Process and Productivity* (New York: Academic Press, 1972).
13. Ibid.
14. B. Latane, K. Williams, and S. Harkins, "Social Loafing," *Psychology Today* (1979), p. 104.

15. D. B. Porter, M. Bird, and A. Wunder, "Competition, Cooperation, Satisfaction, and the Performance of Complex Tasks among Air Force Cadets," *Current Psychology Research and Reviews* 9, no. 4 (1991), pp. 347–54.

16. R. Zajonc, "Social Facilitation," *Science* 149 (1965), pp. 269–74.

17. B. W. Tuckman, "Developmental Sequence in Small Groups," *Psychological Bulletin* 63 (1965), pp. 384–99.

18. Ibid.

19. E. Mayo, *The Human Problems of an Industrial Civilization* (New York: Macmillan, 1933).

20. R. M. Stogdill, "Group Productivity, Drive, and Cohesiveness," *Organizational Behavior and Human Performance* 8 (1972), pp. 26–43.

21. Ibid.

22. J. R. Terborg, C. H. Castore, and J. A. DeNinno, "A Longitudinal Field Investigation of the Impact of Group Composition on Group Performance and Cohesion," paper presented at the annual meeting of the Midwestern Psychological Association, Chicago, 1975.

23. C. J. G. Gersick, "Time and Transition in Work Teams: Toward a New Model of Group Development," *Academy of Management Journal* 31 (1988), pp. 9–41.

24. R. C. Ginnett, "Airline Cockpit Crew," in *Groups That Work (and Those That Don't)*, ed. J. Richard Hackman (San Francisco: Jossey-Bass, 1990).

25. M. Jamal, "Job Stress and Job Performance Controversy: An Empirical Assessment," *Organizational Behavior and Human Performance* 33 (1984), pp. 1–21.

26. P. Zimbardo, C. Haney, W. Banks, and D. Jaffe, "The Mind Is a Formidable Jailer: A Pirandellian Prison," *New York Times Magazine,* April 8, 1973, pp. 38–60.

27. R. J. House, R. S. Schuler, and E. Levanoni, "Role Conflict and Ambiguity Scales: Reality or Artifact?" *Journal of Applied Psychology* 68 (1983), pp. 334–37.

28. J. R. Rizzo, R. J. House, and S. I. Lirtzman, "Role Conflict and Ambiguity in Complex Organizations," *Administrative Science Quarterly* 15 (1970), pp. 150–63.

29. C. D. Fisher, and R. Gitleson, "A Meta-analysis of the Correlates of Role Conflict and Ambiguity," *Journal of Applied Psychology* 68 (1983), pp. 320–33.

30. J. R. Hackman, "Group Influences on Individuals," in *Handbook of Industrial and Organizational Psychology,* ed. M. D. Dunnette (Chicago: Rand McNally, 1976).

31. R. Reilly, *Sports Illustrated* 104, no. 15 (2006), p. 76.

32. D. C. Feldman, "The Development and Enforcement of Group Norms," *Academy of Management Review,* January 1984, pp. 47–53.

33. J. R. Hackman, *Leading Teams—Setting the Stage for Great Performances* (Boston, MA: Harvard Business School Press, 2002).

34. C. P. Alderfer, "Group and Intergroup Relations," in *Improving Life at Work,* eds. J. R. Hackman and J. L. Suttle (Santa Monica, CA: Goodyear, 1977).

35. R. C. Ginnett, "The Formation Process of Airline Flight Crews," *Proceedings of the Fourth International Symposium on Aviation Psychology* (Columbus, OH, 1987).

36. I. L. Janis, *Groupthink,* 2nd ed. (Boston: Houghton Mifflin, 1982).

37. Ibid.

38. Ibid.

39. J. E. Shephard, "Thomas Becket, Ollie North, and You," *Military Review* 71, no. 5 (1991), pp. 20–33.

40. S. P. Robbins, *Organizational Behavior: Concepts, Controversies, and Applications* (Englewood Cliffs, NJ: Prentice Hall, 1986).

41. G. L. Hallam and D. P. Campbell, "Selecting Team Members? Start with a Theory of Team Effectiveness," paper presented at the Seventh Annual Meeting of the Society of Industrial/Organizational Psychologists, Montreal, Canada, May 1992.

42. Ibid.

43. J. R. Hackman, *Groups That Work (and Those That Don't)* (San Francisco: Jossey-Bass, 1990).

44. R. C. Ginnett, "Crews as Groups: Their Formation and Their Leadership," in *Crew Resource Management*, eds. B. Kanki, R. Hemreich, and J. Anca (San Diego, CA: Academic Press, 2010).

45. R. C. Ginnett, "Team Effectiveness Leadership Model: Identifying Leverage Points for Change," *Proceedings of the 1996 National Leadership Institute Conference* (College Park, MD: National Leadership Institute, 1996).

46. J. R. Hackman, "Group Level Issues in the Design and Training of Cockpit Crews," in *Proceedings of the NASA/MAC Workshop on Cockpit Resource Management*, eds. H. H. Orlady and H. C. Foushee (Moffett Field, CA: NASA Ames Research Center, 1986).

47. Ginnett, "Crews as Groups."

48. Ibid.

49. Ginnett, "Team Effectiveness Leadership Model: Identifying Leverage Points for Change."

50. R. C. Ginnett, "Team Effectiveness Leadership Model: Design & Diagnosis," *12th Annual International Conference on Work Teams* (Dallas, TX: 2001).

51. J. E. McGrath, *Leadership Behavior: Some Requirements for Leadership Training* (Washington, DC: Office of Career Development, U.S. Civil Service Commission, 1964).

52. Hackman, *Groups That Work (and Those That Don't)*.

53. K. W. Smith, E. Salas, and M. T. Brannick, "Leadership Style as a Predictor of Teamwork Behavior: Setting the Stage by Managing Team Climate," paper presented at the Ninth Annual Conference of the Society for Industrial and Organizational Psychology, Nashville, TN, 1994.

54. Hackman, *Groups That Work (and Those That Don't)*.

55. S. A. Wheelan, *Group Processes* (Needham Heights, MA: Allyn & Bacon, 1994).

56. McGrath, *Leadership Behavior*.

57. J. R. Katzenbach and B. K. Smith *The Wisdom of Teams* (Boston: HarperBusiness, 1994).

58. D. P. Campbell, S. Hyne, and D. L. Nilsen, *Campbell Interests and Skill Survey Manual* (Minneapolis, MN: National Computer Systems, 1992).

59. Ginnett, "Crews as Groups."

440   Part Three   *Focus on the Followers*

60. Ibid.

61. A. Bandura, "Self-Efficacy: Toward a Unifying Theory of Behavioral Change," *Psychological Review* 84 (1977), pp. 191–215.

62. D. H. Lindsley, D. J. Brass., and J. B. Thomas, " Efficacy-Performance Spirals: A Multilevel Perspective," *Academy of Management Review* 20 (1995), pp. 645–78.

63. R. A. Guzzo, P. R. Yost, R. J. Campbell, and G. P. Shea, "Potency in Teams: Articulating a Construct," *British Journal of Social Psychology* 32 (1993), pp. 87–106.

64. Hackman, *Groups That Work (and Those That Don't).*

65. I. D. Steiner, *Group Process and Productivity* (New York: Academic Press, 1972).

66. M. Kossler, and S. Prestridge, "Geographically Dispersed Teams," *Issues and Observations* 16 (1996), pp. 2–3.

67. J. Lipnack and J. Stamps, *Virtual Teams: Reaching across Space, Time and Organizations with Technology* (New York: John Wiley, 1997).

68. Conference Board, "Global Management Teams: A Perspective," *HR Executive Review* 4 (1996).

69. D. J. Armstrong and P. Cole, "Managing Distances and Differences in Geographically Distributed Work Groups," in *Distributed Work,* eds. P. Hinds and S. Kiesler (Cambridge, MA: MIT Press, 2002), pp. 167–89.

70. A. Majchrzak, A Malhotra, J. Stamps, and J. Lipnack, "Can Absence Make a Team Grow Stronger?" *Harvard Business Review,* May 2004, pp. 131–37.

71. P. Dvorak, "How Teams Can Work Well Together from Far Apart," *The Wall Street Journal,* September 17, 2007, p. B-4.

72. F. J. Yammarino, E. Salas, A. Serban, K. Shirreffs, and M. Shuffler, "Collective Leadership Approaches: Putting the 'We' in Leadership Science and Practice," *Industrial and Organizational Psychology Perspectives on Science and Practice* 5 (2012), pp. 382–402.

73. D. Aron, "The Future of Talent is in Clusters," *Harvard Business Review Blog Network*, February 1, 2013.

74. Hackman, *Groups That Work (and Those That Don't).*

75. Ginnett, "Effectiveness Begins Early."

76. G. L. Hallam and D. P. Campbell, "Selecting Team Members? Start with a Theory of Team Effectiveness," paper presented at the Seventh Annual Meeting of the Society of Industrial/Organizational Psychologists, Montreal, Canada, May 1992.

Chapter

11

Skills for Developing Others

The skills chapter in Part 2 addressed what might be considered relatively basic leadership skills such as listening and communication. In this chapter we will cover a number of additional leadership skills that are somewhat more advanced and that pertain particularly to the leader's relationship with followers. The skills addressed in this section include

- Setting goals.
- Providing constructive feedback.
- Team building for work teams.
- Building high-performance teams—the Rocket Model.
- Delegating.
- Coaching.

Setting Goals

The Roman philosopher Seneca wrote, "When a man does not know what harbor he is making for, no wind is the right wind." Setting goals and developing plans of action to attain them are important for individuals and for groups. For example, the purpose or goal is often the predominant norm in any group. Once group goals are agreed on, they induce member compliance, act as a criterion for evaluating the leadership potential of group members, and become the criteria for evaluating group performance.[1]

Perhaps the most important step in accomplishing a personal or group goal is stating it right in the first place. The reason many people become frustrated with the outcomes of their New Year's resolutions is that their resolutions are so vague or unrealistic that they are unlikely to lead to demonstrable results. It is possible to keep New Year's resolutions, but we must set them intelligently. In a more general sense, some ways of writing goal statements increase the likelihood that we will successfully achieve the desired goals. Goals should be specific and observable, attainable and challenging, based on top-to-bottom commitment, and designed to provide feedback to personnel about their progress toward them. The following is a more detailed discussion of each of these points.

Goals Should Be Specific and Observable

As described in Chapter 9, research provides strong support for the idea that specific goals lead to higher levels of effort and performance than general goals. General goals do not work as well because they often do not provide enough information regarding which particular behaviors are to be changed or when a clear end state has been attained. This may be easiest to see with a personal example.

Assume that a student is not satisfied with her academic performance and wants to do something about it. She might set a general goal such as "I will do my best next year" or "I will do better in school next year." At first such a goal may seem fine; after all, as long as she is motivated to do well, what more would be needed? However, on further thought you can see that "do my best" or "do better" are so ambiguous as to be unhelpful in directing her behavior and ultimately assessing her success. General goals have relatively little impact on energizing and directing immediate behavior, and they make it difficult to assess, in the end, whether someone has attained them. A better goal statement for this student would be to attain a B average or to get no deficient grades this semester. Specific goals like these make it easier to chart progress. A more business-oriented example might be improving productivity at work. Specific goal statements in this case might include a 20 percent increase in the number of products produced by the work unit over the next three months or a 40 percent decrease in the number of products returned by quality control next year.

The idea of having specific goals is closely related to that of having observable goals. It should be clear to everyone when a goal has or has not been reached. It is easy to say your goal is to go on a diet, but a much better goal is "to lose 10 pounds by March." Similarly, it is easy to say a team should do better next season, but a better goal is to say the team will win more than half of next season's games. Note that specific, observable goals are also time limited. Without time limits for accomplishing goals, there would be little urgency associated with them. Neither would there be a finite point at which it is clear whether a person or group has accomplished the goals. For example, it is better to set a goal of improving the next quarter's sales figures than just improving sales.

Goals Should Be Attainable but Challenging

Some people seem to treat goals as a sort of loyalty oath they must pass, as if it would be a break with their ideals or reflect insufficient motivation if any but the loftiest goals were set. Yet to be useful, goals must be realistic. The struggling high school student who sets a goal of getting into Harvard may be unrealistic, but it may be realistic to set a goal of getting into the local state university. A civil rights activist may wish to eliminate prejudice completely, but a more attainable goal might be to eliminate racial discrimination in the local housing project over the next five years. A track team is not likely to win every race, but it may be realistic to aim to win the league championship.

The corollary to the preceding point is that goals should also be challenging. If goals merely needed to be attainable, then there would be nothing wrong with setting goals so easy that accomplishing them would be virtually guaranteed. As we have seen previously, setting easy goals does not result in high levels of performance; higher levels of performance come about when goals stretch and inspire people toward doing more than they thought they could. Goals need to be challenging but attainable to get the best out of ourselves.

Goals Require Commitment

There is nothing magical about having goals; having goals per se does not guarantee success. Unless supported by real human commitment, goal statements are mere words. Organizational goals are most likely to be achieved if there is commitment to them at both the top and the bottom of the organization. Top leadership needs to make clear that it is willing to put its money where its mouth is. When top leadership sets goals, it should provide the resources workers need to achieve the goals and then should reward those who do. Subordinates often become committed to goals simply by seeing the sincere and enthusiastic commitment of top leadership to them. Another way to build subordinate acceptance and commitment to goals is to have subordinates participate in setting the goals. Research on the effects of goal setting demonstrates that worker acceptance and satisfaction tend to increase when workers are allowed to participate in setting goals.[2,3]

On the other hand, research is less conclusive about whether participation in goal setting actually increases performance or productivity. These mixed findings about participation and performance may be due to various qualities of the group and the leader. In terms of the group, groupthink may cause highly cohesive groups to commit to goals that are unrealistic and unachievable. Group members may not have realistically considered equipment or resource constraints or have the technical skills needed to successfully accomplish the goal. In addition, group members may not have any special enthusiasm for accomplishing a goal if the leader is perceived to have little expert power or is unsupportive, curt, or inept.[4-6] However, if leaders are perceived as competent and supportive, followers may have as much goal commitment as they would if they had participated in setting the goal. Thus participation in goal setting often leads to higher levels of commitment and performance if the leader is perceived to be incompetent, but it will not necessarily lead to greater commitment and performance than are achieved when a competent leader assigns a goal. Again, these findings lend credence to the importance of technical competence in leadership effectiveness.

Goals Require Feedback

One of the most effective ways to improve any kind of performance is to provide feedback about how closely a person's behavior matches some criterion, and research shows that performance is much higher when goals are accompanied by feedback than when either goals or feedback are used alone. Goals that are specific, observable, and time limited are conducive to ongoing assessment and performance-based feedback, and leaders and followers should strive to provide and seek regular feedback. Moreover, people should seek feedback from a variety of sources or provide feedback using a variety of criteria. Often, different sources and criteria can paint diverse pictures of goal progress, and people can get a better idea of the true level of their progress by examining the information provided and integrating it across the various sources and criteria.

Providing Constructive Feedback

Giving constructive feedback involves sharing information or perceptions with another about the nature, quality, or impact of that person's behavior. It can range from giving feedback pertaining specifically to a person's work (performance feedback) to impressions of how aspects of that person's interpersonal behavior may be pervasively affecting relationships with others. Our use of the term *feedback* here is somewhat different from its use in the systems view of communication (Figure 8.2 in Chapter 8). In the communication model, the feedback loop begins with actively checking the receiver's interpretation of your own message and then initiating or modifying subsequent communications as necessary. A simple example of that meaning of feedback might be noting another person's quizzical expression when you try to explain a complicated point and realizing you'd better say it differently. The skill of giving constructive feedback, however, inherently involves actively giving feedback to someone else.

Getting helpful feedback is essential to a subordinate's performance and development. Without feedback, a subordinate will not be able to tell whether she's doing a good job or whether her abrasiveness is turning people off and hurting her chances for promotion. And it's not just subordinates who need constructive feedback to learn and grow. Peers may seek feedback from peers, and leaders may seek feedback from subordinates. Besides fostering growth, effective supervisory feedback also plays a major role in building morale.

In many ways, the development of good feedback skills is an outgrowth of developing good communication, listening, and assertiveness skills. Giving good feedback depends on being clear about the purpose of the feedback and on choosing an appropriate context and medium for giving it. Giving good feedback also depends on sending the proper nonverbal signals and trying to detect emotional signals from whoever may be receiving the feedback. In addition, giving good feedback depends on being somewhat assertive in providing it, even when it may be critical of a person's performance or behavior. Although feedback skills are related to communication, listening, and assertiveness skills, they are not the same thing. Someone may have good communication, listening, and assertiveness skills but poor feedback skills. Perhaps this distinction can be made clearer by examining the knowledge, behavior, and evaluative components of feedback skills.

The knowledge component of feedback concerns knowing when, where, and what feedback is to be given. For example, knowing when, where, and how to give positive feedback may be very different from knowing when, where, and how to give negative feedback. The behavioral component of feedback concerns how feedback actually is delivered (as contrasted with knowing how it should be delivered). Good feedback is specific, descriptive, direct, and helpful; poor feedback is often too watered down to be useful to the recipient. Finally, one way to evaluate feedback is to examine whether recipients actually modify their behavior accordingly after receiving it. Of course this should not be the only way to evaluate feedback skills. Even when feedback is accurate in content and delivered skillfully, a recipient may fail to acknowledge it or do anything about it.

Although most leaders probably believe that feedback is an important skill, research has shown that leaders also believe they give more feedback than their subordinates think they do.[7] There are many reasons why leaders may be reluctant to give feedback. Leaders may be reluctant to give positive feedback because of time pressures, doubts about the efficacy of feedback, or lack of feedback skills.[8] Sometimes supervisors hesitate to use positive feedback because they believe subordinates may see it as politically manipulative, ingratiating, or insincere.[9] Leaders also may give positive feedback infrequently if they rarely leave their desks, if their personal standards are too high, or if they believe good performance is expected and should not be recognized at all.[10] Other reasons may explain the failure to give negative feedback,[11] such as fear of disrupting leader–follower relations[12] or fear of employee retaliation.[13]

Although there are a number of reasons why leaders are hesitant to provide both positive and negative feedback, leaders need to keep in mind that followers, committee members, or team members will perform at a higher level if they are given accurate and frequent feedback. It is difficult to imagine how work group or team performance could improve without feedback. Positive feedback is necessary to tell followers they should keep doing what they are doing well, and negative feedback is needed to give followers or team members ideas for how to change their behavior to improve their performance. Although accurate and frequent feedback is necessary, there are several other aspects of feedback that everyone can work on to improve their feedback skills, including making sure it's helpful, being direct, being specific, being descriptive, being timely, being flexible, giving both positive and negative feedback, and avoiding blame and embarrassment when giving feedback. Highlight 11.1 gives examples of each of these different aspects of feedback, and the following is a more complete description of ways leaders can improve their feedback skills.

Make It Helpful

The purpose of feedback is to provide others with information they can use to change their behavior. Being clear about the intent and purpose is important because giving feedback sometimes can become emotional for both the person giving it and the person receiving it. If the person giving feedback is in an emotional state (such as angry), she may say things that make her temporarily feel better but that only alienate the receiver. To be helpful, individuals need to be clear and unemotional when giving feedback, and they should give feedback only about behaviors actually under the other person's control.

Tips for Improving Feedback Skills

HIGHLIGHT 11.1

BE HELPFUL

Do not: "I got better scores when I was going through this program than you just did."

Do: "This seems to be a difficult area for you. What can I do to help you master it better?"

BE DIRECT

Do not: "It's important that we all speak loud enough to be heard in meetings."

Do: "I had a difficult time hearing you in the meeting because you were speaking in such a soft voice."

BE SPECIFIC

Do not: "Since you came to work for us, your work has been good."

Do: "I really like the initiative and resourcefulness you showed in solving our scheduling problem."

BE DESCRIPTIVE

Do not: "I'm getting tired of your rudeness and disinterest when others are talking."

Do: "You weren't looking at anyone else when they were talking, which gave the impression you were bored. Is that how you were feeling?"

BE TIMELY

Do not: "Joe, I think I need to tell you about an impression you made on me in the staff meeting last month."

Do: "Joe, do you have a minute? I was confused by something you said in the meeting this morning."

BE FLEXIBLE

Do not (while a person is crying, or while they are turning red with clenched teeth in apparent anger): "There's another thing I want to tell you about your presentation yesterday . . . "

Do: When a person's rising defenses or emotionality gets in the way of really listening, deal with those feelings first, or wait until later to finish your feedback. Do not continue giving information.

People can improve the impact of the feedback they give when it is addressed to a specific individual. A common mistake in giving feedback is addressing it to "people at large" rather than to a specific individual. In this case, the individuals for whom the feedback was intended may not believe the feedback pertains to them. To maximize the impact of the feedback, people should try to provide it to specific individuals, not large groups.

Be Specific

Feedback is most helpful when it identifies particular behaviors that are positive or negative. One of the best illustrations of the value of specific feedback is in compositions or term papers written for school. If someone turned in a draft of a paper to the instructor for constructive comments and the instructor's comments about the paper were "Good start, but needs work in several areas," the writer would not know what to change or correct. More helpful feedback from the instructor would be specific comments like "This paragraph does not logically follow the preceding one" or "Cite an example here." The same is true of feedback in work situations. The more specifically leaders can point out which behaviors to change, the more clearly they let the other person know what to do.

Be Descriptive

In giving feedback, it is good to stick to the facts as much as possible, being sure to distinguish them from inferences or attributions. A behavior description reports actions that others can see, about which there can be little question or disagreement. Such descriptions must be distinguished from inferences about someone else's feelings, attitudes, character, motives, or traits. It is a behavior description, for example, to say that Sally stood up and walked out of a meeting while someone else was talking. It is an inference, though, to say she walked out because she was angry. However, sometimes it is helpful to describe both the behavior itself and the corresponding impressions when giving feedback. This is particularly true if the feedback giver believes that the other person does not realize how the behavior negatively affects others' impressions.

Another reason to make feedback descriptive is to distinguish it from evaluation. When a person gives feedback based mostly on inferences, he often conveys evaluations of the behavior as well. For example, saying "You were too shy" has a more negative connotation than saying "You had little to say." In the former case, the person's behavior was evaluated unfavorably and by apparently subjective criteria. Yet evaluation is often an intrinsic part of a supervisor's responsibilities, and good performance feedback may necessitate conveying evaluative information to a subordinate. In such cases, leaders are better off providing evaluative feedback when clear criteria for performance have been established. Filley and Pace have described criteria that can be used to provide evaluative feedback; some are listed in Highlight 11.2.[14]

Types of Criteria to Use for Evaluative Feedback

HIGHLIGHT 11.2

1. Compare behavior with others' measured performance. With this method, the subordinate's behavior is compared with that of her peers or co-workers; this is also called norm-referenced appraisal. For example, a subordinate may be told her counseling load is the lightest of all 10 counselors working at the center.

2. Compare behavior with an accepted standard. An example of this method would be a counselor being told her workload was substantially below the standard of acceptable performance set at 30 cases per week. This is known as criterion-referenced appraisal.

3. Compare behavior with a previously set goal. With this method, the subordinate must participate in setting and agree with a goal. This is a form of criterion-referenced appraisal, with the subordinate's "ownership" and acceptance of the goal before the fact critical to the feedback procedure.

4. Compare behavior with past performance.

Source: Adapted from A. C. Filley and L. A. Pace, "Making Judgments Descriptive," in *The 1976 Annual Handbook for Group Facilitators,* eds. J. E. Jones and J. W. Pfeiffer (La Jolla, CA: University Associates Press, 1976), pp. 128–31.

An issue related to impressions and evaluative feedback concerns the distinction between job-related (that is, performance) feedback and more personal or discretionary feedback. Although leaders have a right to expect followers to listen to their performance feedback, that is not necessarily true concerning feedback about other behaviors. Sharing perceptions of a person's behavior could be helpful to that person even when the behavior doesn't pertain specifically to his formal responsibilities; in such cases, however, it is the follower's choice whether to hear it or, if he hears it, whether to act on it.

Be Timely

Feedback usually is most effective when it is given soon after the behavior occurs. The context and relevant details of recent events or behaviors are more readily available to everyone involved, thus facilitating more descriptive and helpful feedback.

Be Flexible

Although feedback is best when it is timely, sometimes waiting is preferable to giving feedback at the earliest opportunity. In general, everyone should remember that the primary purpose of feedback is to be helpful. Feedback sessions should be scheduled with that in mind. For example, a subordinate's schedule may preclude conveniently giving him feedback right away, and it may not be appropriate to give him feedback when it will distract him from a more immediate and pressing task. Furthermore, it may not be constructive to give someone else feedback when the person receiving it is in an emotional state (whether about the behavior in question or other matters entirely). Moreover, it is important to be attentive to the other person's emotional responses while giving feedback and to be ready to adjust your own behavior accordingly.

A final important part of being flexible is to give feedback in manageable amounts. In giving feedback, you do not need to cover every single point at one time; doing so would only overload the other person with information. Instead, anyone who needs to give a lot of feedback to someone else may want to spread out the feedback sessions and focus on covering only one or two points in each session.

Give Positive as Well as Negative Feedback

Giving both positive and negative feedback is more helpful than giving only positive or negative feedback alone. Positive feedback tells the other person or the group only what they are doing right, and negative feedback tells the other person or group only what they are doing wrong. Providing both kinds of feedback is best.

Avoid Blame or Embarrassment

Because the purpose of feedback is to give useful information to other people to help them develop, talking to them in a way merely intended (or likely) to demean or make them feel bad is not helpful. Followers tend to be more likely to believe feedback if it comes from leaders who have had the opportunity to observe their behavior and are perceived to be credible, competent, and trustworthy.[15–17] Bass has pointed out that followers will continue to seek feedback even if their leaders are not competent or trustworthy—though they will not seek it from their leaders.[18] They will seek it from others they trust, such as peers or other superiors.

Team Building for Work Teams

Few activities have become more commonplace in organizations these days than "team-building workshops." One reason for this level of activity is the powerful shift that has occurred in the workplace from a focus primarily on individual work to team-centered work. Unfortunately, however, these activities do not always achieve their objectives. As noted earlier in this text, it doesn't make sense to hold teams responsible for work if nothing else in the organizational environment changes. Team-building interventions, at the team level, may help team members understand why they are having so much difficulty in achieving team objectives, and even suggest coping strategies for an intolerable situation. They are not, however, likely to remove root causes of problems. To better understand the importance of looking at teams this way, let's use an example of this kind of erroneous thinking from a different context.

Team-Building Interventions

Suppose you have decided that the next car you drive must have outstanding ride and handling characteristics. Some cars you test, such as some huge American-made automobiles, have outstanding ride characteristics, but you are not happy with their handling. They sway and "float" in tight slalom courses. Other cars you test have just the opposite characteristics. They are as tight and as stable as you could hope for in turns and stops, but their ride is so hard that your dental work is in jeopardy. But you do find one car that seems to meet your requirements: a Mercedes-Benz provides both a comfortable ride and tremendous road handling characteristics in high-performance situations. There is, however, one small problem. The Mercedes costs a lot of money up front—more than you are willing to put into this project. So you arrive at an alternative solution. You find a used Yugo, a small car built in Yugoslavia and no longer imported into the United States, largely because of inferior quality. But it is cheap, and after purchasing it, you know you will have lots of money left over to beef up the suspension, steering, and braking systems to provide you with the Mercedes-Benz ride you really want.

Ludicrous! Obviously you are never going to get a Mercedes-Benz ride unless you are willing to put in considerable money and effort *up front* rather than doing little up front and putting all your money into repair work. But that is precisely what many organizations attempt to do with teams. They do not seem willing to create the conditions necessary for teamwork to occur naturally (a point we will discuss in the section "Team Building at the Top" in Chapter 16), but when the teams struggle in a hostile environment, as they invariably will, the leaders seem willing to pour tremendous amounts of money into team-building interventions to fix the problem. These types of team-building problems are those we would categorize as "top-down."

An equally vexing problem occurs when organizations are committed to teamwork and are willing to change structures and systems to support it, but are not committed to the "bottom-up" work that is required. This is best illustrated in the rationale for team training shown in Figure 11.1. In our work with organizations, we are frequently asked to help teams that are struggling. In Figure 11.1 we would place these requests at the "TEAM" level, which is the third platform up from the bottom. We believe this type of intervention will work only if the team members have achieved a stable platform from which to work. In this case, that would include the two previous platforms in Figure 11.1. If the foundation is not well established, the solely team-based intervention often leads to intrateam competition or apathy and withdrawal.

As a basis for any work at the team level, individual team members must first be comfortable with themselves. They must be able to answer the questions "What do I bring to the team?" and "What do I need from the team?" Not answering these questions breeds inherent fear and mistrust. When

FIGURE 11.1
A Rationale for Individual, Interpersonal, Team, and Organizational Training

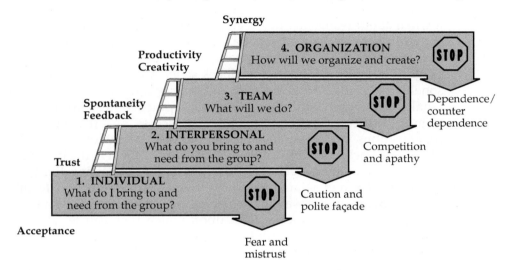

these questions have been answered, team members are in a position to begin dealing at the interpersonal level, where they may now comfortably ask, "What do *you* bring to the team and what do *you* need from the team?" Not resolving these issues results in caution in dealing with other members, and interactions at the "polite façade" level rather than at the level of truth and understanding. If the first- and second-level platforms are in place, a true team-building intervention can be useful. (Incidentally, just because team members have not stabilized themselves at levels 1 and 2 does not mean an intervention cannot be conducted. Rather, it means a more extensive intervention will be required than a solely team-based effort.)

What Does a Team-Building Workshop Involve?

Hundreds, if not thousands, of team-building interventions are being conducted today. Many good sources, such as the *Team and Organization Development Sourcebook*, contain team-based activities such as conflict resolution, problem solving, development of norms, trust building, or goal setting, to name a few.[19] Rather than trying to describe all these suggestions, however, we will describe a few recommendations that we have found useful and then share a few examples of interventions we have used.

At the Center for Creative Leadership, staff are frequently asked to design custom team interventions for mid- to upper-level teams. While we enter these design meetings with no agenda of activities, neither do we enter with a completely blank slate. We believe an intervention at the team level must meet three general requirements to be successful, and at least one activity must be included in the intervention pertaining to each of those three requirements.

The first requirement involves awareness raising. As we noted in our previous chapters, not all cultures are equally prepared or nurtured in the concepts of teamwork. In fact, many of the lessons we think we have learned about teams are incorrect. So we need to dispel such myths and include a healthy dose of team-based research findings about how teams *really* work as a critical element of a workshop. Second, we need some diagnostic, instrument-based feedback so team members can have a reasonably valid map of where they and their teammates now are located. Finally, each intervention must include a practice field, to use Senge's term.[20] Practice is necessary for athletic success, and it is necessary in organizations too. It would be foolish to design a whole new series of plays for a hockey team to implement, talk about them in the locker room, but never actually practice any of them before expecting the team to implement them in a game. Similarly, if you are asking people to change their behaviors in the way they interact to improve teamwork, it is only fair to give them a practice field upon which they can test their new behaviors in a reasonably risk-free, protected environment.

This is where experiential exercises can be useful, and here the quality of the team-building facilitator is important. Conducting a pencil-and-paper exercise in the classroom does not require the same facilitator skill set as that required to conduct, say, a team-rappelling exercise off the face of a cliff—few facilitators get those requirements wrong, and we have seldom discovered problems here. Where we have seen a significant breakdown in facilitator skills is in being able to link the exercise to the real world in which the team will be asked to perform. Facilitators must have not only a good sense of real-time team dynamics but also a sense of the business in which the team operates. They must help the participants make the links back to team dynamics that occur on the manufacturing floor or in the boardroom, and this seems to be the skill that distinguishes highly effective facilitators.

Examples of Interventions

Now let us provide a few examples of the range of interventions that can be included in team building. Ginnett conducted an intervention with three interdependent teams from a state youth psychiatric hospital. The teams included members of the administrative services, the professional staff, and the direct care providers. The members of each team were dedicated to their roles in providing high-quality service to the youths under their care, but the three groups experienced difficulty in working with each other. Extensive diagnosis of the groups revealed two underlying problems. First, each group had a different vision of what the hospital was or should be. Second, each group defined themselves as "care givers," thus making it difficult for them to ask others for help because, in their minds, asking for help tended to put them in the role of their patients. We conducted a series of workshops to arrive at a common vision for the hospital, but the second problem required considerably more work. Because the staff members needed to experientially understand that asking for help did not place them in an inherently inferior position, a "wilderness experience" was designed where the entire staff was asked to spend four days together in a primitive wilderness environment with difficult hiking, climbing, and mountaineering requirements. By the end of the experience, everyone had found an occasion to ask someone else for help. Even more important, everyone found that actually asking others for help—something they had previously resisted—moved the overall team much higher in its ability to perform. Considerable time was spent each evening linking the lessons of the day with the work in the hospital.[21]

In one of the more interesting programs we've conducted, a team of senior executives spent a week together at a ranch in Colorado. Each morning the team met for a series of awareness sessions and data feedback sessions. Afternoons were reserved by the chief operating officer for fun and relaxation, with the only requirement being that attendees participate as a team or subteams. As facilitators, we actively participated with the teams and related their team experiences each day to the lessons of the next morning, as well as to challenges facing the team in its normal work. In interventions like this we have learned that team building can be fun, and that the venues for it are almost limitless. Second, we have learned that being able to observe and process team activity in a real-time mode is essential for team-building facilitators. There is no substitute for firsthand observation as a basis for discerning group dynamics and noting the variety of revealing behaviors that emerge in unstructured team activities.

Building High-Performance Teams: The Rocket Model

As stated throughout this text, leadership is not an individual process. Rather, it involves influencing a group to pursue some type of overarching goal. From Chapter 10 we know that teams vary in a number of important factors, such as group size, norms, development stages, and cohesion. We also know leaders need to take these factors into consideration when creating and leading teams. The Team Leadership Model in Chapter 10 provides a comprehensive description of team dynamics and what leaders must do if they want to create high-performing teams. What follows is a simpler model of team effectiveness that provides both prescriptive and diagnostic advice for building high-performing teams. The Rocket Model of Team Effectiveness is prescriptive in that it tells leaders what steps to take and when to take them when building new teams. The model can also be used as a diagnostic tool for understanding where existing teams are falling short and what leaders need to do to get them back on track.[22–25]

The Rocket Model is based on extensive research with hundreds of teams in the health care, education, retail, manufacturing, service, software, telecommunications, energy, and financial service industries. The model has been used with executive teams at AMD, Williams-Sonoma, e Recycling Corporation, Avanade, Toro, Home Depot, Dell, Waste Management, and the Strategic Health Authority in the United Kingdom; mid-management teams at Symantec, 3M, AT&T, MassMutual, Cummins, Tellabs, Husky Energy, and a number of rural hospitals and school districts; and project teams at Pfizer and Hewlett-Packard. The model seems to work equally well with different types of teams at different organizational levels in different industries. Leaders particularly like the Rocket Model because of its straightforward and practical approach to team building.

A diagram of the Rocket Model can be found in Figure 11.2. As shown, building a team can be analogous to building a rocket. Just as rockets operate in different environments (i.e., low altitude, high altitude, or outer space), so must teams clearly define the context in which they operate. The booster stage is critical for getting a rocket off the ground, so are the mission and talent stages critical next steps for a team. Once the mission and talent issues have been addressed, leaders need to work with team members to sort out team norms and buy-in, and so on. Research shows that the teams with the best results are usually those who report a high level of team functioning on all the components of the Rocket Model.

FIGURE 11.2
The Rocket Model

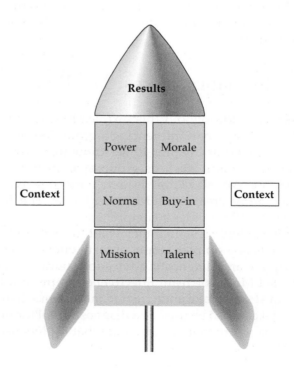

Teams reporting a high level of functioning in only some of these components usually report mediocre results, and those with low functioning on all the components usually achieve few if any results. The following is a more in-depth description of the eight components of the Rocket Model.

Context: What Is the Situation?

A critical first step to building high-performing teams is gaining alignment on team context. Most teams either influence or are influenced by competitors, suppliers, customers, government regulators, market conditions, other internal teams, the larger organization, and more. All too often team members have different assumptions about these constituencies, and as a result they may take well-intended but misguided actions that inadvertently destroy team morale and performance. One noteworthy aspect of team context is the implicit nature of team member assumptions—team members rarely if ever articulate their assumptions about the situation. That being the case, an important step leaders need to take when building high-performing teams is to identify all the constituencies affecting the team, and ask team members to share their assumptions about customers, competitors, and the like. This sharing of information about the situation helps ensure everyone is on the same page about the challenges facing the team.

Assume you were a store manager at a new Starbucks coffee shop that was about to open and wanted to use the Rocket Model to transform your two assistant store managers and 16 baristas into a high-performing team. One of the first things you would do is have everyone identify the constituencies affecting the team. These constituencies might include different customer segments, other coffee shops, key suppliers, the local business environment, other Starbucks stores, the city health inspector, the district manager (your boss), and the larger Starbucks corporation. You and your staff would then need to agree on a set of assumptions for each constituency—will the other coffee shops lower prices or go out of business over the next year? Will corporate be launching new products or opening new stores in the city? Is the local community thriving or declining? After discussing and agreeing on the assumptions for each constituency the team would then identify the greatest challenges facing the store over the next year.

Mission: What Are We Trying to Accomplish?

Once the situation has been clearly defined the next thing a leader must do is to clarify the team's purpose and goals. Thus the mission component of the Rocket Model is concerned with setting a common direction for the team. In some cases the leader works closely with team members to sort out these issues; in other cases the leader makes these determinations; and in still other cases the organization may make these decisions. For this component of the model, who makes these decisions is not as important as ensuring that all the team members understand what the team is trying to accomplish and how they contribute to team success.

There are several aspects of Mission that are worth noting. First, leaders need to realize that individual goals drive individual behavior; team goals drive team behavior. Therefore, if leaders want to encourage collaboration then they need to set team goals. Second, a common problem plaguing many teams is that they set vague or ill-defined team goals. Good team goals are specific, measurable, achievable, realistic, time-bound, and benchmarked. Benchmarking is a critical aspect of team goals, as far too many teams only set internal, continuous improvement type goals (e.g., sell X% more coffee than last month). Continuous improvement goals are helpful, but high-performing teams also set goals that allow them to see how they stack up against the competition (e.g., win-loss record or sales rankings against other stores in the area). Third, mission may be the most important component in the Rocket Model as it impacts all the other components. The mission of the team should determine the number and skills of people needed to achieve results (talent), the rules by which the team operates (norms), the equipment and budget needed (power), and so forth. Because mission plays such a vital role in team building, leaders of underperforming teams often find it worthwhile to clarify the team's goals and benchmarks when striving to improve team performance.

Applying the Rocket Model to the Starbucks scenario, the store manager would work with the team to set goals for the upcoming year. These might include the specific revenue, profitability, cost, customer satisfaction, customer complaint, employee turnover, staff coverage, and health inspection rating goals to be achieved each month or quarter. The team might also set revenue or customer satisfaction goals against the other Starbucks in the city, such as being in the top 5 out of 25 stores in customer satisfaction each month. The team leader would then build a team scorecard that included all the goals and tracked actual team performance on a monthly and quarterly basis.

Talent: Who Is on the Bus?

The talent component of the Rocket Model is about answering the five right questions: Does this team have the right number of people, with the right organizational structure, in the right roles, with the right skills, and for the right reasons? Teams with too many or too few people in ill-defined roles or with team members lacking the skills needed to achieve team goals often will report lower talent scores than teams having the right number of people with the right skills. Clarifying the reporting structure, defining roles and responsibilities, selecting the right kind of people, and continuously developing those skills needed to achieve team goals are the key leadership activities in this component of the Rocket Model. Professional athletic and elite military combat teams are very good at managing talent, as they ensure roles and responsibilities are clear, obsess over hiring decisions, and spend countless hours practicing; they actually spend little time performing. Many private- and public-sector teams seem to do just the opposite: they throw a group of available people together and expect them to produce. These latter teams do not think through who needs to be on the team and how they should be organized, spend little if any time developing needed skills, and never practice.

In the Starbucks example, talent would come into play when the store manager determined how many people would be needed to staff the store, defined the roles that need to be played in order to achieve the team goals, and moved the two assistant store managers and 16 baristas into their respective roles. The team leader would also want to provide ongoing training to his staff to make sure they were gaining the knowledge and skills needed to run shifts, make new drinks, serve customers, clean the equipment, open and close the shop, and other tasks.

Norms: What Are the Rules?

Once team members are in place and clearly understand the team's situation, goals, and roles, leaders need to address the norms component of the Rocket Model. Norms are the rules that govern how teams make decisions, conduct meetings, get work done, hold team members accountable for results, and share information. Several important aspects of norms are worth noting. First, the decisions the team makes, the way in which it makes decisions, how often and how long the team meets, and so forth should all be driven by the team's goals. Second, norms happen. If the team or team leader is not explicit about setting the rules that govern team behavior, they will simply evolve over time. And when they are not explicitly set, these rules may run counter to the team's goals. For example, one of the authors was working with a software development team that was responsible for delivering several new products in a six-month period. The time frame was aggressive, but one of the team norms that had evolved was that it was okay for team members to show up late to team meetings, if they even bothered to show up. However, the team meetings were important to the success of the team because they were the only time the team could discuss problems and coordinate its software development efforts. Team performance did not improve until a new norm was explicitly was set for team meeting participation.

Third, there are many team norms. These norms might include where people sit in meetings, what time team members come in to work, what team members wear, the acronyms and terms they use, and so on. But of the domain of possible norms, those involving decision making, communication, meetings, and accountability seem to be the most important to team functioning. High-performance teams are explicit about what decisions the team makes and how it makes those decisions. These teams have also set rules about the confidentiality of team meetings, how and when information gets shared, and how difficult or controversial topics are raised in team meetings. High-performance teams also have explicit rules about behavior in team meetings and team member accountability. In our Starbucks example, the store manager would work with the team to decide how often and what it would talk about during meetings, who gets to make the call on different store and customer issues, how information gets shared across shifts, how to handle staff tardiness, and other relevant issues.

Buy-In: Is Everyone Committed and Engaged?

Just because team members understand the team's goals, roles, and rules does not necessarily mean they will automatically be committed to them. Many times team members will nod their agreement to the team's goals and rules in team meetings, but then turn around and do something entirely different afterward. This is an example of a team that lacks buy-in. Teams with high levels of buy-in have team members who believe in what the team is trying to accomplish and will enthusiastically put forth the effort needed to complete their assigned tasks and make the team successful.

There are three basic ways team leaders can build buy-in. One way to build buy-in is to develop a compelling team vision or purpose. Many times team members want to be part of something bigger than themselves, and serving on a team can be one venue for fulfilling this need. Whether or not team members will perceive the team to have a compelling vision will depend to a large extent on the degree to which the team's purpose and goals match up to their personal values. Charismatic or transformational leaders (Chapter 14) are particularly adept at creating visions aligned with followers' personal values. A second way to create buy-in is for the team leader to have a high level of credibility. Leaders with high levels of relevant expertise who share trusting relationships with team members often enjoy high levels of buy-in. Team members often question the judgment of team leaders who lack relevant expertise, and they question the agendas of team leaders they do not trust. And because people prefer to make choices as opposed to being told what to do, a third way to enhance team buy-in is to involve team members in the goal, role, and rule-setting process.

In our Starbucks example the store manager could articulate a compelling vision for the store, work on building strong relationships with all the employees, and get the team involved with defining the context, setting team goals, clarifying role expectations, and the like. The store manager could determine whether buy-in was waxing or waning by observing whether team members were exhibiting the behaviors needed to achieve team goals and could provide coaching, clear obstacles, or clarify work expectations for those less committed to team success.

Power: Do We Have Enough Resources?

The power component of the Rocket Model concerns the decision-making latitude and resources the team has to accomplish its goals. Teams reporting high levels of power have considerable decision-making authority and all the equipment, time, facilities, and funds needed to accomplish team goals. Teams with low power often lack the necessary decision-making authority or resources needed to get things done. One of the authors was working with a group of public school administrators who felt they had little power to make decisions affecting the school district. The district had had three superintendents over the past four years, and as a result the school board had stepped in to take over the day-to-day operation of the schools.

To improve the power component of the Rocket Model, team leaders will first need to determine if they have all the decision-making latitude and resources they need to accomplish group goals. If they do not have enough power, they will need to lobby higher-ups to get what they need, devise ways to get team goals accomplished with limited resources, or revise team goals in light of the resource shortfalls. Most teams do not believe they have all the time, resources, or decision-making latitude they need to succeed, but more often than not they have enough of these things to successfully accomplish their goals. Good teams figure out ways to make do with what they have or devise ways to get what they need; dysfunctional teams spend their time and energy complaining about a perceived lack of resources rather than figuring out ways to achieve team goals. Along these lines, many poorly performing teams often make false assumptions or erect barriers that do not really exist. Team leaders need to challenge these assumptions and break barriers if they are to help the team succeed.

Because Starbucks coffee shops have a consistent look and feel, the store manager may not have a lot of latitude in determining the store location and layout, paint scheme, furniture, coffee making equipment, supplies, refrigerators, cash registers, computers, software, uniforms, and so forth needed to achieve team goals. Any shortfalls of equipment or supplies could negatively impact team performance, however, so he or she would also need to secure new supplies, such as coffee, milk, pastries, or napkins as needed.

Morale: Can't We All Just Get Along?

Just because individual team members understand what the team is trying to accomplish, are committed to achieving team objectives, and understand the rules by which the team gets work done does not necessarily mean team members will all get along with each other. Teams that report high levels of morale tend to deal effectively with interpersonal conflict and have high levels of cohesion. This does not mean that highly cohesive teams do not experience interpersonal conflict. Instead, teams with high morale scores have learned how to get conflict out in the open and deal with it in an effective manner. One way leaders can improve morale is to work with team members to determine the rules for addressing team conflict. On the other hand, some of the best techniques for destroying team morale are for leaders to either ignore interpersonal conflict or to tell team members to "quit fighting and just get along."

Morale may be the most easily observed component of the Rocket Model, as it is relatively easy to see if the team is "tight" and team members are getting along. However, when it comes to team morale many teams either suffer from artificial harmony or play dysfunctional *Family Feud*. Teams suffer from artificial harmony when team members refuse to raise controversial topics in team meetings yet complain about these issues to their teammates. Something (usually fear of retaliation by the team leader or bad communication norms) prevents these issues from being raised and resolved, and as a result team members disengage and team morale and performance suffer. At the other extreme some teams have members engaging in open warfare and are no fun to be on. When this occurs team leaders often resort to sending the team to some sort of team-building program, such as an outdoor learning or high ropes course. In almost all these cases, these interventions have little if any long-term effect on team cohesiveness because the morale component of the Rocket Model is often a symptom of a deeper team problem. More often than not, team members do not get along because of unclear goals and roles, ill-defined decision-making or accountability norms, a lack of commitment or resources, and so forth. In other words, the reason why team members fight has to do with a problem in one or more of the other components of the Rocket Model. Successfully identifying and addressing these problem components will not only improve results but will also help develop team morale. In our Starbucks example, the store manager should be on the lookout for areas of disagreement, identify their underlying cause, and get these issues quickly raised and resolved. These discussions should focus on the facts rather than on the personalities of those involved.

Results: Are We Winning?

The context through morale components of the Rocket Model describe the "how" of team building. In other words, these components tell team leaders what they specifically need to do to improve team mission, norms, and so forth. The results component of the Rocket model describes the "what" of team building—what did the team actually accomplish? Like morale, results are a symptom or an outcome of the other components of the Rocket Model. High-performing teams get superior results because they have attended to the other seven components of the Rocket Model. Those teams achieving suboptimal results can improve their performance by focusing on problematic components of the Rocket Model. In our Starbucks example, if the store was failing to achieve its customer service or financial goals then it could reexamine the goals, determine if it had any staffing shortfalls or talent gaps, review its rules to see if people were being held accountable for poor performance, acquire upgraded equipment, and so on.

One thing we know about successful military leaders and athletic coaches is that they teach their teams how to win. They are continually devising strategies and tactics to leverage their teams' strengths, minimize weaknesses, and do just the opposite to their opponents. Private- and public-sector leaders rarely teach their teams how to win. To do this, team leaders need to set well-defined team goals, create executable action plans with clear time lines and accountable parties to achieve these goals, and conduct periodic progress reviews to identify key learnings and revise plans as needed.

Implications of the Rocket Model

As stated at the beginning of this section, the Rocket Model is both prescriptive and diagnostic. When building a new team or determining where an existing team is falling short, leaders should always start with the context, mission, and talent components before moving to other parts of the model. Just as a rocket needs a large booster to get off the ground, so do teams need to have a common understanding of the situation, a set of well-defined team goals, and the right players to succeed. Along these lines, the Team Assessment Survey II was designed to give teams feedback on where they stand with respect to the eight components of the Rocket Model.[26] Figures 11.3 and 11.4 show the assessment results for

FIGURE 11.3
Team Assessment Results for a Dysfunctional Construction Leadership Team

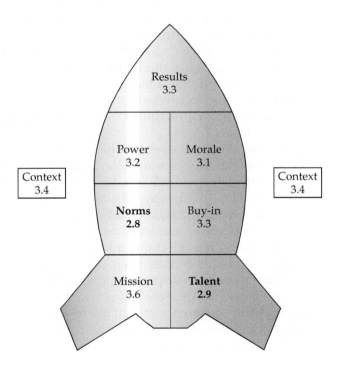

Results
3.3

Power
3.2

Morale
3.1

Context
3.4

Context
3.4

Norms
2.8

Buy-in
3.3

Mission
3.6

Talent
2.9

462   Part Three   *Focus on the Followers*

FIGURE 11.4
Team Assessment
Results for a High-
Performing
Leadership
Development Team

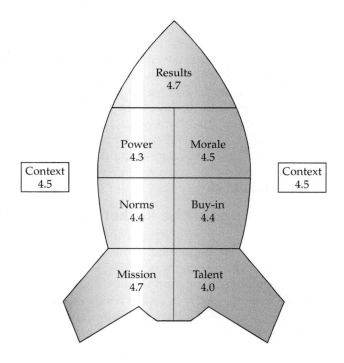

two business teams. Figure 11.3 is a highly dysfunctional group of executives who led a multimillion-dollar construction company. These executives were brought together after the merger of two construction companies, and after 18 months were floundering as a team. Figure 11.4 shows the results for a leadership development team for a Fortune 50 company. This team was more or less hitting on all cylinders and was recognized as one of the top leadership training organizations in the United States.

Second, although everyone has been on groups and teams for most of their lives, most leaders and leaders-to-be do not know how to transform collections of individuals into high-performing teams. The Rocket Model was created to fill this gap. The model is very practical, can be applied to virtually any team, and is based on the premise that the best way to build teams is to identify and work on the issues that matter. The model is also predicated on the belief that a key leader role is to make the implicit explicit; this means leaders need to ensure everyone has the same understanding of team context, goals, roles, rules, and other details. Books such as *The Rocket Model: Practical Advice for Building High-Performing Teams* provide step-by-step instructions to leaders wanting to improve team functioning and performance.

Delegating

Delegation is a relatively simple way for leaders to free themselves of time-consuming chores; give followers developmental opportunities; and increase the number of tasks accomplished by the work group, team, or committee. However, delegation is often an overlooked and underused management option.[26,27] Delegation implies that someone has been empowered by a leader, boss, or coach to take responsibility for completing certain tasks or engaging in certain activities. Delegation gives the responsibility for decisions to those individuals most likely to be affected by or to implement the decision, and delegation is more concerned with autonomy, responsibility, and follower development than with participation. Research has shown that leaders who delegate authority more frequently often have higher-performing businesses,[28] but followers are not necessarily happier when their leaders frequently delegate tasks.[29] Bass maintained that the latter findings were due to subordinates who felt they were not delegated the authority needed to accomplish delegated tasks, monitored too closely, or delegated only tasks leaders did not want to do.[30] Nevertheless, Wilcox showed that leaders who delegated skillfully had more satisfied followers than leaders who did not delegate well.[31] Because leaders who delegate skillfully often have more satisfied and higher-performing work groups, teams, or committees, the following suggestions from Taylor are provided to help leadership practitioners delegate more effectively and successfully. Taylor provided useful ideas about why delegating is important, common reasons for avoiding delegation, and principles of effective delegation.[32]

Why Delegating Is Important

Delegation Frees Time for Other Activities

The essence of leadership is achieving goals through others, not trying to accomplish them by oneself. Learning to think like a leader partly involves developing a frame of mind wherein you think in terms of the whole group's or organization's capabilities and not just your own. This requires a new frame of reference for many individuals, especially those whose past successes resulted primarily from personal achievement in interpersonally competitive situations. Still, leaders typically have so many different responsibilities that they invariably must delegate some of them to others.

It is not just the mere quantity of work that makes delegation necessary. There is a qualitative aspect, too. Because leaders determine what responsibilities will be delegated, the process is one by which leaders can ensure that their time is allocated most judiciously to meet group needs. The leader's time is a precious commodity that should be invested wisely in those activities that the leader is uniquely suited or situated to accomplish and that will provide the greatest long-term benefits to the group. What the leader *can* delegate, the leader *should* delegate.

Delegation Develops Followers

Developing subordinates is one of the most important responsibilities any leader has, and delegating significant tasks to them is one of the best ways to support their growth. It does so by providing opportunities for initiative, problem solving, innovation, administration, and decision making. By providing practical experience in a controlled fashion, delegation allows subordinates the best training experience of all: learning by doing.

Delegation Strengthens the Organization

Delegation is an important way to develop individual subordinates, but doing so also strengthens the entire organization. For one thing, an organization that uses delegation skillfully will be a motivating one to work in. Delegation sends an organizational signal that subordinates are trusted and their development is important. Moreover, skillful delegation inherently tends to increase the significance and satisfaction levels of most jobs, thus making subordinates' jobs better. Delegation also can be seen as a way of developing the entire organization, not just the individuals within it. To the extent that a whole organization systematically develops its personnel using delegation, its overall experience level, capability, and vitality increase. Finally, delegation stimulates innovation and generates fresh ideas and new approaches throughout the whole organization.

Common Reasons for Avoiding Delegation

Delegation Takes Too Much Time

Delegation saves time for the leader in the long run, but it costs the leader time in the short run. It takes time to train a subordinate to perform any new task, so it often really does take less time for a leader to do the task herself than to put in the effort to train someone else to do it. When a task is a recurring or repetitive one, however, the long-term savings will make the additional effort in initial training worth it—both for the leader and for the subordinate.

Delegation Is Risky

It can feel threatening to delegate a significant responsibility to another person because doing so reduces our direct personal control over the work we will be judged by.[33] Delegation may be perceived as a career risk by staking our own reputation on the motivation, skill, and performance of others. It is the essence of leadership, though, that the leader will be evaluated in part by the success of the entire team. Furthermore, delegation need not and should not involve a complete loss of control by the leader over work delegated to others. The leader has a responsibility to set performance expectations, ensure that the task is understood and accepted, provide training, and regularly monitor the status of all delegated tasks and responsibilities.[34]

The Job Will Not Be Done as Well

Often the leader can do many specific tasks or jobs better than anyone else. That is not surprising—the leader is often the most experienced person in the group. This fact, however, can become an obstacle to delegation. The leader may rationalize not delegating a task to someone else because the follower lacks technical competence and the job would subsequently suffer.[35] However, this may be true only in the short term, and letting subordinates make a few mistakes is a necessary part of their development, just as it was for the leader at an earlier stage in her own development. Few things are likely to be so stifling to an organization as a leader's perfectionist fear of mistakes. When thinking about delegating tasks to others, leaders should remember what their own skill levels used to be, not what they are now. Leaders should assess subordinates' readiness to handle new responsibilities in terms of the former, not the latter.

The Task Is a Desirable One

A leader may resist delegating tasks that are a source of power or prestige. He may be willing to delegate relatively unimportant responsibilities but may balk at the prospect of delegating a significant one having high visibility.[36,37] The greater the importance and visibility of the delegated task, though, the greater will be the potential developmental gains for the subordinate. Furthermore, actions always speak louder than words, and nothing conveys trust more genuinely than a leader's willingness to delegate major responsibilities to subordinates.

Others Are Already Too Busy

A leader may feel guilty about increasing a subordinate's already full workload. It is the leader's responsibility, though, to continually review the relative priority of all the tasks performed across the organization. Such a review might identify existing activities that could be eliminated, modified, or reassigned. A discussion with the subordinate about her workload and career goals would be a better basis for a decision than an arbitrary and unilateral determination by the leader that the subordinate cannot handle more work. The new responsibility could be something the subordinate wants and needs, and she might also have some helpful ideas about alternative ways to manage her present duties.

Principles of Effective Delegation

Decide What to Delegate

The first step leaders should take when deciding what to delegate is to identify all their present activities. This should include those functions regularly performed and decisions regularly made. Next leaders should estimate the actual time spent on these activities. This can be done fairly easily by developing and maintaining a temporary log. After collecting this information, leaders need to assess whether each activity justifies the time they are spending on it. In all likelihood, at least some of the most time-consuming recurring activities should be delegated to others. This process will probably also identify some activities that could be done more efficiently (either by the leader or someone else) and other activities that provide so little benefit they could be eliminated completely.

Decide Whom to Delegate To

There might be one individual whose talent and experience make her the logical best choice for any assignment. However, leaders must be careful not to overburden someone merely because that individual always happens to be the best worker. Additionally, leaders have a responsibility to balance developmental opportunities among all their followers. Leaders should look for ways to optimize, over a series of assignments, the growth of all subordinates by matching particular opportunities to their respective individual needs, skills, and goals.

Make the Assignment Clear and Specific

As with setting goals, leaders delegating an assignment must be sure the subordinate understands what the task involves and what is expected of him. Nevertheless, at times leaders provide too brief an explanation of the task to be delegated. A common communication error is overestimating our own clarity, and in the case of delegation this can happen when the leader already knows the ins and outs of the particular task. Some of the essential steps or potential pitfalls in an assignment that seem self-evident to the leader may not be as obvious to someone who has never done the assignment before. Leaders should welcome questions and provide a complete explanation of the task. The time leaders invest during this initial training will pay dividends later. When giving an assignment, leaders should ensure that they cover all the points listed in Highlight 11.3.

Points to Cover When Delegating a Task

HIGHLIGHT 11.3

How does the task relate to organizational goals?

When does the subordinate's responsibility for the task begin?

How has the task been accomplished in the past?

What problems were encountered with the task in the past?

What sources of help are available?

What unusual situations might arise in the future?

What are the limits of the subordinate's authority?

How will the leader monitor the task (such as by providing feedback)?

Finally, in covering these points, be sure to convey high confidence and expectations.

Assign an Objective, Not a Procedure

Indicate what is to be accomplished, not *how* the task is to be accomplished. End results are usually more important than the methods. It is helpful to demonstrate procedures that have worked before, but not to specify rigid methods to follow in the future. Leaders should not assume their ways always were and always will be best. Leaders need to be clear about the criteria by which success will be measured, but allowing subordinates to achieve it in their own ways will increase their satisfaction and encourage fresh ideas.

Allow Autonomy, but Monitor Performance

Effective delegation is neither micromanagement of everything the subordinate does nor laissez-faire indifference toward the subordinate's performance. Leaders need to give subordinates a degree of autonomy (as well as time, resources, and authority) in carrying out their new responsibilities, and this includes the freedom to make certain kinds of mistakes. An organizational climate where mistakes are punished suppresses initiative and innovation. Furthermore, mistakes are important sources of development. Knowing this, one wise executive reassured a subordinate who expected to be fired for a gigantic mistake by saying, "Why should I fire you when I've just invested $100,000 in your development?"[38]

Once a task has been delegated, even though the subordinate's training and development are continuing, the leader should be cautious about providing too much unsolicited advice or engaging in "rescue" activities. An exception would be when a subordinate's mistake would put significant organizational assets at risk. On the other hand, the leader needs to establish specific procedures for periodically reviewing the subordinate's performance of the delegated task. Leaders need to maintain good records of all the assignments they have delegated, including appropriate milestones and completion dates for each one.

Give Credit, Not Blame

Whenever leaders delegate, they must give subordinates *authority* along with responsibility. In the final analysis, however, leaders always remain fully responsible and accountable for any delegated task. If things should go wrong, the leaders should accept responsibility for failure fully and completely and never try to pass blame on to subordinates. On the other hand, if things go well, as they usually will, leaders should give all the public credit to the subordinates. Also, when providing performance feedback privately to a subordinate, emphasize what went right rather than what went wrong. Leaders should not ignore errors in judgment or implementation, but they need not dwell on them, either. One helpful approach to performance feedback is called the "sandwich technique." With this technique, negative feedback is placed between two pieces of positive feedback. It affirms the subordinate's good work, puts the subordinate at least somewhat at ease, and keeps the ratio of positive and negative comments in balance. The idea of a sandwich, however, should not be taken too literally. There is nothing magical about two pieces of positive feedback for one piece of negative feedback. In fact, from the receiver's point of view the balance between positive and negative feedback may seem "about right" when the ratio is considerably higher than 2:1.

Coaching

> *People who are coaches will be the norm. Other people won't get promoted.*
>
> **Jack Welch,
> former General
> Electric CEO**

A key success factor in most organizations today is having leaders and followers with the right knowledge and skills. More and more, companies are looking at "bench strength" as a competitive advantage. There are essentially two ways to acquire bench strength: employers can either buy (that is, hire) the talent they need, or they can build their existing talent through development and coaching programs. Given that many employers face a labor shortage in certain critical positions, many are looking to build their own internal talent.[39] Much of this talent is being developed through informal coaching. As we noted in Chapter 2, most leaders engage in some form of informal coaching. But how good are they at coaching? The authors' conversations with a multitude of leaders indicate that almost every single one was unsure what to do as a coach. Some thought coaching involved directing their employees in how to do tasks. Others thought it involved counseling employees on personal problems. One stated that his only example of coaching came from his high school football coach, and he wouldn't wish that on anyone.

Two thought leaders in this area are Peterson and Hicks,[40] who have described coaching as the "process of equipping people with the tools, knowledge, and opportunities they need to develop themselves and become more successful." According to Peterson and Hicks, good coaches orchestrate rather than dictate development. Good coaches help followers clarify career goals, identify and prioritize development needs, create and stick to development plans, and create environments that support learning and coaching. Coaching is really a blend of several different leadership skills. Being a good coach means having well-developed skills, determining where a follower is in the coaching process, and intervening as appropriate. The five steps of coaching give leaders both a good road map and a diagnostic model for improving the bench strength of their followers.

Peterson and Hicks pointed out that this model works particularly well for high performers—individuals who tend to benefit the most from, but are often overlooked by, leaders when coaching. We noted in Chapter 9 that high performers produce 20 to 50 percent more than average employees,[41] so coaching can have a considerable impact on the bottom line if it is targeted at high performers. Further support for the idea that top performers may benefit the most from coaching comes from athletics. If you watch the Olympics, you have probably seen that many of the world's top athletes have at least one and sometimes two or three coaches. If these world-class athletes feel that coaching can enhance their performance, it is likely that good coaches can also enhance the performance of any organization's top employees. Although the five-step model described here also works with poorly performing employees, more appropriate interventions might also include diagnosing performance problems, goal setting, providing rewards and constructive feedback, and punishing these individuals, particularly if informal coaching is not achieving desired results.

Forging a Partnership

The first step in informal coaching involves establishing a relationship built on mutual trust and respect with a follower. If a follower does not trust or respect her leader, it is unlikely that she will pay much attention to his ideas for her development. There are several things leaders can do to forge a partnership with coachees. First, it will be much easier for leaders with high credibility to build strong partnerships with followers than this will be for leaders with low credibility. Therefore, leaders need to assess their credibility (see Chapter 8), and they may need to take appropriate developmental steps to improve their credibility before their coaching suggestions will have much impact. These developmental steps may include building technical and organizational knowledge as well as building strong relationships with the individuals they want to coach. Understanding the context in which the employee operates can be as important as the relationship the leader shares with the employee.

In Chapter 8 we noted that leaders also need to spend time listening to their coachees; they need to understand coachees' career aspirations, values, intrinsic motivators, view of the organization, and current work situation. Good coaches can put themselves in their coachees' shoes and can understand how coachees may view issues or opportunities differently than themselves. While forging a partnership, leaders can also provide coachees with realistic career advice—sometimes coachees have unrealistic estimations of their skills and opportunities. For example, a new graduate from a top MBA program might want to be a partner at a consulting firm after two years with the company, but company policy may dictate that this decision will not be made until she has been with the firm for at least eight years. Her coach should inform her of this policy and then work with her to map out a series of shorter-term career objectives that will help her become a partner in eight years. If coaches do not know what drives their coachees' behaviors, then another step to forging a partnership is to start asking questions. This is an excellent opportunity for leaders to practice their listening skills so as to better understand their coachees' career aspirations and intrinsic motivators.

Inspiring Commitment: Conducting a GAPS Analysis

This step in the coaching process is similar to the GAPS analysis and the gaps-of-the-GAPS analysis that were discussed in the "Development Planning" section in Chapter 3. The only difference is that these two analyses are now done from the coachee's perspective. Figure 11.5 might help to clarify this difference in perspective. In the goals quadrant of the GAPS analysis the leader should write the coachee's career objectives, and in the perceptions quadrant the leader would write how the coachee's behavior

FIGURE 11.5
A GAPS Analysis for an Employee

Goals: Where do you want to go?	Abilities: What can you do now?
Step 1: Career objectives: Career strategies:	*Step 2:* What strengths do you have for your career objectives? *Step 3:* What development needs will you have to overcome?
Standards: What does your boss or the organization expect?	Perceptions: How do others see you?
Step 5: Expectations:	*Step 4:* 360-degree and performance review results, and feedback from others: • *Boss* • *Peers* • *Direct reports*

Source: D. B. Peterson and M. D. Hicks, *Leader as Coach* (Minneapolis, MN: Personnel Decisions International, 1996); G. J. Curphy, *The Leadership Development Process Manual* (Minneapolis, MN: Personnel Decisions International, 1998).

affects others. It is possible that the leader may not be able to complete all of the quadrants of the GAPS for a coachee. If so, the leader will need to gather more information before going any further. This information gathering may include discussing career goals and abilities with the coachee, reviewing the coachee's 360-degree feedback results, asking peers about how the coachee comes across or impacts others, or asking human resources about the educational or experience standards relevant to the coachee's career goals. One way to gather additional information is to have both the leader and the coachee complete a GAPS analysis independently, and then get together and discuss areas of agreement and disagreement. This can help ensure that the best information is available for the GAPS analysis and also help to build the partnership between the leader and coachee. During this discussion the leader and coachee should also do a gaps-of-the-GAPS analysis to identify and prioritize development needs. Usually leaders will get more commitment to development needs if coachees feel they had an important role in determining these needs, and a gaps-of-the-GAPS discussion is a way to build buy-in. This discussion can also help ensure that development needs are aligned with career goals.

Growing Skills: Creating Development and Coaching Plans

Once the coachee's development needs are identified and prioritized, coachees will need to build development plans to overcome targeted needs. These plans are identical to those described in the "Development Planning" section in Chapter 3. Leaders generally do not build development plans for their coachees. Instead they may want to go over a sample (or their own) development plan and coach their coachees on the seven steps in building a plan. They can then either jointly build a plan or have the coachee individually build a plan for the leader to review. Giving coachees an important role in development planning should increase their level of commitment to the plan. Once a draft development plan is created, the leader and coach can use the development planning checklist in Table 11.1 to review the plan.

In addition to the development plan, leaders must build a coaching plan that outlines the actions they will take to support their coachees' development. Some of these actions might include meeting with the coachees regularly to provide developmental feedback, identifying developmental resources or opportunities, or helping coachees reflect on what they have learned. As with development plans, leaders should share their coaching plans so coachees know what kind of support they will be getting. This will also publicly commit the leaders to the coachees' development, which will make it more likely that they will follow through with the coaching plan.

Table 11.1 Development Plan Checklist

Objectives
- One-year career objective identified?
- No more than a total of two or three development goals?
- Areas in which the employee is motivated and committed to change and develop?

Criteria for Success
- Is the new behavior clearly described?
- Can the behavior be measured or observed?

Action Steps
- Specific, attainable, and measurable steps?
- Mostly on-the-job activities?
- Includes a variety of types of activities?
- Are activities divided into small, doable steps?

Seek Feedback and Support
- Involvement of a variety of others?
- Includes requests for management support?
- Are reassessment dates realistic?

Stretch Assignments
- Do the stretch assignments relate to the employee's career objectives?

Resources
- Uses a variety of books, seminars, and other resources?

Reflect with a Partner
- Includes periodic reviews of learning?

Source: G. J. Curphy, *The Leadership Development Process Manual* (Minneapolis, MN: Personnel Decisions International, 1998).

Promoting Persistence: Helping Followers Stick to Their Plans

Having development and coaching plans in place is no guarantee that development will occur. Sometimes coachees build development plans with great enthusiasm, but then take no further action. This step in the coaching process is designed to help coachees "manage the mundane." An example of managing the mundane might be illustrative. One of the authors successfully completed a triathlon. The most difficult part of this accomplishment was not the event itself, but rather doing all the training needed to successfully complete the event. Similarly, the inability to stick to a diet or keep a New Year's resolution is primarily due to an inability to manage the mundane; people are initially committed to these goals but have a difficult time sticking to them. The same is true with development planning. Conducting a GAPS analysis and creating a development plan are relatively easy; sticking to the plan is more difficult. From the leader's perspective, a large part of coaching is helping followers stick to their development plans.

Several development planning steps are specifically designed to promote persistence. For example, ensuring alignment between career and development objectives, getting feedback from multiple sources on a regular basis, and reflecting with a partner can help keep coachees focused on their development. If the leader is a coachee's developmental partner, then reflection sessions can help followers persist with their development. If leaders are not designated as partners in the development plan, they should commit to meeting regularly with the coachees to discuss progress, what the leaders can do to support development, developmental opportunities, developmental feedback, and so forth.

Leaders can also help to promote persistence by capitalizing on coachable moments. Say a coachee was working on listening skills, and the leader and coach were in a staff meeting together. If the leader provides feedback to the coachee about her listening skills immediately after the staff meeting, the leader has capitalized on a coachable moment. To capitalize on a coachable moment, leaders must know the followers' developmental objectives, be in situations where they can observe followers practicing their objectives, and then provide immediate feedback on their observations. Few coaches capitalize on coachable moments, but they can go a long way toward promoting persistence in coachees. Note that capitalizing on coachable moments should take little time, often less than two minutes. In the example here, the leader could provide feedback to the coachee during their walk back to the office after the staff meeting.

Transferring Skills: Creating a Learning Environment

To build bench strength, leaders need to create a learning environment so that personal development becomes an ongoing process rather than a one-time event. As Tichy and Cohen[42] aptly point out, the most successful organizations are those that emphasize the learning and teaching process—they focus on constantly creating leaders throughout the company. In reality, leaders have quite a bit of control over the learning environments they want to create for their followers, and they can use several interventions to ensure that development becomes an ongoing process. Perhaps the most important intervention is for leaders to role-model development. In that regard, if leaders are not getting regular feedback from followers, they are probably not doing a good job of role-modeling development. By regularly soliciting feedback from followers, leaders are also likely to create a feedback-rich work environment. Once feedback becomes a group norm, people will be much more willing to help build team member skills, which in turn can have a catalytic effect on group performance. The leader will play a large role in this group norm because if the leader is feedback averse, feedback will be difficult to encourage among followers.

Leaders can also create learning environments by regularly reviewing their followers' development. Perhaps the easiest way to do this is by making leaders and followers development partners; then both parties can provide regular feedback and ongoing support. During these discussions leaders and followers should review and update their development plans to capitalize on new development opportunities or acquire new skills. Leaders and followers can also review coaching plans to see what is and is not working and make the necessary adjustments.

Concluding Comments

Perhaps one of the greatest misperceptions of coaching, and the primary reason why leaders state that they do not coach others, is that it takes a lot of time. In reality, nothing could be further from the truth. Leaders are working to build credibility, build relationships with followers, and understand followers' career aspirations and views of the world. Although these take time, they are also activities leaders should be engaged in even if they are not coaching followers. Doing GAPS analyses, identifying and prioritizing development needs, helping followers create development plans, and creating coaching plans often take less than four hours. Although leaders will need to take these steps with all their followers, this time can be spread out over a four- to six-week period. As stated earlier, meeting with followers regularly to review development (perhaps monthly) and capitalizing on coachable moments also take little time. Finally, many of the actions outlined in "Transferring Skills: Create a Learning Environment" in Chapter 3 either take little time or are extensions of actions outlined earlier. The bottom line is that coaching really takes little additional time; it is more a function of changing how you spend time with followers so you can maximize their development.

Another note about the coaching model is that good coaches are equally versatile at all five steps of coaching. Some leaders are good at forging a partnership but then fail to carry development to the next level by conducting GAPS analyses or helping followers build development plans. Other leaders may help followers build development plans but do nothing to promote persistence or create a learning environment. Just as leaders need to develop their technical skills, so might they need to assess and develop coaching skills. It is important to remember that coaching is a dynamic process—good coaches assess where followers are in the coaching process and intervene appropriately. By regularly assessing where they are with followers, they may determine that the relationship with a particular follower is not as strong as they thought, and this lack of relationship is why followers are not sticking to their development plans. In this case a good coach would go back to forging a partnership with the follower and, once a trusting relationship had been created, go through another GAPS analysis, and so forth.

Do what you can, where you are at, with what you have.
Theodore Roosevelt

Inside every old company is a new company waiting to be born.
Alvin Toffler

Finally, it is important to note that people can and do develop skills on their own. Nevertheless, leaders who commit to the five steps of informal coaching outlined here will both create learning organizations and help to raise development to a new level. Given the competitive advantage of companies that have a well-developed and capable workforce, in the future it will be hard to imagine leadership excellence without coaching. Good leaders are those who create successors, and coaching may be the best way to make this happen.

End Notes

1. B. M. Bass, *Bass and Stogdill's Handbook of Leadership,* 3rd ed. (New York: Free Press, 1990).

2. M. Erez, P. C. Earley, and C. L. Hulin, "The Impact of Participation on Goal Acceptance and Performance: A Two-Step Model," *Academy of Management Journal* 28, no. 1 (1985), pp. 359–72.

3. E. A. Locke, G. P. Latham, and M. Erez, "Three-Way Interactive Presentation and Discussion," "A Unique Approach to Resolving Scientific Disputes," and "Designing Crucial Experiments," papers presented at the Society of Industrial and Organizational Psychology Convention, Atlanta, GA, 1987.

4. R. J. House, "Power in Organizations: A Social Psychological Perspective," unpublished manuscript, University of Toronto, 1984.

5. G. P. Latham and T. W. Lee, "Goal Setting," in *Generalizing from Laboratory to Field Settings,* ed. E. A. Locke (Lexington, MA: Lexington Books, 1986).

6. Locke et al., "Three-Way Interactive Presentation and Discussion," "A Unique Approach to Resolving Scientific Disputes," and "Designing Crucial Experiments."

7. M. M. Greller, "Evaluation of Feedback Sources as a Function of Role and Organizational Development," *Journal of Applied Psychology* 65 (1980), pp. 24–27.

8. J. L. Komacki, "Why We Don't Reinforce: The Issues," *Journal of Organizational Behavior Management* 4, nos. 3–4 (1982), pp. 97–100.

9. Bass, *Bass and Stogdill's Handbook of Leadership.*

10. S. Deep and L. Sussman, *Smart Moves* (Reading MA: Addison-Wesley, 1990).

11. J. R. Larson Jr. "Supervisors' Performance Feedback to Subordinates: The Impact of Subordinate Performance Valence and Outcome Dependence," *Organizational Behavior and Human Decision Processes* 37 (1986), pp. 391–408.

12. E. L. Harrison, "Training Supervisors to Discipline Effectively," *Training and Development Journal* 36, no. 11 (1982), pp. 111–13.

13. C. K. Parsons, D. M. Herold, and M. L. Leatherwood, "Turnover during Initial Employment: A Longitudinal Study of the Role of Causal Attributions," *Journal of Applied Psychology* 70 (1985), pp. 337–41.

14. A. C. Filley and L. A. Pace, "Making Judgments Descriptive," in *The 1976 Annual Handbook for Group Facilitators,* eds. J. E. Jones and J. W. Pfeiffer (La Jolla, CA: University Associates Press, 1976).

15. R. W. Coye, "Subordinate Responses to Ineffective Leadership," *Dissertation Abstracts International* 43, no. 6A (1982), p. 2070.

16. P. L. Quaglieri and J. P. Carnazza, "Critical Inferences and the Multidimensionality of Feedback," *Canadian Journal of Behavioral Science* 17 (1985), pp. 284–93.

17. D. L. Stone, H. G. Gueutal, and B. MacIntosh, "The Effects of Feedback Sequence and Expertise of Rater of Perceived Feedback Accuracy," *Personal Psychology* 37 (1984), pp. 487–506.

18. Bass, *Bass and Stogdill's Handbook of Leadership.*

19. M. Silberman and P. Philips (Eds.). *2005 ASTD Team & Organization Development Sourcebook* (Alexandria VA: ASTD Press, 2005).

20. P. M. Senge, *The Fifth Discipline: The Art and Practice of the Learning Organization* (New York: Doubleday/Currency, 1994).

21. R. C. Ginnett, "To the Wilderness and Beyond: The Application of a Model for Transformal Change," *Proceedings of the Ninth Psychology in the Department of Defense Symposium* (Colorado Springs, CO, 1984).

22. G. J. Curphy and R. T. Hogan, *The Rocket Model: Practical Advice for Building High Performing Teams* (Tulsa, OK: Hogan Press, 2012).

23. G. J. Curphy, *The Rocket Model,* pre-conference workshop delivered to the American Psychological Association Division 13 Midwinter Conference, Atlanta, GE, February, 2013.

24. G. J. Curphy, "Applying the Rocket Model to Virtual Teams," unpublished manuscript, 2013.

25. G. J. Curphy, *Building High Performing Teams Training Manual* (North Oaks, MN: Curphy Consulting Corporation, 2013.)

26. G. J. Curphy, *Team Assessment Survey II* (St Paul, MN: Advantis Research and Consulting, 2012.)

27. C. R. Leana, "Power Relinquishment vs. Power Sharing: Theoretical Clarification and Empirical Comparison of Delegation and Participation," *Journal of Applied Psychology* 72 (1987), pp. 228–33.

28. D. Miller and J. M. Toulouse, "Strategy, Structure, CEO Personality and Performance in Small Firms," *American Journal of Small Business,* Winter 1986, pp. 47–62.

29. R. M. Stogdill and C. L. Shartle, *Methods in the Study of Administrative Performance* (Columbus, OH: Ohio State University, Bureau of Business Research, 1955).

30. Bass, *Bass and Stogdill's Handbook of Leadership.*

31. W. H. Wilcox, "Assistant Superintendents' Perceptions of the Effectiveness of the Superintendent, Job Satisfaction, and Satisfaction with the Superintendent's Supervisory Skills," PhD dissertation, University of Missouri, Columbia, 1982.

32. H. L. Taylor, *Delegate: The Key to Successful Management* (New York: Warner Books, 1989).

33. H. D. Dewhirst, V. Metts, and R. T. Ladd, "Exploring the Delegation Decision: Managerial Responses to Multiple Contingencies," paper presented at the Academy of Management Convention, New Orleans, LA, 1987.

34. Bass, *Bass and Stogdill's Handbook of Leadership*.

35. H. D. Dewhirst, V. Metts, and R. T. Ladd, "Exploring the Delegation Decision: Managerial Responses to Multiple Contingencies," paper presented at the Academy of Management Convention, New Orleans, LA, 1987.

36. Bass, *Bass and Stogdill's Handbook of Leadership*.

37. Dewhirst et al., "Exploring the Delegation Decision."

38. M. W. McCall Jr., M. M. Lombardo, and A. M. Morrison, *The Lessons of Experience: How Successful Executives Develop on the Job* (Lexington, MA: Lexington Books, 1988).

39. N. M. Tichy and E. Cohen, *The Leadership Engine: How Winning Companies Build Leaders at Every Level* (New York: HarperCollins, 1997).

40. D. B. Peterson and M. D. Hicks, *Leader as Coach: Strategies for Coaching and Developing Others* (Minneapolis, MN: Personnel Decisions International, 1996), p. 14.

41. J. E. Hunter, F. L. Schmidt, and M. K. Judiesch, "Individual Differences in Output Variability as a Function of Job Complexity," *Journal of Applied Psychology* 74 (1990), pp. 28–42.

42. Tichy and Cohen, *The Leadership Engine*.

Focus on the Situation

Focus on the Situation

Part

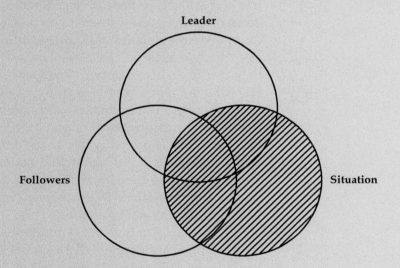

In previous chapters we noted that understanding leaders and followers is much more complicated than many people think. For example, we examined how leaders' personality characteristics, behaviors, and attitudes affect the leadership process. Similarly, followers' attitudes, experience, personality characteristics, and behaviors, as well as group norms and cohesiveness, also affect the leadership process. Despite the complexities of leaders and followers, however, perhaps no factor in the interactional framework is as complex as the situation. Not only do a variety of task, organizational, and environmental factors affect behavior, but the relative salience or strength of these factors varies dramatically across people. What one person perceives to be the key situational factor affecting his or her behavior may be relatively unimportant to another person.

Moreover, the relative importance of the situational factors also varies over time. Even during a single soccer game, for example, the situation changes constantly: the lead changes, the time remaining in the game changes, weather conditions change, injuries occur, and so on. Given the dynamic nature of situations, it may be a misnomer to speak of "the" situation in reference to leadership.

Because of the complex and dynamic nature of situations and the substantial role that perceptions play in the interpretation of situations, no one has been able to develop a comprehensive taxonomy describing all the situational variables affecting a person's behavior. In all likelihood, no one ever will. Nevertheless, considerable research about situational influences on leadership has been accomplished. Leadership researchers have examined how different task, organizational, and environmental factors affect both leaders' and followers' behavior, though most have examined only the effects of one or two situational variables on leaders' and followers' behavior. For example, a study might have examined the effects of task difficulty on subordinates' performance yet ignored how broader issues, such as organizational policy or structure, might also affect their performance. This is primarily due to the difficulty of studying the effects of organizational and environmental factors on behavior. As you might imagine, many of these factors, such as societal culture or technological change, do not easily lend themselves to realistic laboratory experiments where conditions can be controlled and interactions analyzed. Nonetheless, it is virtually impossible to understand leadership without taking the situation into consideration. We examine various factors and theories pertaining especially to the situation in Part 4.

Chapter 12

The Situation

Introduction

April 16, 2007, was a dark day at Virginia Tech. On that day Cho Seung Hui went on a shooting rampage that killed 32 students and faculty and injured a host of others. There is no doubt that Cho was a villain, if not a deranged one, as he created a situation of terror in Norris Hall. But in that same awful situation, heroes were created. One was Zach Petkewicz.

Zach and his fellow classmates were in a classroom near the one where Cho initiated his massacre. They heard the initial gunshots through the walls and could hear them getting closer. At first everyone experienced fear and hid behind whatever they could find for protection. But it occurred to Zach that "there's nothing stopping him from coming in here. We were just sitting ducks." And that's when Zach and others took action.

Zach grabbed a table and shoved it against the door. Seeing his plan, other students joined him, pinning the table against the cinderblock walls around the door frame. They were just in time. Cho tried to get into their classroom next. Having tried the door handle and then brute force, Cho emptied a clip of ammunition through the door before giving up and moving on to another room.

Days after the assault, Zach Petkewicz was interviewed by Matt Lauer on NBC's *Today Show.* Lauer asked Zach if he could have predicted, before the shooting, how he would react. The young hero, whose first reaction had been fear, said that's not possible for anyone. "There's no way of telling what I would have done until you're put in that situation."

Zach was right about two things. First, as he said, it is difficult to predict anyone's behavior unless you take the situation into account. Second, we are coming to understand that the situation is one of the most powerful variables in the leadership equation. And that is the topic of this chapter. It is important to understand how the situation influences leaders and followers and, furthermore, that the situation is not just a "given" that leaders and followers must adapt to; sometimes, at least, leaders and followers can change the situation and thereby enhance the likelihood of

482 Part Four   *Focus on the Situation*

desired outcomes. That's what Zach did: he changed the situation. Of course Zach reacted to a situation he was tragically confronted with, but leaders do not always need to be reactive. Leaders also can use their knowledge of how the situation affects leadership to proactively *change* the situation in order to enhance the likelihood of success. All too often, leaders and followers overlook how changing the situation can help them to change their behavior. This is called **situational engineering.**

Suppose, for example, that a leader received developmental feedback that she needed to spend more time interacting with subordinates. Even with the best intentions, such a goal can prove difficult to achieve, just as numerous New Year's resolutions fail. In both cases an important barrier to success is that the person does not adequately address challenges posed by the situation in which they find themselves. After the holidays, many well-intentioned dieters don't lose weight because they fail to reduce the number of food cues around them. And a leader who may genuinely desire greater interaction with subordinates may nonetheless unwittingly subvert her own goal by continuing to define her tasks in the same way she always had. A better strategy could be to review her own tasks and then delegate some of them to subordinates. This would free up some of the leader's time and also create opportunities to interact with subordinates in ways like mutually setting performance goals and meeting regularly to review their progress.[1]

Highlight 12.1 presents ways in which various versions of a familiar situation may significantly affect your own likelihood of being a "good follower." Highlight 12.2 examines how leaders in dangerous situations might have to adopt different strategies to be successful than they would in more normal situations.

In a book designed to introduce students to the subject of leadership, a chapter about "the situation" poses some challenging obstacles and dilemmas. The breadth of the topic is daunting: it could include almost everything else in the world that has not been covered in the previous chapters! To the typical student who has not yet begun a professional career, pondering the magnitude of variables making up the situation is a formidable request. For one thing, the situation you find yourself in is often seen as completely beyond your control. How many times have you heard someone say, "Hey, I don't make the rules around here—I just follow them"? The subject is made more difficult by the fact that most students have limited organizational experience as a frame of reference. So why bother to introduce the material in this chapter? Because the situation we are in often explains far more about what is going on and what kinds of leadership behaviors will be best than any other single variable we have discussed so far!

In this chapter we will try to sort out some of the complexity and magnitude of this admittedly large topic. First, we will review some of the research that has led us to consider these issues. Then, after considering a

The College Classroom as Situation

HIGHLIGHT 12.1

One way to appreciate the variety of ways in which the situation affects leadership is to look at one of the most familiar situations to you: the college classroom and its associated work. Let's define the leadership challenge in every case as "getting the best out of you" in terms of your study, your work on assignments, and enhancing the experience of the course for everyone. With those criteria of effective leadership (or followership, if you prefer), reflect on how the challenges you face as a follower are affected by the variations in the series of classroom situations described here:

Situation 1	Situation 2	Situation 3 (in some Cases)
You're in a seminar with 15 other students.	You're in a 200-student lecture hall.	You're taking the course virtually over the Internet.
This is an elective course in your major.	This is a required general education course at your school.	
There's much student autonomy in the course in determining course paper topics.	Highly specific writing assignments are prescribed for you.	
A group project is an important part of your grade, and you're working on it with three good friends who are all good students.	A group project is an important part of your grade, and you're working on it with three strangers who are doing poorly in the course.	
Your class meets at 8 a.m.	Your class meets at 2 p.m.	Your class meets at 7 p.m.
You're a full-time student living in a dorm at your college.	You're a part-time student taking the class at a "commuter college" after you finish your regular day job.	

huge situational change that is now occurring, we will present a model to help us consider key situational variables. Finally, we will take a look forward through an interesting lens. Throughout the chapter, though, our objective will be primarily to increase awareness rather than to prescribe specific courses of leader action.

The appropriateness of a leader's behavior with a group of followers often makes sense only when you look at the situational context in which the behavior occurs. For example, severely disciplining a follower might seem a poor way to lead; but if the follower in question had just committed a safety violation endangering the lives of hundreds of people, the leader's actions might be exactly right. In a similar fashion, the situation may be the primary reason personality traits, experience, or cognitive abilities are related less consistently to leadership effectiveness

---

Leading in Extremis

HIGHLIGHT 12.2

Colonel Tom Kolditz is head of the Department of Behavioral Sciences and Leadership at the U.S. Military Academy at West Point. He's the author of a book called *In Extremis Leadership*, which looks at leadership in dangerous contexts. In doing research for the book, Kolditz and his colleagues interviewed leaders of SWAT teams, parachuting teams, special operations soldiers, mountain climbing guides, and others who led in dangerous situations. Kolditz identified several characteristics of effective in extremis leaders:

- They embrace continuous learning because dangerous situations demand it.
- They share risks with their followers.
- They share a common lifestyle with their followers.
- They are highly competent themselves in ways specific to the dangerous situation.
- They inspire high competence and mutual trust and loyalty with others.

Source: T. Kolditz, *In Extremis Leadership: Leading as If Your Life Depended on It* (San Francisco: Jossey-Bass, 2007).

The way of the superior is threefold, but I am not equal to it. Virtuous, he is free from anxieties; wise, he is free from perplexities; bold, he is free from fear.

Confucius

---

than to leadership emergence.[2,3] Most leadership emergence studies have involved leaderless discussion groups, and for the most part the situation is quite similar across such studies. In studies of leadership effectiveness, however, the situation can and does vary dramatically. The personal attributes needed by an effective leader of a combat unit, chemical research and development division, community service organization, or fast-food restaurant may change considerably. Because the situations facing leaders of such groups may be so variable, it is hardly surprising that studies of leader characteristics have yielded inconsistent results when looking at leadership effectiveness across jobs or situations. Thus the importance of the situation in the leadership process should not be overlooked.

Historically, some leadership researchers emphasized the importance of the situation in the leadership process in response to the Great Man theory of leadership. These researchers maintained that the situation, not someone's traits or abilities, plays the most important role in determining who emerges as a leader.[4-6] As support for the situational viewpoint, these researchers noted that great leaders typically emerged during economic crises, social upheavals, or revolutions; great leaders were generally not associated with periods of relative calm or quiet. For example, Schneider[7] noted that the number of individuals identified as great military leaders in the British armed forces during any period depended on how many conflicts the country was engaged in—the higher the number of conflicts, the higher the number of great military leaders. Moreover, researchers advocating the situational viewpoint believed leaders were made, not born, and that prior leadership experience helped forge effective leaders.[8] These early situational theories of leadership tended to be popular in the United States because they fit more closely with American ideals of equality and meritocracy and ran counter to the genetic views of leadership that were popular among European researchers at the time.[9] (The fact that many of these European researchers had aristocratic backgrounds probably had something to do with the popularity of the Great Man theory in Europe.)

More recent leadership theories have explored how situational factors affect leaders' behaviors. In **role theory,** for example, a leader's behavior was said to depend on a leader's perceptions of several critical aspects of the situation: rules and regulations governing the job; role expectations of subordinates, peers, and superiors; the nature of the task; and feedback about subordinates' performance.[10] Role theory clarified how these situational demands and constraints could cause role conflict and role ambiguity.[11] Leaders may experience role conflict when subordinates and superiors have conflicting expectations about a leader's behavior or when company policies contradict how superiors expect tasks to be performed. A leader's ability to successfully resolve such conflicts may well determine leadership effectiveness.[12]

Another effort to incorporate situational variables into leadership theory was Hunt and Osborn's[13] **multiple-influence model.** Hunt and Osborn distinguished between microvariables (such as task characteristics) and macrovariables (such as the external environment) in the situation. Although most researchers looked at the effects tasks had on leader behaviors, Hunt and Osborn believed macrovariables have a pervasive influence on the ways leaders act. Both role theory and the multiple-influence model highlight a major problem in addressing situational factors, which was noted previously: that situations can vary in countless ways. Because situations can vary in so many ways, it is helpful for leaders to have an abstract scheme for conceptualizing situations. This would be a step in knowing how to identify what may be most salient or critical to pay attention to in any particular instance.

One of the most basic abstractions is **situational levels.** The idea behind situational levels may best be conveyed with an example. Suppose someone asked you, "How are things going at work?" You might respond by commenting on the specific tasks you perform ("It is still pretty tough. I am under the gun for getting next year's budget prepared, and I have never done that before"). Or you might respond by commenting on aspects of the overall organization ("It is really different. There are so many rules you have to follow. My old company was not like that at all"). Or you might comment on factors affecting the organization itself ("I've been really worried about keeping my job—you know how many cutbacks there have been in our whole industry recently"). Each response deals with the situation, but each refers to a different level of abstraction: the task level, the organizational level, and the environmental level. Each of these three levels provides a different perspective with which to examine the leadership process (see Figure 12.1).

FIGURE 12.1
An Expanded
Leader–Follower–
Situation Model

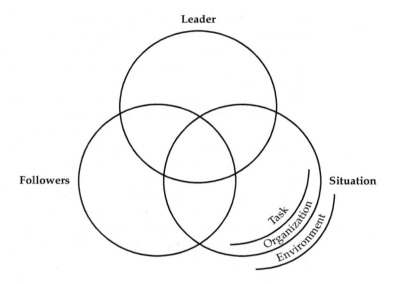

These three levels certainly do not exhaust all the ways in which situations vary. Situations also differ in terms of physical variables like noise and temperature levels, workload demands, and the extent to which work groups interact with other groups. Organizations also have unique "corporate cultures," which define a context for leadership. And there are always even broader economic, social, legal, and technological aspects of situations within which the leadership process occurs. What, amid all this situational complexity, should leaders pay attention to?

The Task

How Tasks Vary, and What That Means for Leadership

The most fundamental level of the situation involves the tasks to be performed by individuals or teams within the organization. Several ways in which tasks vary are particularly relevant to leadership. Industrial and organizational psychologists spent much of the last half-century classifying and categorizing tasks to better understand how to enhance worker satisfaction and productivity. Some of this research has great relevance to leadership, particularly the concepts of task autonomy, feedback, structure, and interdependence.

Task autonomy is the degree to which a job provides an individual with some control over what he does and how he does it. Someone with considerable autonomy would have discretion in scheduling work and deciding the procedures used in accomplishing it. Autonomy often covaries with technical expertise: workers with considerable expertise will be given more latitude, and those with few skills will be given more instruction

The brain is a wonderful organ; it begins working the moment you get up in the morning and does not stop until you get to the office.

Robert Frost

If you want to give a man credit, put it in writing. If you want to give him hell, do it on the phone.

Charles Beacham

and coaching when accomplishing tasks.[14,15] Moreover, responsibility and job satisfaction often increase when autonomy increases.[16]

Another important way in which tasks vary is in terms of **task feedback,** which refers to the degree to which a person accomplishing a task receives information about performance *from performing the task itself.* In this context feedback is received not from supervisors but rather from what is intrinsic to the work activity itself. Driving a car is one example of feedback intrinsic to a task. If you are a skilled driver on a road with a number of twists and turns, you get all the feedback you need about how well you are accomplishing the task merely by observing how the car responds to your inputs. This is feedback from the job itself as opposed to feedback from another person (who in this example would be a classic backseat driver). Extending this example to work or team settings, leaders sometimes may want to redesign tasks so that they (the tasks) provide more intrinsic feedback. Although this does not absolve the leader from giving periodic performance feedback, it can free up some of the leader's time for other work-related activities. Additionally, leaders should understand that followers may eventually become dissatisfied if leaders provide high levels of feedback for tasks that already provide intrinsic feedback.[17–19]

Perhaps the easiest way to explain **task structure** is by using an example demonstrating the difference between a structured task and an unstructured task. Assume the task to be accomplished is solving for x given the formula $3x + 2x = 15$. If that problem were given to a group of people who knew the fundamental rules of algebra, everyone would arrive at the same answer. In this example there is a known procedure for accomplishing the task; there are rules governing how one goes about it; and if people follow those rules, there is one result. These features characterize a *structured task.*

On the other hand, if the task is to resolve a morale problem on a team, committee, or work group, there may be no clear-cut method for solving it. There are many different ways, perhaps none of which is obvious or necessarily best for approaching a solution. Different observers may not see the problem in the same way; they may even have different ideas of what morale is. Solving a morale problem, therefore, exemplifies an *unstructured task.*

People vary in their preferences for, or ability to handle, structured versus unstructured tasks. With the Myers-Briggs Type Indicator (MBTI), for example, perceivers are believed to prefer unstructured situations, whereas judgers prefer activities that are planned and organized.[20] Individuals with high tolerance for stress may handle ambiguous and unstructured tasks more easily than people with low tolerance for stress.[21] Aside from these differences, however, we might ask whether there are any general rules for how leaders should interact with followers as a function of task structure. One consideration here is that while it is *easier* for a leader or coach to give instruction in structured tasks, it is not necessarily the most helpful thing to do.

We can see this by returning to the algebra problem described earlier. If a student had never seen such an algebra problem before, it would be relatively easy to teach the student the rules needed to solve the problem. Once any student has learned the procedure, however, she can solve similar problems on her own. Extending this to other situations, once a subordinate knows or understands a task, a supervisor's continuing instruction (that is, initiating structure or directive behavior) may provide superfluous information and eventually become irritating.[22,23] Subordinates *need* help when a task is unstructured, when they do not know what the desired outcome looks like, and when they do not know how to achieve it. Anything a supervisor or leader can do to increase subordinates' ability to perform unstructured tasks is likely to increase their performance and job satisfaction.[24] Paradoxically, though, unstructured tasks are by nature somewhat ill defined. Thus they often are more difficult for leaders themselves to analyze and provide direction in accomplishing. Nonetheless, reducing the degree of ambiguity inherent in an unstructured situation is a leadership behavior usually appreciated by followers.

Finally, **task interdependence** concerns the degree to which tasks require coordination and synchronization for work groups or teams to accomplish desired goals. Task interdependence differs from autonomy in that workers or team members may be able to accomplish their tasks in an autonomous fashion, but the products of their efforts must be coordinated for the group or team to succeed. Tasks with high levels of interdependence place a premium on leaders' organizing and planning, directing, and communication skills.[25] In one study, for example, coaches exhibiting high levels of initiating-structure behaviors had better-performing teams for sports requiring relatively interdependent effort, such as football, hockey, lacrosse, rugby, basketball, and volleyball; the same leader behaviors were unrelated to team performance for sports requiring relatively independent effort, such as swimming, track, cross-country, golf, and baseball.[26] Thus the degree of task interdependence can dictate which leader behaviors will be effective in a particular situation.

Problems and Challenges

Astronaut Jim Lovell's words during the *Apollo 13* lunar mission, "Houston, we have a problem," launched a remarkable tale of effective teamwork and creative problem solving by NASA engineers working to save the lives of the imperiled crew when two oxygen tanks exploded en route to the moon. The problem they faced was urgent, critical, and novel: no one had ever confronted a problem like this before, no one had even anticipated it, and there were no established checklists, emergency procedures, or backup equipment that could be counted on to reach a viable solution. We might say, of course, that the engineers' task was to devise a solution, but we want to stress a distinction here between the connotation of *task* as it was examined in the preceding section and that of completely novel problems or challenges for which routine solutions do not exist. As we noted earlier, up to this point our treatment of tasks has derived largely from the perspective of industrial and organizational psychology wherein the task dimensions just described (and many others) represent ways to systematically and objectively describe relatively enduring aspects of routine work or jobs. Obviously the situation that the NASA engineers and astronauts faced was anything but routine.

Ronald Heifetz has been studying the leadership implications of problems and challenges like that for many years. He says that often we face problems or challenges for which the problem-solving resources already exist. In general, you can think of these resources as having two aspects: specialized methods and specialized expertise. There are many technical problems that we can solve by applying widely known though specialized methods for solution. A simple example might be determining the gas mileage your car gets on a cross-country trip. The rules are simple to follow, and they always work if you follow them correctly. At other times we may not know the answers, but it may be relatively easy to find the people who do. Maybe we can't fix the rattle coming from the car engine, but we believe the mechanic can do so. We may not know how to fix our ailment, but we believe the physician will know what to do. We may not know how to use a new software system, but we believe we can master it with assistance from an expert. Problems like these are what Heifetz calls **technical problems.** Even though they may be complex, there are expert solutions to them, and experts know how to solve them even if we don't.[27]

Rough waters are truer tests of leadership. In calm water every ship has a good captain.
Swedish proverb

But not all problems are like that. Some problems, by their nature, defy even expert solution. Some problems cannot be solved using currently existing resources and ways of thinking. In fact, it's the nature of such problems that *it can be quite difficult even reaching a common definition of what the problem really is.* Solving such problems requires that the systems facing them make fundamental changes of some kind. Heifetz calls these **adaptive problems.** Whereas technical problems can be solved without changing the nature of the social system itself within which they occur, *adaptive problems can only be solved by changing the system itself.*

At work, the most important issue in addressing technical problems is making sure they get to someone with the authority to manage the solution. According to Heifetz, however, most social problems turn out to be adaptive in nature. Almost by definition, then, significant organizational change is at least in part an adaptive challenge. Even a seemingly simpler leadership challenge at work, like getting someone else to take more seriously some constructive feedback, is actually an adaptive challenge rather than a technical one. But here is where the distinction between technical problems and adaptive problems can become blurred. Go back to our earlier example of seeing a physician for a medical problem—but let's assume

490   Part Four   *Focus on the Situation*

TABLE 12.1
Adaptive and Technical Challenges

	What's the Work?	Who Does the Work?
Technical	Applying current know-how.	Authorities.
Adaptive	Discovering new ways.	The people facing the challenge.

it's your elderly parent rather than yourself who is the patient. Let's further assume that the physician correctly solves the technical problem and provides the correct technical solution—a particular medication that has a noticeable but tolerable side effect. Getting your parent to take the medicine if he doesn't want to turns this seemingly simple technical problem into a challenging adaptive one.

How do you know when a challenge is mostly a technical challenge or mostly an adaptive challenge? It's an adaptive challenge either wholly or mostly

- When people's hearts and minds need to change, and not just their standard or habitual behaviors.
- By a process of elimination—if every technical solution you can think of has failed to improve the situation, it is more likely to be an adaptive challenge.
- If there is continuing conflict among people struggling with the challenge.
- In a crisis, which may reflect an underlying or unrecognized adaptive problem.

Some problems are so complex that you have to be highly intelligent and well informed just to be undecided about them.

Laurence J. Peter, management consultant

Different leadership approaches are required to solve adaptive problems than are required to solve technical problems. That's because adaptive problems involve people's *values*, and finding solutions to problems that involve others' values requires the active engagement of *their* hearts and minds—not just the leader's. This is what Heifetz calls **adaptive leadership.** The importance of the difference between adaptive and technical problems will become clearer as we look later in the chapter at the organizational and environmental levels of the situation.

To summarize, Table 12.1 shows the relationship between whether a problem or a challenge is mostly technical or adaptive in nature, the kind of work required to effectively address the challenge, and whom should be thought of as the "problem solver."[28]

The Organization

From the Industrial Age to the Information Age

All of us have grown up in the age of industry, but perhaps in its waning years. Starting just before the American Civil War and continuing through the last quarter of the 20th century, the industrial age supplanted the age of agriculture. During the industrial age, companies succeeded according to how well they could capture the benefits from "economies of scale and scope."[29] Technology mattered, but mostly to the extent that companies could increase the efficiencies of mass production. Now a new age is emerging, and in this information age many of the fundamental assumptions of the industrial age are becoming obsolete.

Kaplan and Norton[30] have described a new set of operating assumptions underlying the information age and contrasted them with their predecessors in the industrial age. They described changes in the following ways companies operate.

Cross Functions   Industrial age organizations gained competitive advantage through specialization of functional skills in areas like manufacturing, distribution, marketing, and technology. This specialization yielded substantial benefits, but over time also led to enormous inefficiencies and slow response processes. The information age organization operates with integrated business processes that cut across traditional business functions.

Links to Customers and Suppliers   Industrial age companies worked with customers and suppliers via arm's-length transactions. Information technology enables today's organizations to integrate supply, production, and delivery processes and to realize enormous improvements in cost, quality, and response time.

Customer Segmentation   Industrial age companies prospered by offering low-cost but standardized products and services (remember Henry Ford's comment that his customers "can have whatever color they want as long as it is black"). Information age companies must learn to offer customized products and services to diverse customer segments.

Global Scale   Information age companies compete against the best companies throughout the entire world. In fact, the large investments required for new products and services may require customers worldwide to provide adequate returns on those costs.

Innovation   Product life cycles continue to shrink. Competitive advantage in one generation of a product's life is no guarantee of success for future generations of that product. Companies operating in an environment of rapid technological innovation must be masters at anticipating customers' future needs, innovating new products and services, and rapidly deploying new technologies into efficient delivery processes.

Knowledge Workers   Industrial companies created sharp distinctions between an intellectual elite on the one hand (especially managers and engineers) and a direct labor workforce on the other. The latter group performed tasks and processes under direct supervision of white-collar engineers and managers. This typically involved physical rather than mental capabilities. Now all employees must contribute value by what they know and by the information they can provide.

Growing Up with The Gap

HIGHLIGHT 12.3

The Gap, Inc., is growing up in the information age. The retail company got its start in 1969 when Don and Doris Fisher opened the first Gap store in San Francisco. The Fishers' goal was to appeal to young consumers and bridge "the generation gap" they saw in most retail stores. Their first store sold only jeans and targeted customers mainly in their 20s. As Gap customers have grown up, so has the brand. In 1983 The Gap acquired Banana Republic mainly for its thriving catalog business and evolved the company from its original travel theme to an upscale alternative to the more casual Gap stores. In 1990 Baby Gap was born, appealing to young parents looking for stylish alternatives for their children. In 1994 Old Navy stores were introduced as the Gap looked for ways to appeal to value-oriented shoppers. The Piperline brand was created in 2006, retailing footwear online, and Athleta, a women's athletic wear line was added in 2009. From young adult, to career professional, to parent, to cost-conscious family, to aging baby boomer, The Gap has stuck close to its customers and evolved to offer products that would appeal to their changing needs.

Sources: http://www.sfgate.com/cgi-bin/article.cgi?file=/c/a/2004/08/20/BUG8288V9244.DTL&type=printable; http://www.gapinc.com/financmedia/press_releases.htm; http://www.gapinc.com/about/ataglance/milestones.htm.

One needs only to reflect upon Kaplan and Norton's list of changing operating assumptions to recognize that the situation leaders find themselves in today is different from the situation of 20 years ago. What's more, it is probably changing at an ever-increasing rate. In a real sense, the pace of change today is like trying to navigate whitewater rapids; things are changing so rapidly it can be difficult to get one's bearings. You can see how one well-known company has been trying to navigate these changing waters in Highlight 12.3. To understand how organizations cope with change, it will be helpful to look at two different facets of organizations: the formal organization and the informal organization, or organizational culture.

The Formal Organization

The study of the **formal organization** is most associated with the disciplines of management, organizational behavior, and organizational theory. Nonetheless, many aspects of the formal organization have a profound impact on leadership, and so we will briefly review some of the most important of them.

A man may speak very well in the House of Commons, and fail very completely in the House of Lords. There are two distinct styles requisite.

Benjamin Disraeli

Level of authority concerns our hierarchical level in an organization. The types of behaviors most critical to leadership effectiveness can change substantially as we move up an organizational ladder. First-line supervisors, lower-level leaders, and coaches spend a considerable amount of time training followers, resolving work unit or team performance problems, scheduling practices or arranging work schedules, and implementing policies. Leaders at higher organizational levels have more autonomy and spend relatively more time setting policies, coordinating activities, and making staffing decisions.[31,32] Moreover, leaders at higher organizational levels often perform a greater variety of activities and are more apt to use participation and delegation.[33,34] A quite different aspect of how level of authority affects leadership is presented in Highlight 12.4.

Organizational structure refers to the way an organization's activities are coordinated and controlled, and represents another level of the situation in which leaders and followers must operate. Organizational structure is a conceptual or procedural reality, however, not a physical or tangible one. Typically it is depicted in the form of a chart that clarifies formal authority relationships and patterns of communication within the organization. Most people take organizational structure for granted and fail to realize that structure is really just a tool for getting things done in organizations. Structure is not an end in itself, and different structures might exist for organizations performing similar work, each having unique advantages and disadvantages. There is nothing sacrosanct or permanent about any structure, and leaders may find that having a basic

The Glass Ceiling and the Wall

HIGHLIGHT 12.4

While the past 25 years have been marked by increasing movement of women into leadership positions, women still occupy only a small percentage of the highest leadership positions. Researchers at the Center for Creative Leadership embarked on the Executive Woman Project to understand why.[35]

They studied 76 women executives in 25 companies who had reached the general management level or the one just below it. The average woman executive in the sample was 41 and married. More than half had at least one child, and the vast majority were white.

The researchers expected to find evidence of a "glass ceiling," an invisible barrier that keeps women from progressing higher than a certain level in their organizations *because they are women.* One reason the women in this particular sample were interesting was precisely because they had apparently "broken" the glass ceiling, thus entering the top 1 percent of the workforce. These women had successfully confronted three different sorts of pressure throughout their careers, a greater challenge than their male counterparts faced. One pressure was that from the job itself, and this was no different for women than for men. A second level of pressure, however, involved being a female executive, with attendant stresses such as being particularly visible, excessively scrutinized, and a role model for other women. A third level of pressure involved the demands of coordinating personal and professional life. It is still most people's expectation that women will take the greater responsibility in a family for managing the household and raising children. And beyond the sheer size of such demands, the roles of women in these two spheres of life are often at odds (such as being businesslike and efficient, maybe even tough, at work yet intimate and nurturing at home).

Resear Researchers identified the "lessons for success" of this group of women who had broken through the glass ceiling, and they also reported a somewhat unexpected finding. Breaking through the glass ceiling presented women executives with an even tougher obstacle. They "hit a wall" that kept them out of the very top positions. The researchers estimated that only a handful of the women executives in their sample would enter the topmost echelon, called senior management, and that none would become president of their corporation.

understanding of organizational structure is not only useful but imperative. Leaders may wish to design a structure to enhance the likelihood of attaining a desired outcome, or they may wish to change a structure to meet future demands.

One important way in which organizational structures vary is in terms of their complexity. Concerning an organizational chart, **horizontal complexity** refers to the number of "boxes" at any particular organizational level. The greater the number of boxes at a given level, the greater the horizontal complexity. Typically greater horizontal complexity is associated with more specialization within subunits and an increased likelihood for communication breakdowns between subunits. **Vertical complexity** refers to the number of hierarchical levels appearing on an organizational chart. A vertically simple organization may have only two or three levels from the highest person to the lowest. A vertically complex organization, on the other hand, may have 10 or more. Vertical complexity can affect leadership by impacting other factors such as authority dynamics and communication networks. **Spatial complexity** describes geographical dispersion. An organization that has all its people in one location is typically less spatially complex than an organization that is dispersed around the country or around the world. Obviously spatial complexity makes it more difficult for leaders to have face-to-face communication with subordinates in geographically separated locations, and to personally administer rewards or provide support and encouragement. Generally all three of these elements are partly a function of organizational size. Bigger organizations are more likely to have more specialized subunits (horizontal complexity) and a greater number of hierarchical levels (vertical complexity), and to have subunits that are geographically dispersed (spatial complexity).

Organizations also vary in their degree of **formalization,** or degree of standardization. Organizations having written job descriptions and standardized operating procedures for each position have a high degree of formalization. The degree of formalization in an organization tends to vary with its size, just as complexity generally increases with size.[36] Formalization also varies with the nature of work performed. Manufacturing organizations, for example, tend to have fairly formalized structures, whereas research and development organizations tend to be less formalized. After all, how could there be a detailed job description for developing a nonexistent product or making a scientific discovery?

The degree of formalization in an organization poses both advantages and disadvantages for leaders and followers. Whereas formalizing procedures clarifies methods of operating and interacting, it also may constitute demands and constraints on leaders and followers. Leaders may be constrained in the ways they communicate requests, order supplies, or reward or discipline subordinates.[37] If followers belong to a union, then union rules may dictate work hours, the amount of work accomplished per day, or who will be the first to be laid off.[38] Other aspects of the impact

Is There Any Substitute for Leadership?

HIGHLIGHT 12.5

Are leaders always necessary? Or are certain kinds of leader behaviors, at least, sometimes unnecessary? Kerr and Jermier proposed that certain situational or follower characteristics may effectively neutralize or substitute for leaders' task or relationship behaviors. *Neutralizers* are characteristics that reduce or limit the effectiveness of a leader's behaviors. *Substitutes* are characteristics that make a leader's behaviors redundant or unnecessary.

Kerr and Jermier developed the idea of **substitutes for leadership** after comparing the correlations between leadership behaviors and follower performance and satisfaction with correlations between various situational factors and follower performance and satisfaction. Those subordinate, task, and organizational characteristics having higher correlations with follower performance and satisfaction than the two leadership behaviors were subsequently identified as substitutes or neutralizers. The following are a few examples of the situational factors Kerr and Jermier found to substitute for or neutralize leaders' task or relationship behaviors:

- A subordinate's ability and experience may substitute for task-oriented leader behavior. A subordinate's indifference toward rewards overall may neutralize a leader's task and relationship behavior.

- Tasks that are routine or structured may substitute for task-oriented leader behavior, as can tasks that provide intrinsic feedback or are intrinsically satisfying.

- High levels of formalization in organizations may substitute for task-oriented leader behavior, and unbending rules and procedures may even neutralize the leader's task behavior. A cohesive work group may provide a substitute for the leader's task and relationship behavior.

Source: S. Kerr and J. M. Jermier, "Substitutes for Leadership: Their Meaning and Measurement," *Organizational Behavior and Human Performance* 22 (1978), pp. 375–403.

of formalization and other situational variables on leadership are presented in Highlight 12.5

Centralization refers to the diffusion of decision making throughout an organization. An organization that allows decisions to be made by only one person is highly centralized. When decision making is dispersed to the lowest levels in the organization, the organization is very decentralized. Advantages of decentralized organizations include increased participation in the decision process and, consequently, greater acceptance and ownership of decision outcomes. These are both desirable outcomes. There are also, however, advantages to centralization, such as uniform policies and procedures (which can increase feelings of equity) and clearer coordination procedures.[39] The task of balancing the degree of centralization necessary to achieve coordination and control, on one hand, and gaining desirable participation and acceptance, on the other, is an ongoing challenge for the leader.

The Informal Organization: Organizational Culture

The word that sums up the **informal organization** better than any other is its *culture*. Although most people probably think of culture in terms of very large social groups, the concept also applies to organizations. **Organizational culture** has been defined as a system of shared backgrounds, norms, values, or beliefs among members of a group,[40] and **organizational climate** concerns members' subjective reactions to the organization.[41,42] These two concepts are distinct in that organizational climate is partly a function of, or reaction to, organizational culture; our feelings or emotional reactions about an organization are probably affected by the degree to which we share the prevailing values, beliefs, and backgrounds of organizational members.[43] If a person does not share the values or beliefs of the majority of members, then in all likelihood this person would have a fairly negative reaction about the organization overall. Thus organizational climate (and indirectly organizational culture) is related to how well organizational members get along with each other.[44,45] Also note that organizational climate is narrower in scope but highly related to job satisfaction. Generally, organizational climate has more to do with nontask perceptions of work, such as feelings about co-workers or company policies, whereas job satisfaction usually also includes perceptions of workload and the nature of the tasks performed.

Just as there are many cultures across the world, there are a great number of different cultures across organizations. Members of military organizations typically have different norms, background experiences, values, and beliefs, for example, from those of the faculty at most colleges or universities. Similarly, the culture of an investment firm is different from the culture of a research and development firm, a freight hauling company, or a college rugby team. Cultural differences can even exist between different organizations within any of these sectors. The culture of the U.S. Air Force is different from the culture of the U.S. Marine Corps, and Yale University has a different culture than the University of Colorado even though they are both fine institutions of higher learning. Questions that suggest further ways in which organizational cultures may differ are listed in Table 12.2.

One of the more fascinating aspects of organizational culture is that it often takes an outsider to recognize it; organizational culture becomes so second nature to many organizational members that they are unaware of how it affects their behaviors and perceptions.[46] Despite this transparency to organizational members, a fairly consistent set of dimensions can be used to differentiate between organizational cultures. For example, Kilmann and Saxton[47] stated that organizational cultures can be differentiated based on

TABLE 12.2   **Some Questions That Define Organizational Culture**

- What can be talked about or not talked about?
- How do people wield power?
- How does a person get ahead or stay out of trouble?
- What are the unwritten rules of the game?
- What are the organization's morality and ethics?
- What stories are told about the organization?

Source: Adapted from R. H. Kilmann and M. J. Saxton, *Organizational Cultures: Their Assessment and Change* (San Francisco: Jossey-Bass, 1983).

Schein's Four Key Organizational Culture Factors

HIGHLIGHT 12.6

Myths and stories are the tales about the organization that are passed down over time and communicate a story of the organization's underlying values. Virtually any employee of Walmart can tell you stories about Sam Walton and his behavior—how he rode around in his pickup truck, how he greeted people in the stores, and how he tended to "just show up" at different times. The Center for Creative Leadership has stories about its founder, H. Smith Richardson, who as a young man creatively used the mail to sell products. Sometimes stories and myths are transferred between organizations even though the truth may not lie wholly in either one. A story is told in AT&T about one of its founders and how he trudged miles and miles through a blizzard to repair a faulty component so that a woman living by herself in a rural community could get phone service. Interestingly enough, this same story is also told in MCI (now Verizon).

Symbols and artifacts are objects that can be seen and noticed and that describe various aspects of the culture. In almost any building, for example, symbols and artifacts provide information about the organization's culture. For example, an organization may believe in egalitarian principles, and that might be reflected in virtually everyone having the same size office. Or there can be indications of opulence, which convey a very different message. Even signs might act as symbols or artifacts of underlying cultural values. At one university that believed students should have first priority for facilities, an interesting sign showed up occasionally to reinforce this value. It was not a road sign, but a sign appearing on computer monitors. When the university's main computer was being overused, the computer was

programmed to identify nonstudent users, note the overload, and issue a warning to nonstudent users to sign off. This was a clear artifact, or symbol, underlying the priority placed on students at that school.

Rituals are recurring events or activities that reflect important aspects of the underlying culture. An organization may have spectacular sales meetings for its top performers and spouses every two years. This ritual would be an indication of the value placed on high sales and meeting high quotas. Another kind of ritual is the retirement ceremony. Elaborate or modest retirement ceremonies may signal the importance an organization places on its people.

Language concerns the jargon, or idiosyncratic terms, of an organization and can serve several different purposes relevant to culture. First, the mere fact that some know the language and some do not indicates who is in the culture and who is not. Second, language can also provide information about how people within a culture view others. Third, language can be used to help create a culture. A good example of the power of language in creating culture is in the words employees at Disneyland or Walt Disney World use in referring to themselves and park visitors. Employees—all employees, from the costumed Disney characters to popcorn vendors—are told to think of themselves as members of a cast, and never to be out of character. Everything happening at the park is part of the "show," and those who paid admission to enter the park are not mere tourists, but rather "the audience." Virtually everyone who visits the Disney parks is impressed with the consistently friendly behavior of its staff, a reflection of the power of words in creating culture. (Of course a strict and strongly enforced policy concerning courtesy toward park guests also helps.)

members' responses to questions like those found in Table 12.2. Another way to understand an organization's culture is in terms of myths and stories, symbols, rituals, and language.[48] A more detailed description of the four key factors identified by Schein can be found in Highlight 12.6.

Here is an example of how stories contribute to organizational culture. A consultant was asked to help a plant that had been having morale and production problems for years. After talking with several individuals at the plant, the consultant believed he had located the problem. It seems everyone he talked to told him about Sam, the plant manager. He was a giant of a man with a terrible temper. He had demolished unacceptable products with a sledgehammer, stood on the plant roof screaming at workers, and done countless other things sure to intimidate everyone around. The consultant decided he needed to talk to this plant manager. When he did so, however, he met an agreeable person named Paul. Sam, it seems, had been dead for nearly a decade, but his legacy lived on.[49]

Leaders must realize that they can play an active role in changing an organization's culture, not just be influenced by it.[50-53] Leaders can change culture by attending to or ignoring particular issues, problems, or projects. They can modify culture through their reactions to crises, by rewarding new or different kinds of behavior, or by eliminating previous punishments or negative consequences for certain behaviors. Their general personnel policies send messages about the value of employees to the organization (such as cutting wages to avoid layoffs). They can use role modeling and self-sacrifice as a way to inspire or motivate others to work more vigorously or interact with each other differently. Finally, leaders can also change culture by the criteria they use to select or dismiss followers.

Changing an organization's culture, of course, takes time and effort, and sometimes it may be extremely difficult. This is especially true in very large organizations or those with strong cultures. New organizations, on the other hand, do not have the traditions, stories or myths, or established rites to the same extent that older companies do, and it may be easier for leaders to change culture in these organizations. Still another way to think about organizational culture change is described in Highlights 12.7 and 12.8.

Why would a leader *want* to change an organization's culture? It all should depend on whether the culture is having a positive or a negative impact on various desirable outcomes. We remember one organization with a very polite culture, an aspect that seemed positive at first. There were never any potentially destructive emotional outbursts in the organization, and there was an apparent concern for other individuals' feelings in all interactions. However, a darker side of that culture gradually became apparent. When it was appropriate to give feedback for performance appraisals or employee development, supervisors were hesitant to raise negative aspects of behavior; they interpreted doing so as not being polite. And so the organization continued to be puzzled by employee behavior that tended not to improve; the organization was a victim of its own culture.

At other times, organizational culture itself can be a victim of changes initially considered to be merely technical. A classic example of this pertains to the coal mining industry in England. For hundreds of years coal was mined by teams of three people each. In England coal is layered in narrow seams, most only a few feet high. In the past the only practical means to get the coal out was to send the three-person teams of miners

Stages of Leadership Culture Development

HIGHLIGHT 12.7

Researchers at the Center for Creative Leadership have been studying different kinds of leadership cultures, which they define as the values, beliefs, and often taken-for-granted assumptions about how people work together in an organization, reflecting its collective approach to achieving direction, alignment, and commitment. While virtually all large organizations include aspects of all three types, often one of these cultures will be most dominant. Furthermore, these types of leadership culture are thought to represent successive stages of culture development, each one better adapted to deal with increasingly complex challenges. An important practical purpose of this work is to help organizations transform their cultures in ways better suited to the organization's current and future challenges.

Dependent leadership cultures are characterized by widespread beliefs and practices that it's primarily people in positions of authority who are responsible for leadership. This assumption may lead to organizations that emphasize top-down control and deference to authority. In general, you can think of dependent cultures as "conforming" cultures. Other characteristics often associated with dependent cultures include these:

- There may be a command and control mind-set.
- Seniority and position levels are important bases of respect.
- There's great emphasis on keeping things running smoothly.
- Most people operate with the philosophy that it's usually safest to check things out with one's boss before taking a new direction.

Independent leadership cultures are characterized by widespread beliefs and practices that leadership emerges as needed from a variety of individuals, based on knowledge and expertise. There's great emphasis on individual responsibility; decentralized decision making; and the promotion of experts, professionals, and individual contributors into positions of authority. In general, you can think of independent cultures as "achievement-oriented" cultures. Other characteristics associated with independent cultures include these:

- The results that leaders achieve, whatever it takes, are an important basis of respect.
- Even during times of stress, there is great pressure not to let performance numbers go down.
- Bold and independent action that gets results is highly prized.
- The organization is successful because of its large number of highly competent and ambitious individuals.

Interdependent leadership cultures are characterized by widespread beliefs and practices that leadership is a collective activity requiring mutual inquiry and learning. There's widespread use of dialogue, collaboration, horizontal networks, valuing of differences, and a focus on learning. In general, you can think of interdependent cultures as "collaborative" cultures. Other characteristics associated with interdependent cultures include these:

- Many people wear several hats at once, and roles change frequently as the organization continually adapts to changing circumstances.
- People believe it's important to let everyone learn from your experience, even your mistakes.
- There's a widely shared commitment to doing what it takes to make the entire organization be successful, not just one's own group.
- Openness, candor, and building trust across departments are valued.

500   Part Four   *Focus on the Situation*

Metaphors of Leadership Culture

HIGHLIGHT 12.8

Highlight 12.7 described a theory of organizational culture based on the idea that different cultures represent different stages of development. In that theory, interdependent cultures represent a higher stage of development than independent cultures, and independent cultures represent a higher stage of development than dependent cultures. In line with the old saying that a picture is worth a thousand words, here are some pictures that represent different metaphors of leadership culture. Try your hand at aligning each picture (thinking of it as a metaphor) with the type of culture it most represents: dependent, independent, or interdependent.

Evangelistic Preachers

Player Coaches

Pool of Sharks

Motivational Coaches

Network of Peers

Nurturing Parents

Answers: evangelistic preachers = dependent culture; player coaches = interdependent culture; pool of sharks = independent culture; motivational coaches = independent culture; network of peers = interdependent culture; nurturing parents = dependent culture.

down into the mines to dig coal from the seam and then haul it to the surface on a tram. These mining teams had extremely high levels of group cohesiveness. A technological development called the long-wall method of coal extraction upset these close relationships, however. In the long-wall method, workers were arrayed all along an entire seam of coal rather than in distinct teams, and the method should have resulted in higher productivity among the miners. However, the breakdown of the work teams led to unexpected decreases in productivity, much higher levels of worker dissatisfaction, and even disruption of social life among the miners' families. Although the long-wall method was technically superior to the three-person mining team, the leaders of the coal-mining companies failed to consider the cultural consequences of this technological advancement.[54]

These examples help make the point that while organizational culture is a powerful aspect of the situation, it can also seem fairly elusive and unresponsive to simple executive orders to change. For those reasons and others changing an organization's culture is usually both difficult and time-consuming, usually taking years in large organizations. To put it differently, it is much easier to change formal aspects of the organization like its structure or policies than it is to change its culture. In our view, however, it is precisely those organizational change efforts that focus solely or primarily on the formal organization that tend to fail. Truly significant organizational change or transformation is unlikely to be successful without addressing organizational culture as well as the formal organization.

Furthermore, a change effort is more likely to be successful if it is based on an established theory of organizational culture, and not merely subjective preferences about what needs to change. Absent a guiding theory, misguided and superficial targets of change may be selected that miss the point and usually create problems rather than produce desired results. For example, efforts to create a more collaborative culture that only target surface behaviors such as "we'll dress and talk less formally" and "we'll spend more time in meetings together" invariably miss the point, waste energy, and breed cynicism.

You may not be surprised to learn that there are a number of theories of organizational culture, and we will not try to summarize or even list them all here. It will be sufficient for our purposes to examine just one to illustrate how culture theories systematically use abstract dimensions to depict the variety of ways in which living and working in one organization can feel so different from another. The theory we will focus on is Cameron and Quinn's **Competing Values Framework**.[55]

A Theory of Organizational Culture

The Competing Values Framework is depicted in Figure 12.2. It derives its name from the fact that the values depicted on opposite ends of each axis are inherently in tension with each other. They represent competing assumptions about the desired state of affairs in the organization. The core

502 Part Four *Focus on the Situation*

FIGURE 12.2
The Competing Values Framework

Source: K. S. Cameron and R. E. Quinn, *Diagnosing and Changing Organizational Culture* (Reading, MA: Addison-Wesley, 1999), p. 32.

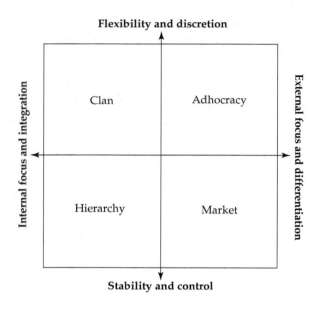

values at one end of each axis or continuum are opposed to the core values at the opposite end. Thus it's impossible that an organization could be both extremely flexible and extremely stable all the time. An organization's culture represents a balance or trade-off between these competing values that tends to work for that organization in its particular competitive environment.

Organizational cultures are not usually designed intentionally. That's one reason we noted earlier in this section that people tend not to be consciously aware of their own organization's culture. In fact, it's usually only when an organization's culture is impeding organizational performance (typically in a changing competitive environment) that people become aware of any need for culture change. It's at just such times that it can be useful for people within an organization to consider something different. The Competing Values Framework was designed to help organizations be more deliberate in identifying a culture more likely to be successful given their respective situations, and in transitioning to it.

As you can see in Figure 12.2, the intersection of the competing values axes creates four quadrants describing four different combinations of values. The distinctive sets of values in these quadrants define four unique organizational cultures.

Organizations that emphasize stability and control, and also focus their attention inward (on how people within the organization interact with each other, on whether internal operating procedures are followed, and so forth), have a **hierarchy culture.** Organizations with a hierarchy culture tend to have formalized rules and procedures; they tend to be highly structured places to work. Following standard operating procedures, or

SOPs, is the rule of the day. The emphasis is on ensuring continuing efficiency, smooth functioning, and dependable operations. Examples of hierarchy cultures are government agencies, fast-food chains, and traditional large manufacturing companies.[56]

Organizations that, like hierarchy cultures, emphasize stability and control but focus their attention primarily on the external environment (outside the organization itself) are called **market cultures.** Their interest is more on interactions with external constituencies like customers and suppliers. Market cultures are competitive and results-oriented, and the results that count most are typically financial measures of success such as profit. To ensure discipline in achieving these ends, there is great emphasis on achieving measurable goals and targets. Fundamentally, what characterizes market cultures is a pervasive emphasis on winning, often defined simply as beating the competition.[57]

Organizations that emphasize having a high degree of flexibility and discretion, and that also focus primarily inward rather than outward, are known as **clan cultures** because in many ways they can be thought of as an extended family. A strong sense of cohesiveness characterizes clan cultures along with shared values and a high degree of participativeness and consensus building. Clan cultures believe their path to success is rooted in teamwork, loyalty, and taking care of people within the organization, including their continuing development. In a real sense clan cultures can be thought of as *relationship* cultures.[58]

Finally, organizations that emphasize having a high degree of flexibility and discretion, and that focus primarily on the environment outside the organization, are called **adhocracy cultures.** In many ways adhocracy cultures represent an adaptation to the transition from the industrial age to the information age described earlier in that this form of organizational culture is most responsive to the turbulent and rapidly changing conditions of the present age. The name *adhocracy* has roots in the phrase *ad hoc*, which means temporary or specialized. Adhocracy cultures are by nature dynamic and changing so as to best foster creativity, entrepreneurship, and staying on the cutting edge. This requires a culture that emphasizes individual initiative and freedom.[59]

In actuality, these four cultures represent idealized forms; no real organization probably exists whose culture can be completely described by just one quadrant. The complexities and necessities of organizational life and survival inevitably require that all cultures include elements from all four of the cultures (that is, all cultures put some value on all the competing values). What differentiates one culture from another, then, is the relative predominance of one culture type over the others. Nonetheless, it should be apparent that quite different approaches to leadership are called for based on which of these four distinctive cultures dominates any organization.

Leadership in hierarchy cultures, for example, emphasizes careful management of information, monitoring detailed aspects of operations, and assuring operational dependability and reliability. In contrast, leadership in market cultures places a premium on aggressiveness, decisiveness, productivity (which is not the same thing as stability or continuity), and outperforming external competitors. Leadership in a clan culture focuses on process more than output, especially as it pertains to minimizing conflict and maximizing consensus. A premium is placed on leadership that is empathetic and caring and that builds trust. And leadership in adhocracy cultures requires vision, creativity, and future-oriented thinking.

An Afterthought on Organizational Issues for Students and Young Leaders

Let us conclude this section by adding an afterthought about what relevance organizational issues may have for students or others at the early stages of their careers, or at lower levels of leadership within their organizations. It is unlikely that such individuals will be asked soon to redesign their organization's structure or change its culture. As noted earlier, this chapter is not intended as a how-to manual for changing culture. On the other hand, it has been our experience that younger colleagues sometimes develop biased impressions of leaders or have unrealistic expectations about decision making in organizations, based on their lack of familiarity with, and appreciation of, the sorts of organizational dynamics discussed in this section. In other words, a primary reason for being familiar with such organizational variables is the context they provide for understanding the leadership process at your own level in the organization. Finally, we have worked with some senior leaders of huge organizations who have been with their companies for their entire careers. They have often been unable to identify *any* of the dimensions of their culture because they have never seen anything else. In these cases we were amazed by how junior managers were far better at describing the culture of the large organization. While these junior people may have had only five to eight years of total work experience, if that experience was obtained in several different organizations, they were much better prepared to describe the characteristics of their new large organization's culture than were the senior executives.

The Environment

The environmental level of the situation refers to factors outside the task or organization that still affect the leadership process. We will focus on two interrelated aspects of these extra-organizational aspects of the situation: (1) the ways in which leaders increasingly confront situations that are unexpected, unfamiliar, complex, and rapidly changing; and (2) the growing importance of leadership across different societal cultures.

Are Things Changing More Than They Used To?

One general aspect of the situation that affects leadership is the degree of change that's occurring. Leading in a relatively stable situation presents different challenges—generally simpler ones—than does leading in a dynamic situation. Many people think things *are* changing more than they used to, and at an increasing pace, but that's not so simple a question as it first might appear. For example, it may seem as though no age could possibly rival ours in terms of the transformative effect technology has had on our lives. On the other hand, an interesting case can be made that technologies introduced to most Americans during the early to mid-20th century like indoor electric lighting, refrigerators, electric and natural gas ovens, and indoor plumbing, changed everyday life to a greater degree than new technologies of the past decade.[60]

Nonetheless, while there's no argument that the generations growing up in the early part of the 20th century experienced profound transformations in life (television, the automobile, air travel, and atomic energy, to name a few), we believe that the nature of challenges facing leaders is changing as never before. Ronald Heifetz argues that leaders not only are facing more crises than ever before but that a new mode of leadership is needed because we're in a *permanent* state of crisis.[61] Thomas Friedman provocatively titled his book *The World Is Flat* to convey how globalization and technology are radically changing how we live and work.[62] And Army General David Petraeus used an oddly anachronistic painting in speaking with the troops he was soon to take command of in what was widely known as "the surge" in Iraq. The painting was *The Stampede*, painted by western artist Frederic Remington in 1908. It depicts a cowboy in the 1800s riding desperately to survive a stampeding herd of cattle panicked by a thunderstorm. As Thomas Ricks tells the story in his account of the surge *The Gamble*, Petraeus used the painting to convey to his subordinates his notion of command. "I don't need to be hierarchical," he explained. "I want to flatten organizations. I'm comfortable with a slightly chaotic environment. I know that it's okay if some of you get out ahead of us. Some of the cattle will get out ahead and we will catch up with them. And some will fall behind and we will circle back and we won't leave them behind. . . . We're just trying to get the cattle to Cheyenne."[63]

To appreciate the significance of what Petraeus was saying, contrast the language and images used here ("don't need to be hierarchical," "some of the cattle will get out") with the stereotypical notions of command and control in the military. Situational changes are being met with new approaches to leadership even within what is often regarded as the epitome of traditional top-down leadership.

We think Heifetz, Friedman, and Petraeus illuminate important ways in which the challenge of leadership is changing. It might be useful, therefore, to introduce a variation of Figure 12.1, which depicted the task, organizational, and environmental levels of the situation. In Figure 12.3 we've

506 Part Four *Focus on the Situation*

FIGURE 12.3
Contrasting
Different
Environments in the
Situational Level

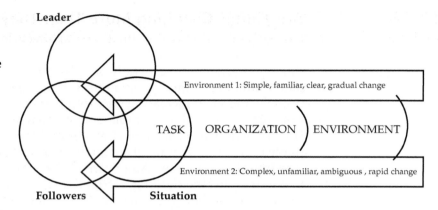

added two vectors to the original diagram to highlight how two contrasting and multidimensional kinds of environments affect leadership. We don't intend the two vectors to imply there's a simple categorization of environments (either simple or complex); we use the representation in the figure to illustrate a range of possible environments. Nonetheless, change has become so fast and so pervasive that it impacts virtually every organization everywhere, and everyone in them. And appropriate to our times, an acronym has been given to this new state of affairs: **VUCA.** Coined by the Army War College, the term *VUCA* describes a world that is volatile, uncertain, complex, and ambiguous.

Another purpose of the vectors in Figure 12.3 is to underscore how different levels of the situation interact. Thus relatively narrow and specific descriptions of job tasks tend to be most common and most appropriate in more formal and highly structured organizations having more hierarchical cultures. This set of situational levels is reasonably aligned to deal with what Heifetz called technical problems. Adaptive or wicked problems, on the other hand, are more likely to be effectively addressed when tasks for individuals and teams are more fluid, in organizations that are less formal, less structured, and more agile and that have adhocracy-like cultures.

Of course we are not saying that once situational variables have been identified as corresponding more closely to the bottom vector, it's a simple matter for a leader to just "turn on" adaptive leadership. The whole point is that such leadership is inherently more than an individual leader or his behavior or skills. Certain kinds of established relationships with followers are vital, and distinctive skill sets on their parts are needed, as is a certain kind of organizational culture.

In addition, Heifetz has described a thorny leadership challenge that can raise its head even after a challenge is recognized as an adaptive one. Followers generally want their leaders to be experts having all the answers (recall that by definition, adaptive problems don't have expert solutions). He said, "When you attain a position of significant authority, people inevitably expect you to treat adaptive challenges as if they were technical—to provide

Workplace Trends

HIGHLIGHT 12.9

In response to increasing competitiveness, uncertainty, globalization, and the pace of change, a number of leadership trends have been identified in how organizations can best face the future:

- Recognize that complex challenges are on the rise, and therefore that new approaches to leadership and leadership development will be required.

- Embrace innovation as a driver of future organizational success.

- Prepare for ever-greater levels of and need for virtual leadership, and that the skills it requires are different than those needed for face-to-face leadership.

- Collaboration across organizational boundaries (across teams, departments, units, regions, and so on) will be essential to organizational success.

- Because trust and respect will be vital, leaders will need to be more authentic in their roles than ever before.

- The next generation of leaders will place new kinds of leadership demands on their organizations.

- A crisis of talent in organizations is coming, and so organizations that have credible and established programs of talent development and succession planning will be at an advantage.

- Ensuring the health and fitness of all employees, leaders included, must become an organizational priority.

Source: A. Martin, *What's Next: The 2007 Changing Nature of Leadership Survey*, CCL Research White Paper (Greensboro, NC: Center for Creative Leadership). Center for Creative Leadership, CCL®, and its logo are registered trademarks owned by the Center for Creative Leadership. © 2007 Center for Creative Leadership. All rights reserved.

I claim not to have controlled events, but confess plainly that events have controlled me.

Abraham Lincoln

---

for them a remedy that will restore equilibrium with the least amount of pain and in the shortest amount of time."[64] Furthermore, leaders themselves easily fall prey to the same expectation. People in positions of authority often take personal pride in being able to solve problems that others can't solve. When facing an adaptive challenge, it can be difficult for them to admit they've come to the limit of their expertise.[65] To put it differently, leadership has never been easy and appears to be growing more difficult. A number of trends driving the changing nature of leadership are listed in Highlight 12.9. And a situational challenge that has always confronted leaders taking over new responsibilities is addressed in Profiles in Leadership 12.1.

Leading across Societal Cultures

A telling illustration of the role societal culture can play in leadership is provided by Malcolm Gladwell in his book *Outliers*. It concerns the role that culture played in a series of airline crashes, including that of Korean Air Flight 801 in 1997, which killed 228 of the 254 people on board. In fact, the loss rate (deaths per number of departing passengers) for Korean Air in the period from 1988 to 1998 was 17 times what it was for a representative American carrier. It may seem initially that the likely cause of such a difference would be deficiencies in the Korean pilots' technical flying expertise or knowledge, but that was not the case—nor is it usually the case. The kinds of errors that cause crashes are almost always errors of teamwork and communication rather than errors of flying skill. Careful

Taking Charge

PROFILE IN LEADERSHIP 12.1

A critical period for any leader often involves those first few moments and days of assuming command. This is a time when first impressions are formed and expectations are set. It is especially challenging when the situation is stressful and the stakes are high.

That was precisely the situation facing Coast Guard Admiral Thad Allen when he took responsibility for overall leadership of the 2005 Hurricane Katrina search-and-rescue recovery efforts. Allen was replacing Michael Brown, then director of the Federal Emergency Management Agency, who had received harsh criticism for mishandling the relief efforts.

The first thing that happened on the day Allen was told of his new responsibility was a joint press conference with his new boss, the Director of Homeland Security, to announce Allen's appointment. The very next thing Allen did was ask to have a meeting with all 4,000 people assigned to the recovery effort. Although they couldn't find a space large enough to hold that many, they did find a place that could accommodate 2,000 of them.

Here is Allen's account of how he handled those critical first moments:

> I got up on a desk, with a loudspeaker, and told everybody that I was giving one order: They were to treat anybody they came into contact with who had been affected by the storm like a member of their own family. Their mother, father, brother, sister, whatever. And I said, "If you do that, two things are going to happen. Number one, if you make a mistake, you're going to err on the side of doing too much, and that's okay. Number two, if somebody has a problem with what you've done, their problem's not with you; their problem's with me."
>
> After I said that, a cheer broke out, because there had been so much stress from the pressure that had been exerted on the response and the perception that it wasn't going well. Just a simple set of core values—a North Star to steer by—was, I think, what they were looking for.

Source: "You Have to Lead from Everywhere," *Harvard Business Review,* November 2010, pp. 76–79.

analysis of those crashes reveals that a root cause was the Korean pilots' customary cultural deep respect for authority. The same factor also played a role in crashes of airliners piloted by crews of other nationalities sharing a similar respect for authority. Respect for authority in itself is neither a good nor a bad thing, but it can be a problem when it interferes with clear and direct communication about an emergency situation. That's just what was happening in these crashes. Strange as it may sound, the crews did not make the criticality of their situations crystal clear to air traffic controllers. Conversing with the controllers as equals, such as by correcting the controllers' understanding of the actual situations, would have seemed disrespectful from the crew's cultural perspective. (As a footnote, Korean Air has corrected its procedures and now has an exemplary safety record.)[66]

This is admittedly a dramatic illustration, and airline crashes are fortunately rare events. The point the story makes, however, applies to leaders of all sorts and in all places: cultural differences—especially when they are not recognized and addressed—can create significant challenges to communication and teamwork. It's no surprise, then, that in recent years an increasing number of empirical studies have examined the challenges of leading across societal cultures. One value of such studies is that their findings can

". . . Then it's agreed. As a crowd, we'll be subdued in innings one through seven, then suddenly become a factor in innings eight and nine . . ."

point out myths, mistaken assumptions, or invalid generalizations people have or make about leadership.

For example, a person regarded as an effective leader in one society may not be perceived as effective in another. That's what one study found in comparing evaluations by supervisors of the leadership effectiveness of female managers in Malaysia with those by supervisors of female managers in Australia. These findings appeared to be based not on an objective appraisal of the female managers' capability but rather on strongly held cultural beliefs about appropriate roles for women in society. There was a clear culturally based readiness by both male and female supervisors in Australia to value equality between the roles of men and women generally and in organizational roles specifically; this was not the case in Malaysia, where more gender-specific stereotypes were held. While these findings were not unexpected, they point out how research findings in Western cultures may not be transferable to developing cultures.[67]

Such findings have a practical importance beyond mere academic or scholarly interest. A survey of executives in the 500 largest corporations in the world showed that having competent global leaders was the most important contributor to business success (as discussed further in Highlight 12.10). What's more, 85 percent of those executives did not think their companies had sufficient numbers of competent global leaders.[68]

Global Leadership

HIGHLIGHT 12.10

There is no doubt about it: the world is getting smaller. Globalization has allowed goods and services to be manufactured, traded, and delivered in places no one thought possible just 10 or 20 years ago. World business leaders, such as Jeffery Immelt of General Electric, Carlos Ghosn of Renault and Nissan Motors, and Steve Ballmer of Microsoft all believe these global trends are irreversible and gaining momentum. But what are the implications of globalization for leadership? It is clear that the ways in which leaders get results through others and build cohesive, goal-oriented teams will vary somewhat from one country to the next. For example, Malaysian leadership culture inhibits assertive, confrontational behavior and puts a premium on maintaining harmony. Effective leaders are expected to show compassion while demonstrating more of an autocratic than participatory leadership style. German leadership culture does not value compassion, and interpersonal relationships are straightforward and stern. Effective leaders in Germany generally value autonomy and participation but have a low team orientation.

So how does one lead in a global economy? Certainly appreciating what different cultures value and how things get done in different countries is an important first step. But do leaders need to do fundamentally different things to build teams or get results through others in India, Zimbabwe, or Estonia? Will leaders of the future need to speak multiple languages or actually live in other countries to be effective? The answers to these questions will depend to some extent on the global orientation of the organization. Some organizations, such as Waste Management or ServiceMaster, operate primarily in Canada and the United States and probably will not need to have leaders who have lived in other countries or speak multiple languages. Other organizations, such as 3M, Hewlett-Packard, Pfizer, BP, Levono, Nike, Toyota, or the British military have significant manufacturing, marketing, sales, or other operations in multiple countries. These organizations often use a global competency model to outline the expectations for leaders in all countries, and these models tend to vary more by company than by country (see Figure 7.3 for an example of a competency model).

It seems likely that leaders who have spent time in other countries, have applied the action–observation–reflection model to maximize the lessons learned from their expatriot experiences, and can speak multiple languages would be better able to lead international organizations. But currently this is conjecture; more research is needed before we can definitively say whether international experience matters, how much and what kinds of experience are needed, what the key lessons to be learned from these experiences are, and how we should select and develop leaders to successfully lead international organizations. The good news here is that a group of 150 social scientists working on the GLOBE (Global Leadership and Organizational Behavior Effectiveness) project are actively seeking the answers to these questions and will soon be publishing their findings.

Sources: S. Green, F. Hassan, J. Immelt, M. Marks, and D. Meiland, "In Search of Global Leaders," *Harvard Business Review,* August 2003, pp. 38–45; J. C. Kennedy, "Leadership in Malaysia: Traditional Values, International Outlook," *The Academy of Management Executive,* 16, no. 3 (2002), pp. 15–24; F. Brodbeck, M. Frese, M. Javidan, and F. G. Kroll, "Leadership Made in Germany: Low on Compassion, High in Performance," *The Academy of Management Executive* 16, no. 1 (2002), pp. 16–30; GLOBE program: http://mgmt3.ucalgary.ca/web/globe.nsf/index.

Without competent global leaders, misunderstandings and slights can occur when people from different cultures are working together. Here are two specific examples. First consider the historic U.S. emphasis on individualism (the focus on *self*-confidence, *self*-control, *self*-concept, *self*-expression, or the way rugged individualists are heroically portrayed in film, television, and literature) and how it might impact work. Given an individualist perspective, certain management practices and expectations seem self-evident, such as the idea of individual accountability for work. When individual accountability is valued, for example, decision-making authority tends to be delegated to individual managers. What's more, those same managers may be inclined to take personal credit when the job is well done. A different norm, however, applies in industrialized Japan. Decision making is often time-consuming to ensure that everyone who will be affected by a decision has input on it beforehand. Another self-evident principle to the U.S. mind is that individual career progress is desirable and good. In some other cultures, however, managers resist competing with peers for rewards or promotions so as not to disturb the harmony of the group or appear self-interested.

Another example of potential conflict or misunderstanding can be seen in the case of orientation to authority—how people should handle power and authority relationships with others. The United States is a relatively young and mobile country, populated mostly by immigrants. Relative to other countries, there is little concern with family origin or class background. There is a belief that success should come through an individual's hard work and talent, not by birthright or class standing. This all leads to relative informality at work, even among individuals of strikingly different position within a company. Subordinates expect their bosses to be accessible, even responsive in some ways to their subordinates. In some other cultures, however, higher status in a company confers nearly unchallengeable authority, and an expectation as well that most decisions will be referred *up* to them (as distinguished from delegated down to others).

What Is Societal Culture?

Before we look at more specific findings about leading across societal cultures, it will be useful first to clarify what the term *societal culture* means. **Societal culture** refers to those learned behaviors characterizing the total way of life of members within any given society. Cultures differ from one another just as individuals differ from one another. To outsiders, the most salient aspect of any culture typically involves behavior—the distinctive actions, mannerisms, and gestures characteristic of that culture. Americans visiting Thailand, for example, may find it curious and even bothersome to see male Thais hold hands with each other in public. They may react negatively to such behavior because it is atypical to them and laden with North American meaning ("It's okay for women to hold hands in public, but men shouldn't do that"). Salient as such behaviors are, however, they are just the tip of the iceberg. The mass of culture is not so readily visible, just as most of an iceberg lies beneath the water. Hidden from view are the beliefs, values, and myths that provide context to manifest behaviors.[69] A clear implication for business leaders in the global context, therefore, is the need to become aware and respectful of cultural differences and cultural perspectives. Barnum pointed out the importance of being able to look at one's own culture through the eyes of another:

> Consciously or unconsciously they will be using their own beliefs as the yardsticks for judging you, so know how to compare those yardsticks by ferreting out their values and noting where they differ the least and most from yours. For example, if their belief in fatalism outweighs your belief in accountability, there will be conflicts down the road. This is a severe problem in the Middle East, for instance, and affects management styles in companies and even the ability to market life insurance, which is frowned upon in communities where Muslim observances are strong.[70]

The GLOBE Study

GLOBE is an acronym for a research program called the Global Leadership and Organizational Behavior Effectiveness Research Program. It is the most comprehensive study of leadership and culture ever attempted, involving data collected from over 17,000 managers representing 950 companies in 62 countries.[71,72]

I do believe in the spiritual nature of human beings. To some it's a strange or outdated idea, but I believe there is such a thing as a human spirit. There is a spiritual dimension to man which should be nurtured.

Aung San Suu Kyi

Hofstede was one of the pioneers in the study of beliefs and culture, and his seminal work provided some of the early roots of the GLOBE study.[73] He identified five fundamental dimensions of cultural values and beliefs, and these, as well as dimensions drawn from the work of other researchers, became the nine dimensions of societal culture used in the GLOBE study. Because of the number of scales and complexity of findings, we'll look at representative findings from just two of those scales to convey the flavor of some of these cross-cultural findings. We'll look at the dimensions of future orientation and collectivism–individualism. Here's a brief definition of each of them:[74]

Future orientation: The degree to which individuals in organizations or societies engage in future-oriented behaviors like planning and investing in the future.

Collectivism: The degree to which individuals express pride, loyalty, and cohesiveness in their organizations, families, or similar small groups.

Table 12.3 presents some of the representative findings that differentiate cultures high or low on each of these dimensions. Cross-cultural differences on these and the other seven dimensions of culture used in GLOBE constitute a foundation for the GLOBE findings on differences in leadership across cultures.

The heart of the conceptual model in the GLOBE research is what's called **implicit leadership theory.** This theory holds that individuals have implicit beliefs and assumptions about attributes and behaviors that distinguish leaders from followers, effective leaders from ineffective leaders, and moral from immoral leaders. The GLOBE model further posits that relatively distinctive implicit theories of leadership characterize different

TABLE 12.3 **Representative Societal Differences on Two GLOBE Dimensions**

Societies Higher on Collectivism Tend to	Societies Higher on Individualism Tend to
• Have a slower pace of life. • Have lower heart attack rates. • Assign less weight to love in marriage decisions. • Have fewer interactions, but interactions tend to be longer and more intimate.	• Have a faster pace of life. • Have higher heart attack rates. • Assign greater weight to love in marriage decisions. • Have more social interactions, but interactions tend to be shorter and less intimate.
Societies Higher on Future Orientation Tend to	Societies Lower on Future Orientation Tend to
• Achieve economic success. • Have flexible and adaptive organizations and managers. • Emphasize visionary leadership that is capable of seeing patterns in the face of chaos and uncertainty.	• Have lower rates of economic success. • Have inflexible and maladaptive organizations and managers. • Emphasize leadership that focuses on repetition of reproducible and routine sequences.

societal cultures from each other as well as organizational cultures within those societal cultures. GLOBE calls these **culturally endorsed implicit theories of leadership** (CLT).

After detailed analysis of findings, GLOBE researchers identified six dimensions that were determined to be applicable across all global cultures for assessing CLT. Here are those six dimensions and a brief description of each:[75]

- **Charismatic/value-based leadership** reflects the ability to inspire, motivate, and expect high performance from others on the basis of firmly held core values.
- **Team-oriented leadership** emphasizes effective team building and implementation of a common purpose or goal among team members.
- **Participative leadership** reflects the degree to which managers involve others in making and implementing decisions.
- **Humane-oriented leadership** reflects supportive and considerate leadership as well as compassion and generosity.
- **Autonomous leadership** refers to independent and individualistic leadership.
- **Self-protective leadership** focuses on ensuring the safety and security of the individual or group member.

After analyzing the data from all the societies in the study, GLOBE researchers categorized them into 10 different societal clusters (such as Eastern Europe, Nordic Europe, Latin America, Southern Asia, and Anglo). Societies were included in a cluster based on criteria of relative similarity of

TABLE 12.4   **Relative Rankings of Selected Societal Clusters on CLT Leadership Dimensions**

Societal Cluster	Charismatic/ Value-Based	Team-Oriented	Participative	Humane-Oriented	Self-Protective
Eastern Europe	Medium	Medium	Low	Medium	High
Anglo	High	Medium	High	High	Low
Middle East	Low	Low	Low	Medium	High

values and beliefs *within* each cluster, and *differentiation* from other societal clusters. Again, it is beyond our purposes here to present a comprehensive description of all these societal clusters. It will suffice to look at just three of them so you will have a general sense of the nature of the GLOBE findings. Table 12.4 presents the relative rankings (high, medium, or low) for three different societal clusters on each of the six global CLT dimensions.[76]

The considerable variation in views of what constitutes good leadership across different societal clusters evident in Table 12.4 makes it clear that behaving effectively as a leader (and being perceived as effective) requires awareness of the cultural values and practices in the society within which one is working.

A final set of interesting findings coming out of GLOBE concerns the **universality of leadership attributes.** These findings both refine and temper the distinctiveness of societal CLTs exemplified in Table 12.4. They temper the impression we may get that different societies have completely different notions of what constitutes good and bad leadership by demonstrating that actually there is consensus across cultures on a number of desirable leadership attributes as well as consensus on what are considered to be universally negative leadership traits. But these findings also provide further insight into which attributes see much of the variability across cultures. GLOBE researchers identified 22 specific attributes and behaviors that are viewed universally across cultures as contributing to leadership effectiveness.[77] They are listed in Table 12.5. In addition,

TABLE 12.5
Leader Attributes and Behaviors Universally Viewed as Positive

Trustworthy	Positive	Intelligent
Just	Dynamic	Decisive
Honest	Motive arouser	Effective bargainer
Foresighted	Confidence builder	Win–win problem solver
Plans ahead	Motivational	Administratively skilled
Encouraging	Dependable	Communicative
Informed	Coordinator	Team builder
Excellence oriented		

Source: Adapted from House et al., *Cultural Influences on Leadership and Organizations: Project Globe. Advances in Global Leadership*, vol. 1 (JAI Press, 1999), pp. 171–233.

TABLE 12.6   Leader Attributes and Behaviors Universally Viewed as Negative

Loner	Nonexplicit
Asocial	Egocentric
Noncooperative	Ruthless
Irritable	Dictatorial

Source: Adapted from House et al., *Cultural Influences on Leadership and Organizations: Project Globe. Advances in Global Leadership*, vol. 1 (JAI Press, 1999), pp. 171–233.

TABLE 12.7   Examples of Leader Behaviors and Attributes That Are Culturally Contingent

Ambitious	Logical
Cautious	Orderly
Compassionate	Sincere
Domineering	Worldly
Independent	Formal
Individualistic	Sensitive

Source: Adapted from House et al., *Cultural Influences on Leadership and Organizations: Project Globe. Advances in Global Leadership*, vol. 1 (JAI Press, 1999), pp. 171–233.

the project identified eight characteristics that are universally viewed as impediments to leader effectiveness (see Table 12.6). And GLOBE researchers identified 35 leader characteristics that are viewed as positive in some cultures but negative in others (some of these are listed in Table 12.7). This large set of culturally contingent characteristics apparently accounts for most of the variance across societal cultures.

Implications for Leadership Practitioners

The perspectives and findings presented in this chapter have significant implications for leadership practitioners. Perhaps most important, leadership practitioners should expect to face a variety of challenges to their own systems of ethics, values, or attitudes during their careers. Additionally, values often are a source of interpersonal conflict. Although we sometimes say two people don't get along because of a personality conflict, often these conflicts are due to differences in value systems, not personality traits. Often people on either side of an issue see only themselves and their own side as morally justifiable. Nonetheless, people holding seemingly antithetical values may need to work together, and dealing with diverse values will be an increasingly common challenge for leaders. As noted earlier, interacting with individuals and groups holding divergent and conflicting values will be an inevitable fact of life for future leaders. This does not mean, however, that increased levels of interpersonal conflict are inevitable. Both leaders and followers might be well advised to minimize the conflict and tension often associated with value differences. Leaders in particular have a responsibility not to let their own personal values interfere with professional leader–subordinate relationships unless the conflicts pertain to issues clearly relevant to the work and the organization.

Summary

The situation may be the most complex factor in the leader–follower–situation framework. Moreover, situations vary not only in complexity but also in strength. Situational factors can play such a pervasive role that they can effectively minimize the effects of personality traits, intelligence, values, and preferences on leaders' and followers' behaviors, attitudes, and relationships. Given the dynamic nature of leadership situations, finding fairly consistent results is a highly encouraging accomplishment for leadership researchers.

As an organizing framework, this chapter introduced the concept of situational levels as a way to consider many situational factors. At the lowest level, leaders need to be aware of how various aspects of tasks can affect both their own and their followers' behaviors, and how they might change these factors to improve followers' satisfaction and performance. The organizational level includes both the formal organization and informal organization. The formal organization involves the ways authority is distributed across various organizational levels and how organizational structure impacts the way activities in the organization are coordinated and controlled. The informal organization or the organizational culture can have a profound impact on the way both leaders and followers behave—and may be the least recognizable because it is the water in the bowl where all the fish are swimming. An increasingly important variable at the environmental level is societal culture, which involves learned behaviors that guide the distinctive mannerisms, ways of thinking, and values within particular societies.

Key Terms

situational engineering, *482*
role theory, *485*
multiple-influence model, *485*
situational levels, *485*
task autonomy, *486*
task feedback, *487*
task structure, *487*

task interdependence, *488*
technical problems, *489*
adaptive problems, *489*
adaptive leadership, *490*
formal organization, *492*

level of authority, *492*
organizational structure, *493*
horizontal complexity, *494*
vertical complexity, *494*
spatial complexity, *494*
formalization, *494*

substitutes for
  leadership, *495*
centralization, *495*
informal
  organization, *495*
organizational
  culture, *495*
organizational
  climate, *496*
myths and stories, *497*
symbols and
  artifacts, *497*
rituals, *497*
language, *497*
dependent leadership
  culture, *499*
independent
  leadership culture,
  499

interdependent
  leadership culture,
  499
Competing Values
  Framework, *501*
hierarchy culture, *502*
market culture, *503*
clan culture, *503*
adhocracy culture, *503*
VUCA, *506*
societal culture, *511*
GLOBE, *512*
future orientation, *512*
collectivism, *512*
implicit leadership
  theory, *512*
culturally endorsed
  implicit theories of
  leadership, *513*

charismatic/values-
  based leadership,
  513
team-oriented
  leadership, *513*
participative
  leadership, *513*
humane-oriented
  leadership, *513*
autonomous
  leadership, *513*
self-protective
  leadership, *513*
universality of
  leadership
  attributes, *514*

Questions

1. The term *bureaucratic* has a pejorative connotation to most people. Can you think of any positive aspects of a bureaucracy?

2. Think of a crisis situation you are familiar with involving a group, team, organization, or country, and analyze it in terms of the leader–follower–situation framework. For example, were the followers looking for a certain kind of behavior from the leader? Did the situation demand it? Did the situation, in fact, contribute to a particular leader's emergence?

3. Can you identify reward systems that affect the level of effort students are likely to put forth in team or group projects? Should these reward systems be different than those for individual effort projects?

Activity

Your instructor has several exercises available that demonstrate the impact of situational factors on behavior. They are not described here because identifying the situational factors being manipulated in an exercise undercuts the purpose of that exercise.

Minicase

Innovation at IKEA

Redecorating and renovating have become a popular international pastime. In a world facing persistent terrorist alerts and lagging economies, more and more people are opting to stay home and make their homes safe havens. This phenomenon has contributed tremendously to the success of IKEA, the Swedish home furniture giant. In monetary terms alone, that success is measured by sales for the fiscal year ending in 2013 totaling 27.9 billion euros - that's a lot of furniture!

Much of IKEA's success can be attributed to its founder, Ingvar Kamprad. Kamprad used graduation money to start IKEA in the small Swedish village where he was born. He started off selling belt buckles, pens, and watches—whatever residents in the small local village of Agunnaryd needed. Eventually Kamprad moved on to selling furniture. One day in 1952, while struggling to fit a large table in a small car, one of Kamprad's employees came up with the idea that changed the furniture industry forever—he decided to remove the legs. IKEA's flat-pack and self-assembly methodology was born, and it rocketed the company past the competition. "After that [table] followed a whole series of other self-assembled furniture, and by 1956 the concept was more or less system-atized," writes Kamprad.

Kamprad is dedicated to maintaining the corporate culture he has helped define over the past 50 years. He is a simple man—his idea of a luxury vacation is riding his bike. He is fiercely cost-conscious and, even though his personal wealth has been estimated in the billions, he refuses to fly first class. He values human interaction above all, and, even though retired, he still visits IKEA stores regularly to keep tabs on what is going on where the business really happens.

The culture at IKEA is a culture closely connected with Kamprad's simple Swedish farm roots. It is a culture that strives "to create a better everyday for the many people." IKEA supports this culture by

- Hiring co-workers (IKEA prefers the word *co-workers* to *employees*) who are supportive and work well in teams.
- Expecting co-workers to look for innovative, better ways of doing things in every aspect of their work.
- Respecting co-workers and their views.
- Establishing mutual objectives and working tirelessly to realize them.
- Making cost consciousness part of everything they do from improving processes for production to purchasing wisely to traveling cost-effectively.
- Complicated solutions—simplicity is a strong part of the IKEA culture.
- Leading by example, so IKEA leaders are expected to pitch in when needed and create a good working environment.
- Believing that a diverse workforce strengthens the company overall.

The IKEA culture is one that resonates for many. The buildings are easy to identify—the giant blue and gold warehouses that resemble oversized Swedish flags are hard to miss. Millions of customers browse through the Klippan sofas and Palbo footstools (Nordic names are given to all IKEA products) in the stark, dimly lit warehouses. The surroundings may not be lavish and the service may be minimal, but customers keep going back not just for the bargains but to experience the IKEA culture as well.

1. Discuss the three input components of the Congruence Model as they apply to the success of IKEA.
2. Consider Schein's four key organizational culture factors as described in Highlight 12.6. What examples can you identify within the IKEA organization that contribute to the company's strong corporate culture?
3. Based on the level of technological complexity and the degree of environmental uncertainty present at IKEA, what type of organizational structure would you expect?

Sources: http://archive.cinweekly.com/content/2004/03/24/0324travelikea.asp; http://www.azcentral.com/home/design/articles/0812ikea12.html; http://strategis.ic.gc.ca/epic/internet/inimr-ri.nsf/en/gr-76894e.html; http://www.geocities.com/TimesSquare/1848/ikea.html; http://www.sustainability.com/news/press-room/JE-teflon-shield-Mar01.asp?popup=1; http://www.benefitnews.com/retire/detail.cfm?id=345.

End Notes

1. T. J. Peters and R. H. Waterman, *In Search of Excellence* (New York: Harper & Row, 1982).
2. R. T. Hogan and J. Hogan, *Manual for the Hogan Personality Inventory* (Tulsa, OK: Hogan Assessment Systems, 1992).
3. G. Yukl, *Leadership in Organizations*, 2nd ed. (Englewood Cliffs, NJ: Prentice Hall, 1989).
4. A. J. Murphy, "A Study of the Leadership Process," *American Sociological Review* 6 (1941), pp. 674–87.
5. H. S. Person, "Leadership as a Response to Environment," *Educational Record Supplement*, no. 6 (1928), pp. 9–21.
6. G. Spiller, "The Dynamics of Greatness," *Sociological Review* 21 (1929), pp. 218-32.
7. J. Schneider, "The Cultural Situation as a Condition for the Condition of Fame," *American Sociology Review* 2 (1937), pp. 480–91.
8. Person, "Leadership as a Response to Environment."
9. B. M. Bass, *Bass and Stogdill's Handbook of Leadership*, 3rd ed. (New York: Free Press, 1990).
10. R. K. Merton, *Social Theory and Social Structure* (New York: Free Press, 1957).
11. J. Pfeffer and G. R. Salancik, "Determinants of Supervisory Behavior: A Role Set Analysis," *Human Relations* 28 (1975), pp. 139–54.
12. A. Tsui, "A Role Set Analysis of Managerial Reputation," *Organizational Behavior and Human Performance* 34 (1984), pp. 64–96.

13. J. G. Hunt and R. N. Osborn, "Toward a Macro-Oriented Model of Leadership: An Odyssey," in *Leadership: Beyond Establishment Views*, eds. J. G. Hunt, U. Sekaran, and C. A. Schriesheim (Carbondale: Southern Illinois University Press, 1982), pp. 196–221.

14. P. Hersey and K. H. Blanchard, *Management of Organizational Behavior: Utilizing Human Resources*, 3rd ed. (Englewood Cliffs, NJ: Prentice Hall, 1977).

15. P. Hersey and K. H. Blanchard, *Management of Organizational Behavior: Utilizing Human Resources*, 4th ed. (Englewood Cliffs, NJ: Prentice Hall, 1984).

16. J. R. Hackman and G. R. Oldham, *Work Redesign* (Reading, MA: Addison-Wesley, 1980).

17. R. J. House and G. Dressler, "The Path-Goal Theory of Leadership: Some Post Hoc and A Priori Tests," in *Contingency Approaches to Leadership*, eds. J. G. Hunt and L. L. Larson (Carbondale: Southern Illinois University Press, 1974).

18. J. P. Howell and P. W. Dorfman, "Substitute for Leadership: Test of a Construct," *Academy of Management Journal* 24 (1981), pp. 714–28.

19. S. Kerr and J. M. Jermier, "Substitutes for Leadership: Their Meaning and Measurement," *Organizational Behavior and Human Performance* 22 (1978), pp. 375–403.

20. I. B. Myers and B. H. McCaulley, *Manual: A Guide to the Development and Use of the Myers-Briggs Type Indicator* (Palo Alto, CA: Consulting Psychologists Press, 1985).

21. Bass, *Bass and Stogdill's Handbook of*.

22. J. D. Ford, "Department Context and Formal Structure as Constraints on Leader Behavior," *Academy of Management Journal* 24 (1981), pp. 274–88.

23. Yukl, *Leadership in Organizations*.

24. M. Siegall and L. L. Cummings, "Task Role Ambiguity, Satisfaction, and the Moderating Effect of Task Instruction Source," *Human Relations* 39 (1986), pp. 1017–32.

25. J. Galbraith, *Designing Complex Organizations* (Menlo Park, CA: Addison-Wesley, 1973).

26. L. Fry, W. Kerr, and C. Lee, "Effects of Different Leader Behaviors under Different Levels of Task Interdependence," *Human Relations* 39 (1986), pp. 1067–82.

27. R. A. Heifetz, *Leadership without Easy Answer* (Cambridge, MA: Belknap, 1998).

28. R. A. Heifetz and M. Linsky, *Leadership on the Line: Staying Alive through the Dangers of Leading* (Boston: Harvard Business School Press, 2002).

29. A. D. Chandler, *Scale and Scope: The Dynamics of Industrial Capitalism* (Cambridge: Harvard University Press, 1990).

30. R. S. Kaplan and D. P. Norton, *The Balanced Scorecard: Translating Strategy into Action* (Boston: Harvard Business School Press, 1996).

31. F. Luthans, S. A. Rosenkrantz, and H. W. Hennessey, "What Do Successful Managers Really Do? An Observational Study of Managerial Activities," *Journal of Applied Behavioral Science* 21 (1985), pp. 255–70.

32. R. C. Page and W. W. Tornow, "Managerial Job Analysis: Are We Any Further Along?" paper presented at a meeting of the Society of Industrial Organizational Psychology, Atlanta, GA, 1987.

33. G. Chitayat and I. Venezia, "Determinates of Management Styles in Business and Nonbusiness Organizations," *Journal of Applied Psychology* 69 (1984), pp. 437–47.

34. L. B. Kurke and H. E. Aldrich, "Mintzberg Was Right! A Replication and Extension of the Nature of Managerial Work," *Management Science* 29 (1983), pp. 975–84.

35. A. M. Morrison, R. P. White, and E. Van Velsor, *Breaking the Glass Ceiling* (Reading, MA: Addison-Wesley, 1987). Morse, G. "Why We Misread Motives," *Harvard Business Review,* January 2003, p. 18.

36. S. P. Robbins, *Organizational Behavior: Concepts, Controversies, and Applications* (Englewood Cliffs, NJ: Prentice Hall, 1986).

37. P. M. Podsakoff, "Determinants of a Supervisor's Use of Rewards and Punishments: A Literature Review and Suggestions for Future Research," *Organizational Behavior and Human Performance* 29 (1982), pp. 58–83.

38. T. H. Hammer and J. Turk, "Organizational Determinants of Leader Behavior and Authority," *Journal of Applied Psychology* 71 (1987), pp. 674–82.

39. Bass, *Bass and Stogdill's Handbook of Leadership.*

40. E. H. Schein, *Organizational Culture and Leadership: A Dynamic View* (San Francisco: Jossey-Bass, 1985).

41. Bass, *Bass and Stogdill's Handbook of Leadership.*

42. S. W. J. Kozlowski and M. L. Doherty, "Integration of Climate and Leadership: Examination of a Neglected Issue," *Journal of Applied Psychology* 74 (1989), pp. 546–53.

43. B. Schneider, P. J. Hanges, D. B. Smith, and A. N. Salvaggio, " Which Comes First: Employee Attitudes or Organizational Financial and Market Performance?" *Journal of Applied Psychology* 88, no. 5 (2003), pp. 836–51. J. Schneider, "The Cultural Situation as a Condition for the Condition of Fame," *American Sociology Review* 2 (1937), pp. 480–91.

44. Bass, *Bass and Stogdill's Handbook of.*

45. Kozlowski and Doherty, "Integration of Climate and Leadership".

46. Bass, *Bass and Stogdill's Handbook of Leadership.*

47. R. H. Kilmann and M. J. Saxton, *Organizational Cultures: Their Assessment and Change* (San Francisco: Jossey-Bass, 1983).

48. Schein, *Organizational Culture and Leadership.*

49. B. Dumaine, "Creating a New Company Culture," *Fortune,* 1990, pp. 127–131.

50. B. M. Bass, *Leadership and Performance beyond Expectations* (New York: Free Press, 1985).

51. J. M. Kouzes and B. Z. Posner, *The Leadership Challenge: How to Get Extraordinary Things Done in Organizations* (San Francisco: Jossey-Bass, 1987).

52. Schein, *Organizational Culture and Leadership.*

522 Part Four *Focus on the Situation*

53. N. M. Tichy and M. A. Devanna, *The Transformational Leader* (New York: John Wiley, 1986).

54. F. E. Emery and E. L. Trist, "The Causal Texture of Organizational Environments," *Human Relations* 18 (1965), pp. 21–32.

55. C. S. Cameron and R. E. Quinn, *Diagnosing and Changing Organizational Culture* (Reading, MA: Addison-Wesley, 1999).

56. Ibid.

57. Ibid.

58. Ibid.

59. Ibid.

60. M. Lind, "The Boring Age," *Time,* March 22, 2010, pp. 58–59.

61. R. Heifetz, A. Grashow, and M. Linsky, "Leadership in a (Permanent) Crisis," *Harvard Business Review,* July–August 2009, pp. 62–69.

62. T. Friedman, *The World Is Flat: A Brief History of the Twenty-First Century* (New York: Farrar, Straus and Giroux, 2005).

63. T. Ricks, *The Gamble* (New York: The Penguin Press, 2009).

64. R. Heifetz, "An Interview with Ronald A. Heifetz: Interview by James Nelson," http://www.managementfirst.com/management_styles/interviews/heifetz.htm, accessed June 5, 2006.

65. Ibid.

66. M. Gladwell, *Outliers* (New York: Little, Brown and Company, 2005).

67. U. D. Jogulu and G. J. Wood, "A Cross-Cultural Study into Peer Evaluations of Women's Leadership Effectiveness," *Leadership & Organization Development Journal* 29, no. 7 (2008), pp. 606–16.

68. M. Javidan and R. J. House, "Cultural Acumen for the Global Manager: Lessons from Project GLOBE," *Organizational Dynamics* 29 (2001), pp. 289-305.

69. L. R. Kohls, *Survival Kit for Overseas Living* (Boston: Intercultural Press, 2001).

70. D. F. Barnum, "Effective Membership in the Global Business Community," in *New Traditions in Business,* ed. J. Renesch (San Francisco: Berrett-Koehler, 1992), p. 153.

71. R. House, P. Hanges, M. Javidan, P. Dorfman, and V. Gupta (ed.), *Culture, Leadership and Organizations: The GLOBE Study of 62 Societies* (Thousand Oaks, CA: Sage, 2004).

72. J. S. Chhokar, F. C. Brodbeck, and R. J. House (eds.), *Culture and Leadership around the World: The GLOBE Book of In-Depth Studies of 25 Societies* (Mahwah, NJ: Lawrence Erlbaum, 2007).

73. G. Hofstede, *Cultural Consequences: Comparing Values, Behaviors, Institutions and Organizations across Nations,* 2nd ed. (Thousand Oaks, CA: Sage Publications, 2001).

74. J. S. Chhokar, F. C. Brodbeck, and R. J. House, "Introduction," in *Culture and Leadership around the World: The GLOBE Book of In-Depth Studies of 25 Societies,* eds. J. S. Chhokar, F. C. Brodbeck, and R. J. House (Mahwah, NJ: Lawrence Erlbaum, 2007), pp. 1–6.

75. P. W. Dorfman, P. J. Hanges, and F. C. Brodbeck, "Leadership and Cultural Variation: The Identification of Culturally Endorsed Leadership Profiles," in *Culture, Leadership and Organizations: The GLOBE Study of 62 Societies*, eds. R. House, P. Hanges, M. Javidan, P. Dorfman, and V. Gupta (Thousand Oaks, CA: Sage, 2004), pp. 669–719.

76. Ibid.

77. R. House, House, R. J., Hanges, P. J., Ruiz-Quintanilla, S. A., Dorfman, P. W., Javidan, M. and Dickson, M. W. *Cultural Influences on Leadership and Organizations: Project Globe. Advances in Global Leadership*, vol. 1 (JAI Press, 1999), pp. 171–233.

Chapter

13

Contingency Theories of Leadership

Introduction

If we were to provide an extremely short summary of the book to this point, we would say leadership is a process that involves aspects of the leader, the followers, and the situation. In Part 1 we discussed the process aspects, while Part 2 was devoted to the leader. Part 3 focused on the followers, and in the previous chapter we discussed the situational components of leadership. You may have also noted that while we attempted to focus exclusively on the component of interest for each section, there were often overlapping areas in our leader–follower–situation (L-F-S) model. The overlap is true, and our attempts to segregate the concepts were done merely for simplicity. The world of leadership is a complex one where multiple aspects of the L-F-S model come into play. Leadership is contingent on the interplay of all three aspects of our model, and these contingencies are the focus of this chapter.

This chapter reviews five well-known contingency theories of leadership. The first, leader–member exchange (LMX) theory, focuses on the contingencies and interactions between the leader and the followers. The remaining four theories address certain aspects of the leader, the followers, and the situation. These theories also share several other similarities. First, because they are theories rather than someone's personal opinions, these models have been the focus of a considerable amount of empirical research over the years. Second, these theories implicitly assume that leaders are able to accurately diagnose or assess key aspects of the followers or the leadership situation. Third, with the exception of Fiedler's contingency model,[1,2] leaders are assumed to be able to act in a flexible manner. In other words, leaders can and should change their behaviors as situational and follower characteristics change. Fourth, a correct match between situational and follower characteristics and leaders' behaviors is

It is a capital mistake to theorize before one has data.

Sir Arthur Conan Doyle

assumed to have a positive effect on group or organizational outcomes. Thus these theories maintain that leadership effectiveness is maximized when leaders correctly make their behaviors *contingent* on certain situational and follower characteristics. Because of these similarities,[3] Chemers argued that these contingency theories are more similar than different. He said they differ primarily in terms of the types of situational and follower characteristics upon which various leader behaviors should be contingent.

Leader–Member Exchange (LMX) Theory

In Chapter 1 we first noted a contingency when we mentioned the "in-group" and "out-group" interactions between leaders and followers. These relationships were originally described as vertical dyad linkages[4] but have developed over time into what is most often referred to today as **leader–member exchanges** (LMX). The main premise of these theories has remained unchanged, however. Fundamentally, LMX argues that leaders do not treat all followers as if they were a uniform group of equals. Rather, the leader forms specific and unique linkages with each subordinate, thus creating a series of dyadic relationships. In general, as just noted, the linkages tend to be differentiated into two major groups.

In the out-group, or low-quality exchange relationships, interpersonal interaction is largely restricted to fulfilling contractual obligations.[5] With other subordinates (the in-group), leaders form high-quality exchange relationships that go well beyond "just what the job requires." These high-quality relationships are indeed "exchanges" because both parties benefit. In exchange for higher levels of task performance[6] from subordinates, leaders may contribute empowerment,[7] sponsorship of subordinates in social networks,[8] and mentoring.[9]

There has been considerable evolution in leader–member exchange research and thinking in the last 20 years. Early on, the focus was on stages of development as the process of the relationship developed over time. These stages typically were described as follows:

1. **Role-taking** happens early in a follower's work experience. Here the leader offers opportunities and evaluates the follower's performance and potential.
2. **Role-making** is the next phase where a role is created based on a process of trust building. This is a fragile stage, and any perceived betrayals can lead to the follower being dropped from the developing in-group and assigned to the out-group.
3. **Routinization** occurs as the relationship becomes well established. It is in this phase that similarities (for the in-group) and differences (often accentuated for the out-group) become cemented.

TABLE 13.1
The Cycle of Leadership Making

Source: Adapted from G. B. Graen and M. Uhl-Bien, "Relationship-Based Approach to Leadership: Development of Leader–Member Exchange (LMX) Theory over 25 Years: Applying a Multi-Level Multi-Domain Perspective," *Leadership Quarterly* 6 (1995), pp. 219–47.

TIME			
Characteristic	**Stranger**	**Acquaintance**	**Maturity**
Relationship building phase	Role-taking	Role-making	Role routinization
Reciprocity	Cash and carry	Mixed	In-kind
Time span of reciprocity	Immediate	Some delay	Indefinite
Leader–member exchange	Low	Medium	High
Incremental influence	None	Limited	Almost unlimited

Perhaps the biggest leap forward in LMX came 25 years after its introduction, in an article by Graen and Uhl-Bien.[10] In this publication, the authors expanded the descriptive portion of the model, which continued to focus on the dyadic processes between the leader and followers. However, the model also changed from merely describing the process to proposing a prescriptive process that would enhance organizational effectiveness. Most of us can identify with the descriptive components of LMX portion by thinking back to coaches or teachers from our past that had in-groups and out-groups. Now the model suggests behaviors that the leader should engage in to actively develop relationships (hence the prescriptive label) and build more in-group relations across the follower pool. This process of leadership is outlined in Table 13.1.

The LMX leadership making process moves from left to right in the table as indicated by the time arrow. Perhaps most important in the prescriptive notion of the model is the focus on the leader's responsibility to enhance overall organizational effectiveness by developing more in-groups and reducing the number of out-groups. In summary, the leadership making process prescribes that the leader should work to develop special relationships with *all* followers, should offer each follower an opportunity for new roles, responsibilities, and challenges, should nurture high-quality exchanges with all followers, and should focus on ways to build trust and respect with all subordinates—resulting in the entire work group becoming an in-group rather than accentuating the differences between in-groups and out-groups.

Concluding Thoughts about the LMX Model

In its earlier form (the vertical dyad linkage model), LMX was one of the simplest of the contingency models. Looking at our leader–follower–situation model, it is easy to see that LMX, even today, is largely about the process of relationship building between the leader and the follower. The situation has barely crept in, and only if we consider the desire to increase organizational effectiveness by maximizing the number of in-groups the leader might develop. From an application perspective, perhaps the biggest limitation of LMX is that it does not describe the specific behaviors that lead to high-quality relationship exchanges between the leader and the follower. Nonetheless, LMX, as opposed to some of the subsequent contingency models, continues to generate research into the present decade.[11,12]

In fact, of all the contingency models presented here, we see more research articles related to LMX than to any of the other theories. The research addresses topics related to LMX including follower proactive personality,[13] the extent of the leader's social network,[14] the degree to which employees identify their supervisor with the organization,[15] employees' perceptions of both the procedural and distributive justice climate,[16] and the degree that followers perceive that the leaders treat all members fairly (not necessarily "equally") and that the leaders represent the group's values and norms.[17] On a broader level, LMX is being studied both across various countries[18] and with globally distributed teams.[19]

The Normative Decision Model

Obviously in some situations leaders can delegate decisions to subordinates or should ask subordinates for relevant information before making a decision. In other situations, such as emergencies or crises, leaders may need to make a decision with little, if any, input from subordinates. The level of input that subordinates have in the decision-making process varies substantially depending on the issue at hand, followers' level of technical expertise, or the presence or absence of a crisis. Although the level of participation changes due to various leader, follower, and situational factors,[20] Vroom and Yetton maintained that leaders can often improve group performance by using an optimal amount of participation in the decision-making process. Thus the normative decision model is directed solely at determining how much input subordinates should have in the decision-making process. Precisely because the normative decision model is limited only to decision making and is not a grand, all-encompassing theory, it is a good model to examine next.

Levels of Participation

Like the other theories in this chapter, the **normative decision model**[21] was designed to improve some aspects of leadership effectiveness. In this case Vroom and Yetton explored how various leader, follower, and situational factors affect the degree of subordinates' participation in the decision-making process and, in turn, group performance. To determine which situational and follower factors affect the level of participation and group performance, Vroom and Yetton first investigated the decision-making processes leaders use in group settings. They discovered a continuum of

Levels of Participation in the Normative Decision Model

HIGHLIGHT 13.1

Autocratic Processes

AI: The leader solves the problem or makes the decision by himself or herself using the information available at the time.

AII: The leader obtains any necessary information from followers, then decides on a solution to the problem herself. She may or may not tell followers the purpose of her questions or give information about the problem or decision she is working on. The input provided by them is clearly in response to her request for specific information. They do not play a role in the definition of the problem or in generating or evaluating alternative solutions.

Consultative Processes

CI: The leader shares the problem with the relevant followers individually, getting their ideas and suggestions without bringing them together as a group. Then he makes a decision. This decision may or may not reflect the followers' influence.

CII: The leader shares the problem with her followers in a group meeting. In this meeting, she obtains their ideas and suggestions. Then she makes the decision, which may or may not reflect the followers' influence.

Group Process

GII: The leader shares the problem with his followers as a group. Together they generate and evaluate alternatives and attempt to reach agreement (consensus) on a solution. The leader's role is much like that of a chairman, coordinating the discussion, keeping it focused on the problem, and making sure the critical issues are discussed. He can provide the group with information or ideas that he has, but he does not try to press them to adopt "his" solution. Moreover, leaders adopting this level of participation are willing to accept and implement any solution that has the support of the entire group.

Source: Adapted from V. H. Vroom and P. W. Yetton, *Leadership and Decision Making* (Pittsburgh, PA: University of Pittsburgh Press, 1973).

decision-making processes ranging from completely autocratic (labeled "AI") to completely democratic, where all members of the group have equal participation (labeled "GII"). These processes are listed in Highlight 13.1.

Decision Quality and Acceptance

After establishing a continuum of decision processes, Vroom and Yetton[22] established criteria to evaluate the adequacy of the decisions made—criteria they believed would be credible to leaders and equally applicable across the five levels of participation. Although a wide variety of criteria could be used, Vroom and Yetton believed decision quality and decision acceptance were the two most important criteria for judging the adequacy of a decision.

Decision quality means simply that if the decision has a rational or objectively determinable "better or worse" alternative, the leader should select the better alternative. Vroom and Yetton[23] intended quality in their model to apply when the decision could result in an objectively or measurably better outcome for the group or organization. In the for-profit sector, this criterion can be assessed in several ways, but perhaps the easiest to understand is, "Would the decision show up on the balance sheet?" In this case, a high-quality (or, conversely, low-quality) decision would have a direct and measurable impact on the organization's bottom line. In the public sector, we might determine if there was a quality component to a decision by asking, "Will one alternative have a greater cost saving than the other?" or "Does this decision improve services to the client?" Although it may seem that leaders should always choose the alternative with the highest decision quality, this is not always the case. Often leaders have equally good (or bad) alternatives. At other times, the issue in question is trivial, rendering the quality of the decision relatively unimportant.

Decision acceptance implies that followers accept the decision as if it were their own and do not merely comply with the decision. Acceptance of the decision outcome by the followers may be critical, particularly if the followers will bear principal responsibility for implementing the decision. With such acceptance, there will be no need for superiors to monitor compliance, which can be a continuing and time-consuming activity (and virtually impossible in some circumstances, such as with a geographically dispersed sales staff).

As with quality, acceptance of a decision is not always critical for implementation. For example, most organizations have an accounting form that employees use to obtain reimbursement for travel expenses. Suppose a company's chief financial officer (CFO) has decided to change the format of the form for reimbursing travel expenses and has had the new forms printed and distributed throughout the company. Further, she has sent out a notice that, effective June 1, the old forms will no longer be accepted for reimbursement—only claims made using the new forms will be processed and paid. Assuming the new form has no gross errors, problems, or omissions, our CFO really has no concern with acceptance as defined here. If people want to be reimbursed for their travel expenses, they will use the new form. This decision, in essence, implements itself.

On the other hand, leaders sometimes assume that they do not need to worry about acceptance because they have so much power over their followers that overt rejection of a decision is not likely to occur. A corporate CEO is not apt to see a junior accountant stand up and openly challenge the CEO's decision to implement a new policy, even though the young accountant may not buy into the new policy at all. Because followers generally do not openly object to the decisions made by leaders with this much power, these leaders often mistakenly assume that their decisions have been accepted and will be fully implemented. This is a naive view of what really goes on in organizations. Just because the junior subordinate does not publicly voice his opposition does not mean he will rush to wholeheartedly implement the decision. In fact, the junior accountant has a lot more time to destructively undermine the policy than the CEO does to ensure that it is being carried out to the letter.

The Decision Tree

Having settled on quality and acceptance as the two principal criteria for effective decisions, Vroom and Yetton then developed a normative decision model. (A normative model is based on what ought to happen rather than

530 Part Four *Focus on the Situation*

FIGURE 13.1
Vroom and Yetton's Leadership Decision Tree

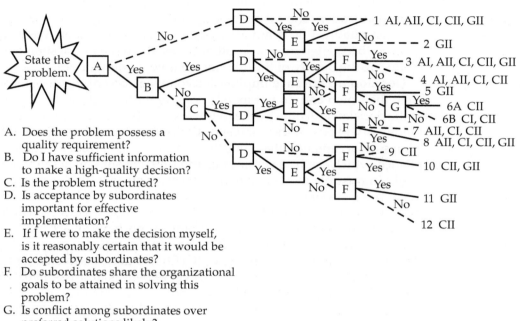

A. Does the problem possess a
   quality requirement?
B. Do I have sufficient information
   to make a high-quality decision?
C. Is the problem structured?
D. Is acceptance by subordinates
   important for effective
   implementation?
E. If I were to make the decision myself,
   is it reasonably certain that it would be
   accepted by subordinates?
F. Do subordinates share the organizational
   goals to be attained in solving this
   problem?
G. Is conflict among subordinates over
   preferred solutions likely?

Source: Reprinted from V. H. Vroom and P. W. Yetton, *Leadership and Decision Making*, by permission of the University of Pittsburgh Press, © 1973 University of Pittsburgh Press.

describing what does happen.) They also developed a set of questions to protect quality and acceptance by eliminating decision processes that would be wrong or inappropriate. Generally, these questions concern the problem itself, the amount of pertinent information possessed by the leader and followers, and various situational factors.

To make it easier for leaders to determine how much participation subordinates should have to optimize decision quality and acceptance, Vroom and Yetton[24] incorporated these questions into a decision tree (see Figure 13.1). To use the decision tree, we start at the left by stating the problem and then proceed through the model from left to right. Every time a box is encountered, the question associated with that box must be answered with either a yes or a no response. Eventually all paths lead to a set of decision processes that, if used, will lead to a decision that protects both quality and acceptance.

Having reached a set of feasible alternatives that meet the desirable criteria for quality and acceptance among followers, the leader may then wish to consider additional criteria. One practical consideration is the amount of time available (see Highlight 13.2). If time is critical, the leader should select the alternative in the feasible set that is farthest to the *left*, again noting that the feasible set is arranged from AI through GII. It

How Much Time Do I Have?

HIGHLIGHT 13.2

In a world of instant messages that require lightning-fast responses, Steven B. Sample, president of the University of Southern California, is touting the benefits of "artful procrastination." In his course on leadership and his book *The Contrarian's Guide to Leadership,* a key lesson is never make a decision today that can reasonably be put off to tomorrow:

> With respect to timing, almost all great leaders have understood that making quick decisions is typically counterproductive. I'm not talking about what to have for breakfast or what tie to wear today. President Harry Truman almost personified this concept. When anyone told him they needed a decision, the first thing he would ask is "How much time do I have—a week, 10 seconds, six months?" What he understood was that the nature of the

decision that a leader makes depends to a large extent on how much time he has in which to make it. He also understood that delaying a decision as long as reasonably possible generally leads to the best decisions being made.

Other lessons from Sample include these:

- Think gray. Don't form opinions if you don't have to.
- Think free. Move several steps beyond traditional brainstorming.
- Listen first, talk later. And when you listen, do so artfully.
- You can't copy your way to the top.

Sources: http://www.usc.edu/president/book/; http://www.refresher.com/!enescontrarian.html; http://bottomlinesecrets.com/blpnet/article.html?article_id=33302.

generally takes less time to make and implement autocratic decisions than it does to make consultative or group decisions. Nevertheless, the first step is to protect quality and acceptance (by using the model). Only *after* arriving at an appropriate set of outcomes should leaders consider time in the decision-making process. This tenet is sometimes neglected in the workplace by leaders who overemphasize time as a criterion. Obviously there are some situations where time is absolutely critical, as in life-or-death emergencies. Certainly no one would have expected U.S. Airways Captain Chesley "Sully" Sullenberger to pull out his Vroom-Yetton decision model after his Airbus A320 struck a flock of geese and he found himself plummeting toward the Hudson River in what had become a very large glider. But too often leaders ask for a decision to be made as if the situation were an emergency when, in reality, they (the leaders, not the situation) are creating the time pressure. Despite such behavior, it is difficult to imagine a leader who would knowingly prefer a fast decision that lacks both quality and acceptance among the implementers to one that is of high quality and acceptable to followers but that takes more time.

Another important consideration is follower development. Again, after quality and acceptance have been considered using the decision tree, and if the leader has determined that time is not a critical element, she may wish to follow a decision process more apt to allow followers to develop their own decision-making skills. This can be achieved by using the decision tree and

532 Part Four *Focus on the Situation*

then selecting the alternative within the feasible set that is farthest to the *right*. The arrangement of processes from AI to GII provides an increasing amount of follower development by moving from autocratic to group decisions.

Finally, if neither time nor follower development is a concern and multiple options are available in the feasible set of alternatives, the leader may select a style that best meets his or her needs. This may be the process with which the leader is most comfortable ("I'm a CII kind of guy"), or it may be a process in which he or she would like to develop more skill.

Concluding Thoughts about the Normative Decision Model

Having looked at this model in some detail, we will now look at it from the perspective of the leader–follower–situation (L-F-S) framework. To do this, we have used the different decision processes and the questions from the decision tree to illustrate different components in the L-F-S framework (see Figure 13.2). Several issues become apparent in this depiction. First,

FIGURE 13.2
Factors from the Normative Decision Model and the Interactional Framework

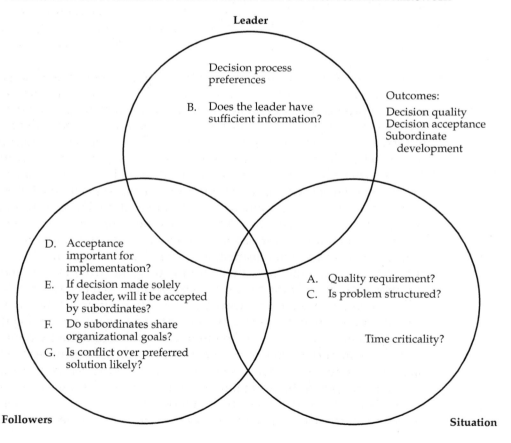

for ease of presentation we have placed each question or factor solely within one circle or another. Nevertheless, we could argue that some of the questions could or should be placed in another part of the model. For example, the question "Do I have sufficient information to make a high-quality decision?" is placed in the leader block. It might be argued, however, that no leader could answer this question without some knowledge of the situation. Strictly speaking, therefore, perhaps this question should be placed in the intersection between the leader and the situation. Nonetheless, in keeping with our theme that leadership involves interactions among all three elements, it seems sufficient at this point to illustrate them in their simplest state.

A second issue also becomes apparent when the normative decision model is viewed through the L-F-S framework. Notice how the Vroom and Yetton[25] model shifts focus away from the leader toward both the situation and, to an even greater degree, the followers. There are no questions about the leader's personality, motivations, values, or attitudes. In fact, the leader's preference is considered only after higher-priority factors have been considered. The only underlying assumption is that the leader is interested in implementing a high-quality decision (when quality is an issue) that is acceptable to followers (when acceptance is critical to implementation). Given that assumption and a willingness to consider aspects of the situation and aspects of the followers, the leader's behavior can be channeled into more effective decision-making processes.

A third issue is that the L-F-S framework organizes concepts in a familiar conceptual structure. This is an advantage even for a theory with as limited a focus as the normative decision model (that is, decision making); it will be even more helpful later as we consider more complex theories.

Finally, because the normative decision model is a *leadership theory* rather than Vroom and Yetton's personal opinions, a number of empirical studies have investigated the model's efficacy. Research conducted by Field[26] and Vroom and Jago[27,28] provided strong support for the model; these studies showed that leaders were much more likely to make effective or successful decisions when they followed its tenets than when they ignored them. Nevertheless, although leaders may be more apt to make effective decisions when using the model, there is no evidence to show that these leaders are more effective overall than leaders not using the model.[29] The latter findings again point out that both the leadership process and leadership effectiveness are complex phenomena; being a good decision maker is not enough to be a good leader (although it certainly helps). Other problems with the model are that it views decision making as taking place at a single point in time,[30] assumes that leaders are equally skilled at using all five decision procedures,[31] and assumes that some of the prescriptions of the model may not be the best for a given situation. For example, the normative decision model prescribes that leaders use a GII decision process if conflict may occur over a decision, but leaders may be more effective if they instead make an AI decision and avoid intra-group conflict.[32] Despite these problems, the normative model is one of the best supported of the five major contingency theories of leadership, and leaders would be wise to consider using the model when making decisions. Vroom has also converted the decision tree depicted on page 530 to an expert system entitled Decision Making for Leaders that can be used interactively on laptop computers. This advance allows more input into the aspects of the decision variables by the leader.

The Situational Leadership® Model

It seems fairly obvious that leaders do not interact with all followers in the same manner. For example, a leader may give general guidelines or goals to her highly competent and motivated followers but spend considerable time coaching, directing, and training her unskilled and unmotivated followers. Or leaders may provide relatively little praise and assurances to followers with high self-confidence but high amounts of support to followers with low self-confidence. Although leaders often have different interactional styles when dealing with individual followers, is there an optimum way for leaders to adjust their behavior with different followers and thereby increase their likelihood of success? And if there is, what factors should the leader base his behavior on—the follower's intelligence? Personality traits? Values? Preferences? Technical competence? A model called **Situational Leadership**® offers answers to these two important leadership questions.

Leader Behaviors

The Situational Leadership® model has evolved over time. Its essential elements first appeared in 1969,[33] with roots in the Ohio State studies, in which the two broad categories of leader behaviors, initiating structure and consideration, were initially identified (see Chapter 7). As Situational Leadership® evolved, so did the labels (but not the content) for the two leadership behavior categories. Initiating structure changed to **task behaviors,** which were defined as the extent to which a leader spells out the responsibilities of an individual or group. Task behaviors include telling people what to do, how to do it, when to do it, and who is to do it. Similarly, consideration changed to **relationship behaviors,** or how much the leader engages in two-way communication. Relationship behaviors include listening, encouraging, facilitating, clarifying, explaining why a task is important, and giving support.

When the behavior of actual leaders was studied, there was little evidence to show these two categories of leader behavior were consistently related to leadership success; the relative effectiveness of these two behavior dimensions often depended on the situation. Hersey's Situational Leadership® model explains why leadership effectiveness varies across these two behavior dimensions and situations. It arrays the two

FIGURE 13.3
**Situational
Leadership®**

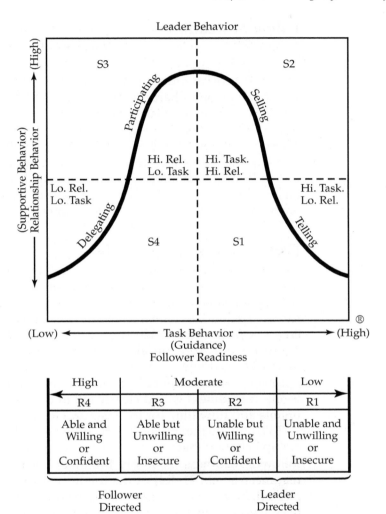

orthogonal dimensions as in the Ohio State studies and then divides each of them into high and low segments (see Figure 13.3). According to the model, depicting the two leadership dimensions this way is useful because certain combinations of task and relationship behaviors may be more effective in some situations than in others.

For example, in some situations high levels of task but low levels of relationship behaviors are effective; in other situations, just the opposite is true. So far, however, we have not considered the key follower or situational characteristics with which these combinations of task and relationship behaviors are most effective. Hersey says these four combinations of task and relationship behaviors would increase leadership effectiveness if they were made contingent on the readiness level of the individual follower to perform a given task.

Follower Readiness

In Situational Leadership®, **follower readiness** refers to a follower's ability and willingness to accomplish a particular task. Readiness is not an assessment of an individual's personality, traits, values, age, and so on. It's not a personal characteristic, but rather how ready an individual is to perform a particular task. Any given follower could be low on readiness to perform one task but high on readiness to perform a different task. An experienced emergency room physician would be high in readiness on tasks like assessing a patient's medical status, but could be relatively low on readiness for facilitating an interdepartmental team meeting to solve an ambiguous and complex problem like developing hospital practices to encourage collaboration across departments.

Prescriptions of the Model

Now that the key contingency factor, follower readiness, has been identified, let us move on to another aspect of the figure—combining follower readiness levels with the four combinations of leader behaviors described earlier. The horizontal bar in Figure 13.3 depicts follower readiness as increasing from right to left (not in the direction we are used to seeing). There are four segments along this continuum, ranging from R1 (the lowest) to R4 (the highest). Along this continuum, however, the assessment of follower readiness can be fairly subjective. A follower who possesses high levels of readiness would clearly fall in the R4 category, just as a follower unable and unwilling (or too insecure) to perform a task would fall in R1.

To complete the model, a curved line is added that represents the leadership behavior that will most likely be effective given a particular level of follower readiness. To apply the model, leaders should first assess the readiness level (R1–R4) of the follower relative to the task to be accomplished. Next a vertical line should be drawn from the center of the readiness level up to the point where it intersects with the curved line in Figure 13.3. The quadrant in which this intersection occurs represents the level of task and relationship behavior that has the best chance of producing successful outcomes. For example, imagine you are a fire chief and have under your command a search-and-rescue team. One of the team members is needed to rescue a backpacker who has fallen in the mountains, and you have selected a particular follower to accomplish the task. What leadership behavior should you exhibit? If this follower has both substantial training and experience in this type of rescue, you would assess his readiness level as R4. A vertical line from R4 would intersect the curved line in the quadrant where both low task and low relationship behaviors by the leader are most apt to be successful. As the leader, you should exhibit a low level of task and relationship behaviors and delegate this task to the follower. On the other hand, you may have a brand-new member of the fire department who still has to learn the ins and outs of firefighting.

A Developmental Intervention Using SLT

HIGHLIGHT 13.3

Dianne is a resident assistant in charge of a number of students in a university dorm. One particular sophomore, Michael, has volunteered to work on projects in the past but never seems to take the initiative to get started on his own. Michael seems to wait until Dianne gives him explicit direction, approval, and encouragement before he will get started. Michael can do a good job, but he seems to be unwilling to start without some convincing that it is all right, and unless Dianne makes explicit what steps are to be taken. Dianne has assessed Michael's readiness level as R2, but she would like to see him develop, both in task readiness and in psychological maturity. The behavior most likely to fit Michael's current readiness level is selling, or high task, high relationship. But Dianne has decided to implement a developmental intervention to help Michael raise his readiness level. Dianne can be most helpful in this intervention by moving up one level to participating, or low task, high relationship. By reducing the amount of task instructions and direction while encouraging Michael to lay out a plan on his own and supporting his steps in the right direction, Dianne is most apt to help Michael become an R3 follower. This does not mean the work will get done most efficiently, however. As we saw in the Vroom and Yetton model earlier, if part of the leader's job is development of followers, then time may be a reasonable and necessary trade-off for short-term efficiency.

Because this particular follower has low task readiness (R1), the model maintains that the leader should use a high level of task and a low level of relationship behaviors when initially dealing with this follower.

Hersey suggests one further step leaders may wish to consider. The model just described helps the leader select the most appropriate behavior given the current level of follower readiness. However, there may be cases when the leader would like to see followers increase their level of readiness for particular tasks by implementing a series of **developmental interventions** to help boost follower readiness levels. The process would begin by first assessing a follower's current level of readiness and then determining the leader behavior that best suits that follower in that task. Instead of using the behavior prescribed by the model, however, the leader would select the next higher leadership behavior. Another way of thinking about this would be for the leader to select the behavior pattern that would fit the follower if that follower were one level higher in readiness. This intervention is designed to help followers in their development, hence its name (see Highlight 13.3).

Concluding Thoughts about the Situational Leadership® Model

In Figure 13.4 we can see how the factors in Situational Leadership® fit within the L-F-S framework. In comparison to the Vroom and Yetton model, there are fewer factors to consider in each of the three elements. The only situational consideration is knowledge of the task, and the only

FIGURE 13.4
Factors from the Situational Leadership® Model and the Interactional Framework

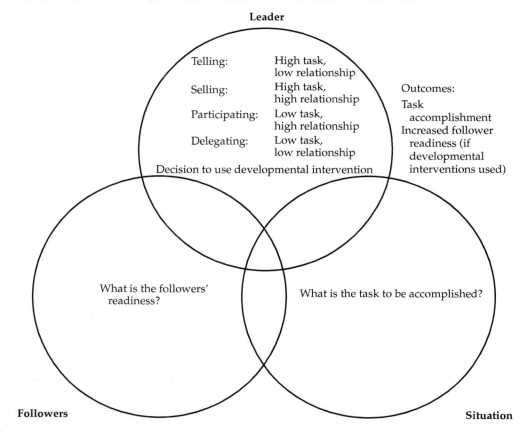

follower factor is readiness. On the other hand, the theory goes well beyond decision making, which was the sole domain of the normative decision model.

Situational Leadership® is usually appealing to students and practitioners because of its commonsense approach as well as the ease of understanding it. Unfortunately there is little published research to support the predictions of Situational Leadership® in the workplace.[34,35] A great deal of research has been done within organizations that have implemented Situational Leadership®, but most of those findings are not available for public dissemination.

In 2007 Blanchard modified the Situational Leadership® prescriptions to specify more clearly the four definitions of follower developmental level and their four corresponding optimal styles of leadership.[36] Although this revision of the model, perhaps as a result of much criticism concerning the lack of prescriptive specificity, does create a more discrete typology of follower styles, recent research suggests that the original model is a better predictor of subordinate performance and attitudes than the revised version.[37]

Nevertheless, even with these shortcomings, Situational Leadership® is a useful way to get leaders to think about how leadership effectiveness may depend somewhat on being flexible with different subordinates, not on acting the same way toward them all.

The Contingency Model

Although leaders may be able to change their behaviors toward individual subordinates, leaders also have dominant behavioral tendencies. Some leaders may be generally more supportive and relationship-oriented, whereas others may be more concerned with task or goal accomplishment. The contingency model[38] recognizes that leaders have these general behavioral tendencies and specifies situations where certain leaders (or behavioral dispositions) may be more effective than others.

Fiedler's[39] **contingency model** of leadership is probably the earliest and most well-known contingency theory, and is often perceived by students to be almost the opposite of SLT. Compared to the contingency model, SLT emphasizes flexibility in leader behaviors, whereas the contingency model maintains that leaders are much more consistent (and consequently less flexible) in their behavior. Situational Leadership theory maintains that leaders who *correctly base their behaviors* on follower maturity will be more effective, whereas the contingency model suggests that leader effectiveness is primarily determined by *selecting the right kind of leader for a certain situation or changing the situation* to fit the particular leader's style. Another way to say this is that leadership effectiveness depends on both the leader's style and the favorableness of the leadership situation. Some leaders are better than others in some situations but less effective in other situations. To understand contingency theory, therefore, we need to look first at the critical characteristics of the leader and then at the critical aspects of the situation.

The Least Preferred Co-worker Scale

To determine a leader's general style or tendency, Fiedler developed an instrument called the **least preferred co-worker (LPC) scale.** The scale instructs a leader to think of the single individual with whom he has had the greatest difficulty working (that is, the least preferred co-worker) and then to describe that individual in terms of a series of bipolar adjectives (such as friendly–unfriendly, boring–interesting, and sincere–insincere). Those ratings are then converted into a numerical score.

In thinking about such a procedure, many people assume that the score is determined primarily by the characteristics of whatever particular individual the leader happened to identify as his least preferred co-worker. In the context of contingency theory, however, the score is thought to *represent something about the leader, not the specific individual the leader evaluated.*

The current interpretation of these scores is that they identify a leader's *motivation hierarchy.*[40] Based on their LPC scores, leaders are categorized into two groups: **low-LPC leaders** and **high-LPC leaders.** In terms of their motivation hierarchy, low-LPC leaders are motivated primarily by the task, which means these leaders gain satisfaction primarily from task accomplishment. Thus their dominant behavioral tendencies are similar to the initiating structure behavior described in the Ohio State research or the task behavior of SLT. However, if tasks are being accomplished in an acceptable manner, low-LPC leaders will move to their secondary level of motivation, which is forming and maintaining relationships with followers. Thus low-LPC leaders will focus on improving their relationships with followers *after* they are assured that assigned tasks are being satisfactorily accomplished. If tasks are no longer being accomplished in an acceptable manner, however, low-LPC leaders will refocus their efforts on task accomplishment and persist with these efforts until task accomplishment is back on track.

In terms of motivation hierarchy, high-LPC leaders are motivated primarily by relationships, which means these leaders are satisfied primarily by establishing and maintaining close interpersonal relationships. Thus their dominant behavioral tendencies are similar to the consideration behaviors described in the Ohio State research or the relationship behaviors in SLT. If high-LPC leaders have established good relationships with their followers, they will move to their secondary level of motivation, which is task accomplishment. As soon as leader–follower relations are jeopardized, however, high-LPC leaders will cease working on tasks and refocus their efforts on improving relationships with followers.

You can think of the LPC scale as identifying two different sorts of leaders, with their respective motivational hierarchies depicted in Figure 13.5. Lower-level needs must be satisfied first. Low-LPC leaders will move "up" to satisfying relationship needs when they are assured the task is being satisfactorily accomplished. High-LPC leaders will move "up" to emphasizing task accomplishment when they have established good relationships with their followers.

Because all tests have some level of imprecision, Fiedler[41] suggested that the LPC scale cannot accurately identify the motivation hierarchy for individuals with intermediate scores. Research by Kennedy[42] suggested an alternative view. Kennedy has shown that individuals within the intermediate range of LPC scale scores may more easily or readily switch between being task- or relationship-oriented leaders than those individuals with more extreme scale scores. They may be equally satisfied by working on the task or establishing relationships with followers.

FIGURE 13.5
Motivational
Hierarchies for
Low- and High-LPC
Leaders

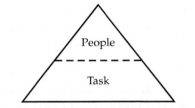

Low-LPC leader motivational hierarchy

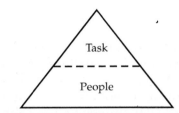

High-LPC leader motivational hierarchy

Situational Favorability

The other important variable in the contingency model is **situational favorability,** which is the amount of control the leader has over the followers. Presumably the more control a leader has over followers, the more favorable the situation is, at least from the leader's perspective. Fiedler included three subelements in situation favorability. These were leader–member relations, task structure, and position power.

Leader–member relations are the most powerful of the three subelements in determining overall situation favorability. They involve the extent to which relationships between the leader and followers are generally cooperative and friendly or antagonistic and difficult. Leaders who rate leader–member relations as high feel they have the support of their followers and can rely on their loyalty.

Task structure is second in potency in determining overall situation favorability. Here the leader objectively determines task structure by assessing whether there are detailed descriptions of work products, standard operating procedures, or objective indicators of how well the task is being accomplished. The more one can answer these questions affirmatively, the higher the structure of the task.

Position power is the weakest of the three elements of situational favorability. Leaders who have titles of authority or rank, the authority to administer rewards and punishments, and the legitimacy to conduct follower performance appraisals have greater position power than leaders who lack them.

The relative weights of these three components, taken together, can be used to create a continuum of situational favorability. When using the

FIGURE 13.6
Contingency Model Octant Structure for Determining Situational Favorability

High ⟵ Overall situation favorability							Low

Leader–member relations	Good				Poor			
Task structure	Structured		Unstructured		Structured		Unstructured	
Position power	High	Low	High	Low	High	Low	High	Low
Octant	1	2	3	4	5	6	7	8

contingency model, leaders are first asked to rate items that measure the strength of leader–member relations, the degree of task structure, and their level of position power. These ratings are then weighted and combined to determine an overall level of situational favorability facing the leader.[43] Any particular situation's favorability can be plotted on a continuum Fiedler divided into octants representing distinctly different levels of situational favorability. The relative weighting scheme for the subelements and how they make up each of the eight octants are shown in Figure 13.6.

You can see that the octants of situational favorability range from 1 (highly favorable) to 8 (very unfavorable). The highest levels of situational favorability occur when leader–member relations are good, the task is structured, and position power is high. The lowest levels of situational favorability occur when there are high levels of leader–member conflict, the task is unstructured or unclear, and the leader does not have the power to reward or punish subordinates. Moreover, the relative weighting of the three subelements can easily be seen by their order of precedence in Figure 13.6, with leader–member relations appearing first, followed by task structure, and then position power. For example, because leader–member relations carry so much weight, it is impossible for leaders with good leader–member relations to have anything worse than moderate situational favorability, regardless of their task structure or position power. In other words, leaders with good leader–member relations will enjoy situational favorability no worse than octant 4; leaders with poor leader–member relations will face situational favorability no better than octant 5.

Prescriptions of the Model

Fiedler and his associates have conducted numerous studies to determine how different leaders (as described by their LPC scores) have performed in different situations (as described in terms of situational favorability). Figure 13.7 describes which type of leader (high or low LPC) Fiedler found to be most effective, given different levels of situation favorability. The solid dark line represents the relative effectiveness of a low-LPC

FIGURE 13.7
Leader Effectiveness Based on the Contingency between Leader LPC Score and Situation Favorability

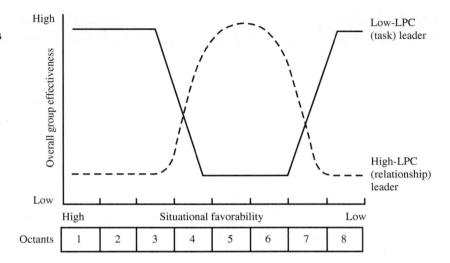

leader, and the dashed line represents the relative effectiveness of a high-LPC leader. It is obvious from the way the two lines cross and recross that there is some interaction between the leader's style and the overall situation favorability. If the situational favorability is moderate (octants 4, 5, 6, or 7), then those groups led by leaders concerned with establishing and maintaining relationships (high-LPC leaders) seem to do best. However, if the situation is either very unfavorable (octant 8) or highly favorable (octants 1, 2, or 3), then those groups led by the task-motivated (low-LPC) leaders seem to do best.

Fiedler suggested that leaders will try to satisfy their primary motivation when faced with unfavorable or moderately favorable situations. This means that low-LPC leaders will concentrate on the task and high-LPC leaders will concentrate on relationships when faced with these two levels of situational favorability. Nevertheless, leaders facing highly favorable situations know that their primary motivations will be satisfied and thus will move to their secondary motivational state. This means that *leaders will behave according to their secondary motivational state only when faced with highly favorable situations* (see Highlight 13.4).

Several interesting implications of Fiedler's[44] model are worthy of additional comment. Because leaders develop their distinctive motivation hierarchies and dominant behavior tendencies through a lifetime of experiences, Fiedler believed these hierarchies and tendencies would be difficult to change through training. Fiedler maintained it was naive to believe that sending someone to a relatively brief leadership training program could substantially alter any leader's personality or typical way of acting in leadership situations; after all, such tendencies had been developed over many years of experience. Instead of trying to change the leader,

High- and Low-LPC Leaders and the Contingency Model

HIGHLIGHT 13.4

Suppose we have two leaders, Tom Low (a low-LPC or task-motivated leader) and Brenda High (a high-LPC or relationship-motivated leader). In unfavorable situations, Tom will be motivated by his primary level and will thus exhibit task behaviors. In similar situations, Brenda will also be motivated by her primary level and as a result will exhibit relationship behaviors. Fiedler found that in unfavorable situations, task behavior will help the group to be more effective, so Tom's behavior would better match the requirements of the situation. Group effectiveness would not be aided by Brenda's relationship behavior in this situation.

In situations with moderate favorability, both Tom and Brenda are still motivated by their primary motivations, so their behaviors will remain the same. Because the situation has changed, however, group effectiveness no longer requires task behavior. Instead the combination of situational variables leads to a condition where a leader's relationship behaviors will make the greatest contribution to group effectiveness. Hence Brenda will be the most effective leader in situations of moderate favorability.

In highly favorable situations, Fiedler's explanation gets more complex. When leaders find themselves in highly favorable situations, they no longer have to be concerned about satisfying their primary motivations. In highly favorable situations, leaders switch to satisfying their secondary motivations. Because Tom's secondary motivation is to establish and maintain relationships, in highly favorable situations he will exhibit relationship behaviors. Similarly, Brenda will also be motivated by her secondary motivation, so she would manifest task behaviors in highly favorable situations. Fiedler believed that leaders who manifested relationship behaviors in highly favorable situations helped groups to be more effective. In this case, Tom is giving the group what it needs to be more effective.

Fiedler concluded, training would be more effective if it showed leaders how to recognize and change key situational characteristics to better fit their personal motivational hierarchies and behavioral tendencies. Thus, according to Fiedler, the content of leadership training should emphasize situational engineering rather than behavioral flexibility in leaders. Relatedly, organizations could become more effective if they matched the characteristics of the leader (in this case LPC scores) with the demands of the situation (situational favorability) than if they tried to change the leader's behavior to fit the situation. These suggestions imply that high- or low-LPC leaders in mismatched situations should either change the situation or move to jobs that better match their motivational hierarchies and behavioral patterns.

Concluding Thoughts about the Contingency Model

Before reviewing the empirical evidence, perhaps we can attain a clearer understanding of the contingency model by examining it through the L-F-S framework. As shown in Figure 13.8, task structure is a function of the situation, and LPC scores are a function of the leader. Because position power is not a characteristic of the leader but of the situation the leader finds himself

FIGURE 13.8
Factors from Fiedler's Contingency Theory and the Interactional Framework

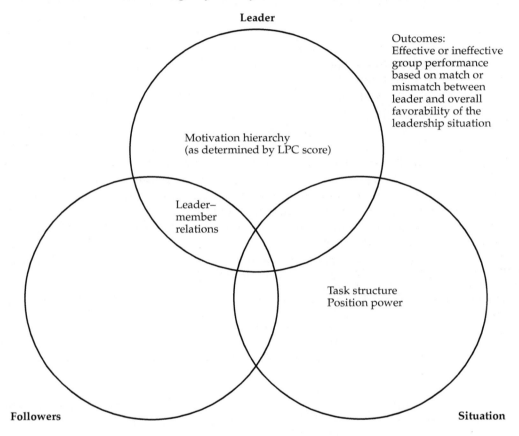

or herself in, it is included in the situational circle. Leader–member relations are a joint function of the leader and the followers; thus they belong in the overlapping intersection of the leader and follower circles.

As opposed to the dearth of evidence for Hersey and Blanchard's[45,46] situational theory, Fiedler and his fellow researchers have provided considerable evidence that the predictions of the model are empirically valid, particularly in laboratory settings.[47–51] However, a review of the studies conducted in field settings yielded only mixed support for the model.[52] Moreover, researchers have criticized the model for the uncertainties surrounding the meaning of LPC scores,[53–55] the interpretation of situational favorability,[56,57] and the relationships between LPC scores and situational favorability.[58–60] Despite such questions, however, the contingency model has stimulated considerable research and is the most validated of all leadership theories.

The Path–Goal Theory

Perhaps the most sophisticated (and comprehensive) of the five contingency models is path–goal theory. The underlying mechanism of **path–goal theory** deals with expectancy—a cognitive approach to understanding motivation where people calculate effort-to-performance probabilities (If I study for 12 hours, what is the probability I will get an A on the final exam?), performance-to-outcome probabilities (If I get an A on the final, what is the probability of getting an A in the course?), and assigned valences or values of outcomes (How much do I value a higher GPA?). Theoretically at least, people are assumed to make these calculations on a rational basis, and the theory can be used to predict what tasks people will put their energies into, given some finite number of options.

Path–goal theory uses the same basic assumptions as expectancy theory. At the most fundamental level, the effective leader will provide or ensure the availability of valued rewards for followers (the goal) and then help them find the best way of getting there (the path). Along the way, the effective leader will help the followers identify and remove roadblocks and avoid dead ends; the leader will also provide emotional support as needed. These task and relationship leadership actions essentially involve increasing followers' probability estimates for effort-to-performance and performance-to-reward expectancies. In other words, the leader's actions should strengthen followers' beliefs that if they exert a certain level of effort, they will be more likely to accomplish a task, and if they accomplish the task, they will be more likely to achieve some valued outcome.

Although uncomplicated in its basic concept, the model has added more variables and interactions over time. Evans[61] is credited with the first version of path–goal theory, but we will focus on a later version developed by House and Dressler.[62] Their conceptual scheme is ideally suited to the L-F-S framework because they described three classes of variables that include leader behaviors, followers, and the situation. We will examine each of these in turn.

Leader Behaviors

The four types of leader behavior in path–goal theory can be seen in Table 13.2. Like SLT, path–goal theory assumes that leaders not only may use varying styles with different subordinates but might also use differing styles with the same subordinates in different situations. Path–goal theory suggests that, depending on the followers and the situation, these different leader behaviors can increase followers' acceptance of the leader, enhance their level of satisfaction, and raise their expectations that effort will result in effective performance, which in turn will lead to valued rewards (see Highlight 13.5).

**TABLE 13.2
The Four Leader
Behaviors of
Path–Goal Theory**

Directive leadership. These leader behaviors are similar to the task behaviors from SLT. They include telling the followers what they are expected to do, how to do it, when it is to be done, and how their work fits in with the work of others. This behavior would also include setting schedules, establishing norms, and providing expectations that followers will adhere to established procedure and regulations.

Supportive leadership. Supportive leadership behaviors include having courteous and friendly interactions, expressing genuine concern for the followers' well-being and individual needs, and remaining open and approachable to followers. These behaviors, which are similar to the relationship behaviors in SLT, also are marked by attention to the competing demands of treating followers equally while recognizing status differentials between the leader and the followers.

Participative leadership. Participative leaders engage in the behaviors that mark the consultative and group behaviors described by Vroom and Yetton.[26] As such, they tend to share work problems with followers; solicit their suggestions, concerns, and recommendations; and weigh these inputs in the decision-making process.

Achievement-oriented leadership. Leaders exhibiting these behaviors would be seen as both demanding and supporting in interactions with their followers. First they would set challenging goals for group and follower behavior, continually seek ways to improve performance en route, and expect the followers to always perform at their highest levels. But they would support these behaviors by exhibiting a high degree of ongoing confidence that subordinates can put forth the necessary effort; will achieve the desired results; and, even further, will assume even more responsibility in the future.

The Followers

Path–goal theory contains two groups of follower variables. The first relates to the *satisfaction of followers,* and the second relates to the *followers' perception of their own abilities* relative to the task to be accomplished. In terms of followers' satisfaction, path–goal theory suggests that leader behaviors will be acceptable to followers to the degree that followers see the leader's behavior either as an immediate source of satisfaction or as directly instrumental in achieving future satisfaction. In other words, followers will actively support a leader as long as they view the leader's actions as a means for increasing their own levels of satisfaction. However, there is only so much a leader can do to increase followers' satisfaction levels because satisfaction also depends on characteristics of the followers themselves.

A frequently cited example of how followers' characteristics influence the impact of leader behaviors on followers' levels of satisfaction involves the trait of locus of control. People who believe they are "masters of their own ship" are said to have an internal locus of control; people

Shifting Behaviors at Caterpillar

HIGHLIGHT 13.5

James Despain was a leader with a very directive leadership style. He began his career at Caterpillar Inc. as a young man, sweeping the factory floor. He followed the lead of others of his generation—the 1950s were a time when leaders were the ultimate authority and words like *participative* and *consultative* were unheard of. Despain worked his way into supervisory positions and finally was named vice president of the track-type tractor division. Despain claims he "spent much of [his] career as a manager focusing on what employees were doing wrong." He focused on the tasks at hand and little else. But in the early 1990s Despain had to face some hard facts: his $1.2 billion division was losing millions of dollars per year, his management team was getting hundreds of grievances from their employees, and morale at the Caterpillar plant was extremely low.

Despain and his leadership group identified the need for a strategic plan to transform the working culture. Key to the plan was determining a strategy for dealing with employee attitudes and behavior. Despain and his transformation team identified nine behaviors or "common values" that they wanted every employee to emulate every day— trust, mutual respect, customer satisfaction, a sense of urgency, teamwork, empowerment, risk taking, continuous improvement, and commitment.

Employee evaluations were based on the manifestation of these behaviors. Above and beyond those behaviors, top executives and management were expected to lead by example and commit themselves to practice 100 positive leadership traits. Statements such as "I will know every one of my employees by name . . . will recognize their accomplishments with praise . . . will trust my employees to do their work" became the new mantras for those in charge.

Through this process, Despain came to understand that "the most important thing for employees in the workplace is to achieve self-worth." The principal change he was striving to achieve was to make employees accountable for how their jobs got done; for workers that meant stretching a little more every day to achieve their full potential. For managers it meant shifting away from achieving traditional metrics and toward drawing desired behavior from workers. "And we found that the more we focused on behavior, the better the metrics got." The result: Despain's division cut its break-even point in half within five years of launching the transformation.

Sources: http://www.tribuneindia.com/2004/20040509/ spectrum/book2.htm; http://www.sodexho-usa.com/ printer_friendly.htm; http://www.stchas.edu/press/ despain.shtml

who believe they are (relatively speaking) "pawns of fate" are said to have an external locus of control. Mitchell, Smyser, and Weed[63] found that follower satisfaction was not directly related to the degree of participative behaviors manifested by the leader; that is, followers with highly participative leaders were no more satisfied than followers with more autocratic leaders. However, when followers' locus-of-control scores were taken into account, a contingency relationship was discovered. As shown in Figure 13.9, internal-locus-of-control followers, who believed outcomes were a result of their own decisions, were much more satisfied with leaders who exhibited participative behaviors than they were with leaders who were directive. Conversely, external-locus-of-control followers were more satisfied with directive leader behaviors than they were with participative leader behaviors.

FIGURE 13.9
Interaction between Followers' Locus of Control Scores and Leader Behavior in Decision Making

Source: Adapted from T. R. Mitchell, C. M. Smyser, and S. E. Weed, "Locus of Control: Supervision and Work Satisfaction," *Academy of Management Journal* 18 (1975), pp. 623–30.

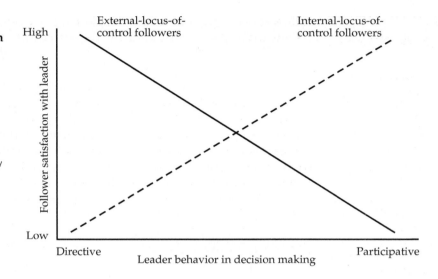

Followers' perceptions of their own skills and abilities to perform particular tasks can also affect the impact of certain leader behaviors. Followers who believe they are perfectly capable of performing a task are not as apt to be motivated by, or as willing to accept, a directive leader as they would a leader who exhibits participative behaviors. Using the same rationale as for locus of control, we can predict the opposite relationship for followers who do not perceive that they have sufficient abilities to perform a task. Once again, the acceptability of the leader and the motivation to perform are in part determined by followers' characteristics. Thus path–goal theory suggests that both leader behaviors and follower characteristics are important in determining outcomes.

The Situation

Path–goal theory considers three situational factors that impact or moderate the effects of leader behavior on follower attitudes and behaviors. These include *the task, the formal authority system,* and *the primary work group.* Each of these three factors can influence the leadership situation in one of three ways. These three factors can serve as an independent motivational factor, as a constraint on the behavior of followers (which may be either positive or negative in outcome), or as a reward.

However, these variables can often affect the impact of various leader behaviors. For example, if the task is structured and routine, the formal authority system has constrained followers' behaviors, and the work group has established clear norms for performance, then leaders would be serving a redundant purpose by manifesting directive or achievement-oriented behaviors. These prescriptions are similar to some of those noted in substitutes for leadership theory[64] because everything the

550 Part Four *Focus on the Situation*

Although people object when a scientific analysis traces their behavior to external conditions and thus deprives them of credit and the chance to be admired, they seldom object when the same analysis absolves them of blame.

B. F. Skinner

follower needs to understand the effort-to-performance and performance-to-reward links is provided by the situation. Thus redundant leader behaviors might be interpreted by followers as either a complete lack of understanding or empathy by the leader, or an attempt by the leader to exert excessive control. Neither of these interpretations is likely to enhance the leader's acceptance by followers or increase their motivation.

Although we have already described how follower characteristics and situational characteristics can impact leader behaviors, path–goal theory also maintains that follower and situational variables can impact each other. In other words, situational variables, such as the task performed, can also impact the influence of followers' skills, abilities, or personality traits on followers' satisfaction. Although this seems to make perfect sense, we hope you are beginning to see how complicated path–goal theory can be when we start considering how situational variables, follower characteristics, and leader behaviors interact in the leadership process.

Prescriptions of the Theory

In general, path–goal theory maintains that leaders should first assess the situation and select a leadership behavior appropriate to situational demands. By manifesting the appropriate behaviors, leaders can increase followers' effort-to-performance expectancies, performance-to-reward expectancies, or valences of the outcomes. These increased expectancies and valences will improve subordinates' effort levels and the rewards attained, which in turn will increase subordinates' satisfaction and performance levels and the acceptance of their leaders. Perhaps the easiest way to explain this complicated process is through an example. Suppose we have a set of followers who are in a newly created work unit and do not understand the requirements of their positions. In other words, the followers have a high level of role ambiguity. According to path–goal theory, leaders should exhibit a high degree of directive behaviors to reduce the role ambiguity of their followers. The effort-to-performance link will become clearer when leaders tell followers what to do and how to do it in ambiguous situations, which in turn will cause followers to exert higher effort levels. Because role ambiguity is assumed to be unpleasant, these directive leader behaviors and higher effort levels should eventually result in higher satisfaction levels among followers. Figure 13.10 illustrates this process. Similarly, leaders may look at the leadership situation and note that followers' performance levels are not acceptable. The leader may also conclude that the current situation offers few, if any, incentives for increased performance. In this case the leader may use directive behaviors to increase the value of the rewards (or valence), which in turn will increase followers' effort levels and performance.

FIGURE 13.10
Examples of Applying Path–Goal Theory

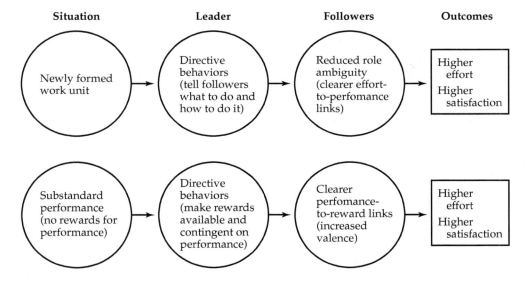

Concluding Thoughts about the Path–Goal Theory

Before getting into the research surrounding path–goal theory, you may wish to examine the theory using the L-F-S framework. As shown in Figure 13.11, the components of path–goal theory fit nicely into the L-F-S model. The four leader behaviors fit into the leader circle, the characteristics of the followers fit into the follower circle, and the task and the formal authority system fit into the situation circle. Of all the components of path–goal theory, the only "mismatch" with the L-F-S model deals with the primary work group. The norms, cohesiveness, size, and stage of development of groups are considered to be part of the follower function in the L-F-S model but are part of the situation function in path–goal theory. In that regard, we hasten to note we use the L-F-S framework primarily for heuristic purposes. Ultimately the concepts described in these five theories are sufficiently complex and ambiguous that there probably is no right answer in any single depiction.

In terms of research, the path–goal theory has received only mixed support to date.[65–68] Although many of these mixed findings may be due to the fact that the path–goal theory excludes many of the variables found to impact the leadership process, that may also be due to problems with the theory. Yukl[69] maintained that most of these criticisms deal with the methodology used to study path–goal theory and the limitations of expectancy theory. Moreover, the path–goal theory assumes that the only way to increase performance is to increase followers'

FIGURE 13.11
Factors from Path–Goal Theory and the Interactional Framework

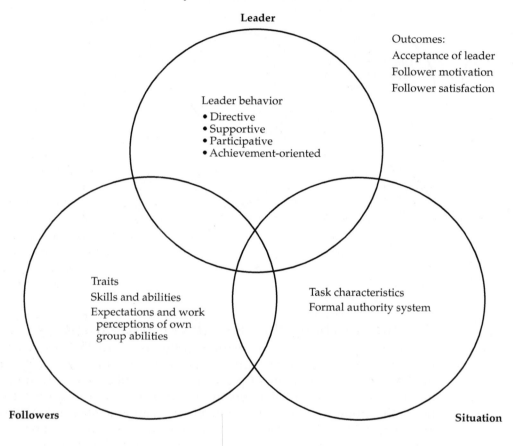

Leader

Leader behavior
- Directive
- Supportive
- Participative
- Achievement-oriented

Outcomes:
Acceptance of leader
Follower motivation
Follower satisfaction

Traits
Skills and abilities
Expectations and work
perceptions of own
group abilities

Task characteristics
Formal authority system

Followers

Situation

To act is easy; to think is hard.

Goethe

motivation levels. The theory ignores the roles leaders play in selecting talented followers, building their skill levels through training, and redesigning their work.[70]

Nonetheless, path–goal theory is useful for illustrating two points. First, as noted by Yukl,[71] "path–goal theory has already made a contribution to the study of leadership by providing a conceptual framework to guide researchers in identifying potentially relevant situational moderator variables." Path–goal theory also illustrates that, as models become more complicated, they may be more useful to researchers and less appealing to practitioners. Our experience is that pragmatically oriented students and in-place leaders want to take something from a model that is understandable and can be applied in their work situation right away. This does not mean they prefer simplicity to validity—they generally appreciate the complexity of the leadership process. But neither do they want a model that is so complex as to be indecipherable.

Summary

This chapter has provided an overview of five well-known contingency theories of leadership, which include leader–member exchange theory, the normative decision model,[72] the Situational Leadership® model, the contingency model[73] and the path–goal theory.[74] All five models are similar in that they specify that leaders should make their behaviors contingent on certain aspects of the followers or the situation to improve leadership effectiveness. In addition, all five theories implicitly assume that leaders can accurately assess key follower and situational factors. However, as the material regarding perception in Chapter 2 shows, it is entirely possible that two leaders in the same situation may reach different conclusions about followers' levels of knowledge, the strength of leader–follower relationships, the degree of task structure, or the level of role ambiguity being experienced by followers. These differences in perception could lead these two leaders to reach different conclusions about the situation, which may in turn cause them to take different actions in response to the situation. Furthermore, these actions may be in accordance or in conflict with the prescriptions of any of these five theories. Also, the fact that leaders' perceptions may have caused them to act in a manner not prescribed by a particular model may be an underlying reason why these five theories have reported conflicting findings, particularly in field settings.

Another reason these theories have generally found mixed support in field settings is that they are all limited in scope. Many factors that affect leader and follower behaviors in work group, team, or volunteer committee settings are not present in laboratory studies but often play a substantial role in field studies. For example, none of the models take into account how levels of stress, organizational culture and climate, working conditions, technology, economic conditions, or types of organizational design affect the leadership process. Nevertheless, the five contingency theories have been the subject of considerable research; and even if only mixed support for the models has been found, this research has added to our knowledge about leadership and has given us a more sophisticated understanding of the leadership process.

Key Terms

leader–member exchange, *525*
role-taking, *525*
role-making, *525*
routinization, *525*
normative decision model, *527*

autocratic processes, *528*
consultative processes, *528*
group process, *528*
decision quality, *528*
decision acceptance, *529*

Situational Leadership®, *534*
task behaviors, *534*
relationship behaviors, *534*
follower readiness, *536*

554   Part Four   *Focus on the Situation*

developmental
  interventions, *537*
contingency
  model, *539*
least preferred
  co-worker (LPC)
  scale, *539*
low-LPC leaders, *540*

high-LPC
  leaders, *540*
situational
  favorability, *541*
path–goal theory, *546*
directive
  leadership, *547*

supportive
  leadership, *547*
participative
  leadership, *547*
achievement-oriented
  leadership, *547*

Questions

1. Given the description of the leadership situation facing the airplane crash survivors described in Chapter 1, how would leader–member exchange, the normative decision model, the situational leadership theory, the contingency model, and the path–goal theory prescribe that a leader should act?

2. Can leaders be flexible in how they interact with others? Do you believe leaders can change their behavior? Their personalities?

3. Think of a leadership situation with which you are familiar. Apply each of the theories in this chapter to the situation. Which theory best fits the interaction of the leader, followers, and situation in your example? Does any theory allow you to predict a likely or preferred outcome for a current challenge?

Minicase

Big Changes for a Small Hospital

As F. Nicholas Jacobs toured the Windber Medical Center facility, he was dismayed by the industrial pink-painted walls, the circa-1970 furniture, and the snow leaking through the windows of the conference room. Employees earned 30 percent less than their counterparts in the area, and turnover was steep. As Windber's newest president, Jacobs knew he was the facility's last hope—if he couldn't successfully turn around the aging facility, it would mean closing the doors forever.

Coming to Windber Medical Center in 1997, Jacobs was keenly aware that the hospital could be the next in a series of small hospitals that had fallen victim to a struggling economy. Determined to see that not happen, he began by making connections with the employees of the hospital and the community at large. Jacobs's first step was to interview the employees to find out firsthand what they wanted for the Windber community and the medical center. He also looked to members of local community groups like the local library, the Agency on Aging, and local politicians and asked these groups what they wanted from their local medical facility. When Jacobs realized that octogenarians made up a larger percentage of the population in Windber, Pennsylvania, than in all of Dade County, Florida, he made it a priority to provide more options to seniors for improving their health and quality of life. He set forth a vision of a medical center that was more of a community center—a center that would allow members of the community to exercise in a state-of-the-art facility while having access to professionals to answer health-related questions. Jacobs realized that keeping people in the community both physically and mentally healthy also meant keeping the hospital financially healthy. He made the center's new preventative care philosophy clear to the public: "Work out at our hospital so you can stay out of our hospital."

Jacobs's efforts have paid off—in an era when small hospitals are closing left and right, Windber Medical Center is thriving. Under Jacobs's leadership Windber has established an affiliation with the Planetree treatment system, which integrates meditation, massage, music, and other holistic methods into traditional health care. Windber's wellness center, which offers fitness training, yoga, and acupuncture, among other treatments, opened in January 2000 and now generates over $500,000 annually. Gone are the pink walls and dated furniture—replaced with fountains, plants, and modern artwork. Jacobs recruited a former hotel manager to oversee food service. And despite the dismissal of about 32 employees (those used to a more traditional hospital setting had a tough time in the new environment), the staff has nearly doubled to 450 employees, and pay has improved. Windber has raised more than $50 million in public and private funding and has forged research partnerships with the Walter Reed Army Health System and the University of Pittsburgh, among others. The Windber Research Institute, Windber's heart disease reversal program, has treated about 250 patients.

1. Consider the factors from the situational leadership theory outlined in Figure 13.4. Apply these factors to Jacobs and Windber.
2. How do you think Jacobs would score on the least preferred co-worker (LPC) scale? Why?
3. Based on the success of Windber, in what range would you guess the overall situational favorability might fall for Jacobs on the continuum illustrated in Figure 13.6?

Sources: http://www.careerjournaleurope.com/columnists/inthelead/20030827 inthelead.html; http://www.haponline.org/ihc/hospitalshealthsystems/models2.asp; http://www.post-gazette.com/pg/04013/260747.stm.

End Notes

1. F. E. Fiedler, "Reflections by an Accidental Theorist," *Leadership Quarterly* 6, no. 4 (1995), pp. 453–61.
2. F. E. Fiedler, *A Theory of Leadership Effectiveness* (New York: McGraw-Hill, 1967).
3. M. M. Chemers, "The Social, Organizational, and Cultural Contest of Effective Leadership," in *Leadership: Multidisciplinary Perspectives*, ed. B. Kellerman (Englewood Cliffs, NJ: Prentice Hall, 1984).

4. G. Graen and J. F. Cashman, "A Role-Making Model of Leadership in Formal Organization: A Developmental Approach," in *Leadership Frontiers,* eds. J. G. Hunt and L. L. Larson (Kent, OH: Kent State University Press), pp. 143–65, 1976.

5. R. C. Linden and G. Graen, "Generalizability of the Vertical Dyad Linkage Model of Leadership," *Academy of Management Journal* 23 (1980), pp. 451–65.

6. S. J. Wayne, L. M. Shore, and R. C. Linden, "Perceived Organizational Support and Leader-Member Exchange: A Social Exchange Perspective," *Academy of Management Journal* 40 (1997), pp. 82–111.

7. G. Chen, B. L. Kirkman, R. Kanfer, D. Allen, and B. Rosen, "A Multilevel Study of Leadership Empowerment and Performance in Teams," *Journal of Applied Psychology* 92 (2007), pp. 331–46.

8. R. T. Sparrowe and R. C. Linden, "Two Routes to Influence: Integrating Leader-Member Exchange and Social Network Perspectives," *Administrative Science Quarterly* 50 (2005), pp. 505–35.

9. T. A. Scandura and C. A. Schriesheim, "Leader-Member Exchange and Supervisor Career Mentoring as Complementary Constructs in Leadership Research," *Academy of Management Journal* 37 (1994), pp. 1588–1602.

10. G. B. Graen and M. Uhl-Bien, "Relationship-Based Approach to Leadership: Development of Leader-Member Exchange (LMX) Theory over 25 Years: Applying a Multi-Level Multi-Domain Perspective," *Leadership Quarterly* 6 (1995), pp. 219–47.

11. D. J. Henderson, R. C. Liden, B. C. Glibkowski, and A. Chaudhry, "LMX Differentiation: A Multilevel Review and Examination of Its Antecedents and Outcomes," *Leadership Quarterly* 20 (2009), pp. 517–34.

12. L. Atwater and A. Carmeli, "Leader-Member Exchange, Feelings of Energy, and Involvement in Creative Work," *Leadership Quarterly* 20 (2010), pp. 264–75.

13. Z. Zhang, M. Wang, and J. Shi, "Leader-Follower Congruence in Proactive Personality and Work Outcomes: The Mediating Role of Leader-Member Exchange," *Academy of Management Journal* 55, no. 1 (2009) pp. 111–30.

14. V. Venkataramani, S. Green, and D. Schleicher, "Well-Connected Leaders: The Impact of Leaders' Social Network Ties on LMX and Members' Work Attitudes," *Journal of Applied Psychology* 95, no. 6 (2010), pp. 1071–84.

15. R. Eisenberger, G. Karagonlar, F. Stinglhamber, P. Neves, T. Becker, M. G. Gonzalez-Morales, and M. Steiger-Mueller, "Leader-Member Exchange and Affective Organizational Commitment: The Contribution of Supervisor's Organizational Embodiment," *Journal of Applied Psychology* 95, no. 6 (2010), pp. 1085–103.

16. B. Erdogan, and T. N. Bauer, "Differentiated Leader-Member Exchanges: The Buffering Role of Justice Climate," *Journal of Applied Psychology* 95, no. 6 (2010), pp. 1104–120.

17. D. DeCremer, M. van Dijke, and D. M. Mayer, "Cooperating When 'You' and 'I' Are Treated Fairly: The Moderating Role of Leaders Prototypicality," *Journal of Applied Psychology* 95, no. 6 (2010), pp. 1121–133.

18. T. Rockstuhl, J. H. Dulebohn, S. Ang, and L. M. Shore, "Leader-Member Exchange (LMX) and Culture: A Meta-Analysis of Correlates of LMX Across 23 Countries," *Journal of Applied Psychology* 97, no. 6 (2012), pp. 1097–130.

19. R. S. Gajendran, and A. Joshi, "Innovation in Globally Distributed Teams: The Role of LMX, Communication Frequency, and Member Influence on Team Decisions," *Journal of Applied Psychology* 97, no. 6 (2012), pp. 1252–261.

20. V. H. Vroom and P. W. Yetton, *Leadership and Decision Making* (Pittsburgh, PA: University of Pittsburgh Press, 1973).

21. Ibid.

22. Ibid.

23. Ibid.

24. Ibid.

25. Ibid.

26. R. H. G. Field, "A Test of the Vroom-Yetton Normative Model of Leadership," *Journal of Applied Psychology* 67 (1982), pp. 523–32.

27. V. H. Vroom and A. G. Jago, "Leadership and Decision Making: A Revised Normative Model," paper presented at the Academy of Management Convention, Boston, MA, 1974.

28. V. H. Vroom and A. G. Jago, *The New Theory of Leadership: Managing Participation in Organizations* (Englewood Cliffs, NJ: Prentice Hall, 1988).

29. J. B. Miner, "The Uncertain Future of the Leadership Concept: An Overview," in *Leadership Frontiers*, ed. J. G. Hunt and L. L. Larson (Kent, OH: Kent State University, 1975).

30. G. Yukl, *Leadership in Organizations*, 2nd ed. (Englewood Cliffs, NJ: Prentice Hall, 1989).

31. G. A. Yukl and D. D. Van Fleet, "Theory and Research on Leadership in Organizations," in *Handbook of Industrial & Organizational Psychology*, vol. 3, ed. M. D. Dunnette and L. M. Hough (Palo Alto, CA: Consulting Psychologists Press, 1992), pp. 1–51.

32. A. Couch and P. W. Yetton, "Manager Behavior, Leadership Style, and Subordinate Performance: An Empirical Extension of the Vroom-Yetton Conflict Rule," *Organizational Behavior and Human Decision Processes* 39 (1987), pp. 384–96.

33. P. Hersey and K. H. Blanchard, "Life Cycle Theory of Leadership," *Training and Development Journal* 23 (1969), pp. 26–34.

34. R. P. Vecchio, "Situational Leadership Theory: An Examination of a Prescriptive Theory," *Journal of Applied Psychology* 72 (1987), pp. 444–51.

35. Yukl and Van Fleet, "Theory and Research on Leadership in Organizations."

36. K. H. Blanchard, *Leading at a Higher Level* (Upper Saddle River, New Jersey: Prentice-Hall, 2007).

37. G. Thompson and R. P. Vecchio, "Situational Leadership Theory: A Test of Three Versions," *Leadership Quarterly* 20 (2009), pp. 837–48.

38. Fiedler, "Reflections by an Accidental Theorist."

39. Ibid.

40. F. E. Fiedler, "The Contingency Model and the Dynamics of the Leadership Process," in *Advances in Experimental Social Psychology*, ed. L. Berkowitz (New York: Academic Press, 1978).

41. Ibid.

42. J. K. Kennedy, "Middle LPC Leaders and the Contingency Model of Leader Effectiveness," *Organizational Behavior and Human Performance* 30 (1982), pp. 1–14.

43. F. E. Fiedler and M. M. Chemers, *Improving Leadership Effectiveness: The Leader Match Concept,* 2nd ed. (New York: John Wiley, 1982).

44. Fiedler, "Reflections by an Accidental Theorist."

45. P. Hersey and K. H. Blanchard, "Life Cycle Theory of Leadership," *Training and Development Journal* 23 (1969), pp. 26–34.

46. P. Hersey and K. H. Blanchard, *Management of Organizational Behavior: Utilizing Human Resources,* 4th ed. (Englewood Cliffs, NJ: Prentice Hall, 1982).

47. Fiedler, "The Contingency Model and the Dynamics of the Leadership Process."

48. F. E. Fiedler, "Cognitive Resources and Leadership Performance," *Applied Psychology: An International Review* 44, no. 1 (1995), pp. 5–28.

49. Fiedler and Chemers, *Improving Leadership Effectiveness.*

50. L. H. Peters, D. D. Hartke, and J. T. Pohlmann, "Fiedler's Contingency Theory of Leadership: An Application of the Meta-analytic Procedures of Schmidt and Hunter," *Psychological Bulletin* 97 (1985), pp. 274–85.

51. M. J. Strube and J. E. Garcia, "A Meta-analytic Investigation of Fiedler's Contingency Model of Leadership Effectiveness," *Psychological Bulletin* 90 (1981), pp. 307–21.

52. L. H. Peters, D. D. Hartke, and J. T. Pohlmann, "Fiedler's Contingency Theory of Leadership: An Application of the Meta-analytic Procedures of Schmidt and Hunter," *Psychological Bulletin* 97 (1985), pp. 274–85.

53. Kennedy, "Middle LPC Leaders and the Contingency Model of Leader Effectiveness."

54. R. W. Rice, "Construct Validity of the Least Preferred Co-Worker Score," *Psychological Bulletin* 85 (1978), pp. 1199–1237.

55. C. A. Schriesheim and S. Kerr, "Theories and Measures of Leadership: A Critical Appraisal of Current and Future Directions," in *Leadership: The Cutting Edge,* eds. J. G. Hunt and L. L. Larson (Carbondale, IL: Southern Illinois University Press, 1977).

56. A. G. Jago and J. W. Ragan, "The Trouble with Leader Match Is That It Doesn't Match Fiedler's Contingency Model," *Journal of Applied Psychology* 71 (1986), pp. 555–59.

57. A. G. Jago and J. W. Ragan, "Some Assumptions Are More Troubling Than Others: Rejoinder to Chemers and Fiedler," *Journal of Applied Psychology* 71 (1986), pp. 564–65.

58. Jago and Ragan, "The Trouble with Leader Match Is That It Doesn't Match Fiedler's Contingency Model.

59. Jago and Ragan, "Some Assumptions Are More Troubling Than Others."

60. R. P. Vecchio, "Assessing the Validity of Fiedler's Contingency Model of Leadership Effectiveness: A Closer Look at Strube and Garcia," *Psychological Bulletin* 93 (1983), pp. 404–8.

61. M. G. Evans, "The Effects of Supervisory Behavior on the Path-Goal Relationship," *Organizational Behavior and Human Performance* 5 (1970), pp. 277–98.

62. R. J. House and G. Dressler, "The Path–Goal Theory of Leadership: Some Post Hoc and A Priori Tests," in *Contingency Approaches to Leadership*, eds. J. G. Hunt and L. L. Larson (Carbondale, IL: Southern Illinois University Press, 1974).

63. T. R. Mitchell, C. M. Smyser, and S. E. Weed, "Locus of Control: Supervision and Work Satisfaction," *Academy of Management Journal* 18 (1975), pp. 623–30.

64. S. Kerr and J. M. Jermier, "Substitutes for Leadership: Their Meaning and Measurement," *Organizational Behavior and Human Performance* 22 (1978), pp. 375–403.

65. C. A. Schriesheim and A. S. DeNisi, "Task Dimensions as Moderators of the Effects of Instrumental Leadership: A Two Sample Replicated Test of Path–Goal Leadership Theory," *Journal of Applied Psychology* 66 (1981), pp. 589–97.

66. C. A. Schriesheim and S. Kerr, "Theories and Measures of Leadership: A Critical Appraisal of Current and Future Directions," in *Leadership: The Cutting Edge*, eds. J. G. Hunt and L. L. Larson (Carbondale, IL: Southern Illinois University Press, 1977).

67. Yukl, *Leadership in Organizations*.

68. C. A. Schriesheim, S. L. Castro, X. Zhou, and L. A. DeChurch, "An Investigation of Path–Goal and Transformational Leadership Theory Predictions at the Individual Level of Analysis," *Leadership Quarterly* 17 (2006), pp. 21–38.

69. Yukl, *Leadership in Organizations*.

70. Yukl and Van Fleet, "Theory and Research on Leadership in Organizations."

71. Yukl, *Leadership in Organizations*.

72. Vroom and Yetton, *Leadership and Decision Making*.

73. Fiedler, "Reflections by an Accidental Theorist."

74. House and Dressler, "The Path–Goal Theory of Leadership."

Chapter 14

Leadership and Change

Introduction

There is nothing more difficult to take in hand, more perilous to conduct, or more uncertain of success, than to take the lead in the introduction of a new order of things.

Niccolò Machiavelli, writer

Organizations today face myriad potential challenges. To be successful they must cope effectively with the implications of new technology, globalization, changing social and political climates, new competitive threats, shifting economic conditions, industry consolidation, swings in consumer preferences, and new performance and legal standards. Think how technology enabled Mark Zuckerberg to create Facebook or the changes the U.S. military had to make as it shifted from stemming the tide of communism to fighting more regionalized conflicts. And consider how the events of September 11, 2001, the wars in Iraq and Afghanistan, the threats of global terrorism, the economic recession in the United States and European Union, the growth of the Chinese and Brazilian economies, the Arab Spring, and global warming have affected leaders in both the private and public sectors around the world. Leading change is perhaps the most difficult challenge facing any leader, yet this skill may be the best differentiator of managers from leaders and of mediocre from exceptional leaders. The best leaders are those who recognize the situational and follower factors inhibiting or facilitating change, paint a compelling vision of the future, and formulate and execute a plan that moves their vision from a dream to reality.

The scope of any change initiative varies dramatically. Leaders can use goal setting, coaching, mentoring, delegation, or empowerment skills to effectively change the behaviors and skills of individual direct reports. But what would you need to do if you led a pharmaceutical company of 5,000 employees and you had just received FDA approval to introduce a revolutionary new drug into the marketplace? How would you get the research and development, marketing, sales, manufacturing, quality, shipping, customer service, accounting, and information technology departments to work together to ensure a profitable product launch? Or what would you do if you had to reduce company expenses by 40 percent for the next two years or deal with a recent acquisition of a competitor?

It is not necessary to change. Survival is not mandatory.

W. Edwards Deming, quality expert

Obviously change on this scale involves more than individual coaching and mentoring. Because this chapter builds on much of the content of the previous chapters, it is fitting that it appears toward the end of the text. To successfully lead larger-scale change initiatives, leaders need to attend to the situational and follower factors affecting their group or organization (Chapters 9, 10, and 12). They must also use their intelligence, problem-solving skills, creativity, and values to sort out what is important and formulate solutions to the challenges facing their group (Chapters 5–7). But solutions in and of themselves are no guarantee for change; leaders must use their power and influence, personality traits, coaching and planning skills, and knowledge of motivational techniques and group dynamics in order to drive change (Chapters 2, 3, 4, 8, 9, 11, and 16). An example of what it takes to drive large-scale organizational change can be found in Highlight 14.1 and 14.2.

As an overview, this chapter begins by revisiting the leadership versus management discussion from Chapter 1. We then describe a rational approach to organizational change and spell out what leaders can do if they want to be successful with their change efforts. This model also provides a good diagnostic framework for understanding why many change efforts fail. We conclude the chapter with a discussion of an alternative approach to change—charismatic and transformational leadership. The personal magnetism, heroic qualities, and spellbinding powers of these leaders can have unusually strong effects on followers, which often lead to dramatic organizational, political, or societal change. Unlike the rational approach to change, the charismatic and transformational leadership framework places considerable weight on followers' heightened emotional levels to drive organizational change. Much of the leadership research over the past 30 years has helped us better understand the situational, follower, and leader characteristics needed for charismatic or transformational leadership to occur. The chapter concludes with an overview of these factors and a review of the predominant theory in the field, Bass's theory of transformational and transactional leadership.[1]

The Rational Approach to Organizational Change

A number of authors have written about organizational change, including O'Toole,[2] Pritchett,[3] McNulty,[4] Heifetz and Linsky,[5] Moss Kanter,[6,7] Krile, Curphy, and Lund,[8] Ostroff,[9] Rock and Schwartz,[10] Kotter,[11] Curphy,[12,13] Burns,[14] Marcus and Weiler,[15] Bennis and Nanus,[16] Tichy and Devanna,[17] Bridges,[18] Collins and Porras,[19] Treacy and Wiersma,[20] Beer,[21,22] Heifetz and Laurie,[23] and Collins.[24,25] All these authors have unique perspectives on leadership and change, but they also share a number of common characteristics. Beer[21,22] has offered a rational and straightforward approach to organizational change that addresses many of the issues raised by the

Change in the Waste Industry

HIGHLIGHT 14.1

Even something as mundane as trash disposal can present some significant leadership challenges. One company, Waste Management, acquired over 1,600 smaller waste disposal companies in the United States, Canada, and Puerto Rico from 1995 to 2004. All of the acquired companies had their own financial systems, pay scales and benefits, trucks and equipment, and operating procedures. None of the IT or financial systems could "talk" to each other, drivers followed different operating procedures and had different performance standards and compensation packages, many of the companies were former competitors that now had to collaborate in order to achieve overall company goals, and few if any supervisors had been through any type of leadership training. The board of directors brought in an outsider, Maury Myers from Yellow Freight, to integrate all these acquisitions into a single company. As CEO, Maury's first task was to create a common financial system so that all the company's revenues and expenses could be consolidated into a single financial statement. And given the large number of acquired companies, this in itself was no small task. He also created a system that allowed supervisors and drivers to set goals and measure daily productivity and customer satisfaction rates and introduced other major organizational change initiatives to improve safety and vehicle maintenance, optimize vehicle use, and reduce operating expenses.

The results of these change initiatives have been nothing short of spectacular. Waste Management is now the industry leader in the waste industry, consisting of approximately 43,000 employees who create $2 billion in profits on a $12 billion annual revenue stream. Driver productivity, customer satisfaction, and driver safety have improved over 50 percent, and operating expenses have been dramatically reduced. Maury Myers retired from the CEO role in November 2004 and was replaced by David Steiner, the former CFO.

Since taking the reins at Waste Management David Steiner has focused on three critical initiatives, which include operational excellence, growth, and rebranding. In terms of operational excellence, the company has implemented a number of companywide initiatives to improve the safety and productivity of employees. Some of these include the Mission for Success Safety program, the Business Process Improvement initiative, and Waste Route, a route optimization program. These programs have helped Waste Management to become the best in the industry in terms of safety and worker productivity. The company is vigorously pursuing a number of organic growth opportunities to generate additional profits, such as capturing landfill gases to fuel garbage trucks, taking the lead in electronic recycling and disposal, placing power generating windmills at landfills, and developing new waste-to-energy power plants. In terms of rebranding, Waste Management has been repositioning itself with its "Think Green" television, radio, and magazine ads; the use of natural gas–powered trucks; and an aggressive landfill remediation program. It is looking at how it can play a lead role in sustainability because many companies, such as Walmart, have corporate goals of reducing store waste by 95 percent in the next five years. If these customers dramatically reduce their waste streams, what will Waste Management have to do to remain a good investment for shareholders? Although Waste Management has seen some dramatic changes over the past 10 years, waste stream reduction, alternative energy sources, and global warming are forcing Waste Management to undergo even more dramatic changes. What would you do if you were running a waste disposal company that made most of its money from landfills and the country adopted a strong sustainability mind-set?

Change in a Rural Community

HIGHLIGHT 14.2

There is no limit to what an organized group can do if it wants to.

George McLean, newspaper editor

Change does not just happen in organizations; it also occurs in communities. Whereas many suburbs are experiencing dramatic growth, most urban and rural communities are experiencing declines in population and business. Some rural communities are working hard to attract new businesses, such as ethanol plants and wind farms, and build new schools or new community centers; others are organizing to prevent Walmart or other large retailers from building stores in their communities. One of the real success stories of how a community transformed itself is Tupelo, Mississippi. Tupelo is famous for being the birthplace of Elvis Presley; in 1940 it also had the distinction of being the county seat of the poorest county in the poorest state in the country. But Lee County now has a medical center with over 6,000 employees, boasts 18 Fortune 500 manufacturing plants, and has added 1,000 new manufacturing jobs in each of the past 13 years. Tupelo now has a symphony, an art museum, a theater group, an 8,000-seat coliseum, and an outstanding recreational program. Its public schools have won national academic honors, and its athletic programs have won several state championships.

So how was Tupelo able to transform itself from a poor to a vibrant rural community? The town had no natural advantages, such as a harbor or natural resources, which would give it a competitive advantage. It also had no interstate highways, and the closest metropolitan centers were over 100 miles away. The key to Tupelo's success was the ability of the town's citizens to work together. More specifically, the citizens of Tupelo were able to (1) collaborate effectively in identifying the problems and needs of the community, (2) achieve a working consensus on goals and priorities, (3) agree on ways and means to implement goals and priorities, and (4) collaborate effectively in the agreed actions.

Tupelo's success started when local community members pooled resources to acquire a siring bull. The bull's offspring were used to start local ranches. Farmers shifted from planting cotton to growing crops needed to support the ranchers and local populace, and farming and ranching equipment distributors started up local operations. George McLean, the local newspaper publisher, kept the community focused on economic development and helped local entrepreneurs by subsidizing office and warehouse space. With various tax breaks and incentives from local bankers, furniture manufacturers started moving to town. A number of other businesses then sprang up to support the manufacturers, and community leaders made a concerted effort to expand and improve local health care and educational facilities to support the new workforce. Despite the successes to date, Tupelo is facing even bigger challenges, as many of the local furniture manufacturers are being threatened by low-cost manufacturers in China. But if any community were to succeed in the face of challenge, it would likely be Tupelo. The community seems to have the leaders needed to help citizens fully understand these new challenges and what to do to meet them. What would you do to preserve jobs and attract new businesses if you were the mayor of Tupelo?

Source: V. L. Grisham Jr., *Tupelo: The Evolution of a Community* (Dayton, OH: Kettering Foundation Press, 1999).

other authors. Beer's model also provides a road map for leadership practitioners wanting to implement an organizational change initiative, as well as a diagnostic tool for understanding why change initiatives fail. According to Beer,

$$C = D \times M \times P > R$$

We've long believed that when the rate of change inside an institution becomes slower than the rate of change outside, the end is in sight. The only question is when.

Jack Welch, former CEO of General Electric

The ultimate curse is to be a passenger on a large ship, to know that the ship is going to sink, to know precisely what to do to prevent it, and to realize that no one will listen.

Myron Tribus, Massachusetts Institute of Technology

The D in this formula represents followers' **dissatisfaction** with the current status quo. M symbolizes the **model** for change and includes the leader's vision of the future as well as the goals and systems that need to change to support the new vision. P represents **process**, which concerns developing and implementing a plan that articulates the who, what, when, where, and how of the change initiative. R stands for **resistance**; people resist change because they fear a loss of identity or social contacts, and good change plans address these sources of resistance. Finally the C corresponds to the **amount of change**. Notice that leaders can increase the amount of change by increasing the level of dissatisfaction, increasing the clarity of vision, developing a well-thought-out change plan, or decreasing the amount of resistance in followers. You should also note that the $D \times M \times P$ is a multiplicative function—increasing dissatisfaction but having no plan will result in little change. Likewise, if followers are content with the status quo, it may be difficult for leaders to get followers to change, no matter how compelling their vision or change plan may be. This model maintains that organizational change is a systematic process, and large-scale changes can take months if not years to implement.[15,21,22] Leadership practitioners who understand the model should be able to do a better job developing change initiatives and diagnosing where their initiatives may be getting stuck. Because change is an important component of leadership, we will go into more detail about each of the components of Beer's model.

Dissatisfaction

Followers' level of satisfaction is an important ingredient in a leader's ability to drive change. Followers who are relatively content are not apt to change; malcontents are much more likely to do something to change the situation. Although employee satisfaction is an important outcome of leadership, leaders who want to change the status quo may need to take action to decrease employee satisfaction levels. Follower's emotions are the fuel for organizational change, and change often requires a considerable amount of fuel. The key for leadership practitioners is to increase dissatisfaction (D) to the point where followers are inclined to take action, but not so much that they decide to leave the organization. So what can leaders do to increase follower dissatisfaction levels? Probably the first step is to determine how satisfied followers are with the current situation. This information can be gleaned from employee satisfaction surveys, grievance records, customer complaints, or conversations with followers. To increase dissatisfaction, leaders can talk about potential competitive, technology, or legal threats or employee concerns about the status quo. They can also capitalize on or even create some type of financial or political crisis, compare benchmarks against other organizations, or substantially increase performance standards. All of these actions can potentially heighten followers' emotional levels; however, leaders must ensure that these emotions are channeled toward the leader's vision for the organization (see Highlight 14.3).

Citizen Dissatisfaction and Guerrilla Warfare

HIGHLIGHT 14.3

Follower dissatisfaction should not be limited to organizations, as people can be just as unhappy with their government as they can be with their employers. The American Revolution, Gandhi's campaign to oust the British, Mao Zedong's and Fidel Castro's campaigns to convert China and Cuba to communist rule, the Arab Spring, and the civil wars in Syria and Libya are good examples of what can happen if those in charge let citizen dissatisfaction spin out of control. If the disenfranchised have no real outlet to vent their anger or change their government then they may resort to guerrilla warfare. Guerrilla warfare can be defined as a conflict with no front lines, no uniforms, no starting and ending points, that often targets civilians and is quite deadly. It is the war of choice whenever someone wants to overthrow a government that has a formal army with superior firepower. But how long has guerrilla warfare been around? Does it work? What role is technology playing in guerrilla warfare?

It turns out that wars between uniformed armies, such as the American Civil War, World War II, or the first Gulf War are fairly rare; guerrilla warfare is much more prevalent. For example, the American Indians, the Vietcong, the African National Congress in South Africa, the Irish Republican Army, the FARC in Columbia, al-Qaeda in Iraq, the Taliban in Afghanistan, and the Syrian Free Army all adopted guerrilla warfare tactics. Guerrilla wars tend to be quite long, 7 to 10 years on average, and the likelihood of success is not particularly high. Guerrilla warriors won 25 percent of the time before 1945, and this percentage has only improved to 40 percent over the last 70 years. For some guerrilla warriors, such as the Irish Republican Army, winning the war may not be as important as gaining valuable concessions from the opposition.

The key to winning or losing a guerrilla war is winning the hearts and minds of the populace. If noncombatants feel they are safer or better off with the opposition they will support the guerrilla movement. Conversely, if civilians believe their government better serves these needs then they will not support the movement. The use of car bombs, human shields, kidnapping, and assassinations is intended to show that the government cannot provide safety and security and win the hearts and minds of the greater population. Governments often play right into the hands of guerrilla warriors by adopting tactics that have little impact on the warriors but anger the greater population. The superior firepower strategy of "bombing people back to the Stone Age" and "Shock and Awe" used by the United States early in the Vietnam and second Iraq wars had minimal impact on enemy combatants but angered the local population. It was only when Generals Abrams and Petraeus introduced counterinsurgency tactics intended to win the hearts and minds of the local populace that the U.S. military started making progress in the Vietnam and Iraq wars.

Technology is playing a more important role in guerrilla warfare. Social media, YouTube videos, the Internet, and 24/7 news coverage all are now being used by both government and guerrilla forces to win popular support. Drones have made it possible for governments to kill guerrilla leaders with minimal civilian casualties. Perhaps the next big front in guerrilla warfare will be cyberattacks. What will happen to the hearts and minds of citizens when their power and water get shut off or when financial systems are corrupted? What if these attacks originate from outside a country's borders? What role is technology playing in the Syrian civil war? What tactics has Bashar Hafez al-Assad adopted to quell the insurgency, and are these tactics working? Do guerrilla leaders use a rational or emotional approach to drive change?

Sources: S. Gorman and S. Hughes, "U.S. Steps Up Alarm Over Cyber Attacks," *The Wall Street Journal,* March 13, 2013, pp. A1 and A8; M. Boot, "The Guerrilla Myth," *The Wall Street Journal,* January 19–20, 2013, pp. C1–C2; M. Boot, *Invisible Armies: An Epic History of Guerrilla Warfare from Ancient Times to the Present* (New York: Liveright, 2013); T. E. Ricks, *Fiasco: The American Military Adventure in Iraq* (New York: The Penguin Press, 2006); T. E. Ricks, *The Generals: American Military Command from World War II to Today* (New York: The Penguin Press, 2012).

Model

Without a compelling vision, there is no way for people who lose the most to reconcile their losses.
Bill Mease, business consultant

There are four key components to the model (*M*) variable in the change formula, and these include environmental scanning, a vision, the setting of new goals to support the vision, and needed system changes. As discussed earlier, organizations are constantly bombarded with economic, technological, competitive, legal, and social challenges. Good leaders constantly scan the external environment to assess the seriousness of these threats. They are also adept at internal scanning; they understand where the organization is doing well and falling short. Thus keeping up to date on current events, spending time reviewing organizational reports, and taking time to listen to followers' concerns are some techniques leaders use to conduct external and internal scans.[2,8,11,12,15,22,26] This information in turn is used to formulate a vision for the change initiative. What would a new organization look like if it were to successfully counter the gravest external threats, take advantage of new market opportunities, and overcome organizational shortcomings? What would be the purpose of the new organization, and why would people want to work in it? A good vision statement should answer these questions. Fortunately a vision statement does not have to be a solo effort on the part of the leader. Often leaders will either solicit followers for ideas or work with a team of followers to craft a vision statement.[8,15–17,27,28] Both of these actions can help to increase followers' commitment to the new vision.

Without a clear vision and an explicit set of goals, all decisions are based on politics.
Pete Ramstad, Toro

It is important to understand the difference between an organization's vision and goals. Just as ancient mariners used the stars to navigate, so should a vision provide guidance for an organization's actions. A vision helps an organization make choices about what it should and should not do, the kind of people it should hire and retain, the rules by which it should operate, and so on.[10,20,27–29] But just as the stars were not the final destination for the mariners, a vision is not the final destination for an organization. An organization's goals are the equivalent of the mariners' final destination, and they should spell out specifically what the organization is trying to accomplish and when they will get done.[2,8,19,26–29] Depending on the organization, these goals might concern market share, profitability, revenue or customer growth, quality, the implementation of new customer service or information technology systems, the number of patents awarded, school test scores, fund-raising targets, or the reduction of crime rates. Thus an organization's goals can be externally or internally focused or both, depending on the results of the environmental scan and the vision of the organization. Highlight 14.4 provides an example of a vision statement and organizational goals for a waste-to-energy power company. (This company burns trash to create electricity.)

After determining the organization's goals, the leader will need to determine which systems need to change for the organization to fulfill its vision and accomplish its goals. In other words, how do the marketing, sales,

An Example of a Vision Statement and Organizational Goals

HIGHLIGHT 14.4

Vision Statement

To be the industry leader in waste-to-energy operating companies.

Selected Organizational Goals

- Increase profitability growth from 5 to 8.5 percent.
- Hold maintenance and repair spending to 2015 levels.
- Maintain 92 percent boiler availability rate across all plants.
- Reduce unscheduled boiler downtime by 29 percent.

- Reduce accounting costs by 12 percent by centralizing the accounting function.
- Achieve zero recordables and zero lost time safety incidents across all plants.
- Implement a metals recovery system across all plants in order to boost recycle revenues by 26 percent.
- Win five new waste-to energy plant operating contracts in 2015.

Source: G. J. Curphy, *The Competitive Advantage Program for Wheelabrator Technologies Incorporated* (North Oaks, MN: Author, 2010).

manufacturing, quality, human resource, shipping, accounting, or customer service systems need to change if the organization is to succeed? And does the current organizational structure or culture support or interfere with the new vision? Leaders wanting their organizational change initiatives to succeed will need to take a systems thinking approach after setting organizational goals.[15,26,27,30] A **systems thinking approach** asks leaders to think about the organization as a set of interlocking systems, and explains how changes in one system can have intended and unintended consequences for other parts of the organization. For example, if a company wanted to grow market share and revenue, it might change the compensation system to motivate salespeople to go after new customers. However, this approach could also cause a number of problems in the manufacturing, quality, shipping, accounting, and customer service departments. Leaders who anticipate these problems make all of the necessary systems changes to increase the odds of organizational success. Leaders may need to set goals and put action plans in place for each of these system changes. These actions can be contrasted to **siloed thinking**, where leaders act to optimize their part of the organization at the expense of suboptimizing the organization's overall effectiveness.[15,26,27,30] For example, the vice president of sales could change the sales compensation plan if she believed her sole concern was annual revenues. This belief could be reinforced if her compensation was based primarily on hitting certain revenue targets. If she were a siloed thinker, she would also believe that profitability, quality, or customer service were not her concerns. However, this mode of thinking could ultimately lead to her downfall: quality and order fulfillment problems might cause customers to leave faster than new customers buy products.

568   Part Four   *Focus on the Situation*

FIGURE 14.1
The Components of Organizational Alignment

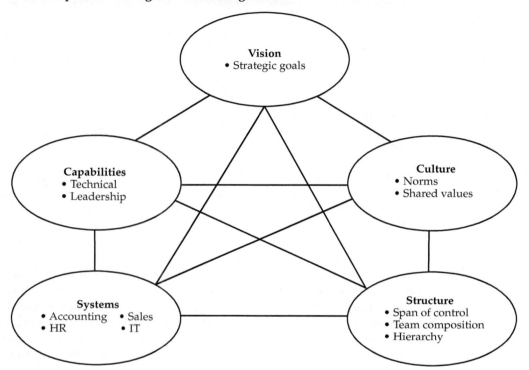

Figure 14.1 is a graphic depiction of a systems model for leadership practitioners. All the components of this model interact with and affect all the other components of the model. Therefore, leaders changing organizational vision or goals will need to think through the commensurate changes in the organization's structure, culture, systems, and leader and follower capabilities. Similarly, changes in the information or hiring systems can affect the organization's capabilities, culture, structure, or ability to meet its goals. One of the keys to successful organizational change is ensuring that all components in Figure 14.1 are in alignment. A common mistake for many leaders is to change the organization's vision, structure, and systems and overlook the organization's culture and leader and follower capabilities. This makes sense in that it is relatively easy to create a new vision statement, organizational chart, or compensation plan. Leaders either discount the importance of organizational culture and capabilities, falsely believe they are easy to change, or believe they are a given because they are so difficult to change. It is possible to change the culture and capabilities of an organization, but it takes considerable time and focused effort. Unfortunately about 70 percent of change initiatives fail, and the underlying cause for many of these failures is the leader's inability or unwillingness to address these culture and capabilities issues.[5–8,11,22,23,27,31–35]

Process

At this point in the change process, the leader may have taken certain steps to increase follower dissatisfaction. She may also have worked with followers to craft a new vision statement, set new team or organizational goals, and determined what organizational systems, capabilities, or structures need to change. In many ways, the D and M components of the change model are the easiest for leadership practitioners to alter. The process (P) component of the change model is where the change initiative becomes tangible and actionable because it consists of the development and execution of the **change plan**.[8,12,27,33,36] Good change plans outline the sequence of events, key deliverables, timelines, responsible parties, metrics, and feedback mechanisms needed to achieve the new organizational goals. They may also include the steps needed to increase dissatisfaction and deal with anticipated resistance, an outline of training and resource needs, and a comprehensive communication plan to keep all relevant parties informed.

Depending on the depth and breadth of change, change plans can be detailed and complicated. For example, the waste-to-energy company described earlier could no longer do what it had always done if it were to reach its goals outlined in Highlight 14.3. The company needed new behaviors, metrics, and feedback systems to achieve these goals. The company's change plan was quite extensive and consisted of an overall plan for the company as well as plant-specific goals and change plans. Each of these plans outlined the action steps, responsible parties, metrics, and due dates; progress against the plans was regularly reviewed in monthly plant business and operational reviews. The goals and change plans were constantly adjusted in these meetings to take into account unforeseen barriers, sooner-than-expected progress, and so on.

Of course the plan itself is only a road map for change. Change will occur only when the action steps outlined in the plan are actually carried out. This is another area where leadership practitioners can run into trouble. One of the reasons why CEOs fail is an inability to execute, and this is also one of the reasons why first-line supervisors through executives derail.[36–39] Perhaps the best way to get followers committed to a change plan is to have them create it. This way followers become early adopters and know what, why, when, where, who, and how things are to be done. Nevertheless, many times it is impossible for all the followers affected by the change to be involved with plan creation. In these cases follower commitment can be increased if the new expectations for behavior and performance are explicit, the personal benefits of the change initiative are made clear, and followers already have a strong and trusting relationship with their leader.[8,15,28] Even after taking all of these steps, leadership practitioners will still need to spend considerable time regularly reviewing progress and holding people accountable for their roles and responsibilities in the change plan. Followers face competing demands for time and effort,

Organizational change initiatives will only succeed when the changes are specified down to the individual employee level. Employees need to understand which old attitudes and behaviors are to be discarded and which new ones are to be acquired.

**Jerry Jellison,
University of
Southern California**

Muhammad Yunus

PROFILES IN LEADERSHIP 14.1

Muhammad Yunus was born as the third of nine children. He graduated 16th out of the 39,000 high school students who took national graduation exams in East Pakistan that year and attended Chittagong College to obtain bachelor's and master's degrees in economics. Yunus then worked in the Bureau of Economics and was a lecturer in Chittagong College before winning a Fulbright Scholarship. He used his scholarship to earn a PhD in economics at Vanderbilt University before returning to East Pakistan. East Pakistan had always been a poor country, but became even poorer after suffering the Bangladesh Liberation War in the early 1970s. Upon his return to Bangladesh Yunus began looking for effective ways to reduce the country's high poverty levels.

It was right after the war that Yunus lent a group of 42 women the equivalent of $27 to buy bamboo. The women had started up a small chair building business, but their money lenders charged such high interest rates that all their profits were used up paying off their loans. The women essentially became indentured slaves, as the banks in Bangladesh were unwilling to lend money to any perceived to be a high credit risk. Yunus charged the women the equivalent of 4 percent on their loan and helped them break out of the cycle of poverty. This event was the beginning of Yunus's work in microlending,

which is lending small amounts of money to poor entrepreneurs to help them start up and grow businesses. Yunus lent money to small groups he called "solidarity groups," designating them as people who were more likely to repay loans and also help other members in time of need.

In 1983 Yunus opened Grameen Bank, a bank that specialized in providing group loans to poor entrepreneurs. Over the past 30 years the bank has expanded across multiple countries, has made over $7 billion in loans, and has seen a repayment rate of 96 to 97 percent. Yunus has probably done as much as anyone to improve the lives of the poor, and because of these efforts has been listed as one of the top 12 greatest entrepreneurs of our time by *Money* magazine, one of the 25 most influential business leaders in the past 25 years by Wharton Business School, and received the Nobel Peace prize in 2006.

Do you think Yunus used a rational or emotional approach to drive change in rural communities?

Sources: N. St. Anthony, "Small Loans, Big Results," *The Minneapolis-Star Tribune,* March 10, 2013, p. D3; http://www.pbs.org/opb/thenewheroes/meet/yunus.htm; http://money.cnn.com/galleries/2012/news/companies/1203/gallery.greatest-entrepreneurs.fortune/13.html; http://huffingtonpost.com/john-wellington-ennis/bonsai-people_b_974972.html; http://www.time.com/time/asia/2006/heroes/bl_yunus.html;

In terms of barriers to change, there is not a single rural community that wouldn't benefit from a few timely deaths.

Jim Krile, community researcher

---

and a lack of follow-through will cause many followers to drop the change initiative off of their radar screens. Leaders should also anticipate shifts in followership types once the change plan is implemented. Self-starters may shift to become criticizers, brown-nosers to slackers, or slackers to criticizers. Leaders who address these shifts in types and inappropriate follower behaviors in a swift and consistent manner are more likely to succeed with their change initiatives.

Resistance

Why would followership styles shift as a result of a change initiative? One reason is that it may take some time before the benefits of change are realized. Leaders, followers, and other stakeholders often assume

FIGURE 14.2
The Expectation–
Performance Gap

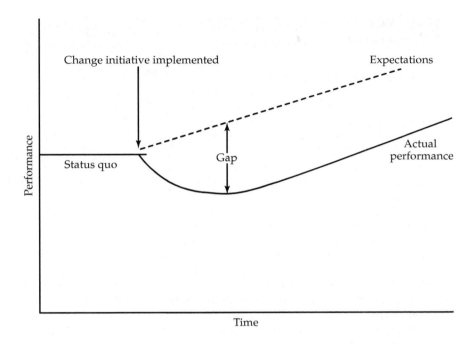

that performance, productivity, or customer service will immediately improve upon the acquisition of new equipment, systems, behaviors, and so on. However, there is often a temporary drop in performance or productivity as followers learn new systems and skills. This difference between initial expectations and reality is called the **expectation–performance gap** and can be the source of considerable frustration (see Figure 14.2). If not managed properly, it can spark resistance (*R*), causing followers to revert back to old behaviors and systems to get things done. Leaders can help followers deal with their frustration by setting realistic expectations, demonstrating a high degree of patience, and ensuring that followers gain proficiency with the new systems and skills as quickly as possible. Good change plans address the expectation–performance gap by building in training and coaching programs to improve follower skill levels.[27,28,39]

Another reason why followers might resist change is a fear of loss.[3–5,8–10,21,23,27,33,34,40] Because of the change, followers are afraid of losing power, close relationships with others, valued rewards, and their sense of identity or, on the other hand, being seen as incompetent. According to Beer,[21] the fear of loss is a predictable and legitimate response to any change initiative, and some of a leader's responses to these fears can be found in Table 14.1. Change initiatives are more likely to be successfully adopted if their change plans identify and address potential areas of resistance. People also seem to go through some predictable

Everybody resists change, particularly those who have to change the most.
**James O'Toole,
Aspen Institute**

572   Part Four   *Focus on the Situation*

TABLE 14.1
Common Losses with Change

Source: J. F. Krile, G. J. Curphy, and D. R. Lund, *The Community Leadership Handbook: Framing Ideas, Building Relationships, and Mobilizing Resources* (St Paul, MN: The Fieldstone Alliance, 2006).

Loss of	Possible Leader Actions
Power	Demonstrate empathy, good listening skills, and new ways to build power.
Competence	Offer coaching, mentoring, training, peer coaching, job aids, and so forth.
Relationships	Help employees build new relationships before change occurs or soon thereafter.
Rewards	Design and implement new reward system to support change initiative.
Identity	Demonstrate empathy; emphasize value of new roles.

reactions when confronted with change. An example might help to clarify the typical stages people go through when coping with change. Suppose you were working for a large company that needed to lay off 30 percent of the workforce due to a slowdown in the economy and declining profits. If you were one of the people asked to leave, your first reaction might be shock or surprise. You might not have been aware that market conditions were so poor or that you would be among those affected by the layoff. Next you would go through an anger stage. You might be angry that you had dedicated many long evenings and weekends to the company and now the company no longer wanted your services. After anger would come the rejection stage. In this stage you would start to question whether the company really knew what it was doing by letting you go and perhaps rationalize that they would probably be calling you back. In the final stage, acceptance, you would realize that the company might not ask you back, and you would start to explore other career options. These four reactions to change—shock, anger, rejection, and acceptance—make up what is known as the **SARA model**.[41] Most people go through these four stages whenever they get passed over for a promotion, receive negative feedback on a 360-degree report, get criticized by their boss, or the like.

But what should a leadership practitioner do with the SARA model? Perhaps the first step is to simply recognize the four reactions to change. Second, leaders need to understand that individual followers can take more or less time to work through the four stages. Leaders can, however, accelerate the pace in which followers work though the four stages by maintaining an open door policy, demonstrating empathy, and listening to concerns. Third, it is important to note that people are not likely to take any positive action toward a change initiative until they reach the acceptance stage. This does not mean they are happy with the change—only that they accept the inevitability of the change. Fourth, leaders also need to understand that where people are in the SARA model often varies

FIGURE 14.3
Reactions to Change

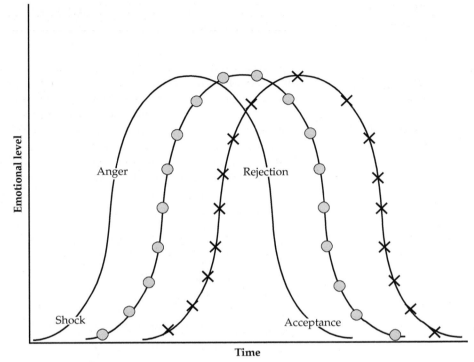

— Top leaders

⬤ Middle managers

✕ Individual contributors

Commitment is nice, but doses of compliance may be necessary.
**Michael Beer,
Harvard Business
School**

according to organization level. Usually the first people to realize that a change initiative needs to be implemented are the organization's top leaders. Like everyone else, they go through the four stages, but they are the first to do so. The next people to hear the news are middle managers, followed by first-line supervisors and individual contributors. These three groups also go through the emotional stages of the SARA model but do so at different times. These differences in emotional reactions by organizational level are depicted in Figure 14.3. What is interesting in Figure 14.3 is that just when top executives have reached the acceptance stage, first-line supervisors and individual contributors are in the anger or rejection stages. By this time top leaders are ready to get on with the implementation of the change initiative and may not understand why the rest of the organization is still struggling. Because they are already at the acceptance stage, top leaders may fail to demonstrate empathy and listening skills, and this may be another reason for the depressed performance depicted in Figure 14.2.

574   Part Four   *Focus on the Situation*

Concluding Comments about the Rational Approach to Organizational Change

The situational, follower, and leader components of the rational approach to organizational change are shown in Figure 14.4. Although organizational vision, goals, and change plans are often a collaborative effort between the leader and followers, they are the primary responsibility of the leader. Leaders also need to think about the importance of critical mass for driving change.[8,15,27,28,35] They may be more successful by initially focusing their change efforts on early adopters and those on the fence rather than on those followers who are the most adamant about maintaining the status quo. Once a critical mass is reached, the adopters can exert peer pressure on followers who are reluctant to change.[8,22,27,28] This approach also maintains that the leader needs both good leadership and good management skills if a change initiative is to succeed over the long term. Leadership skills are important for determining a new vision for the organization, increasing dissatisfaction, coaching followers on how to do things differently, and overcoming resistance. Management skills are important when setting new goals and creating, implementing, and reviewing progress on change plans. Both sets of skills not only are important components in organizational change but also may play a key role in determining whether a new company

FIGURE 14.4
The Rational Approach to Organization Change and the Interactional Framework

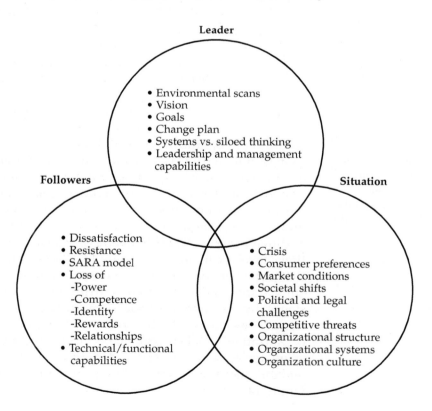

will succeed or fail. Because of their strong leadership skills, entrepreneurs are often good at starting up new organizations. Many of these individuals can get people excited about their vision for the new company. However, if entrepreneurs fail to possess or appreciate the importance of management skills, they may not create the systems, policies, and procedures necessary to keep track of shifting consumer preferences, revenues, customer satisfaction, quality, and costs. As a result, these individuals may not have the information they need to make good operational and financial decisions, and their companies eventually file for bankruptcy. On the other hand, it is hard to see how planning and execution skills alone will result in the formation of a new company or drive organizational change. It is almost impossible to start up a new company—or for an organization to successfully change—if the person in charge does not have a compelling vision or fails to motivate others to do something different. Many of the other reasons why organizational change initiatives fail have their roots in underdeveloped leadership or management skills.[11,37]

Although both sets of skills are important, leadership practitioners should recognize that there is a natural tension between leadership and management skills. In many ways management skills help to maintain the status quo; they help to ensure consistency in behaviors and results. Leadership skills are often used to change the status quo; they help to change the purpose and processes by which an organization gets things done. Leaders who overuse or overemphasize either set of skills are likely to suboptimize team or organizational performance. Nonetheless, two leadership and management skills seem vitally important to driving change and are worth discussing in more detail. **Adaptive leadership** involves behaviors associated with being able to successfully flex and adjust to changing situations. Change, challenge, and adversity seem to be part of most organizations today, and the most effective leaders are those who readily adapt their leadership styles to changing situational demands.[42,43] And because of the constant bombardment of change, learning agility also seems to play a vital role in leadership effectiveness. **Learning agility** is the capability and willingness to learn from experience and apply these lessons to new situations.[44] The most effective leaders are those with high levels of learning agility and adaptability—not only do they know how to build teams and get results through others in changing situations, but also they can flex and adjust their behavior as needed to adapt to situational demands. The first part of this chapter was designed to help leadership practitioners better understand when to use leadership and management skills in the change process, and education and experience can help leadership practitioners improve both sets of skills.

Finally, it is worth noting that the rational approach gives leaders a systematic process for driving change and increasing understanding of why change initiatives succeed or fail in their respective organizations. Leadership practitioners can use the $C = D \times M \times P > R$ model as a road map for

A Tool for Understanding Rational Change: Force Field Analysis

HIGHLIGHT 14.5

If you really want to understand something, then try to change it.

Kurt Lewin, researcher

Force field analysis (FFA) is a tool that can be used to gain a better understanding of organizational change. FFA uses vectors to graphically depict the driving forces and the barriers to an organizational change. Stronger forces and barriers are represented by larger vectors; weaker forces and barriers are represented by smaller vectors. Here is an example of an FFA for a rural school district trying to improve third grade student achievement test scores in math:

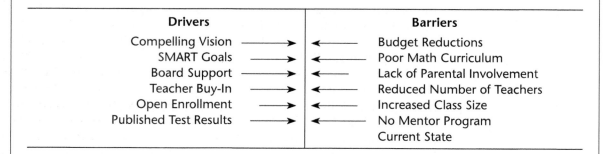

Drivers		Barriers
Compelling Vision ⟶	⟵	Budget Reductions
SMART Goals ⟶	⟵	Poor Math Curriculum
Board Support ⟶	⟵	Lack of Parental Involvement
Teacher Buy-In ⟶	⟵	Reduced Number of Teachers
Open Enrollment ⟶	⟵	Increased Class Size
Published Test Results ⟶	⟵	No Mentor Program
		Current State

The first step in an FFA is to graphically depict the current state as shown here. In many cases the drivers and barriers to change in the current state should more or less balance out because they represent the current status quo. The second step in an FFA is to formulate strategies to increase the drivers or reduce the barriers to organizational change. (Leaders will often get better results if they focus on reducing barriers rather than increasing the number or size of the drivers for change.) The third and final step in an FFA is to create and implement change plans that outline the steps, accountable parties, and timelines for increasing drivers and reducing the barriers to change.

Use an FFA to depict a change initiative going on at your school or in the local community. What would you recommend doing to drive change based on your FFA?

Sources: K. Lewin, "Field Theory and Experiment in Social Psychology: Concepts and Methods," *American Journal of Sociology* 44 (1939) pp. 868–96. G.J. Curphy & R. Hogan, *The Rocket Model: Practical Advice for Building High Performing Teams* (Tulsa, OK: Hogan Press, 2012).

creating a new vision and goals, changing the products and services their organizations provide, or changing the IT, financial, operations, maintenance, or compensation systems used to support organizational goals. Likewise, leadership practitioners can also use this model to diagnose where their change initiatives have fallen short—perhaps followers were reasonably satisfied with the status quo or did not buy into the new vision and goals, critical systems changes were not adequately identified, or change plans were incomplete or improperly implemented. Given the explanatory power of the model, the rational approach to change gives leaders a useful heuristic for driving organizational and community change.

The Emotional Approach to Organizational Change: Charismatic and Transformational Leadership

The comment that best summarized the situation as I moved into the chancellor's role was when somebody told me that the Department of Education was there not to serve the kids, but to serve the employees.

Joel Klein, former Chancellor, New York City Department of Education

Although the rational approach provides a straightforward model for organizational change, it seems that many large-scale political, societal, or organizational changes were not this formulaic. For example, it is doubtful that Jesus Christ, Muhammad, Joan of Arc, Vladimir Lenin, Adolf Hitler, Mahatma Gandhi, Mao Zedong, Martin Luther King Jr., the Ayatollah Khomeini, Nelson Mandela, Fidel Castro, Hugo Chávez, or Osama bin Laden followed some change formula or plan, yet these individuals were able to fundamentally change their respective societies. Although these leaders differ in a number of important ways, one distinct characteristic they all share is charisma. Charismatic leaders are passionate, driven individuals who can paint a compelling vision of the future. Through this vision they can generate high levels of excitement among followers and build particularly strong emotional attachments with them. The combination of a compelling vision, heightened emotional levels, and strong personal attachments often compels followers to put forth greater effort to meet organizational or societal challenges. The enthusiasm and passion generated by charismatic leaders seems to be a dual-edged sword, however. Some charismatic movements can result in positive and relatively peaceful organizational or societal changes; Evo Morales and Hugo Chavez have done a great deal to help the poor in Bolivia and Venezuela. On the downside, when this passion is used for selfish or personal gains, history mournfully suggests it can have an equally devastating effect on society. Examples here might include Zimbabwe President Robert Mugabe or Kim Jung-Un of North Korea.

What is it about charismatic leadership that causes followers to get so excited about future possibilities that they may willingly give up their lives for a cause? Even though many people conjure up images of charismatic individuals when thinking about leadership, the systematic investigation of charismatic leadership is relatively recent. The remainder of this chapter begins with a historical review of the research on charismatic leadership and the leader–follower–situation components of charismatic leadership. We will then review the most popular conceptualization of charisma: Bass's theory of transformational and transactional leadership. We conclude this chapter by comparing and contrasting the rational and emotional approaches to organizational change.

Charismatic Leadership: A Historical Review

Prior to the mid-1970s charismatic leadership was studied primarily by historians, political scientists, and sociologists. Of this early research, Max Weber arguably wrote the single most important work. Weber was a sociologist interested primarily in how authority and religious and economic forces affected societies over time. Weber maintained that societies could

An institution is the lengthened shadow of one man.

Ralph Waldo Emerson, writer

be categorized into one of three types of authority systems: traditional, legal–rational, and charismatic.[45]

In the **traditional authority system,** the traditions or unwritten laws of the society dictate who has authority and how this authority can be used. The transfer of authority in such systems is based on traditions such as passing power to the first-born son of a king after the king dies. Historical examples would include the monarchies of England from the 1400s to 1600s or the dynasties of China from 3000 BC to the 1700s. Some modern examples of the traditional authority system include Saudi Arabia, Kuwait, Jordan, North Korea, and Brunei. But these examples should not be limited to countries—many of the CEOs in privately held companies or publicly traded companies that are controlled by a majority shareholder are often the children or relatives of the previous CEO. Examples include Wal-Mart, BMW, Samsung, Cargill, Amway, and Bechtel.

In the **legal–rational authority system** a person possesses authority not because of tradition or birthright but because of the laws that govern the position occupied. For example, elected officials and most leaders in nonprofit or publicly traded companies are authorized to take certain actions because of the positions they occupy. The power is in the position itself rather than in the person who occupies the position. Thus John Kerry can take certain actions not because of whom he is or is related to but because of his role as U.S. Secretary of State.

These two authority systems can be contrasted to the **charismatic authority system**, in which people derive authority because of their exemplary characteristics. Charismatic leaders are thought to possess superhuman qualities or powers of divine origin that set them apart from ordinary mortals. The locus of authority in this system rests with the individual possessing these unusual qualities; it is not derived from birthright or laws. According to Weber, charismatic leaders come from the margins of society and emerge as leaders in times of great social crisis. These leaders focus society both on the problems it faces and on the revolutionary solutions proposed by the leader. Thus charismatic authority systems are usually the result of a revolution against the traditional and legal–rational authority systems. Examples of these revolutions might be the overthrow of the Shah of Iran by the Ayatollah Khomeini, the ousting of the British in India by Mahatma Gandhi, the success of Martin Luther King Jr. in changing the civil rights laws in the United States, or the economic and social change movements led by Hugo Chavez in Venezuela. Unlike traditional or legal–rational authority systems, charismatic authority systems tend to be short-lived. Charismatic leaders must project an image of success in order for followers to believe they possess superhuman qualities; any failures will cause followers to question the divine qualities of the leader and in turn erode the leader's authority.

A number of historians, political scientists, and sociologists have commented on various aspects of Weber's conceptualization of charismatic authority systems. Of all these comments, however, probably the biggest controversy surrounding Weber's theory concerns the locus of charismatic leadership. Is charisma primarily the result of the situation or social context facing the leader, the leader's extraordinary qualities, or the strong relationships between charismatic leaders and followers? A number of authors have argued that charismatic movements could not take place unless the society was in a crisis.[46–48] Along these lines, Friedland, Gerth and Mills, and Kanter have argued that before a leader with extraordinary qualities would be perceived as charismatic, the social situation must be such that followers recognize the relevance of the leader's qualities.[49–51] Others have argued that charismatic leadership is primarily a function of the leader's extraordinary qualities, not the situation. These qualities include having extraordinary powers of vision, the rhetorical skills to communicate this vision, a sense of mission, high self-confidence and intelligence, and high expectations for followers.[52,53] Finally, several authors have argued that the litmus test for charismatic leadership does not depend on the leader's qualities or the presence of a crisis, but rather on followers' reactions to their leader. According to this argument, charisma is attributed only to those leaders who can develop particularly strong emotional attachments with followers.[54–58]

The debate surrounding charismatic leadership shifted dramatically with the publication of James MacGregor Burns's *Leadership*. Burns was a prominent political scientist who had spent a career studying leadership in the national political arena. He believed that leadership could take one of two forms. **Transactional leadership** occurred when leaders and followers were in some type of exchange relationship to get needs met. The exchange could be economic, political, or psychological, and examples might include exchanging money for work, votes for political favors, loyalty for consideration, and so forth. Transactional leadership is common but tends to be transitory in that there may be no enduring purpose to hold parties together once a transaction is made. Burns also noted that while this type of leadership could be quite effective, it did not result in organizational or societal change and instead tended to perpetuate and legitimize the status quo.[14]

The second form of leadership is **transformational leadership**, which changes the status quo by appealing to followers' values and their sense of higher purpose. Transformational leaders articulate the problems in the current system and have a compelling vision of what a new society or organization could be. This new vision of society is intimately linked to the values of both the leader and the followers; it represents an ideal that is congruent with their value systems. According to Burns, transformational leadership is ultimately a moral exercise in that it raises the standard of human conduct. This implies that the acid test for transformational leadership might be the answer to the question "Do the changes advocated by the leader advance or hinder the development of the organization or

Kleptocracies and Authority Systems

HIGHLIGHT 14.6

The difference between a kleptocrat and a wise statesman, between a robber baron and a benefactor, is merely one of degree.

Jared Diamond, researcher

In the book *Guns, Germs, and Steel* author Jared Diamond describes the historic, geographic, climatic, technologic, demographic, and economic factors that have caused human societies to emerge, thrive, or disappear. One phenomenon that appears across many groups as they grow to 100 or so people is the emergence of some form of government. Sometimes this government is based on the power of a family (traditional authority); other times it is more fomalized (legal–rational authority); and at times it is based on a single leader (charismatic authority). Governments emerge because groups this size begin to recognize that they can solve common problems, such as finding food and shelter and defending against enemies by pooling resources rather than working as individuals. Thus members of the group give up certain liberties and resources but gain services they could ill afford on their own. Some people perceive this exchange to be relatively fair; the services they receive seem to offset their costs in terms of taxes, food, and so on. But at other times these governments appear to be nothing more than kleptocracies—people pay large tributes to a small group of people at the top but get little in return. Kleptocracies can be found in traditional authority systems; what do British citizens get in return

for paying taxes to support having a queen? Kleptocracies can also be found in legal–rational systems; the collapse of the financial services and automobile industries in 2008–2009 are examples of executives ripping off customers, employees, and shareholders. Charismatic leaders can also head up kleptocracies. At one time Robert Mugabe was seen as a charismatic leader by many of his citizens, but with his $2 million birthday party, poverty rates at an all-time high, and inflation hovering at 8,000 percent per year, it seems that most citizens of Zimbabwe are not enjoying the same fruits of success.

Because charismatic leaders are more likely to emerge in a crisis, they may be more likely to appear when citizens believe their fees, taxes, goods, cattle, or people payments are misaligned with the benefits they are getting by keeping their government in place. This is precisely what happened when Mao, Lenin, and Castro led their communist revolutions in China, Russia, and Cuba. More recently this same phenomenon has allowed charismatic leaders to be elected into the presidential suites in Venezuela and Ecuador. The Arab Spring was a revolt against the corrupt and unfair rule found in many Middle Eastern countries and the (un)fairness of the tax versus service exchange is often used by politicians in the United States to get elected into office.

Is your current government a kleptocracy? Why or why not? What information would you use to justify your answer?

Source: J. Diamond, *Guns, Germs, and Steel: The Fates of Human Societies* (New York: W.W. Norton, 1999).

society?" Transformational leaders are also adept at **reframing** issues; they point out how the problems or issues facing followers can be resolved if they fulfill the leader's vision of the future. These leaders also teach followers how to become leaders in their own right and incite them to play active roles in the change movement (see Profiles in Leadership 14.1–14.5).

All transformational leaders are charismatic, but not all charismatic leaders are transformational. Transformational leaders are charismatic because

Nelson Mandela

PROFILES IN LEADERSHIP 14.2

South Africa was ruled by a white minority government for much of the past 200 years. Although blacks made up over 75 percent of the populace, whites owned most of the property, ran most of the businesses, and controlled virtually all the country's resources. Moreover, blacks did not have the right to vote and often worked under horrible conditions for little or no wages. Seeing the frustration of his people, Nelson Mandela spent 50 years working to overturn white minority rule. He started by organizing the African National Congress, a nonviolent organization that protested white rule through work stoppages, strikes, and riots. Several whites were killed in the early riots, and in 1960 the police killed or injured over 250 blacks in Sharpeville. Unrest over the Sharpeville incident caused 95 percent of the black workforce to go on strike for two weeks, and the country declared a state of emergency. Mandela then orchestrated acts of sabotage to further pressure the South African government to change. The organization targeted installations and took special care to ensure that no lives were lost in

the bombing campaign. Mandela was arrested in 1962 and spent the next 27 years in prison. While in prison he continued to promote civil unrest and majority rule, and his cause eventually gained international recognition. He was offered but turned down a conditional release from prison in 1985. After enormous international and internal pressure, South African President F. W. de Klerk "unbanned" the ANC and unconditionally released Nelson Mandela from prison. Nonetheless South Africa remained in turmoil, and in 1992, 4 million workers went on strike to protest white rule. Because of this pressure, Mandela forced de Klerk to sign a document outlining multiparty elections. Mandela won the 1994 national election and was the first democratically elected leader of the country.

Do you think Nelson Mandela is a charismatic leader? Why or why not?

Sources: M. Fatima, *Higher Than Hope: The Authorized Biography of Nelson Mandela* (New York: Harper & Row, 1990); S. Clark, *Nelson Mandela Speaks: Forming a Democratic, Nonracist South Africa* (New York: Pathfinder Press, 1993).

they can articulate a compelling vision of the future and form strong emotional attachments with followers. However, this vision and these relationships are aligned with followers' value systems and help them get their needs met. Charismatic leaders who are not transformational can convey a vision and form strong emotional bonds with followers, but they do so to get their own (that is, the leader's) needs met. Both charismatic and transformational leaders strive for organizational or societal change; the difference is whether the changes are for the benefit of the leader or the followers. Finally, transformational leaders are always controversial. Charismatic leadership almost inherently raises conflicts over values or definitions of the social good. Controversy also arises because the people with the most to lose in any existing system will put up the most resistance to a transformational change initiative. The emotional levels of those resisting the transformational leadership movement are often just as great as those who embrace it, and this may be the underlying cause for the violent ends to Martin Luther King Jr., John F. Kennedy, Mahatma Gandhi, Joan of Arc, and Jesus Christ. Burns stated that transformational leadership always involves conflict and change, and transformational leaders must be willing to embrace conflict,

582   Part Four   *Focus on the Situation*

Osama bin Laden

PROFILES IN LEADERSHIP 14.3

Osama bin Laden was a member of the prestigious bin Laden family in Saudi Arabia and the founder of al-Qaeda. Bin Laden was born in Riyadh, Saudi Arabia, and was brought up as a devout Sunni Muslim. He attended the Al-Thager Model School in Jeddah, "the school of the elite," and was exposed to many teachings of the Muslim Brotherhood while growing up. He attended university after his secondary schooling, but it is uncertain what he majored in or whether he obtained a degree. At the age of 17 he married his first wife and reportedly had up to four wives and fathered anywhere between 12 and 24 children. In person he was said to be soft-spoken, charming, respectful, and polite. He appeared to live a life of discipline, simplicity, and self-sacrifice, preferring that his wealth be used to benefit al-Qaeda rather than improve his personal lifestyle.

Bin Laden first engaged in militant activities in the late 1970s, when he moved to Pakistan to help the mujahedeen fight a guerilla war to oust the Soviet Union from Afghanistan. His family connections and wealth helped to fund many of the mujahedeen's efforts over the next 10 years. Some of his money and arms may have come from the Central Intelligence Agency: the United States also wanted to get the Soviet Union out of Afghanistan.

After Iraq invaded Kuwait in 1990, bin Laden offered to protect Saudi Arabia with 12,000 armed men, but his offer was rebuffed by the Saudi royal family. Shortly thereafter bin Laden publicly denounced the presence of coalition troops ("infidels") on Saudi soil and wanted all U.S. bases on the Arab peninsula to be closed. He eventually left Saudi Arabia to take up residence in Sudan, where he established a new base for mujahedeen operations. The purpose of his African organization was to propagate Islamist philosophy and recruit new members to the cause. In 1996 bin Laden left Sudan and went to Afghanistan to set up a new base of operations, where he forged a close relationship with the leaders of the new Taliban government.

Bin Laden issued fatwas in 1996 and 1998 that stated that Muslims should kill civilians and military personnel from the United States and allied countries until they withdrew support for Israel and withdrew military forces from Islamic countries. It is believed he was either directly involved with or funded the 1992 bombing of the Gold Mihor Hotel in Aden, Yemen; the massacre of German tourists in Luxor, Egypt, in 1997; the 1998 bombings of two U.S. embassies in Africa; and the World Trade Center and Pentagon bombings on September 11, 2001. He, al-Qaeda, and its splinter movements were involved with the London subway bombing, the wars in Afghanistan and Iraq, and unrest in the Philippines, Thailand, Indonesia, and Somalia. Bin Laden was formulating a number of new terrorists attacks when he was killed by a U.S. Navy SEALs team during a raid in Abbottabad, Pakistan, in 2012.

It is clear that bin Laden had a following, and that following has grown into the tens of thousands over the past 20 years. These followers are very devoted; some are so committed that they volunteer to be suicide bombers. A much larger group may not play active roles in al-Qaeda but are clearly sympathetic to its cause. But as strong as these followers' feelings were about bin Laden, others were just as intent to see him dead or behind bars.

Is Osama bin Laden a charismatic leader or a transformational leader? Would your answer to this question change if you were sympathetic to the al-Qaeda cause? Do you think his death helped or hurt others' perceptions of bin Laden's charisma?

Sources: http://topics.nytimes.com/reference/ timestopics/people/b/osama_bin_laden/index.html; http://www.infoplease.com/spot/osamabinladen.html.

make enemies, exhibit a high level of self-sacrifice, and be thick-skinned and focused to perpetuate their cause (see Profiles in Leadership 14.3).[59–65]

Leadership researchers Gary Yukl, Jerry Hunt, and Jay Conger have all maintained that the publication of *Leadership* played a key role in renewing interest in the topic of leadership.[66–68] As a result, research over the past

35 years has explored cross-cultural, gender, succession, leader, follower, situational, and performance issues in charismatic or transformational leadership. From these efforts we now know that charismatic or transformational leadership is both common and rare. It is common because it can occur in almost every social stratum across every culture. For example, a high school student leader in France, a military cadet leader at the U.S. Naval Academy, a Kenyan community leader, an Indonesian hospital leader, or a Russian business executive could all be perceived as charismatic or transformational leaders. But it is also rare because most people in positions of authority are not perceived to be charismatic or transformational leaders. We also know that females such as Dilma Rousseff, Oprah Winfrey, and Julia Gillard tend to be perceived as more charismatic than their male counterparts and that transformational leadership results in higher group performance than transactional leadership.[69-88] Although charismatic or transformational leadership often results in large-scale organizational change and higher organizational performance, there is little evidence that these changes remain permanent in organizational settings after the leader moves on.[89,90] In addition, some researchers have found that charismatic or transformational leaders did not result in higher organizational performance, but they did earn higher paychecks for themselves.[89,91-93] In other words, these leaders were good at garnering attention, hogging credit, and changing their respective organizations, but many of these changes did not result in higher organizational performance.

As a result of this research, we also have three newer theories of charismatic or transformational leadership. Conger and Kanungo used a stage model to differentiate charismatic from noncharismatic leaders. Charismatic leaders begin by thoroughly assessing the current situation and pinpointing problems with the status quo. They then articulate a vision that represents a change from the status quo. This vision represents a challenge and is a motivating force for change for followers. The vision must be articulated in a way that increases dissatisfaction with the status quo and compels followers to take action. In the final stage, leaders build trust in their vision and goals by personal example, risk taking, and their total commitment to the vision.[94] The theory developed by House and his colleagues describes how charismatic leaders achieve higher performance by changing followers' self-concepts. Charismatic leaders are believed to motivate followers by changing their perceptions of work itself, offering an appealing vision of the future, developing a collective identity among followers, and increasing their confidence in getting the job done.[95-97] Avolio and Bass's theory of transformational and transactional leadership is essentially an extension of Burns's theory. Unlike Burns, who viewed transactional and transformational leadership as the extremes of a single continuum, Avolio and Bass viewed these two concepts as independent leadership dimensions. Thus leaders can be transformational and transactional, transactional but not transformational, and so on. Transformational leaders are believed to achieve stronger results because they heighten followers' awareness of goals and the means to achieve them, they convince followers to take action for the collective good of the group, and their vision of the future helps followers satisfy higher order needs. Because Avolio and Bass created a questionnaire to assess a leader's standing on transactional and transformational leadership, this theory is by far the most thoroughly researched and will be discussed in more detail later in this chapter.[98]

What Are the Common Characteristics of Charismatic and Transformational Leadership?

The ultimate measure of a man is not where he stands in moments of comfort and convenience, but where he stands in moments of challenge and controversy.

Martin Luther King Jr., civil rights leader

Although there are some important differences in the theories offered by Conger and Kanungo, House, and Avolio and Bass, in reality they are far more similar than different. These researchers either do not differentiate charismatic from transformational leadership, or see charisma as a component of transformational leadership. Therefore, we will use these terms somewhat interchangeably in the next section, although we acknowledge the fundamental difference between these two types of leadership. A review of the common leader, follower, and situational factors from Burns and the three more recent theories can be found in Figure 14.5. Like the past debates surrounding charismatic leadership, modern researchers are divided on whether charismatic leadership is due to the leader's superhuman qualities, a special relationship between leaders and followers, the situation, or some combination of these factors. Irrespective of the locus of charismatic leadership, the research provides overwhelming support for the notion that transformational leaders are effective at large-scale societal or organizational change.

Leader Characteristics

Charismatic leaders are meaning makers. They pick and choose from the rough materials of reality and construct pictures of great possibilities. Their persuasion then is of the subtlest kind, for they interpret reality to offer us images of the future that are irresistible.

Jay Conger, University of Southern California

Leadership researchers have spent considerably more time and effort trying to identify the unique characteristics of charismatic leaders than they have exploring follower or situational factors. This is partly because some researchers believe that it is possible to drive higher levels of organizational change or performance through the selection or training of charismatic leaders.[64,70,76,77,82,83,99,100] Although some scholars have argued that the leader's personal qualities are the key to charismatic or transformational leadership, we do not believe the leader's qualities alone result in charismatic leadership.[101,102] We do, however, acknowledge several common threads in the behavior and style of both charismatic and transformational leaders, and these include their vision and values, rhetorical skills, ability to build a particular kind of image in the hearts and minds of their followers, and personalized style of leadership.

Vision

Both transformational and charismatic leaders are inherently future-oriented. They involve helping a group move "from here to there."

FIGURE 14.5
Factors Pertaining to Charismatic Leadership and the Interactional Framework

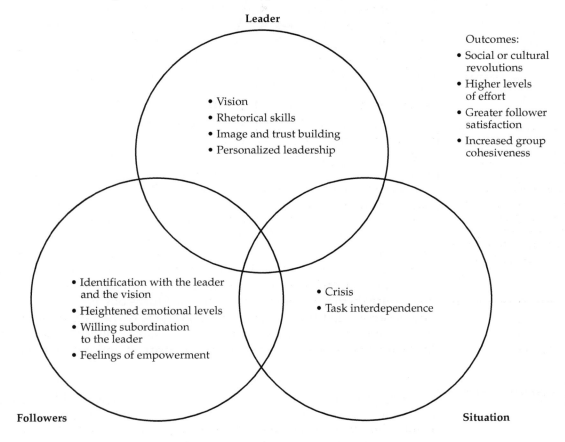

Leader

• Vision
• Rhetorical skills
• Image and trust building
• Personalized leadership

Outcomes:
• Social or cultural revolutions
• Higher levels of effort
• Greater follower satisfaction
• Increased group cohesiveness

• Identification with the leader and the vision
• Heightened emotional levels
• Willing subordination to the leader
• Feelings of empowerment

• Crisis
• Task interdependence

Followers

Situation

Never underestimate the power of purpose.
**Price Pritchett,
consultant**

Charismatic leaders perceive fundamental discrepancies between the way things are and the way things can (or should) be. They recognize the shortcomings of the present order and offer an imaginative **vision** to overcome them. A charismatic leader's vision is not limited to grand social movements; leaders can develop a compelling vision for any organization and organizational level. This vision can have both a stimulating and a unifying effect on the efforts of followers, which can help drive greater organizational alignment and change and higher performance levels by followers (see Figure 14.6).[103–105] Paradoxically, the magic of a leader's vision is often that the more complicated the problem, the more people may be drawn to simplistic solutions.

Rhetorical Skills

In addition to *having* vision, charismatic leaders are gifted in *sharing* their vision. As discussed earlier, charismatic and transformational leaders

586 Part Four *Focus on the Situation*

FIGURE 14.6
A Leader's Vision of the Future Can Align Efforts and Help Groups Accomplish More

Source: Adapted from P. M. Senge, *The Fifth Discipline* (New York: Doubleday, 1990).

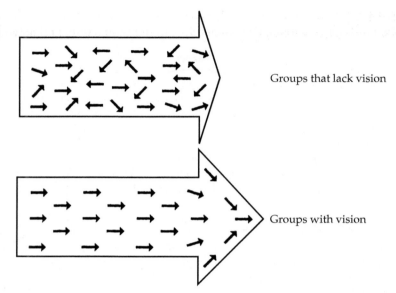

Groups that lack vision

Groups with vision

Facts tell, but stories sell.
Bob Whelan, NCS Pearson

---

have superb **rhetorical skills** that heighten followers' emotional levels and inspire them to embrace the vision. As it turns out, both the content of a transformational leader's speeches and the way they are delivered are vitally important.[104–114] Charismatic leaders make extensive use of metaphors, analogies, and stories rather than abstract and colorless rational discourse to reframe issues and make their points. Often the delivery of the speech is even more important than the content itself—poor delivery can detract from compelling content. Adolf Hitler mastered his delivery techniques so well that his speeches can have hypnotic power even to people who do not understand German. Similarly, many people consider Martin Luther King Jr.'s "I Have a Dream" speech one of the most moving speeches they have ever heard. U-Tube videos of Adolph Hitler, Martin Luther King Jr., Ronald Reagan, or Bill Clinton's speeches show their masterful evocation of patriotic and cultural themes.

Image and Trust Building

As demonstrated in Profiles in Leadership 14.2 and 14.3, transformational leaders build trust in their leadership and the attainability of their goals through an **image** of seemingly unshakable self-confidence, strength of moral conviction, personal example and self-sacrifice, and unconventional tactics or behavior.[63,95,115–120] They are perceived to have unusual insight and ability and act in a manner consistent with their vision and values. Whereas transformational leaders **build trust** by showing commitment to followers' needs over self-interest, some charismatic leaders are so concerned with their image that they are not beyond taking credit for others' accomplishments or exaggerating their expertise.[115]

Setting an example is not the main means of influencing another; it is the only means.
Albert Einstein, physicist

The Trouble with Superheroes

HIGHLIGHT 14.7

All publicly traded companies have boards of directors, whose primary responsibility is to increase shareholder value. People buy stock in companies such as Amazon or Apple, and their boards ensure top management makes the best use of this money to improve business performance. One of the most important decisions boards can make when it comes to improving shareholder value is succession planning. The board of directors make CEO hiring, compensation, and firing decisions and have a major say on who fills the other C-suite positions. Oftentimes changes in economic conditions, consumer preferences, competitive threats, suppliers, or regulatory policy cause business results to suffer, and when this occurs boards are likely to look for new CEOs who are perceived to be charismatic. There are some interesting research findings regarding CEO succession planning and organizational change that are worth discussing further.

One interesting finding is that CEOs only account for 5 percent of a company's performance. A company's revenue may increase from $1 billion to $2 billion dollars or its stock price may rise from $50 to $60, but the CEO has little direct impact on these improvements. CEOs will take full credit but economic conditions, globalization, technology, new products, or failed competitors often play more pervasive roles in company performance. CEOs also will claim that they are critical to motivating and inspiring employees, but research shows immediate supervisors have much greater impact on employee engagement. As such, it may be that immediate supervisors and middle managers play bigger roles in company performance than CEOs. A third research finding is that there is a negative correlation between outside CEO pay and company performance. The more boards pay to hire an outside superstar CEO, the more a company's performance is apt to decline. Other research shows there is very little relationship between CEO compensation, a CEO's ability to build teams, and company performance. CEOs may talk a good game when it comes to driving change and improving the organization, but the facts show that many are better at managing their careers than leading change.

Despite these findings boards are hiring CEOs from the outside more than ever before. Since the 1970s the percentage of outsiders being hired as CEOs increased from 15 to over 33 percent and is even higher in the high-tech industry. Boards can get around the problems associated with hiring outside CEOs by adopting robust **succession planning processes**. Good succession plans identify the key knowledge, skills, and behaviors needed to be successful in top leadership positions; rigorously evaluate internal talent against these criteria; systematically develop those with the most potential to fill these positions; and conduct regular talent reviews. Companies that do this well, such as General Electric and Proctor & Gamble, have several potential internal candidates who could step into the CEO or CFO role. These organizations do such a good job developing leadership talent that potential successors often get hired away by other companies. Despite the findings that internal candidates tend to make the best CEOs, most companies do not have strong succession planning processes, which is why boards go to the outside to hire "charismatic" or "transformational" CEOs.

Hewlett-Packard has hired six outside CEOs since 1999 and the current CEO, Meg Whitman, came from eBay. eBay was faltering when Whitman left and she spent $100M of her own money in a failed campaign to be the governor of California in 2010. How successful do you think Meg Whitman will be as the CEO of HP? What has happened to the company over the past 15 years as a result of all these outside hires?

Sources: "Schrumpeter: The Trouble with Superheros," *The Economist,* October 1, 2011, p. 74; "Schrumpeter: The Tussle for Talent," *The Economist,* January 8, 2011, p. 68; "In Praise of David Brent: Middle Managers Are Not as Useless as People Think," *The Economist,* August 27, 2011, p. 56; T. Hutzschenreuter, I. Kleindiest, and C. Greger, "How New Leaders Affect Strategic Change Following a Succession Event: A Critical Review of the Literature," *The Leadership Quarterly* 23, no. 5 (2012), pp. 729–55; PDI Ninth House, *Getting Succession Right: Six Essential Elements of Effective Succession Plans* (Minneapolis, MN: Author, 2011). B. Groysberg, L. K. Kelly, and B. MacDonald, "The New Path to the C-Suite," *Harvard Business Review* (March 2011), pp. 60–69; J. Collins, *Good to Great* (New York: Harper Business, 2001).

Personalized Leadership

One of the most important aspects of charismatic and transformational leadership is the personal nature of the leader's power. These leaders share strong, personal bonds with followers, even when the leader occupies a formal organizational role. It is this **personalized leadership** style that seems to be responsible for the feelings of empowerment notable among followers of charismatic or transformational leaders. Charismatic leaders seem more adept at picking up social cues and tend to be emotionally expressive, especially through such nonverbal channels as their eye contact, posture, movement, gestures, tone of voice, and facial expressions. Transformational leaders also empower followers by giving them tasks that lead to heightened self-confidence and creating environments of heightened expectations and positive emotions.[1,61,62,64,77,89,116,119,121–124]

Never tell people how to do things. Tell them what to do, and they will surprise you with their ingenuity.

George S. Patton, U.S. Army general

Follower Characteristics

Being attacked by Rush Limbaugh is like being gummed by a newt. It doesn't actually hurt but it leaves you with slimy stuff on your ankle.

Molly Ivins, writer

If charismatic leadership were defined solely by a leader's characteristics, it would be relatively easy to identify individuals with good vision, rhetorical, and impression management skills and place them in leadership positions. Over time we would expect that a high percentage of followers would embrace and act on these leaders' visions. However, a number of leaders appear to possess these attributes yet are not seen as charismatic. They may be good, competent leaders, but they seem unable to evoke strong feelings in followers or to get followers to do more than they thought possible. In reality, charisma is probably more a function of the followers' reactions to a leader than of the leader's personal characteristics. If followers do not accept the leader's vision or become emotionally attached to the leader, then the leader simply will not be perceived to be either charismatic or transformational. Thus **charisma** is in the eyes and heart of the beholder; it is a particularly strong emotional reaction to, identification with, and belief in some leaders by some followers. Note that this definition is value-free—leaders seen as charismatic may or may not share the same values as their followers or meet Burns's criteria for transformational leadership. A recent example of followers' divergent reactions can be seen with U.S. President Barack Obama. Some followers, particularly those in the Democratic party, perceive President Obama to be a very charismatic leader. Most Republicans think he does not share the same values as the American people and is out to destroy the United States, yet he is clearly the same person. Many of the more popular conceptualizations of charisma and charismatic leadership today also define charisma in terms of followers' reactions to the leader.[1,77,94,111,125–127] Defining charisma as a reaction that followers have toward leaders makes it reasonable to turn our attention to the four unique characteristics of these reactions.

Identification with the Leader and the Vision

Two of the effects associated with charismatic leadership include a strong affection for the leader and a similarity of follower beliefs with those of the leader. These effects describe a sort of bonding or **identification with the leader** personally and a parallel psychological investment to a goal or activity (a "cause") bigger than oneself. Followers bond with a leader because they may be intensely dissatisfied with the status quo and see the implementation of the vision as a solution to their problems. Being like the leader, or approved by the leader, also becomes an important part of followers' self-worth.[128–134]

Heightened Emotional Levels

Charismatic leaders are able to stir followers' feelings, and this **heightened emotional level** results in increased levels of effort and performance.[61,62,64,122,132,135–138] Emotions are often the fuel driving large-scale initiatives for change, and charismatic leaders will often do all they can to maintain them, including getting followers to think about their dissatisfaction with the status quo or making impassioned appeals directly to followers. But charismatic leaders need to keep in mind that some people will become alienated with the vision and movement and can have emotions just as intense as those of the followers of the vision. This polarizing effect of charismatic leaders may be one reason why they tend to have violent deaths: those alienated by a charismatic leader are almost as likely to act on their emotions as followers within the movement.[139]

Willing Subordination to the Leader

We're not worthy; we're not worthy!
Wayne and Garth, "Wayne's World"

Whereas the preceding factor dealt with followers' emotional and psychological closeness to the leader, **willing subordination to the leader** involves their deference to his or her authority.[130] Charismatic leaders often seem imbued with superhuman qualities. As a result, followers often naturally and willingly submit to the leader's apparent authority and superiority. Followers seem to suspend their critical thinking skills; they have few doubts about the intentions or skills of the leader, the correctness of the vision or change initiative, or the actions they need to take in order to achieve the vision.

Feelings of Empowerment

Followers of charismatic leaders are moved to expect more of themselves, and they work harder to achieve these higher goals. Charismatic leaders set high expectations while expressing confidence in their abilities and providing ongoing encouragement and support. Somewhat paradoxically, followers feel stronger and more powerful at the same time they willingly subordinate themselves to the charismatic leader. These **feelings of empowerment**, when combined with heightened emotional levels and a leader's vision of the future, often result in increases in organizational, group, or team performance or significant social change.[81,116,122,140,141] (See Table 14.2 for typical reactions to change requests.)

590   Part Four   *Focus on the Situation*

TABLE 14.2
Followers'
Responses to
Change

Source: B. Yager (Boise, ID:
The Bryan Yager Group,
2003).

> **Malicious compliance:** This occurs when followers either ignore or actively sabotage change requests.
> **Compliance:** This takes place when followers do no more than abide by the policies and procedures surrounding change requests.
> **Cooperation:** Followers willingly engage in those activities needed to make the change request become reality.
> **Commitment:** Followers embrace change requests as their own and often go the extra mile to make sure work gets done. Charismatic and transformational leaders are adept at getting followers committed to their vision of the future.

Bob Knowling

PROFILES IN LEADERSHIP 14.4

Bob Knowling was a former member of the Hewlett-Packard, Shell Exploration, Ariba, Aprimo, Immune Response Corporation, and Simdesk Technologies boards of directors and currently serves on the boards of directors for Heidricks & Struggles, an executive search firm, Roper Industries, and Bartech Group. He is also the former vice president of network operations at Ameritech, the executive vice president of network operations and technology for U.S. West, and the CEO of Covad Communications, the New York City Leadership Academy, and Telwares. From a business perspective, Knowling has seen it all, from start-ups to turnarounds, times of rapid growth, major restructurings, mergers and acquisitions, divestitures, working with venture capitalists and private equity firms, launching initial public offerings, and hiring and firing high-visibility CEOs. As the chairman of Eagles Landing Partners, Knowling travels all over the world providing advice to boards of directors, CEOs, C-suite executives, and other senior executives on how to improve their businesses.

Knowling is a testament for what hard work, perseverance, ambition, adaptability, and a winning attitude can do to create teams of loyal followers that achieve superior results. He has accomplished a great deal in his life without having the advantages or privileges associated with many who make it to the top of Corporate America. Growing up in Indiana and Missouri as one of

13 kids, his house had no television or running water, and he often would venture to local lakes and streams to catch fish to help feed the family. Marital problems caused Knowling to live with his mother, father, or grandparents at various times. He got active in organized sports in the sixth grade and became a four sport letterman in high school. Knowling worked in high school and started up several businesses—one involved reselling golf balls retrieved from water hazards and another was running a crew to cut and trim lawns. Because of his academic and athletic performance Knowling received a scholarship to Wabash College, where he majored in theology and continued to excel in basketball and football.

Knowling was able to take these lessons learned while growing up and apply them to the business world. After college he joined Indiana Bell, a telecommunications company, as an installation and repair supervisor. Knowling had no prior knowledge about telephone operations, so he spent the first few months learning how orders came in, trucks were loaded, crews were scheduled, lines were installed, and customers were billed for their services. He did this by being the first one in to work, helping his dispatchers assign jobs, helping load the trucks with the supplies needed for the day, traveling out with his crews to do installations, and being the last one to leave the office. Knowling had inherited one of the worst performing crews in Indiana, but by setting clear goals, holding people accountable for performance, providing needed resources, clearing obstacles, listening to inputs, treating people decently, inspiring and engaging others, building a team, and teaching them how to win he soon had one of the top performing crews in the state. Knowling applied this success formula to every job he has ever had and he rose rapidly through the ranks as a result.

Indiana Bell was part of a larger telecommunications firm named Ameritech, and Knowling was one of 120 people brought in to drive something called Breakthrough Leadership. The chairman and CEO of Ameritech felt the company was ill-equipped to deal with telephone service deregulation and was not prepared to compete in a competitive market. He enlisted his best and brightest people to turn the company around. Knowling had always been able to build a winning team, but the Breakthrough Leadership changes were hundreds of times bigger than anything he had done before. Knowling worked with University of Michigan Professor Dr. Noel Tichy, who had been the

chief learning officer at General Electric under Jack Welch, and was able to implement processes that drove major changes at Ameritech. Because of his successes, Knowling was lured away to U.S. West to drive major change and transform the worst-performing Regional Bell Operating Company, which he quickly accomplished. With these successes he was subsequently named CEO of Covad Communications and was asked to join several Fortune 500 boards of directors. Knowling spent time as CEO of the New York City Leadership Academy teaching administrators, principals, and assistant principals how to lead. He launched Eagles Landing Partners several years ago to help global businesses learn how to lead, build teams, and win.

Do you think it is possible to teach leaders how to implement change? Does Bob Knowling use a rational or emotional approach to drive change?

Sources: B. Knowling, *You Can Get There From Here* (New York: Porfolio/Penguin, 2011); http://www.forbes.com/profile/robert-knowling/; http://www.answers.com/topic/robert-e-knowling-jr;

Situational Characteristics

Many researchers believe that situational factors also play an important role in determining whether a leader will be perceived as charismatic. Perhaps individuals possessing the qualities of charismatic leaders are perceived as charismatic only when confronting certain types of situations. Because the situation may play an important role in the attribution of charisma, it will be useful to review some of the situational factors believed to affect charismatic leadership.

Crises

Perhaps the most important situational factor associated with charismatic leadership is the presence or absence of a **crisis**. Followers who are content with the status quo are relatively unlikely to perceive a need for a charismatic leader or be willing to devote great effort to fundamentally change an organization or society. On the other hand, a crisis often creates "charisma hungry" followers who are looking for a leader to alleviate or resolve their crisis. Leaders are given considerably more latitude and autonomy and may temporarily (or sometimes permanently) suspend accepted rules, policies, and procedures to pull the organization out of the crisis. Some leaders may even create or manufacture crises to increase followers' acceptance of their vision, the range of actions they can take, and followers' level of effort. Although a crisis situation does not necessarily make every leader look charismatic, such a situation may set the stage for particular kinds of leader behaviors to be effective.[80,82,92,101,102,121,142–144]

Social Networks

Celebrity is obscurity biding its time.
Carrie Fisher,
actress

Social networks can also affect the attribution of charisma. Attributions of charisma will spread more quickly in organizations having well-established social networks, where everybody tends to know everyone else. And more often than not charismatic leaders have bigger social networks and play a more central role in their networks than leaders seen as less charismatic.[145,146]

Other Situational Characteristics

Two other situational characteristics may help or hinder the emergence of a charismatic leader. One of these is outsourcing and organizational downsizing. Many people believe that downsizing destroys the implicit contract between employer and employee and leaves many employees disillusioned with corporate life. Because charismatic or transformational leadership is intensely relational in nature, destroying the implicit contract between leaders and followers greatly diminishes the odds of charismatic leadership emergence. But of all the situational variables affecting charismatic leadership, perhaps the most important and overlooked variable is **time**. Charismatic or transformational leadership does not happen overnight. It takes time for leaders to develop and articulate their vision, heighten followers' emotional levels, build trusting relationships with followers, and direct and empower followers to fulfill the vision. A crisis may compress the amount of time needed for charismatic leadership to emerge, whereas relatively stable situations lengthen this period.

Rules are good servants, but not always good masters.
Russell Page,
master landscaper

Concluding Thoughts about the Characteristics of Charismatic and Transformational Leadership

Several final points about the characteristics of charismatic leadership need to be made. First, although we defined charisma as a quality attributed to certain leaders based on the relationships they share with followers, charismatic leadership is most fully understood when we also consider how leader and situational factors affect this attribution process. The special relationships charismatic leaders share with followers do not happen by accident; rather, they are often the result of interaction between the leader's qualities, the degree to which a leader's vision fulfills followers' needs, and the presence of certain situational factors. Second, it seems unlikely that all the characteristics of charismatic leadership need to be present before charisma is attributed to a leader. The bottom line for charisma seems to be the relationships certain leaders share with followers, and there may be a variety of ways in which these relationships can develop. This also implies that charisma may be more of a continuum than an all-or-nothing phenomenon. Some leaders may be able to form particularly strong bonds with a majority, others with a few—and still others may not get along well with any followers. Third, it seems that charismatic leadership can happen anywhere—schools, churches, communities, businesses, government organizations, and nations—and does not happen only on the world stage.

Fourth, given that there are a number of ways to develop strong emotional attachments with followers, one important question is whether it is possible to attribute charisma to an individual based solely on his or her position or celebrity status. Some individuals in positions of high public visibility and esteem (film stars, musicians, athletes, television evangelists, or politicians) can develop (even cultivate) charismatic images among their fans and admirers. In these cases it is helpful to recognize that charismatic leadership is a two-way street. Not only do followers develop strong emotional bonds with leaders, but leaders also develop strong emotional bonds with followers and are concerned with follower development.[14,81,140] It is difficult to see how the one-way communication channels of radio and television can foster these two-way relationships or enhance follower growth. Thus, although we sometimes view certain individuals as charismatic based on media manipulation and hype, this is not transformational leadership.

So what can leadership practitioners take from this research if they want to use an emotional approach to drive organizational change? They will probably be more successful at driving organizational change if they capitalize on or create a crisis. They also need to be close enough to their followers to determine their sources of discontent and ensure that their vision provides a solution to followers' problems and paints a compelling picture of the future. Leaders must passionately articulate their vision of the future; it is difficult to imagine followers being motivated toward a vision that is unclear or presented by a leader who does not seem to really care about it. Leadership practitioners also need to understand that they alone cannot make the vision a reality; they need their followers' help and support to create organizational or societal changes. Along these lines, they will need to be a role model and coach followers on what they should (and should not) be doing, provide feedback and encouragement, and persuade followers to take on more responsibilities as their skills and self-confidence grow. Finally, leadership practitioners using this approach to organizational change also need to be thick-skinned, resilient, and patient (see Highlight 14.8). They will need to cope with the polarization effects of charismatic leadership and understand that it takes time for the effects of this type of leadership to yield results. However, the rewards appear to be

Good to Great: An Alternative Framework to the Rational and Emotional Approaches to Organizational Change

HIGHLIGHT 14.8

An alternative conceptualization of organizational change comes from the book *Good to Great.* Collins and his research team reviewed the financial performance of 1,435 companies that appeared on the Fortune 500 list from 1965 to 1995. From this list, 11 companies made the leap from being a good to a truly great company—a company that yielded financial returns much higher than those for the overall stock market or industry competitors for at least 15 consecutive years. For example, a dollar invested in these 11 companies in 1965 would have yielded $471 in January 2000, whereas the same dollar invested in the stock market would have returned $56. Collins's research indicates that these 11 companies all followed the same six rules:

1. *Level 5 leadership:* The *Good to Great* companies were led not by high-profile celebrity leaders but rather by humble, self-effacing, and reserved individuals who also possessed an incredibly strong drive to succeed.

2. *First who, then what:* Before developing a future vision or goals, these leaders first made sure they had the right people with the right skills in the right jobs. Leadership talent management was a key focus of these top companies.

3. *Confront the brutal facts (yet never lose faith):* These leaders met reality head-on—they did not sugarcoat organizational challenges or difficulties. But they also had an unshakable faith in their organizations' ability to meet these challenges.

4. *The hedgehog concept:* These companies all focused on being the best in the world at what

they did, were deeply passionate about their business, and identified one or two key financial or operational metrics to guide their decision making and day-to-day activities.

5. *A culture of discipline:* Companies that had disciplined people did not need hierarchies, bureaucracies, or excessive controls because the people in the field knew what they needed to do and made sure it happened.

6. *Technology accelerators:* All these companies selectively used technology as a means for enhancing business operations, but they were not necessarily leaders in technical innovation.

There were several other surprising findings in Collins's research. First, none of these top-performing companies was led by transformational or charismatic leaders. Second, because these top companies were constantly undergoing small but noticeable changes, they did not need to launch major change initiatives or organizational restructuring programs. Third, companies need to abide by all six of these rules to go from good to great; three or four of the six rules were not enough for companies to make the leap to becoming top performers.

How do you think a *Good to Great* leader would perform in a crisis? What would he or she do differently than a charismatic leader? What role does talent play in *Good to Great* companies versus those led by charismatic leaders?

Source: J. Collins, *Good to Great* (New York: HarperCollins, 2001); J. Collins, "Level 5 Leadership: The Triumph of Humility and Fierce Resolve," *HBR on Point* (Boston, MA: Harvard Business School Press, 2004).

well worth the efforts. There appears to be overwhelming evidence that charismatic or transformational leaders are more effective than their non-charismatic counterparts, whether they be presidents of the United States,[147] CEOs,[80,84,148] military cadets and officers,[78,79,149,150] college professors,[151] or first-line supervisors and middle-level managers in a variety of public and private sector companies.[77,82,85–88,122,152,153]

Bass's Theory of Transformational and Transactional Leadership

Much of what we know about the leader, follower, and situational characteristics associated with charismatic or transformational leaders comes from research on Bass's **theory of transformational and transactional leadership**.[1,117,121] Bass believed that transformational leaders possessed those leader characteristics described earlier and used subordinates' perceptions or reactions to determine whether a leader was transformational. Thus transformational leaders possess good vision, rhetorical, and impression management skills and use them to develop strong emotional bonds with followers. Transformational leaders are believed to be more successful at driving organizational change because of followers' heightened emotional levels and their willingness to work toward the accomplishment of the leader's vision. In contrast, transactional leaders do not possess these leader characteristics, nor are they able to develop strong emotional bonds with followers or inspire followers to do more than followers thought they could. Instead transactional leaders were believed to motivate followers by setting goals and promising rewards for desired performance.[1,98,116,117,119,124] Avolio and Bass maintained that transactional leadership could have positive effects on follower satisfaction and performance levels, but they also stated that these behaviors were often underutilized because of time constraints, a lack of leader skills, and a disbelief among leaders that rewards could boost performance.[77,98] Bass also maintained that transactional leadership only perpetuates the status quo; a leader's use of rewards does not result in the long-term changes associated with transformational leadership.[117]

Like the initiating structure and consideration behaviors described in Chapter 7, Bass hypothesized that transformational and transactional leadership comprised two independent leadership dimensions. Thus individuals could be high transformational but low transactional leaders, low transformational and low transactional leaders, and so on. Bass developed a questionnaire, known as the **Multifactor Leadership Questionnaire (MLQ)**, to assess the extent to which leaders exhibited transformational or transactional leadership and the extent to which followers were satisfied with their leader and believed their leader was effective. The MLQ is a 360-degree feedback instrument that assesses five transformational and three transactional factors and a nonleadership factor.[117,154–158] The transformational leadership factors assess the degree to which the leader instills pride in others, displays power and confidence, makes personal sacrifices or champions new possibilities, considers the ethical or moral consequences of decisions, articulates a compelling vision of the future, sets challenging standards, treats followers as individuals, and helps followers understand the problems they face. The three transactional leadership factors assess the extent to

Bill Roberts

PROFILES IN LEADERSHIP 14.5

Although transformational leaders come from all walks of life, one common characteristic they share is their ability to drive change and get things done. One of the best examples of a transformational leader is Bill Roberts, the vice president of operations for Wheelabrator Technologies, Inc. (WTI). Wheelabrator Technologies runs a fleet of 22 waste-to-energy facilities—power plants that burn trash to create electricity and steam for residential and commercial customers. These plants are environmentally friendly in that only 10 percent of the trash they burn is returned to landfills; they have much lower air pollution emissions than coal-fired plants; and all the metals in the trash are recovered and recycled. As the vice president of operations, Roberts is responsible for the financial, operational, safety, and environmental performance of the fleet. When he took over operations three years ago, Roberts recognized that the fleet was not performing nearly as well as it could. Boiler availability (a measure of operating capacity) was down, safety performance was eroding, and the fleet's financial performance had substantial room for improvement. At about the same time WTI embraced an aggressive growth strategy and was looking to expand both domestically and internationally. The fleet needed to perform at a much higher level to fund these business development efforts as well as provide the operating, safety, and environmental statistics needed to give WTI a competitive advantage when bidding for new business.

Since taking over, Roberts has driven a number of major changes across the fleet. An engaging and dynamic speaker, Roberts painted a compelling picture of the future of WTI and set clear expectations of performance for all his plant managers. He empowered his plant managers to find ways to improve boiler availability, safety, and financial performance and provided training to help them think more like business owners. By constantly reviewing results with the plant managers, Roberts kept challenging and encouraging his staff to find ways to continuously improve performance. He rewarded plant managers who improved plant performance and coached or removed those who could not meet his expectations. By getting plant managers to work together to solve mutual problems, Roberts also broke down the walls that had previously existed between his staff and got them to work together as a high-performing team.

From an operational perspective, the 22 plants are running about 10 percent better than they were when he took over. The fleet now has an impeccable environmental and safety record, and the plant managers have a much stronger understanding of plant financials. Because of these efforts, WTI has achieved world-class operational, safety, and environmental performance and has been able to use these results to expand the business in the United States, the United Kingdom, and China.

Given this description of Bill Roberts, do you think he is more of a charismatic or Level 5 leader? What other information would you need to make this assessment?

which leaders set goals, make rewards contingent on performance, obtain necessary resources, provide rewards when performance goals have been met, monitor followers' performance levels, and intervene when problems occur. The MLQ also assesses another factor called laissez-faire leadership, which assesses the extent to which leaders avoid responsibilities, fail to make decisions, are absent when needed, or fail to follow up on requests.

Research Results of Transformational and Transactional Leadership

To date, over 350 studies have used the MLQ to investigate transformational and transactional leadership across a wide variety of situations. These results indicated that transformational leadership can be observed in all countries, institutions, and organizational levels, but it was more prevalent in public institutions and at lower organizational levels.[70,77,78,82,119] In other words, there seemed to be more transformational leaders in the lower levels of the military or other public sector organizations than anywhere else. Second, there is overwhelming evidence that transformational leadership is a significantly better predictor of organizational effectiveness than transactional or laissez-faire leadership. Transformational leaders, whether they are U.S. presidents, CEOs, school administrators, or plant managers, seem to be more effective than transactional leaders at driving organizational change and getting results. Avolio and Bass also believed that transformational leadership augments performance above and beyond what is associated with transactional leadership.[77] Third, as expected, laissez-faire leadership was negatively correlated with effectiveness.

Given that the MLQ can reliably identify transformational leaders and that these leaders can drive higher levels of organizational change and effectiveness than their transactional counterparts, it seems reasonable to ask whether it is possible to train or select charismatic leaders. Fortunately researchers have looked at the effects of transformational leadership training on the performance of military, public sector, and private industry leaders in the United States, Canada, and Israel. Usually these training programs consisted of several one- to five-day training sessions in which participants learned about the theory of transformational and transactional leadership; received MLQ feedback on the extent to which they exhibit transformational, transactional, and laissez-faire leadership; and then went through a series of skill-building exercises and activities to improve their leadership effectiveness. This research provided strong evidence that it is possible for leaders to systematically develop their transformational and transactional leadership skills.[70,77,82,83,99,156,159,160]

An alternative to training leaders to be more transformational is to select leaders with the propensity to be transformational or charismatic in the first place. Several researchers have looked at the importance of childhood experiences, leadership traits, and even genetics in transformational leadership. Zacharatos, Barling, and Kelloway reported that adolescents who were rated by coaches and peers to be more transformational were also more likely to have parents who were transformational leaders.[161] There is also evidence that certain Five Factor Model (FFM) leadership traits (Chapter 6) can be reliably used to identify transformational

TABLE 14.3   **Correlations between Five Factor Model Dimensions and Charismatic Leadership Characteristics for 125 Corporate CEOs and Presidents**

Personality Dimension	Transformational Leadership Characteristics			
	Visionary Thinking	Empowering Others	Inspiring Trust	High-Impact Delivery
Extraversion	.32	.33	.16	.47
Conscientiousness	−.08	−.01	.06	−.04
Agreeableness	.02	.52	.48	.35
Neuroticism	−.03	.29	.38	.22
Openness to experience	.47	.30	.14	.40

Source: D. Nilsen, "Using Self and Observers' Ratings for Personality to Predict Leadership Performance," unpublished doctoral dissertation, University of Minnesota, Minneapolis, 1995.

leaders.[76,124,139,162–166] Some of the most compelling evidence comes from Nilsen, who looked at the relationships between FFM personality traits and 125 CEOs. As shown in Table 14.3, not only are the FFM personality dimensions strongly correlated with certain components of transformational leadership, but the pattern of high and low correlations seems to make sense.[165] Given that certain leadership traits are related to transformational leadership, and that leadership traits have a genetic component, it is not surprising that some researchers also believe that some aspect of transformational leadership is heritable.[100]

Despite this evidence that it may be possible to select and train transformational leaders, the fact remains that charisma ultimately exists in the eye of the beholder. Thus there can be no guarantee that leaders who have the right stuff and are schooled in the appropriate techniques will be seen as charismatic by followers. As discussed earlier, follower and situational variables play a key role in determining whether leaders are perceived as transformational and drive organizational change. Certain leaders may get higher transformational leadership scores as a result of a training program; but do they actually heighten followers' emotional levels, get followers to exert extra effort, and as a result achieve greater organizational change or performance after the program? Given what we know about individual differences and leadership skills training, it seems likely that a leader's personality will also play a major role in determining whether he or she will benefit from such training.

Finally, several other important comments about the theory of transformational and transactional leadership are worth noting. First, and perhaps most important, this theory has generated a considerable amount of interest among leadership researchers. This research has helped leadership practitioners better understand the leader, follower, and situational components of charismatic or transformational leadership, whether transformational leaders are born or made, and so forth. Nevertheless, this approach to leadership may be more a reflection of socially desirable leadership behaviors than the full range of skills needed by leaders. For example, it seems likely that business leaders wanting to drive organizational change or performance need to have a good understanding of the industry, business operations, market trends, finance, strategy, and technical or functional knowledge; they also need to effectively cope with stress, negotiate contracts with vendors, demonstrate good planning skills, and develop and monitor key metrics. Yet none of these attributes and skills is directly measured by the MLQ. This leads us to another point, which is that a primary problem with this theory is that there is only one way to be an effective leader, and that is by demonstrating transformational leadership skills. The contingency theories of leadership no longer matter, and situational or follower factors have little impact on leadership effectiveness. In all likelihood leaders probably need to do more than just exhibit transformational leadership skills if they wish to achieve greater organizational change and performance.

Summary

This chapter has reviewed two major approaches to organizational change. Although independent lines of research were used to develop the rational and emotional approaches to change, in reality these approaches have several important similarities. With the rational approach, leaders increase follower dissatisfaction by pointing out problems with the status quo, systematically identifying areas of needed change, developing a vision of the future, and developing and implementing a change plan. In the emotional approach, leaders develop and articulate a vision of the future, heighten the emotions of followers, and empower followers to act on their vision. Charismatic leaders are also more likely to emerge during times of uncertainty or crisis, and may actually manufacture a crisis to improve the odds that followers will become committed to their vision of the future. The rational approach puts more emphasis on analytic, planning, and management skills, whereas the emotional approach puts more emphasis on leadership skills, leader–follower relationships, and the presence of a crisis to drive organizational change. This chapter also described the steps leadership practitioners must take if they wish to drive organizational change. There is ample evidence to suggest that either the rational or the emotional approach can result in organizational change, but the effectiveness of the change may depend on which approach leadership practitioners are most comfortable with and the skill with which they can carry it out.

600 Part Four *Focus on the Situation*

Key Terms

$C = D \times M \times P > R$, 563
dissatisfaction, 564
model, 564
process, 564
resistance, 564
amount of change, 564
systems thinking approach, 567
siloed thinking, 567
change plan, 569
expectation–performance gap, 571
SARA model, 572
adaptive leadership, 575
learning agility, 575
force field analysis (FFA), 576

traditional authority system, 578
legal–rational authority system, 578
charismatic authority system, 578
transactional leadership, 579
transformational leadership, 579
reframing, 580
vision, 585
rhetorical skills, 586
image, 586
build trust, 586
succession planning process, 587
personalized leadership, 588

charisma, 588
identification with the leader, 589
heightened emotional level, 589
willing subordination to the leader, 589
feelings of empowerment, 589
crisis, 591
social networks, 592
time, 592
theory of transformational and transactional leadership, 595
Multifactor Leadership Questionnaire (MLQ), 595

Questions

1. Was Hugo Chavez a transformational or charismatic leader? What data would you need to gather to answer this question?
2. Are Vladimir Putin and Hamid Karzai charismatic or transformational leaders? Would your answers differ if you were a Russian or Afghanistan citizen?
3. Research shows that females are seen as more transformational leaders, yet they hold relatively few top leadership positions compared to men. Why do you think this is the case? What, if anything, could you do to change this situation?
4. How does the model of community leadership (Chapter 7) compare to the rational and emotional approaches to organizational change?
5. Can leaders lack intelligence (as described in Chapter 6) and still be seen as charismatic?
6. How do charismatic and transformational leadership relate to the four followership types described in the "Focus on the Followers" section of this book?
7. Suppose you wanted to build a new student union at your school. What would you need to do to make this happen if you used a rational versus an emotional approach to organizational change?

Activities

1. Break into teams and identify something that needs to change at your school or at work. Use the rational approach to change (C = D × M × P > R) to develop a plan for your change initiative.
2. Interview a midlevel leader or executive and ask about the biggest change initiative she or he was ever a part of. Did this leader use more of a rational or emotional approach to organizational change, and was the change initiative successful? Why or why not?
3. Create a force field analysis diagram for a change you would like to see happen at your work or school.

Minicase

Keeping Up with Bill Gates

Bill Gates inherited intelligence, ambition, and a competitive spirit from his father, a successful Seattle attorney. After graduating from a private prep school in Seattle, he enrolled in Harvard but dropped out to pursue his passion—computer programming. Paul Allen, a friend from prep school, presented Gates with the idea of writing a version of the BASIC computer language for the Altair 8800, one of the first personal computers on the market. Driven by his competitive nature, Gates decided he wanted to be the first to develop a language to make the personal computer accessible for the general public. He and Allen established the Microsoft Corporation in 1975. Gates's passion and skill were programming—he would work night and day to meet the extremely aggressive deadlines he set for himself and his company. Eventually Gates had to bring in other programmers; he focused on recent college graduates. "We decided that we wanted them to come with clear minds, not polluted by some other approach, to learn the way that we liked to develop software, and to put the kind of energy into it that we thought was key."

In the early days of Microsoft, Gates was in charge of product planning and programming while Allen was in charge of the business side. He motivated his programmers with the claim that whatever deadline was looming, no matter how tight, he could beat it personally if he had to. What eventually developed at Microsoft was a culture in which Gates was king. Everyone working under Gates was made to feel they were lesser programmers who couldn't compete with his skill or drive, so they competed with each other. They worked long hours and tried their best to mirror Gates—his drive, his ambition, his skill. This internal competition motivated the programmers and made Microsoft one of the most successful companies in the computer industry, and one of the most profitable. The corporation has created a tremendous amount of wealth—many of its employees have

602   Part Four   *Focus on the Situation*

become millionaires while working at Microsoft, including, of course, Bill Gates, currently one of the richest men in the world. During the 1990s Bill Gates's net worth grew at an average rate of $34 million per day; that's $200 million per week!

Gates needed a castle for his kingdom, so he built a much-talked-about house on Lake Washington. The house lies mainly underground and looks like a set of separate buildings when viewed from above. The house was conceived as a showcase for Microsoft technology—it took $60 million, seven years of planning and construction, and three generations of computer hardware before it was finally finished. A feature of the house that reveals a lot about its owner is the house's system of electronic badges. These badges let the house computers know where each resident and visitor is in the house. The purpose of the badges is to allow the computer to adjust the climate and music to match the preferences of people in the house as they move from room to room. What happens when more than one person is in a room? The computer defaults to Gates's personal preferences.

1. Would you classify Bill Gates as a charismatic or transformational leader? Why?
2. Consider the followers and employees of Gates. What are some unique characteristics of Gates's followers that might identify him as charismatic or transformational?

Sources: http://www.microsoft.com; http://news.bbc.co.uk/1/hi/programmes/worlds_most_powerful/3284811.stm; http://ei.cs.vt.edu/~history/Gates.Mirick.html; http://www.time.com/time/time100/builder/profile/gates3.html; http://www.pbs.org/cringely/pulpit/pulpit20001123.html.

End Notes

1. B. M. Bass, *Leadership and Performance beyond Expectations* (New York: Free Press, 1985).
2. J. O'Toole, *Leading Change* (San Francisco: Jossey-Bass, 1995).
3. P. Pritchett, *Firing Up Commitment during Organizational Change* (Dallas, TX: Pritchett and Associates, 2001).
4. E. McNulty, "Welcome Aboard (But Don't Change a Thing)," *Harvard Business Review,* October 2002, pp. 32–41.
5. R. A. Heifetz and M. Linsky, "A Survival Guide for Leaders," *Harvard Business Review,* June 2002, pp. 65–75.
6. R. Moss Kanter, "Leadership and the Psychology of Turnarounds," *Harvard Business Review,* June 2003, pp. 58–64.
7. R. M. Kanter, *The Change Masters* (New York: Simon & Schuster, 1983).
8. J. Krile, G. J. Curphy, and D. Lund, *The Community Leadership Handbook: Framing Ideas, Building Relationships and Mobilizing Resources* (St. Paul, MN: Fieldstone Alliance, 2005).

9. F. Ostroff, "Change Management in Government," *Harvard Business Review,* May 2006, pp. 141–53.

10. D. Rock and J. Schwartz, "The Neuroscience of Leadership: Why Organizational Change Hurts," Strategy 1 Business 43 (2006) pp. 71–79.

11. J. Kotter, "Leading Change: Why Transformation Change Efforts Fail," *Harvard Business Review,* January 2007, pp. 96–103.

12. G. J. Curphy, *The Competitive Advantage Program for Wheelabrator Technologies Incorporated* (North Oaks, MN: Author, 2006).

13. G. J. Curphy, *Leadership, Teams, and Change Program for the New York City Leadership Academy* (North Oaks, MN: Author, 2005).

14. J. M. Burns, *Leadership* (New York: Harper & Row, 1978).

15. R. Marcus and R. Weiler, *Aligning Organizations: The Foundation of Performance* (Camden, ME: Brimstone Consulting Group, 2010).

16. W. G. Bennis and B. Nanus, *Leaders: The Strategies for Taking Charge* (New York: Harper & Row, 1985).

17. N. M. Tichy and M. A. Devanna, *The Transformational Leader* (New York: John Wiley, 1986).

18. W. Bridges, *Managing Transitions: Making the Most of Change* (Reading, MA: Addison-Wesley, 1991).

19. J. C. Collins and J. I. Porras, *Built to Last: Successful Habits of Visionary Companies* (Reading, MA: Perseus Books, 1997).

20. M. Treacy and F. Wiersma, *The Discipline of Market Leaders* (Reading, MA: Perseus Books, 1997).

21. M. Beer, *Leading Change,* Reprint No. 9-488-037 (Boston: Harvard Business School Publishing Division, 1988).

22. M. Beer, "Developing Organizational Fitness: Towards a Theory and Practice of Organizational Alignment," paper presented at the 14th Annual Conference of the Society of Industrial and Organizational Psychology, Atlanta, GA, 1999.

23. R. A. Heifetz and D. L. Laurie, "The Work of Leadership," *Harvard Business Review,* December 2001, pp. 131–40.

24. J. Collins, *Good to Great* (New York: HarperCollins, 2001).

25. J. Collins, *How the Mighty Fall* (New York: HarperCollins, 2009).

26. N. M. Tichy and N. Cardwell, *The Cycle of Leadership: How Great Companies Teach Their Leaders to Win* (New York: HarperBusiness, 2002).

27. G. J. Curphy, *The Blandin Education Leadership Program* (Grand Rapids, MN: The Blandin Foundation, 2003).

28. G. J. Curphy and R. T. Hogan, *The Rocket Model: Practical Advice for Building High Performing Teams* (Tulsa, OK: Hogan Press, 2012).

29. G. J. Curphy, *Applying the Rocket Model to Virtual Teams* (North Oaks, MN: Author, 2013).

30. P. M. Senge, *The Fifth Discipline: The Art and Practice of the Learning Organization* (New York: Doubleday/Currency, 1994).

31. G.J. Curphy, *Strategy, Strategy Execution, and Change: The Culture Card Sort Exercise* (North Oaks, MN: Author, 2013).

32. M. L. Marks and P. H. Mirvis, "Making Mergers and Acquisitions Work," *Academy of Management Executive* 15, no. 2 (2001), pp. 80–94.

33. P. Pritchett and R. Pound, *Smart Moves: A Crash Course on Merger Integration Management* (Pritchett and Associates, 2001).

34. C. M. Ruvolo and R. C. Bullis, "Essentials of Cultural Change: Lessons Learned the Hard Way," *Consulting Psychology Journal* 55, no. 3 (2003), pp. 155–68.

35. Q. N. Huy, "In Praise of Middle Managers," *Harvard Business Review,* September 2001, pp. 72–81.

36. L. Bossidy and R. Charan, *Execution: The Discipline of Getting Things Done* (New York: Crown Business Publishing, 2002).

37. G. J. Curphy, A. Baldrica, and R. T. Hogan, Managerial Incompetence, unpublished manuscript, 2009.

38. R. Charan and G. Colvin, "Why CEOs Fail," *Fortune,* June 21, 1999, pp. 69–82.

39. L. Hirschhorn, "Campaigning for Change," *Harvard Business Review,* July 2002, pp. 98–106.

40. S. Oreg and Y. Berson, "Leadership and Employees' Reactions to Change: The Role of Leaders' Personal Attributes and Transformational Leadership Style," *Personnel Psychology* 64, no. 1 (2011), pp. 627–660.

41. E. Kübler-Ross, *Living with Death and Dying* (New York: Macmillan, 1981).

42. R. B. Kaiser, "Introduction to the Special Issue on Developing Flexible and Adaptable Leaders for an Age of Uncertainty," *Consulting Psychology Journal: Practice and Research* 62, no. 2 (2010), pp. 77–80.

43. G. A. Yukl and R. Mahsud, "Why Flexible and Adaptable Leadership Is Essential," *Consulting Psychology Journal: Practice and Research* 62, no. 2 (2010), pp. 81–93.

44. K. De Muese, G. Dai, and G. S. Hallenbeck, "Learning Agility: A Construct Whose Time Has Come," *Consulting Psychology Journal: Practice and Research* 62, no. 2 (2010), pp. 119–30.

45. M. Weber, *The Theory of Social and Economic Organization,* ed. Talcott Parsons, trans. A. M. Henderson and T. Parsons (New York: Free Press, 1964).

46. P. M. Blau, "Critical Remarks on Weber's Theory of Authority," *American Political Science Review* 57, no. 2 (1963), pp. 305–15.

47. E. Chinoy, *Society* (New York: Random House, 1961).

48. H. Wolpe, "A Critical Analysis of Some Aspects of Charisma," *Sociological Review* 16 (1968), pp. 305–18.

49. W. H. Friedland, "For a Sociological Concept of Charisma," *Social Forces,* no. 1 (1964), pp. 18–26.

50. H. H. Gerth and C. W. Mills, *Max Weber: Essays in Sociology* (New York: Oxford University Press, 1946).

51. R. M. Kanter, *Commitment and Community* (Cambridge: Harvard University Press, 1972).

52. R. C. Tucker, "The Theory of Charismatic Leadership," *Daedalus* 97 (1968), pp. 731–56.

53. T. E. Dow, "The Theory of Charisma," *Sociological Quarterly* 10 (1969), pp. 306–18.

54. B. R. Clark, "The Organizational Saga in Higher Education," *Administrative Science Quarterly* 17 (1972), pp. 178–84.

55. G. Deveraux, "Charismatic Leadership and Crisis," in *Psychoanalysis and the Social Sciences,* eds. W. Muensterberger and S. Axelrod (New York: International University Press, 1955).

56. J. V. Downton, *Rebel Leadership: Commitment and Charisma in the Revolutionary Process* (New York: Free Press, 1973).

57. J. T. Marcus, "Transcendence and Charisma," *Western Political Quarterly* 16 (1961), pp. 236–41.

58. E. Shils, "Charisma, Order, and Status," *American Sociological Review* 30 (1965), pp. 199–213.

59. N. Turner, J. Barling, O. Eptiropaki, V. Butcher, and C. Milner, "Transformational Leadership and Moral Reasoning," *Journal of Applied Psychology* 87, no. 2 (2002), pp. 304–11.

60. T. L. Price, "The Ethics of Authentic Transformational Leadership," *Leadership Quarterly* 14, no. 1 (2003), pp. 67–82.

61. J. Gooty, S. Connelly, J. Griffith, and A Gupta, "Leadership, Affect, and Emotions: A State of the Science Review," *The Leadership Quarterly* 21, no. 6 (2010), pp. 979–04.

62. J. E. Bono and R. Ilies, "Charisma, Positive Emotions, and Mood Contagion," *Leadership Quarterly* 17 (2006), pp. 317–34.

63. S. Parameshwar, "Inventing Higher Purpose through Suffering: The Transformation of the Transformational Leader," *Leadership Quarterly* 17 (2006), pp. 454–74.

64. M. Greer, "The Science of Savoir Faire," *Monitor on Psychology,* January 2005, pp. 28–30.

65. J. M. Strange and M. D. Mumford, "The Origins of Vision: Effects of Reflection, Models, and Analysis," *Leadership Quarterly* 16 (2005) pp. 121–48.

66. G. Yukl, "An Evaluation of Conceptual Weaknesses in Transformational and Charismatic Leadership Theories," *Leadership Quarterly* 10, no. 2 (1999), pp. 285–306.

67. J. G. Hunt, "Transformational/Charismatic Leadership's Transformation of the Field: An Historical Essay," *Leadership Quarterly* 10, no. 2 (1999), pp. 129–44.

68. J. A. Conger and J. G. Hunt, "Charismatic and Transformational Leadership: Taking Stock of the Present and Future," *Leadership Quarterly* 10, no. 2 (1999), pp. 121–28.

69. E. E. Duehr and J. E. Bono, "Personality and Transformational Leadership: Differential Prediction for Male and Female Leaders," in *Predicting Leadership: The Good, The Bad, the Different, and the Unnecessary,* J. P. Campbell and M. J. Benson (chairs), annual meeting of Society of Industrial and Organizational Psychology, New York, April 2007.

70. B. M. Bass, "Two Decades of Research and Development in Transformational Leadership," *European Journal of Work and Organizational Psychology* 8, no. 1 (1999), pp. 9–32.

71. D. N. Den Hartog, R. J. House, P. J. Hanges, S. A. Ruiz-Quintanilla, P. W. Dorfman, and associates, "Culture Specific and Cross-Culturally Generalizable Implicit Leadership Theories: Are Attributes of Charismatic/ Transformational Leadership Universally Endorsed?" *Leadership Quarterly* 10, no. 2 (1999), pp. 219–56.

72. A. H. Eagly and L. L. Carli, "The Female Leadership Advantage: An Evaluation of the Evidence," *Leadership Quarterly* 14 (2003), pp. 807–34.

73. J. B. Rosener, "Ways Women Lead," *Harvard Business Review* 68 (1990), pp. 119–25.

74. V. U. Druskat, "Gender and Leadership Style: Transformational and Transactional Leadership in the Roman Catholic Church," *Leadership Quarterly* 5, no. 1 (1994), pp. 99–120.

75. B. M. Bass and F. J. Yammarino, *Long-term Forecasting of Transformational Leadership and Its Effects among Naval Officers: Some Preliminary Findings*, Technical Report No. ONR-TR-2 (Arlington, VA: Office of Naval Research, 1988).

76. S. M. Ross and L. R. Offermann, "Transformational Leaders: Measurement of Personality Attributes and Work Group Performance," paper presented at the Sixth Annual Society of Industrial and Organizational Psychologists Convention, St. Louis, MO, April 1991.

77. B. J. Avolio and B. M. Bass, *Developing a Full Range of Leadership Potential: Cases on Transactional and Transformational Leadership* (Binghamton: State University of New York at Binghamton, 2000).

78. B. M. Bass, "Thoughts and Plans," in *Cutting Edge: Leadership 2000*, eds. B. Kellerman and L. R. Matusak (Carbondale, IL: Southern Illinois University Press, 2000), pp. 5–9.

79. G. J. Curphy, "An Empirical Investigation of Bass' (1985) Theory of Transformational and Transactional Leadership," PhD dissertation, University of Minnesota, 1991.

80. D. A. Waldman, G. G. Ramirez, R. J. House, and P. Puranam, "Does Leadership Matter? CEO Leadership Attributes and Profitability under Conditions of Perceived Environmental Uncertainty," *Academy of Management Journal* 44, no. 1 (2001), pp. 134–43.

81. T. Dvir, D. Eden, B. J. Avolio, and B. Shamir, "Impact of Transformational Leadership on Follower Development and Performance: A Field Experiment," *Academy of Management Journal* 45, no. 4 (2002), pp. 735–44.

82. J. E. Bono, "Transformational Leadership: What We Know and Why You Should Care!" Presentation delivered to the Minnesota Professionals for Psychology Applied to Work, Minneapolis, MN, September 2002.

83. B. M. Bass, B. J. Avolio, D. I. Jung, and Y. Berson, "Predicting Unit Performance by Assessing Transformational and Transactional Leadership," *Journal of Applied Psychology* 88, no. 2 (2003), pp. 207–18.

84. D. A. Waldman, M. Javidan, and P. Varella, "Charismatic Leadership at the Strategic Level: A New Application of Upper Echelons Theory," *Leadership Quarterly* 15, no. 3 (2004), pp. 355–80.

85. T. A. Judge and R. F. Piccolo, "Transformational and Transactional Leadership: A Meta-analytic Test of Their Relative Validity," *Journal of Applied Psychology* 89, no. 5 (2004), pp. 755–68.

86. R. T. Keller, "Transformational Leadership, Initiating Structure, and Substitutes for Leadership: A Longitudinal Study of Research and Development Project Team Performance," *Journal of Applied Psychology* 91, no. 1 (2006), pp. 202–10.

87. J. L. Whittington, V. L. Goodwin, and B. Murray, "Transformational Leadership, Goal Difficulty, and Job Design: Independent and Interactive Effects on Employee Outcomes," *Leadership Quarterly* 15, no. 5 (2004), pp. 593–606.

88. L. A. Nemanich and R. T. Keller, "Transformational Leadership in an Acquisition: A Field Study of Employees," *Leadership Quarterly* 18, no. 1 (2007), pp. 49–68.

89. J. A. Conger, "Charismatic and Transformational Leadership in Organizations: An Insider's Perspective on These Developing Streams of Research," *Leadership Quarterly* 10, no. 2 (1999), pp. 145–80.

90. B. Tranter, "Leadership and Change in the Tasmanian Environmental Movement," *The Leadership Quarterly* 20, no. 5 (2009), pp. 708–24.

91. R. Khurana, "The Curse of the Superstar CEO," *Harvard Business Review*, September 2002, pp. 60–67.

92. H. L. Tosi, V. F. Misangyi, A. Fanelli, D. A. Waldman, and F. J. Yammarino, "CEO Charisma, Compensation, and Firm Performance," *Leadership Quarterly* 15, no. 3 (2004), pp. 405–20.

93. B. R. Agle, N. J. Nagarajan, J. A. Sonnenfeld, and D. Srinivasan, "Does CEO Charisma Matter? An Empirical Analysis of the Relationships among Organizational Performance, Environmental Uncertainty, and Top Management Team Perceptions of Charisma," *Academy of Management Journal* 49, no. 1 (2006), pp. 161–74.

94. J. A. Conger and R. N. Kanungo, *Charismatic Leadership in Organizations* (Thousand Oaks, CA: Sage, 1998).

95. R. J. House, "A 1976 Theory of Charismatic Leadership," in *Leadership: The Cutting Edge,* eds. J. G. Hunt and L. L. Larson (Carbondale, IL: Southern Illinois University Press, 1977).

96. R. J. House and B. Shamir, "Toward an Integration of Transformational, Charismatic, and Visionary Theories," in *Leadership Theory and Research Perspective and Directions,* eds. M. Chemers and R. Ayman (Orlando, FL: Academic Press, 1993), pp. 577–94.

97. B. Shamir, R. J. House, and M. B. Arthur, "The Motivation Effects of Charismatic Leadership: A Self-Concept Based Theory," *Organizational Science* 4 (1993), pp. 577–94.

98. B. J. Avolio and B. M. Bass, "Transformational Leadership, Charisma, and Beyond," in *Emerging Leadership Vistas,* eds. J. G. Hunt, B. R. Baliga, and C. A. Schriesheim (Lexington, MA: D. C. Heath, 1988).

99. A. J. Towler, "Effects of Charismatic Influence Training on Attitudes, Behavior, and Performance," *Personnel Psychology* 56, no. 2, pp. 363–82.

100. R. Hooijberg and J. Choi, "From Selling Peanuts and Beer in Yankee Stadium to Creating a Theory of Transformational Leadership: An Interview with Bernie Bass," *Leadership Quarterly* 11, no. 2 (2000), pp. 291–300.

101. K. M. Boal and J. M. Bryson, "Charismatic Leadership: A Phenomenal and Structural Approach," in *Emerging Leadership Vistas,* eds. J. G. Hunt, B. R. Baliga, H. P. Dachler, and C. A. Schriesheim (Lexington, MA: Heath Company, 1988).

102. M. Kets de Vries, *The Leadership Mystique: A User's Guide for the Human Enterprise* (London: Financial Times/Prentice Hall, 2001).

103. J. M. Strange and M. D. Mumford, "The Origins of Vision: Charismatic versus Ideological Leadership," *Leadership Quarterly* 13, no. 4 (2002), pp. 343–78.

104. J. S. Mio, R. E. Riggio, S. Levin, and R. Reese, "Presidential Leadership and Charisma: The Effects of Metaphor," *Leadership Quarterly* 16 (2005), pp. 287–94.

105. L. J. Naidoo and R. G. Lord, "Speech Imagery and Perceptions of Charisma: The Mediating Role of Positive Affect," *The Leadership Quarterly* 19, no. 3 (2008), pp. 283–96.

106. R. McKee, "Storytelling That Moves People: A Conversation with Screenwriting Coach Robert McKee," *Harvard Business Review,* June 2003, pp. 51–57.

107. C. J. Palus, D. M. Horth, A. M. Selvin, and M. L. Pulley, "Exploration for Development: Developing Leaders by Making Shared Sense of Complex Challenges," *Consulting Psychology Journal* 55, no. 1 (2003), pp. 26–40.

108. Y. Berson, B. Shamir, B. J. Avolio, and M. Popper, "The Relationship between Vision Strength, Leadership Style, and Context," *Leadership Quarterly* 12, no. 1 (2001), pp. 53–74.

109. B. Shamir, M. B. Arthur, and R. J. House, "The Rhetoric of Charismatic Leadership: A Theoretical Extension, a Case Study, and Implications for Research," *Leadership Quarterly* 5 (1994), pp. 25–42.

110. Y. Berson, B. Shamir, B. J. Avolio, and M. Popper, "The Relationship between Vision Strength, Leadership Style, and Context," *Leadership Quarterly* 12, no. 1 (2001), pp. 53–74.

111. A. R. Willner, *The Spellbinders: Charismatic Political Leadership* (New Haven: Yale University Press, 1984).

112. V. Seyranian and M. C. Bligh, "Presidential Charismatic Leadership: Exploring the Rhetoric of Social Change," *The Leadership Quarterly* 19, no. 1 (2008), pp. 54–76.

113. K. B. Boal and P. L. Schultz, "Storytelling, Time, and Evolution: The Role of Strategic Leadership in Complex Adaptive Systems," *The Leadership Quarterly* 18, no. 3 (2007), pp. 411–28.

114. W. Liu, R. Zhu, and Y. Yang, "I Warn You Because I Like You: Voice Behavior, Employee Identifications, and Transformational Leadership," *The Leadership Quarterly* 21, no. 1 (2010), pp. 189–202.

115. J. A. Conger, *The Charismatic Leader* (San Francisco: Jossey-Bass, 1989).

116. B. M. Bass and B. J. Avolio, eds., *Increasing Organizational Effectiveness through Transformational Leadership* (Thousand Oaks, CA: Sage, 1994).

117. B. M. Bass, "Does the Transactional–Transformational Leadership Paradigm Transcend Organizational and National Boundaries?" *American Psychologist* 52, no. 3 (1997), pp. 130–39.

118. B. M. Bass and P. Steidlmeier, "Ethics, Character, and Authentic Transformational Leadership Behavior," *Leadership Quarterly* 10, no. 2 (1999), pp. 181–218.

119. J. J. Sosik, B. J. Avolio, and D. I. Jun, "Beneath the Mask: Examining the Relationship of Self-Presentation and Impression Management to Charismatic Leadership," *Leadership Quarterly* 13, no. 3 (2002), pp. 217–42.

120. R. Pillai, E. A. Williams, K. B. Lowe, and D. I. Jung, "Personality, Transformational Leadership, Trust, and the 2000 Presidential Vote," *Leadership Quarterly* 14, no. 2 (2003), pp. 161–92.

121. B. M. Bass, *Bass and Stogdill's Handbook of Leadership,* 3rd ed. (New York: Free Press, 1990).

122. J. E. Bono and T. A. Judge, "Self-Concordance at Work: Toward Understanding the Motivational Effects of Transformational Leaders," *Academy of Management Journal* 46, no. 5 (2003), pp. 554–71.

123. G. J. Curphy, *Hogan Assessment Systems Certification Workshop Training Manuals* (Tulsa, OK: Hogan Assessment Systems, 2003).

124. J. Antonakis and R. J. House, "On Instrumental Leadership: Beyond Transactions and Transformations," presentation delivered at the UNL Gallup Leadership Summit, June 2004, Lincoln, Nebraska.

125. J. M. Howell and P. Frost, "A Laboratory Study of Charismatic Leadership," *Organizational Behavior and Human Decision Processes* 43 (1988), pp. 243–69.

126. J. M. Howell and B. Shamir, "The Role of Followers in the Charismatic Leadership Process: Relationships and Their Consequences," *Academy of Management Review* 30, no. 1 (2005), pp. 96–112.

127. M. E. Brown and L. K. Trevino, "Leader–Follower Values Congruence: Are Socialized Charismatic Leaders Better Able to Achieve It?" *Journal of Applied Psychology* 94, no. 2 (2009), pp. 478–90.

128. M. G. Ehrhart and K. J. Klein, "Predicting Followers' Preferences for Charismatic Leadership: The Influence of Follower Values and Personality," *Leadership Quarterly* 12, no. 2 (2001), pp. 153–80.

129. R. G. Lord and D. J. Brown, "Leadership, Values, and Subordinate Self-Concepts," *Leadership Quarterly* 12, no. 2 (2001), pp. 133–52.

130. R. Kark, B. Shamir, and G. Chen, "The Two Faces of Transformational Leadership: Empowerment and Dependency," *Journal of Applied Psychology* 88, no. 2 (2003), pp. 246–55.

131. O. Epitopaki and R. Martin, "The Moderating Role of Individual Differences in the Relation between Transformational/Transactional Leadership Perceptions and Organizational Identification," *Leadership Quarterly* 16 (2005), pp. 569–89.

132. S. M. Campbell, A. J. Ward, J. A. Sonnenfeld, and B. R. Agle, "Relational Ties That Bind: Leader–Follower Relationship Dimensions and Charismatic Attribution," *Leadership Quarterly* 19, no. 5 (2008), pp. 556–68.

133. B. M. Galvin, P. Balkundi, and D. D. Waldman, "Spreading the Word: The Role of Surrogates in Charismatic Leadership Processes," *Academy of Management Review* 35, no. 3 (2010), pp. 477–94.

134. F. O. Walumbwa, B. J. Avolio, and W. Zhu, "How Transformational Leadership Weaves Its Influence on Individual Job Performance: The Role of Identification and Efficacy Beliefs," *Personnel Psychology* 61, no. 4 (2008), pp. 793–826.

135. S. Fox and Y. Amichai-Hamburger, "The Power of Emotional Appeals in Promoting Organizational Change Programs," *The Academy of Management Executive* 15, no. 4 (2001), pp. 84–94.

136. J. E. Bono, H. Foldes, G. Vinson, and J. P. Muros, "Workplace Emotions: The Role of Supervision and Leadership," *Journal of Applied Psychology* 92, no. 5 (2007), pp. 1357–67.

137. A. Erez, V. F. Misangyi, D. E. Johnson, M. A. LePine, and K. C. Halverson, "Stirring the Hearts of Followers: Charismatic as the Transferral of Affect," *Journal of Applied Psychology* 93, no. 3 (2008), pp. 602–16.

138. S. K. Johnson, "I Second That Emotion: Effects of Emotional Contagion and Affect at Work on Leader and Follower Outcomes," *Leadership Quarterly* 19, no. 1 (2008), pp. 1–19.

139. R. J. House, J. Woycke, and E. M. Fodor, "Charismatic and Noncharismatic Leaders: Differences in Behavior and Effectiveness," in *Charismatic Leadership: The Elusive Factor in Organizational Effectiveness*, eds. J. A. Conger and R. N. Kanungo (San Francisco: Jossey-Bass, 1988), pp. 98–121.

140. M. Popper and O. Mayseless, "Back to Basics: Applying a Parenting Perspective to Transformational Leadership," *Leadership Quarterly* 14, no. 1 (2003), pp. 41–66.

141. J. M. Beyer, "Training and Promoting Charisma to Change Organizations," *Leadership Quarterly* 10, no. 2 (1999), pp. 307–30.

142. J. G. Hunt, K. B. Boal, and G. E. Dodge, "The Effects of Visionary and Crisis-Responsive Charisma on Followers: An Experimental Examination of Two Kinds of Charismatic Leadership," *Leadership Quarterly* 10, no. 3 (1999), pp. 423–48.

143. B. S. Pawar and K. K. Eastman, "The Nature and Implications of Contextual Influences on Transformational Leadership: A Conceptual Examination," *Academy of Management Review* 22, no. 1 (1997), pp. 80–109.

144. I. Boga and N. Ensari, "The Role of Transformational Leadership and Organizational Change on Perceived Organizational Success," *The Psychologist-Manager Journal* 12, no. 4 (2009), pp. 235–51.

145. J. C. Pastor, J. R. Meindl, and M. C. Mayo, "A Network Effects Model of Charismatic Attributions," *The Academy of Management Journal* 45, no. 2 (2002), pp. 410–20.

146. J. E. Bono and M. H. Anderson, "The Advice and Influence Networks of Transformational Leaders," *Journal of Applied Psychology* 90, no. 6, pp. 1301–14.

147. R. J. Deluga, "American Presidential Proactivity, Charismatic Leadership and Rated Performance," *Leadership Quarterly* 9, no. 2 (1998), pp. 265–92.

148. A. Fanelli and V. F. Misangyi, "Bringing Out Charisma: CEO Charisma and External Stakeholders," *Academy of Management Review* 31, no. 4 (2006), pp. 1049–61.

149. G. J. Curphy, "The Effects of Transformational and Transactional Leadership on Organizational Climate, Attrition, and Performance," in *Impact of Leadership*, eds. K. E. Clark, M. B. Clark, and D. P. Campbell (Greensboro, NC: Center for Creative Leadership, 1992).

150. J. Adams, H. T. Prince, D. Instone, and R. W. Rice, "West Point: Critical Incidents of Leadership," *Armed Forces and Society* 10 (1984), pp. 597–611.

151. A. S. Labak, "The Study of Charismatic College Teachers," *Dissertation Abstracts International* 34 (1973), p. 1258B.

152. S. J. Shin and J. Zhou, "Transformational Leadership, Conservation, and Creativity: Evidence from Korea," *Academy of Management Journal* 46, no. 6, pp. 703–14.

153. A. H. B. De Hoogh, D. N. Den Hartog, P. L. Koopman, H. Thierry, P. T. Van den Berg, J. G. Van der Weide, and C. P. M. Wilderom, "Leader Motives, Charismatic Leadership, and Subordinates' Work Attitude in the Profit and Voluntary Sector," *Leadership Quarterly* 16 (2005), pp. 17–38.

154. A. E. Rafferty and M. A. Griffen, "Dimensions of Transformational Leadership: Conceptual and Empirical Extensions," *Leadership Quarterly* 15, no. 3 (2004), pp. 329–54.

155. J. Antonakis, B. J. Avolio, and N. Sivasubramainiam, "Context and Leadership: An Examination of the Nine Factor Full Range Leadership Theory Using the Multifactor Leadership Questionnaire," *Leadership Quarterly* 15, no. 2 (2003), pp. 261–95.

156. B. M. Bass and B. J. Avolio, *The Multifactor Leadership Questionnaire Report* (Palo Alto, CA: Mind Garden, 1996).

157. J. Rowold and K. Heinitz, "Transformational and Charismatic Leadership: Assessing the Convergent, Divergent, and Criterion Validity of the MLQ and CKS," *Leadership Quarterly* 18, no. 1 (2007), pp. 121–33.

158. R. F. Piccolo, J. E. Bono, T. A. Judge, E. E. Duehr, and J. P. Muros, "Which Leader Behaviors Matter Most: Comparing Dimensions of the LBDQ and MLQ," paper presented in J. P. Campbell and M. J. Benson (chairs), *Predicting Leadership: The Good, The Bad, the Different, and the Unnecessary*, Annual Meeting of Society of Industrial and Organizational Psychology, New York, April, 2007.

159. M. Frese, S. Beimel, and S. Schoenborn, "Action Training for Charismatic Leadership: Two Evaluations of Studies of a Commercial Training Module on Inspirational Communication of a Vision," *Personnel Psychology* 56, no. 3 (2003), pp. 671–97.

160. J. Barling, C. Loughlin, and E. K. Kelloway, "Development and Test of a Model Linking Safety–Specific Transformational Leadership and Occupational Safety," *Journal of Applied Psychology* 87, no. 3 (2002), pp. 488–96.

161. A. Zacharatos, J. Barling, and E. K. Kelloway, "Development and Effects of Transformational Leadership in Adolescents," *Leadership Quarterly* 11, no. 2 (2000), pp. 211–26.

162. T. A. Judge and J. E. Bono, "Five-Factor Model of Personality and Transformational Leadership," *Journal of Applied Psychology* 85, no. 5 (2000), pp. 751–65.

612 Part Four *Focus on the Situation*

163. R. T. Hogan, G. J. Curphy, and J. Hogan, "What Do We Know about Personality: Leadership and Effectiveness?" *American Psychologist* 49 (1994), pp. 493–504.

164. G. J. Curphy, "New Directions in Personality," in Personality and Organizational Behavior, R. T. Hogan (chair). Symposium presented at the 104th Annual Meeting of the American Psychological Association, Toronto, Canada, 1996.

165. D. L. Nilsen, Using Self and Observers' Rating of Personality to Predict Leadership Performance, unpublished doctoral dissertation, University of Minnesota, Minneapolis, 1995.

166. R. J. House, W. D. Spangler, and J. Woycke, "Personality and Charisma in the U.S. Presidency: A Psychological Theory of Leadership Effectiveness," *Administrative Science Quarterly* 36 (1991), pp. 364–96.

Chapter

15

The Dark Side of Leadership

Introduction

Back in May 2005 one of the authors of this book was on a flight from Columbus, Ohio, to Minneapolis, Minnesota. Northwest Airlines Flight 1495 had a heavy passenger load and a crew of two pilots and three flight attendants. The two-hour flight seemed routine, but upon landing the author noticed the runway was lined with ambulances and fire trucks. The plane taxied off the runway and stopped some distance short of the gate. After waiting five minutes, one of the pilots got on the intercom and announced, "The plane has experienced a systems malfunction." The pilots and flight attendants did not say anything more, and about five minutes later the DC-9 began moving again.

The DC-9 had been traveling about 10 seconds when suddenly a loud boom filled the cabin and the plane came to an abrupt stop. Passengers were thrown violently forward in their seats, but luckily everyone was still wearing their seatbelts. The author and other passengers had assumed the plane was taxiing to its gate, but a look out the window showed that the DC-9 had collided with another aircraft. Apparently the pilots of the DC-9 had left the engines running and the plane had experienced a hydraulics failure, which caused it to lose all steering and braking capabilities. The DC-9 collided with a Northwest Airlines A-319 that was being pushed back from its gate, and the wing of the A-319 peeled back the first 10 feet of the roof of the DC-9 during the collision.

After the plane had stopped, the lead flight attendant unbuckled her seat belt and started running up and down the aisle yelling, "Assume the crash position! Assume the crash position!" The passengers were wondering how putting our heads between our knees was going to help when the plane had already come to a stop, but we dutifully complied with the flight attendant's request. After two to three minutes of running up and down the aisle and barking orders, the lead flight attendant hyperventilated and collapsed in a heap behind the first-class bulkhead. The two remaining flight attendants then got out of their seats to check on the lead flight attendant.

Most of the passengers started easing out of the crash position and began looking to the other flight attendants for guidance on what to do, but none was forthcoming. The author then got up and went to the cockpit door because he could tell that the wing of the A-319 had come in through the cockpit, and he was concerned about the pilots. He asked the pilots whether they needed any help, and one of them meekly replied that they needed medical attention. The author tried to open the door, but the door reinforcements added after 9/11/2001 made it impossible to get in.

As the author was tugging on the cockpit door handle, he could overhear the two flight attendants discussing whether they should deplane the aircraft. One attendant asked, "Should we keep them on or get them off?" The other attendant replied, "I don't know, what do you think?" This conversation continued for three to four minutes, with the lead flight attendant still whispering in the background, "Assume the crash position. Assume the crash position." During this time one of the flight attendants came up to the cockpit door and asked the pilots what to do, but there was no response. She then went back to attend to the lead flight attendant.

At this time the author noticed that jet fuel from the wing of the A-319 had leaked into the cockpit of the DC-9 and had seeped into the first-class cabin. He realized that his shoes and pants were covered in jet fuel and an errant spark would light up two planes full of people. He then turned and yelled at the flight attendants, "I am standing in jet fuel. Get everyone off the plane. NOW!" The two coherent flight attendants got up and proceeded to hustle everyone off the plane using the DC-9's rear exit. Being in the front of the cabin at the cockpit door, the author was the last in line to get off the plane. You can imagine how happy he was to see passengers at the rear of the aircraft taking the time to open the overhead bins and retrieve their luggage while he was standing in jet fuel. The flight attendants did not intervene more than giving some mild reminders to passengers to just exit the aircraft and leave the luggage behind.

All the passengers from both aircraft escaped with only a few minor injuries. The flight attendants were okay; the two DC-9 pilots needed some medical attention but were released the next day. But this incident provides several vivid examples of failures in leadership. The pilots failed to warn the passengers of the impending collision and did not use the thrust reversers to stop the plane. The lead flight attendant's instructions to assume the crash position after the plane was at a complete stop and then collapsing two to three minutes later did not instill confidence. The other two flight attendants needed to step into a leadership role and take over the situation but were unable to make a decision or tell passengers what to do. Northwest Airlines failed by having standard operating procedures (SOPs) that instructed pilots to leave the engines running in the event of an aircraft hydraulics failure. Instead the SOP should have instructed pilots to shut down the engines and have the plane towed to a gate. The airline also failed when the author called in several times offering to describe the incident in order to improve training and was ignored. Later he learned that the airline formally rewarded the two pilots and three flight attendants for their outstanding actions during the emergency.

Although this may appear a bit self-serving, in our minds leadership is the most important topic in the world today. Leadership determines whether countries are democracies or dictatorships or are at peace or war, whether businesses are good investments or kleptocracies, whether teams win or lose, whether health care and education reforms fail or succeed, and whether rural communities thrive or merely survive. Leadership plays a role in determining where you live, what schools you get into, what laws and rules you must obey, what occupations you enter, whether you have a successful career, and how your children are raised. It plays such a pervasive part in our lives that it is easy to overlook its impact on our day-to-day behaviors. Because of the profound ways in which leadership affects us all, it would be nice if the people in positions of authority were actually good at it. But research shows that most people are woefully inadequate when it comes to influencing an organized group toward accomplishing its goals. The purpose of this chapter is to describe the most common reasons why people fail in leadership positions and the steps we can take to improve our odds of success.

It is fitting that this chapter appears at the end of the book because it draws on much of the leader, follower, and situation material described in earlier chapters. As an overview, we will review the research pertaining to and some practical steps for avoiding destructive leadership, managerial incompetence, and managerial derailment. **Destructive leadership** is associated with individuals who are effective at building teams and getting results through others, but who obtain results that are morally or ethically challenged or undermine organizational or community success (see Highlight 15.1). An example here might be Adolf Hitler. Hitler was clearly able to rally an entire country around a common cause and conquered a number of countries, yet the end result was a continent in ruins and the death of over 20,000,000 people. Unlike destructive leadership, **managerial incompetence** concerns a person's *inability* to build teams or get results through others. A majority of people in positions of authority can (1) build teams but not get results; (2) get results but destroy team morale and cohesiveness; or (3) neither build teams nor get results. **Managerial derailment** describes the common reasons why people in positions of authority have difficulties building teams or getting results through others. Knowing the six root causes of managerial derailment and what to do to avoid these pitfalls can help you be more effective as a leader.

If you put on a blindfold and threw a dart at a map of the world, then there is a 70 percent chance that whatever country the dart lands on is run by some form of dictatorship.

RT Hogan, Hogan Assessment Systems

The Pursuit of Power and Destructive Leadership

HIGHLIGHT 15.1

Destructive leadership can be defined as the ability to build teams whose results do not serve the common good. Destructive leadership is prevalent in both dictatorships and democracies, but the checks and balances of the latter keep the destructive tendencies of elected leaders in check. Both dictators and those elected play the same game, which is to get into power, stay in power, and control resources. Autocrats are better at playing this game, as they tend to stay in power much longer than their democratically elected counterparts. Dictators only need to reward a small band of loyal followers who can suppress the opposition and control the populace, whereas democratically elected leaders can lose their jobs if they neglect their voters.

The destructive leadership tendencies of democratically led countries are readily evident whenever one political party controls all of the key institutions. Venezuela, Russia, and South Africa are all democracies, yet the Chavez, Putin, and Zuma governments have changed the political, legal, criminal justice, media, and economic institutions in order to maintain power and control funds. These governments are associated with the high

levels of political favoritism, corruption, crime, and media manipulation often found in dictatorships. Fortunately neither political party in the United States has complete control of the legislative, executive, or judicial branches of the government or media. What would happen to workers' rights, reproductive rights, taxes, the national debt, Medicare, Social Security, immigration, gun control, environmental laws, economic competitiveness, and the Department of Defense if the liberal wing of the Democratic Party in the United States controlled all these institutions? What if moderate Republicans or the Tea Party controlled all the major institutions? Would these changes serve the common good or the constituencies represented by these parties? Has the redrawing of congressional districts after the 2010 census increased or decreased the odds of destructive leadership happening in the United States?

Sources: M. Moynihan, "It's Good to Be Boss," *The Wall Street Journal,* September 24–25, 2011, p. C10; B. Bueno de Mesquita and A. Smith, *The Dictator's Handbook: Why Bad Behavior Is Almost Always Good Politics* (New York: PublicAffairs, 2011); R. Hogan, *How to Define Destructive Leadership* (Tulsa, OK: Hogan Assessment Systems, 2012).

Destructive Leadership

One way to evaluate leadership effectiveness is to look at a person's ability to build teams and get results through others. Effective leaders are those who can meet both criteria, where ineffective leaders have trouble building teams or getting results. As described in Chapter 14, James MacGregor Burns has maintained that truly effective leaders need to meet an additional criterion, which is to raise the standard of human conduct and improve the lives of everyone they touch.[1] In other words, effective leaders must make the organizations or societies they belong to better places to work or live. Given these three criteria, we can see that there is a subset of leaders who are good at painting a compelling picture of the future and getting followers to drive the organizational or societal changes needed to make their vision become reality, yet the end result may be morally or ethically reprehensible or work against the common good.

Gulnara Karimova: The Most Hated Person in Uzbekistan

PROFILES IN LEADERSHIP 15.1

The Republic of Uzbekistan is a former Soviet bloc country that gained independence in the early 1990s. A double landlocked country where natural gas, gold, uranium, and cotton production make up most of the country's economic base, Islam Karimov has ruled since the country's independence, and citizens enjoy few civil rights. Dispatches from the U.S. Embassy in Uzbekistan describe the country as a nightmarish world where corruption, organized crime, torture, and forced labor are endemic. Dissidents are reported boiled alive, protesters are summarily executed, and all teachers and students are forced to leave school to pick cotton each fall. Decades without central planning by the Karimov government has allowed the Aral Sea to shrink by 50 percent over the past 25 years and is now a global ecological disaster.

Life for ordinary citizens of Uzbekistan is harsh, but life for the Karimov family is quite good. Perhaps the most privileged of this lot is Gulnara Karimova, the eldest daughter of Islam, who is known as "the most hated person in Uzbekistan." The glamorous and controversial Gulnara has bullied her way into the mobile phone, entertainment, retail, restaurant, beverage, and tourism industries in Uzbekistan and reportedly has a personal net worth of over $600 million. Karimova has an eye for successful companies and, once identified, she secures ownership stakes through taxation, the legal system, intimidation, or confiscation. Because of her lack of popularity at home and abroad, Karimova leads a number of foundations and sponsors events to support social causes. These activities have had little impact on her public reputation, however, as most citizens see Gulnara Karimova as the ruthless, greedy, selfish, corrupt, and spoiled child of a despot.

Sources: http://www.forbescustom.com/Emerging MarketsPgs/WomanofSubstanceP1.html; http://divainternational.ch/spip.php?article487; http://www.gulnarakarimova.com/; http://www.guardian.co.uk/world/2006/aug11/tomparfitt.mainsection; http://www.rferl.org/content/Its_Gulnaras_World_We_Only_Live_In_It/1907693.html; http://www.foreignpolicy.com/articles/2009/08/04/the_worlds_worst-daughters?page=0,0;

The next time a Democrat or Republican claims to be taking a position for the "good of his country," remember to replace the word "country" with "career."
Michael Moynihan, reporter

Some of these leaders are among the most infamous in history and include Alexander the Great, Genghis Kahn, Attila the Hun, Ivan the Terrible, Vlad the Impaler, Napoleon Bonaparte, Adolf Hitler, Joseph Stalin, Mao Zedong, Pol Pot, Idi Amin, Saddam Hussein, Kim Jong-Il, Robert Mugabe, Fidel Castro, and Osama bin Laden. No one could argue about whether these individuals had a major impact on their countries and societies, but their collective influence killed hundreds of millions of innocent people. And such leaders who are still alive lead incredibly repressed societies or followers who are bent on delivering death and destruction (see Profiles in Leadership 15.1 and 15.2.)

Destructive leadership is not limited to government or political leaders—it occurs in virtually all other settings. The recession of 2008 to 2010 can be partially attributed to a number of destructive leaders in the financial services industry. Many greedy bank and insurance executives did a good job of building teams and generating profits, but the profits were gained by cooking the books, selling financial products that were doomed to fail, or funding subprime mortgages that owners could ill

Hugo Chavez: Hero or Destructive Leader?

PROFILES IN LEADERSHIP 15.2

In March 2013 thousands of people filled the streets of Caracas, Venezuela, to mourn the death of their president, Hugo Chavez. Chavez had won three national elections, was one of *Time*'s 25 most influential people in 2005 and 2006, and had led Venezuela since 1999. A gifted politician and orator who connected with the downtrodden, Chavez got elected as an outsider to address Venezuela's pervasive inequality and corruption. Sitting on some of the world's largest oil deposits and with oil prices increasing tenfold while he served as president, Chavez was able to use this windfall in revenues to provide handouts to the poor, open clinics and subsidized grocery stores in poor neighborhoods, and lower the country's poverty rate from 49 to 28 percent.

But is Venezuela better off now than it was when Chavez took over the presidency? Chavez nationalized a number of privately held firms and placed political cronies with little business or technical expertise in key leadership positions. Many of these companies are less productive and competitive than they had been in the past and are being propped up by oil revenues. Foreign investment in Venezuela is virtually nonexistent, as investors worry about their holdings being nationalized. Over 40 television and radio stations have been shut down; the courts, legislative bodies, and remaining media outlets have been filled with Chavez loyalists; corruption and crime are at all-time highs; and 90 percent of murders go unpunished. Despite having the second-highest oil revenues in the world, Venezuela's infrastructure is crumbling, inflation has spiraled out of control, food shortages occur regularly, standards of living have fallen, and the country has a huge national debt.

Was Hugo Chavez a hero or a destructive leader? Would your answer differ if you lived in a Venezuelan slum or were a business owner whose company was nationalized?

Sources: "Hugo Chavez's Rotten Legacy," *The Economist,* March 9, 2013, p. 10; R. Carroll, *Comandante: Hugo Chavez's Venezuela* (New York: Penguin Press, 2013); "Now for the Reckoning," *The Economist,* March 9, 2013, pp. 23–26; M. A. O'Grady, "Chavez the Redeemer," *The Wall Street Journal,* March 11, 2013, p. A15; http://www.bloomberg.com/news/2013-03-07/venezuelans-quality-of-life-improved-in-un-index-under-chavez.html; http://www.nytimes.com/2013/03/06/world/Americas/hugo_chavez_venezuelas_polarizing_figure_dies_at_58.html?_r=0;

afford. The problem was so widespread in the financial services industry that it almost caused the collapse of the entire global economy. Similarly, the massacres at My Lai, Serbia, Bosnia, Croatia, Rwanda, Darfur, and Syria show that destructive leadership also occurs in military settings. In the spirit of seeking revenge or ethnic cleansing, military commanders will rally the troops to kill everyone in particular villages and towns—even those who are not military combatants. Religious leaders can also exhibit destructive leadership. Jim Jones and David Koresh are two examples of highly charismatic religious leaders who developed cultlike followings and lead their adherents to commit suicide (see Profiles in Leadership 15.3). And destructive leadership can occur at a variety of levels in organizations. Sometimes first-line supervisors, midlevel managers, and executives who disagree with company policies and strategies will motivate their followers to pursue courses of action that are not aligned with organizational interests. These actions and their subsequent results often lead to poor customer service, duplicative efforts, high levels of team

David Koresh: Destructive Religious Leader

PROFILES IN LEADERSHIP 15.3

In April 1993 approximately 85 people died at a religious compound outside of Waco, Texas. Many of them died in the fire that consumed the compound, but a single bullet to the head had killed others. Twenty-five of the deceased were children. How did this happen? The story of David Koresh is a classic example of what can go wrong when bad leaders take charge.

By all accounts David Koresh (born as Vernon Wayne Howell) had a miserable childhood. His mother was only 14 when David was born and went through two divorces before she was 20. David was abused by his uncle while growing up and his mother decided to attend the local Seventh Day Adventist church when he turned nine. Apparently David loved church and religion and was spellbound during sermons. He memorized large portions of scripture and could effortlessly recite endless passages. However, in his later teen years Koresh began to question why the church believed in modern-day prophets yet claimed that none had walked the earth for a long time. He also began to question the biblical interpretations of elders and eventually left the Seventh Day Adventists to join the Branch Davidians. The Branch Davidians believed not only in modern-day prophets but also in Armageddon. At the age of 24 Koresh took over

the Branch Davidians by having intimate relations with their 67-year-old leader. He also secretly married a 14-year-old member of the sect and was subsequently kicked out of the church. He and many of the Branch Davidians left to start their own chapter outside Waco, Texas.

While starting his own church Koresh became increasingly temperamental and violent. He made fellow members watch violent war movies and listen to his rock sessions, and he put them through long fasts and strange diets. At first Koresh abided by his own rules, but eventually he claimed that God had told him it was all right for him, and only him, to violate these rules. Koresh took a number of wives, all of whom were under 15. He eventually told the males that all the females in the church were to become his wives and their marriages were no longer valid. This bizarre behavior continued until agents from the Alcohol, Tobacco, and Firearms Bureau came to the compound to investigate allegations of firearms violations and child abuse in early 1993. Rather than allowing the agents to investigate, Koresh burned down the compound, killed many of his followers, and committed suicide.

Source: K. R. Samples, E. M. deCastro, R. Abanes, and R. J. Lyle, *Prophets of the Apocalypse: David Koresh and the Other American Messiahs* (Grand Rapids, MI: Baker Books, 1994).

conflict, and ultimately suboptimal financial performance. Although these leaders and followers may believe they are doing the right thing, their actions harm their organizations.[2–6]

Barbara Kellerman correctly points out that the United States has an overly optimistic outlook on leadership. Most of the leadership books written for U.S. consumption have an overly positive tone and generally maintain that leadership is relatively easy to learn.[7] Similarly, many leadership training programs delivered in the United States are built on the erroneous assumption that leaders are inherently good and effective; destructive or incompetent leadership is the exception rather than the rule.[8] Yet Jared Diamond's book, *Guns, Germs, and Steel: The Fates of Human Societies*, shows that most societies from the earliest times to today have been kleptocracies.[9] Some are legitimized kleptocracies, where kings, queens, and elected officials dictate laws or write rules to increase their

620   Part Four   *Focus on the Situation*

power or personal wealth. Dictators who emerge after violent overthrows of previous governments seem to benefit greatly from their change in status but rarely if ever improve the lot of commoners (see Profiles in Leadership 15.1). Thus destructive leadership occurs when people in positions of authority use their team-building skills to achieve greedy, selfish, or immoral results. And as history mournfully suggests, evil, corrupt, greedy, and selfish leaders will likely be around for a long time.

A final note about destructive leadership is worth discussing further: what may be considered destructive versus good leadership may be in the eye of the beholder. Although most people believe Kim Jong-Un and Alexander Lukashenko are egomaniacal despots, those loyal to these two individuals may see them as great leaders. And in reality those who are loyal to destructive leaders generally are rewarded for their efforts. Sometimes this reward comes in the form of a bullet (Joseph Stalin, Mao Zedong, and Idi Amin did not hesitate to kill loyal followers whom they perceived as rivals), but more often than not loyal followers are richly rewarded with titles, wealth, and power. The same perspective could be applied to Osama bin Laden. Most people from Western cultures see Osama bin Laden as a threat, but his followers see his vision as a path to heaven. This concept of good versus destructive leadership could also be applied to President Barack Obama. Many Democrats see Barack Obama as a great U.S. president, but members of the Tea Party think the United States is heading in the wrong direction and is destined to fail under his leadership. Sometimes political, religious, or business leaders advocate what many believe are the wrong things, but these turn out to be the right things over time. Lee Iacocca's push for a government bailout of Chrysler, Martin Luther King Jr.'s vision for civil rights, and Bill Clinton's intervention in the Yugoslavian civil war are all examples of leaders accused of doing bad things at the time but who in retrospect improved the organizations and societies they led. Thus destructive leadership might not be quite so clear-cut as we might think (see Profiles in Leadership 15.2).

Managerial Incompetence

Whereas destructive leadership is associated with individuals who build teams to achieve corrupt or evil ends, incompetent management is associated with individuals who either cannot build teams or cannot get results through others. In other words, incompetent managers have difficulties building loyal followings or getting anything done. Research shows that there may be more incompetent than competent managers; the **base rate of managerial incompetence** may be 50 to 75 percent.[7-13] You might think the base rate of managerial incompetence could not be this high—too many countries, businesses, government and other nonprofit organizations, or volunteer organizations would simply fail if riddled with such a high percentage of incompetent leaders. But consider the following facts:

- Most countries are run by some form of dictatorship. Most ordinary citizens in Saudi Arabia, Syria, Belarus, Bahrain Sudan, Jordan, Chad, Iran, Turkmenistan, China, and Russia do not have much say over who is in charge, what laws are made, and so on. Although the leaders of these countries have a following among a minority of people, the majority has little input into who leads them.

- Many leaders of democratic countries are perceived as being unable to build teams or get results. U.S. President George W. Bush saw his approval ratings drop from 85 to 30 percent over his eight-year term. Barack Obama experienced a 25-point approval rating drop during his first 18 months in office, and the U.S. Congress has less than a 15 percent approval rating from likely voters.[14–16]

- There were 1,132 CEO departures in the first nine months of 2008, up from 700 per year from 2002 to 2004. Fifty percent of *Fortune* 500 CEOs will be dismissed for poor performance over the next three years. Worldwide confidence in business leaders is the lowest it has ever been for the past 10 years.[15,17–20]

- Employee satisfaction surveys show that more than 75 percent of all respondents indicate that the most stressful part of their job is their immediate boss.[13,15] This finding holds true across countries and industries.

- Sixty percent of the participants in a high-performing division of a Fortune 100 company indicated that that their organization was successful despite their leaders. Thirty-five percent of the participants in a broader research study of high-performing companies said the same thing. Clueless bosses in high-performing companies attribute success to their own efforts, but it may be highly engaged employees working in high-performing teams that make the difference between winning and losing.[21]

- A study published in *Harvard Business Review* reported that only 30 percent of businesses had "healthy and respectful" work climates. A majority of organizations had dysfunctional and unhealthy work climates.[22,23]

- At any one time the 800,000 employees of the U.S. Postal Service have filed 150,000 grievances against their supervisors.[13]

- Research shows that 50–90 percent of all new businesses fail within five years. This finding seems consistent across all business types and countries. Most of the failures can be attributed to managerial incompetence.[24–27]

- BP, the energy company responsible for the Gulf of Mexico environmental disaster in 2010, has been cited 760 times and paid fines of

$373,000,000 for safety and environmental violations since 2005. The root causes of most major industrial accidents and incidents, such as the Bhopal, India, chemical spill, the Exxon Valdez disaster, or the Texas City refinery explosion can be traced back to poor management oversight or management cost-cutting initiatives.[28,29]

- Research also shows that 67 percent of all IT projects fail to deliver promised functionality, are not delivered on time, or do not stay within budgeted costs. This IT project failure rate has not improved much over the past 10 years, and U.S. businesses are now spending over $55 billion annually on poorly scoped or executed IT projects.[30]

- Over 70 percent of all mergers and acquisitions fail to yield projected improvements in profitability and synergies. Examples might include HP's acquisition of Autonomy or Sears merger with Kmart.[31]

- A majority of large-scale organizational change initiatives fail to achieve their intended results.[32]

- Toxic, destructive, or abusive supervision is prevalent in both the public and private sectors. A U.S. Army study indicated that only 27 percent of officers could accurately identify ineffective leaders and 25 percent of the officer corps were either abusive to others or careerists out only for themselves. Another study indicated that over 60 percent of workers reported to an abusive or destructive leader sometime during their career.[6,23,33,34]

- In 2012, three Italian researchers were awarded the Ig Noble prize for demonstrating mathematically that organizations would become more efficient if they promoted people randomly. If the base rate of managerial incompetence ranges between 50 and 75 percent, then random promotions would be the best alternative.[35]

As unflattering as these statistics are, these examples may seem out of the realm of most readers. So let's make the concept of managerial incompetence a little more personal. One easy way to determine the level of incompetence among people in positions of authority is to do the **Dr. Gordy test**.[8,12] To use this test, begin by counting the total number of people you have been led by or worked for in the past. This total should include past bosses, athletic coaches, team captains, choir directors, camp directors, and so on. In other words, it should include anyone with whom you played a formal followership role. Once you have arrived at a total, count the number of people in this group for whom you would willingly play, sing, or work again. In other words, how many of these people would you play a followership role for again if given a choice? Now calculate the percentage of competent leaders in the total group of leaders. When health care, education, business, military, and community leaders are asked the same question, most need only the digits on a single hand to count the number of leaders for whom they would willingly work again. The

FIGURE 15.1
The Two Dimensions of Managerial Incompetence

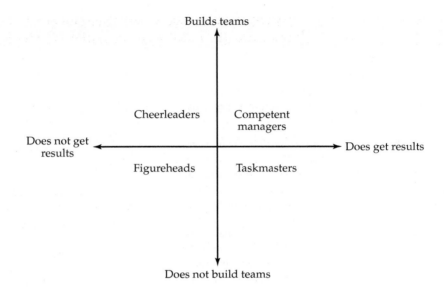

percentage of competent leaders people would willingly work for again varies dramatically across individuals, but the percentage seems to hover between 25 and 40 percent.[8,10,12,13,15] This means that most people would not work for a majority of leaders they have been exposed to.

We believe that those occupying positions of authority are paid to get results, and they get results by building teams.[8,12,13] As shown in Figure 15.1, **competent managers** are good at building teams and getting results through others. Although they are the types of leaders most people aspire to be, most people in positions of authority fall into one of the other three categories. **Taskmasters** are often good at achieving results, such as financial targets or win–loss records, but tend to treat followers so poorly that these results are generally short-lived. Nonetheless, some taskmasters are effective at turning around failing businesses. Because these managers do not care for people, they can make the tough decisions needed to right a sinking ship, and some are so good at turnarounds that they spend their entire careers moving from one floundering company to another. Other taskmasters are good at projecting an image of success by launching **programs for promotions initiatives** that garner a lot of attention but have no real chance of success. Superiors get caught up in the hyperbole and often promote task masters before the consequences of their poorly conceived initiatives and lack of team-building skills become evident (see Highlight 15.2). And because taskmasters have impressive track records, they are often hired away to wreak havoc on other organizations.

Cheerleaders are people in positions of authority who are people-centered and make a point of getting along with everyone. Thanks to their focus on making the workplace warm and fun, most people like

An Example of a Taskmaster

HIGHLIGHT 15.2

The following is a story about a sales manager who is a taskmaster. What advice would you give to the writer to fix the problem?

I've been working in a medium-sized manufacturing company for the past 20 years. I'm not in sales, but interact with salespeople on a daily basis. Over the past year or so, I have noticed the sales force has been frustrated. After numerous conversations not only with the sales force, but also with other people in all aspects of the company, I have realized that the poison is coming from one person: Mike, the sales manager. Mike has been with the company for over 10 years and has successfully maneuvered his way to the position of sales manager. All of his promotions were given to him because of his own self-promotion. He has an enormous ego. His tactics of bulldog management, double standards, and outright lying are driving his sales force out and are frustrating people all over the company. He is disliked, even hated, by almost everyone in the company. Amazingly, Mike doesn't realize what people think of him. I believe the owners tolerate Mike's behavior because he has produced decent sales over the years. This year sales are substantially down. I believe the company is going to start to lose good salespeople because of Mike. Here's why: Nobody will confront him because if they do, he threatens them or makes them do some ridiculous assignment. All conversations with Mike are one-sided. If you bring up a concern that involves him, he will change the subject and dismiss you. It's like he is afraid of the truth. He is dishonest and essentially a loose cannon. I believe the owners know the truth about Mike but they continue to let him act this way. I believe Mike will never leave because he knows he could never get away with the things he does here anywhere else. My concern is that if the owners don't fix the "Mike problem" they will start to lose good salespeople. Any advice?

Source: J. Lloyd, "Good Firms Work to Find Out Truth about Bad Managers," *Milwaukee Journal Sentinel,* August 20, 2000, p. 20.

People don't leave companies, they leave bad bosses.
Beverly Kaye, CEO

During my brother-in-law's first performance review, his boss said, "I'm not quite sure what you do around here. But whatever it is, could you do it faster?"
Jeanie Waara, printer

working for cheerleaders. However, cheerleaders spend so much time making the workplace enjoyable that they forget why they are paid to be in leadership positions, which is to get results. Cheerleaders are involved with a number of different activities but confuse activity with productivity and get little accomplished. They also have a difficult time doing anything that could potentially erode their relationships with followers, which includes dealing with conflict or confronting performance problems. Nevertheless, because they are loyal and dutiful, avoid making enemies, engage in strategic ingratiation, and are well liked by followers, cheerleaders often are promoted into senior positions in organizations (see Highlight 15.3).

Figureheads do not play to win; they play to not lose. They may not be complete failures at building teams and getting results, but they could be a lot better at both of these endeavors. Many times figureheads do just enough to stay out of trouble and avoid the spotlight. The last thing figurehead managers want is attention because this might raise superiors' expectations for their performance. So if their team is starting to exceed expectations, they may hold back or even sabotage team performance to avoid having to meet higher expectations in the future. Thus followers

An Example of a Cheerleader

HIGHLIGHT 15.3

Every business depends on its account receivables department. This department collects payments from customers, and problems in collections will hurt company performance. An office supply company was having serious cash flow problems and had been using its credit line to pay its bills, primarily because accounts receivable time had increased from 36 to 52 days. To try to turn around this problem, Helen was made manager of accounts receivable because of her performance during a major sales software conversion. Helen approached her new role with great enthusiasm, and motivational posters started appearing everywhere. The poster titled "The Power of One" was particularly amusing because she was the one person who did everything but her job.

Helen was easy to get along with and well liked by her staff. She knew everyone's personal problems, regularly organized potluck lunches, and brought in weekly treats. When peers inquired about the status of invoices, Helen always told them she would "get right on it," but it usually took another three to four calls before they could determine what was really happening. After three months the only gains in the department were on the waistlines of the staff, who had made no progress in reducing the time it was taking customers to pay the company. A few months later Helen brought in outside consultants to help fix the accounts receivable problem. Helen constantly extolled the virtues of her hardworking staff and consultants and provided pleasant but somewhat ridiculous excuses for her department's lack of progress. After a year of posters, potlucks, and ever-worsening accounts receivables results, Helen was promoted into another position. The keys to her success were flattering her boss and making everyone on her team happy—team results were not important.

If you were Helen's boss, what would you do to achieve better accounts receivable results?

Source: G. J. Curphy, A. Baldrica, and R. T. Hogan, *Managerial Incompetence,* unpublished manuscript, 2009.

---

who are self-starters can get frustrated and leave organizations when they find out they are working for figureheads (see Highlight 15.4).

There are variations of figureheads. Some have a hard time building teams and getting results because they are so intellectually and interpersonally challenged. It is hard to build a team and get results if you are completely clueless about people and repeatedly demonstrate poor business judgment. Other figureheads want to succeed but demonstrate irritating, counterproductive behaviors that interfere with their ability to build teams or get results through others. Some lack the motivation needed to build teams or get results. Put another way, these individuals simply do not care if they lead cohesive teams or obtain better-than-average results. Situational factors may also affect the prevalence of figureheads in organizations—some managers may find themselves in situations where they lack the equipment, systems, budget, or talent needed to succeed. For example, a fire chief may find it nearly impossible to build a cohesive, effective team of firefighters if the department lacks fire trucks or a fire station or has no budget to train staff.

If the base rate of managerial incompetence is 50 to 75 percent, we might wonder how organizations can succeed with such a high percentage of

Universities are not hierarchies, they are anarchies.

David Campbell, Center for Creative Leadership

An Example of a Figurehead

HIGHLIGHT 15.4

Steve Jones was a salesman who learned the car business and then convinced a local bank to lend him the money to open his own Ford dealership. Over the years Steve added Dodge, Suzuki, BMW, Nissan, Rover, and Volkswagen automobile and Yamaha motorcycle dealerships to his company; annual revenues grew from less than $1,000,000 to over $200,000,000. As Steve grew older he became concerned with succession and wanted his oldest son Scott to take over the business. Growing up in a privileged environment, Scott was a poor student in high school and flunked out of college, but Steve brought him into the business and put him in charge of purchasing. One of his responsibilities was to purchase life and health insurance for employees.

Scott asked a local insurance representative to make an insurance sales presentation for him and 15 other executives from the dealerships. During the presentation Scott asked several irrelevant ques-

tions and criticized the other executives and the representative for not following his line of questioning. He had strong opinions about, but no grasp of, life and health insurance. Unfortunately Scott acted no differently at the sales presentation than he did in his day-to-day interactions with customers, vendors, managers, and employees—he treated everyone with equal distain. Scott did not care about the people on his purchasing team, and the dealership began making bad purchasing decisions. The other managers and employees tried to keep Scott from making mistakes, but Scott ignored any advice on how to obtain better results. After several major purchasing blunders, Steve removed Scott from his position and told him never to return to work. Although Steve saved his business, Scott continues to treat others as "little people" who are unworthy of his presence.

Source: G. J. Curphy, A. Baldrica, and R. T. Hogan, *Managerial Incompetence*, unpublished manuscript, 2009.

ineffective people in positions of authority. Although managerial incompetence can be found in any organization, many businesses still make money, the U.S. military is capable of waging wars, children continue to get educated, and most people receive high-quality health care when they need it. The good news is that organizations may not actually need every person in a position of authority to be a competent manager. The keys to success may be for organizations to ensure that they have a higher percentage of competent managers than their competitors and that these individuals are in pivotal leadership roles. Research shows that organizations with higher percentages of competent managers occupying critical positions are more successful than those with fewer competent managers who are not well placed.[36–38] The purpose of this chapter and book is to increase the odds of you becoming a competent manager and securing positions where you can have an impact on the success of your organization.

Managerial Derailment

So far we have described five different leadership and management types. Destructive leadership is associated with individuals who have good team-building skills but achieve results that are morally reprehensible or undermine organizational success. Taskmasters get good results but run over people and erode team cohesiveness while doing so. Cheerleaders

The Moronization of Management

HIGHLIGHT 15.5

Carl Icahn is a multibillionaire who made his fortune buying up companies that were poorly managed, straightening out their operations and finances, and then reselling them for a profit. Senior managers dislike Icahn because they often lose their jobs when he buys their companies; but many would argue that if they were doing their jobs, the company performance would be so good that Icahn would not see an opportunity to buy the company and flip it to make a profit. Icahn has a theory about U.S. businesses: many senior executives are the "guys you knew in college, the fraternity president—not too bright, back slapping, but a survivor, politically astute, a nice guy." According

to Icahn, to be a chief executive people need to know how not to tread on anyone's toes on the way up. Eventually a person becomes the number two in the company and needs to be just a little worse than number one in order to survive. When the number two gets promoted to be the CEO, he in turn promotes someone a little less capable than him as the second-in-command. "It is survival of the unfittest—eventually we are all going to be run by morons." Icahn calls this phenomenon of promoting people slightly less capable than the incumbent leader the **moronization of management.**

Source: Adapted from *The Economist,* February 11, 2006, p. 42.

are very busy and care about followers but fail to get anything done. Figureheads have difficulties building teams and getting results because they are clueless, do not care, or are in situations that make it impossible to succeed. Competent managers make up a minority of people in positions of authority and are those who can build teams and achieve results that improve organizations, societies, or countries. Of course, if it were easy to be a competent manager, many more people would be in this category. Given that most people in positions of authority are either destructive or incompetent leaders, there must be many ways in which people can fail as leaders. The purpose of this section is to describe the most common reasons why people fail in leading others.

Over the past 30 years a considerable amount of research has been done on managerial derailment, and it is worthwhile to describe the lessons of these efforts because they apply to virtually anyone in a position of authority. Initial research on managerial derailment—whereby individuals who at one time were on the fast track only to have their careers derailed—was conducted in the early 1980s by researchers at the Center for Creative Leadership. The researchers went to the human resources departments in a number of *Fortune* 100 companies seeking lists of their **high-potential managers.** McCall and Lombardo defined *high potentials* as individuals who had been identified as eventually becoming either the CEO/president or one of his or her direct reports sometime in the future. They waited for three years and then returned to these organizations to ask what had happened to the people on the lists. They discovered that roughly a quarter of the high potentials had been promoted to one of the top two levels in the organization, and an equal percentage had not yet been promoted but would be as soon as a position became available. Another 25 percent had left the companies; some had quit to form their own companies, and others were given better offers somewhere else. Finally, about a quarter of the people on the list were no longer being considered for promotion. Most of these individuals were let go or demoted to less influential and visible positions. This last group of individuals represented cases of managerial derailment.[39]

Several other researchers have investigated the managerial derailment phenomenon.[40–54] This additional research used much larger samples (one researcher examined over 3,000 derailed managers), European and cross-generational samples, and more sophisticated assessment tools (such as 360-degree feedback instruments). Moreover, a substantially higher percentage of women and minorities were represented in this later research; the initial high-potential list was dominated by white males. As Van Veslor and Leslie point out, this research focused on identifying factors that helped derailment candidates initially get identified as high potentials as well as factors contributing to their ultimate professional demise.[44] Although these studies varied in many ways, there are many consistent findings across them. Both successful and derailed candidates were smart, ambitious, and willing to do whatever it took to get the job done, and they had considerable technical expertise. In other words, all of the high-potential candidates had impressive track records in their organizations.

On the other hand, the derailed candidates exhibited one or more behavioral patterns not evident in the high potentials who succeeded. Five key derailment themes run through the research results listed in Table 15.1 and are described in more detail here. Note that the derailment themes included in Table 15.1 have been consistently reported by researchers in both the United States and Europe. One derailment pattern identified in Table 15.1 is a **failure to meet business objectives.** Although both successful and derailed managers experienced business downturns, the two groups handled setbacks quite differently. Successful managers took personal responsibility for their mistakes and sought ways to solve the problem. Derailed managers tended to engage in finger-pointing and blamed others for the downturn. *But as long as things were going well,* it was difficult to differentiate these two groups on this factor. Some of these managers were also untrustworthy. They blatantly lied about business results, cooked the books, or failed to keep promises, commitments, or deadlines. Others failed because they were not particularly smart or did not have an in-depth understanding of the business and as a result exercised poor judgment.

Although the research cited in Table 15.1 focused on failed high-potential candidates, the inability to achieve business results is not limited to this audience. Many people in positions of authority may not be high-potential candidates but are nonetheless unable to achieve business or organizational results. These individuals tend to be either cheerleaders or

Volume forgives all sins.
Bernie Marcus,
The Home Depot

When doctors make a poor diagnosis, their patients die and they don't have to deal with it anymore. When lawyers fail to present a good case, their clients go to jail and they don't have to deal with it anymore. But when a hiring manager makes a mistake, they have to say "Good morning" to it every day.
Pete Ramstad, Toro

TABLE 15.1 Common Themes in Derailment Research

			Research Study			
Skill Domain *Definition*	Benz (1985a)	McCall and Lombardo (1983)	Morrison, White, and Van Velsor (1987)	McCauley and Lombardo (1990)	Lombardo and Eichinger (2006)	Rasch, Shen, Davies, and Bono (2008)
Business						
Ability to plan, organize, monitor, and use resources	Lacked business skill	Specific business problems	Performance problems	Difficulty in molding a staff	Poor administrative skills	Poor task performance
	Unable to deal with complexity	Unable to think strategically	Not strategic	Difficulty in making strategic transition	Lack of strategic thinking	Poor planning, organization, and/or communication
	Reactive and tactical	Unable to staff effectively	Restricted business experience	Strategic differences with management	Difficulty making tough choices	
Leadership						
Ability to influence, build, and maintain a team; role modeling	Unable to delegate	Overmanaging—failing to delegate	Can't manage subordinates		Failure to build a team	Failure to nurture and manage talent
	Unable to build a team					Avoiding conflict and people problems Overcontrolling

(continued)

TABLE 15.1   (*Continued*)

Skill Domain / Definition	Benz (1985a)	McCall and Lombardo (1983)	Research Study — Morrison, White, and Van Velsor (1987)	McCauley and Lombardo (1990)	Lombardo and Eichinger (2006)	Rasch, Shen, Davies, and Bono (2008)
Interpersonal						
Social skill, empathy, and maintaining relationships	Unable to maintain relationships with a network	Insensitivity (abrasive, intimidating, bully)	Poor relationships	Problems with interpersonal relationships	Poor political skills	Failure to consider human needs
		Cold, aloof, arrogant			No interpersonal savvy	
					Unable to deal with conflict	
Intrapersonal						
Self-awareness and self-control, emotional maturity, integrity	Lets emotions cloud judgment	Unable to adapt to a boss with a different style	Unable to adapt to boss	Too dependent on an advocate	Questionable integrity	Procrastination. and time delays
	Slow to learn	Too dependent on an advocate	Too ambitious	Lack of follow-through	Low self-awareness	Poor emotional control
	An "overriding personality defect"	Too ambitious				Rumor-mongering and inappropriate use of information
		Betrayal of trust				

Source: J. Hogan, R. T. Hogan, and R. Kaiser, "Managerial Derailment," in *APA Handbook of Industrial and Organizational Psychology*, Vol. 3, ed. S. Zedeck (Washington, DC: American Psychological Association, 2011), pp. 555–76.

figureheads and simply cannot get anything accomplished. As described earlier, some are popular but confuse activity with productivity; others want their teams to get just enough done to stay off their boss's radar screens. Some may be motivated to achieve results but consistently make bad decisions or alienate team members by exhibiting behaviors that interfere with team cohesiveness, such as an inability to make decisions, micromanaging team members, or taking credit for others' work. One hallmark of effective leadership is the ability to get results across a variety of situations; those who cannot get anything noteworthy accomplished are destined to fail the Dr. Gordy test.

The second derailment pattern identified by Hogan, Hogan, and Kaiser was an **inability to build and lead a team.**[43] Some high-potential candidates derailed because they simply did not know how to build teams. Others failed by hiring staff members that were just like themselves, which only magnified their own strengths and weaknesses. Some wanted to stay in the limelight and hired staff less capable than they were. Still others micromanaged their staffs and wanted their followers to "check their brains at the door" before coming to work, even when they lacked relevant subject matter expertise. People in positions of authority who spend too much time doing activities that should be done by direct reports can also have difficulty building teams because they disempower all the managers who work for them. Because these leaders are making the decisions that their followers would normally make, followers become disengaged with work and team performance suffers.[8,12,13,53,55]

Like the failure to meet business objectives, the inability to build or lead teams is a common reason why many people in positions of authority are seen as incompetent managers. Two underlying reasons for the inability to build teams are a lack of team-building know-how and dark-side personality traits. Many people can easily describe the best and worst teams they have ever been on, but when asked what process they would use to build high-performing teams, they are surprisingly inarticulate. In other words, most people in positions of authority understand the importance of teamwork but have no clue how to make it happen.[55] This lack of team-building know-how is one reason why some people are seen as figureheads and taskmasters, but another key reason is the presence of dark-side personality traits. These attributes will be described in more detail later in this chapter.

A third derailment pattern has to do with an **inability to build relationships** with co-workers. The derailed managers exhibiting this pattern of behavior were insensitive to the needs and plights of their followers and co-workers, and they were often overly competitive, demanding, and domineering. They embraced the "my way or the highway" school of management, and many would be categorized as taskmasters. Many were extremely arrogant and truly believed no one in their organizations was as good as they were, and they let their co-workers know this every time

You would be talking with my boss, and suddenly she would snap. She'd lock eyes with you, and her voice would drop very low. It turns out that she learned this technique in an obedience class with her dog, and she found it to be an effective "tool" in managing people.

Anonymous, jobs.aol.com

they could. Some of these derailed managers also did whatever they felt necessary to get the job done, even if it meant stepping on a few toes. Unfortunately this is not a recommended technique for winning friends and influencing people. It is wise to remember the old adage that you should be careful whom you step on going up a ladder because you may meet them again on your way down. Many of these managers left a trail of bruised people who were waiting for the right opportunity to bring these leaders down.

The inability to get along with others is a fairly common derailment pattern among high potentials and anyone else in positions of authority. An example is a female vice president of marketing and sales for a cellular phone company who was fired from her $200,000-a-year job for exhibiting many of the behaviors just listed. She was very bright, had an excellent technical background (she was an engineer), had already been the CEO of several smaller organizations, and worked long hours. Although she also had a strong leaderlike personality, she would quickly identify and capitalize on others' faults, constantly comment on their incompetence, talk down to people, run over her peers when she needed resources or support, promote infighting among her peers and subordinates, and expect to be pampered. Interestingly, she had no idea she was having such a debilitating effect on those she worked with until she received some 360-degree feedback. Had she received this feedback sooner, she might have been able to stop her career from derailing.

The inability to build relationships is not limited to taskmasters; figureheads also have difficulties getting along with others. But rather than exhibiting a "my way or the highway" attitude, figureheads fail to build relationships with followers because they regularly exhibit emotional outbursts and temper tantrums, falsely believe that followers are out to get them, fail to provide followers with needed resources or support, or burn out team members with constantly shifting priorities. These irritating, counterproductive behavioral tendencies are manifestations of dark-side personality traits, which will be described in more detail later in this chapter.

Charan and Colvin, Dotlich and Cairo, Hogan, and Curphy have all stated that people problems are also one of the primary reasons why CEOs fail. However, unlike derailed first-line supervisors or midlevel managers, most CEOs get along with others in the company. The problem with some CEOs is that they get along with some of their direct reports too well and do not take timely action to address problem performers. More specifically, some CEOs fail because they place loyal subordinates into jobs they are incapable of handling, falsely believe they can help poorly performing subordinates to change ineffective behavior, do not want to offend Wall Street or the board by letting popular (but ineffective) executives go, or do not feel comfortable hiring outsiders to fill key executive positions.[8,12,13,40,53,55,56]

Half the CEOs in the world are below average.
**David Campbell,
Center for Creative
Leadership**

Another derailment profile has to do with a leader's **inability to adapt** to new bosses, businesses, cultures, or structures. As pointed out earlier in this chapter, business situations require different leadership behaviors and skills, and some derailed managers could not adapt or adjust their styles to changing bosses, followers, and situations. They persisted in acting the same way when it was no longer appropriate to new circumstances. For example, a first-line supervisor for an electronics firm that built video poker machines was having a difficult time transitioning from his old job as a missile guidance repairman in the U.S. Air Force. He thought he should lead his subordinates the way he led others in the military: his staff should be willing to work long hours and over the weekends without being told to do so and to travel for extended periods with short notice. Their thoughts or opinions about ways to improve work processes did not matter to him, and he expected everyone to maintain cool and professional attitudes at work. After half of his staff quit as a direct result of his supervision, he was demoted and replaced by one of his subordinates.

The inability to adapt is not just a first-line supervisor or midlevel manager phenomenon, as newly hired senior leaders have sometimes tried to transform their organizations into those they had worked for in the past. Robert McNamara tried to turn the Department of Defense into Ford, John Scully tried to turn Apple into Pepsi, Bob Nardelli tried to convert The Home Depot into General Electric, Leo Apotheker tried to transform HP into SAP, and Ron Johnson and Melissa Mayer are trying to reshape JC Penney's into Apple stores and Yahoo into Google. Given the success McNamara, Scully, Nardelli, and Apotheker had with their change initiatives, the future does not bode well for these latter two leaders.

In the past, organizations could afford to take their time in identifying and developing leadership talent. And as described earlier in this book, many of the best organizations today have strong programs for systematically developing leadership bench strength. However, organizations today are under increasing pressure to find good leaders quickly, and they are increasingly asking their own high-potential but inexperienced leadership talent to fill these key roles. Although these new leaders are bright and motivated, they often have narrow technical backgrounds and lack the leadership breadth and depth necessary for the new positions. The unfortunate result is that many of these leaders leave their organizations because of **inadequate preparation for promotion.** For example, a relatively young woman attorney was promoted to be the vice president of human resources in a large telecommunications firm. Although she was bright and ambitious, her previous management experience involved leading a team of six attorneys, whereas her promotion put her in charge of 300 human resources professionals. It soon became apparent that she lacked the skills and knowledge needed to manage a large, geographically

Our investigation revealed that Katrina was a national failure, an abdication of the most solemn obligation to provide for the common welfare. At every level—individual, corporate, philanthropic, and governmental—we failed to meet the challenge that was Katrina. In this cautionary tale, all the little pigs built houses of straw.

Congressional Report on the Government's Response to Hurricane Katrina

The Sea Witch

PROFILES IN LEADERSHIP 15.4

Holly Graf was the first female in the U.S. Navy to command a cruiser, the second largest surface vessel in the fleet. Graf's father was a commander in the U.S. Navy, and as a child she dreamed of someday commanding a ship. Pursuing her dreams, Graf graduated from the U.S. Naval Academy and rapidly advanced through a series of leadership roles in destroyer tenders, frigates, destroyers, and finally a guided missile cruiser. Intelligent and ambitious, she also obtained three masters degrees and did a stint at the Pentagon during her shore assignments. Graf's troubles in leading and managing others were noted relatively early in her career. When a destroyer she was commanding stopped suddenly while leaving port, she began screaming and swearing at the navigator, thinking he had run the ship aground, which would have been a career-ending episode for Graf. It turned out that one of the screws on the destroyer had failed; but when the crew heard about the ship running aground, they all broke out in song: "Ding, dong, the witch is dead!" She allegedly ran over a whale during ship maneuvers; choked one of her subordinates during a "training session"; regularly pushed, screamed, swore at, and questioned the manhood of her staff; routinely tossed coffee cups at those bearing bad news; and thought it was acceptable for junior officers to play piano at her personal Christmas parties and walk her dogs. When a chaplain visiting one of her ships tried to give her feedback about her leadership style and its debilitating effect on the crew, she quickly dismissed the chaplain and did not speak to him for the rest of the cruise. The ship's crew let out a loud cheer when she was formally relieved of command and promoted into another command position.

For a number of years the complaints about Graf fell on deaf ears, but eventually they became so pervasive as to warrant a formal investigation. Based on the results of this investigation, Graf was relieved of command; shortly thereafter a popular Navy blog had 190 posts about Graf. Nearly all the posts were negative; the four supportive posts came from individuals who had never served under Graf. It was evident that Graf had a toxic effect on almost everyone she worked with, yet she continued to get promoted despite strong evidence showing that she was unable to build teams. A key question that remains unanswered is why the navy not only tolerated but actually rewarded these behaviors in a leader. Perhaps the navy's lack of leadership accountability played as much of a role in Graf's promotions and ultimate demise as Graf herself.

What would you have done if you were Graf's commanding officer? Or one of her direct reports?

Sources: http://www.time.com/time/nation/article/0,8599,1969602-2,00.html; http://www.susankatzkeating.com/2010/01/captain-holly-graf-plows-down-whale.html.

dispersed human resources organization. Although she tried hard to succeed, she kept acting as a front-line supervisor instead of a functional leader and failed to earn the respect of her staff. After six months she was given a generous separation package and asked to leave the company.

Most derailed managers manifest several of these themes; the presence of only one of these behavioral patterns is usually not enough for derailment. The only exception to this rule is a failure to meet business objectives. Managers who do not follow through with commitments, break promises, lie, are unethical, and do not get results do not stay on the high-potential list for long. Although this research focused on derailment patterns for high-potential candidates, it seems likely that these five reasons for failure are universal. It would be difficult to perceive someone as a competent manager if he or she could not obtain business results or had difficulties adapting to new situations, building teams, or getting along with others. A bigger concern is why these managerial derailment patterns appear to be fairly obvious, yet so many people fail as leaders. In other words, if you asked a group of people why people in positions of authority fail, it is likely that you would hear the five reasons described in this section. Because these derailment factors are more or less public knowledge, it seems that simply being aware of the reasons why people fail in leadership positions does not seem to be enough to prevent it from happening. If we assume that most people move into managerial positions with positive intent and generally know the pitfalls to avoid in order to be successful, yet they are likely to be perceived as incompetent managers, then there must be something else going on. We believe that managerial incompetence and derailment have some underlying root causes, and knowing what they are and what to do to minimize their impact will improve the odds of being perceived as a competent manager. Many of these root causes are variations of concepts presented earlier in this book.

The Six Root Causes of Managerial Incompetence and Derailment

The research on managerial derailment provides a good starting point for investigating the underlying reasons why most people in positions of authority are seen as taskmasters, cheerleaders, or figureheads. Clearly a failure to achieve business objectives, an inability to build a team, or an inability to adapt to changing conditions will make leaders fail. But what causes people to fail to achieve business results or get along with others? Are these management failures due to character flaws on the part of the leader, pervasive situational factors, problematic followers, or some combination of all three factors? As shown in Figure 15.2, leader, follower, and situational factors all play roles in managerial derailment. Sometimes leaders are put in situations where it is virtually impossible to build teams or achieve results; at other times a leader's own shortcomings cause managerial incompetence and derailment (see Profiles in Leadership 15.4). Looking over Figure 15.2, we might think it is next to impossible to be a competent manager because there are so many ways in which people in positions of authority can fail. For example, the global economy could take a significant downturn, hurricanes or terrorist events could disrupt supply chains, key followers could retire or be hired away by competitors, organizations could downsize or be acquired by other companies, new competitors could develop disruptive technologies and dominate the market, workers could go on strike, or the new CEO could be a taskmaster. The good news is that we can mitigate managerial derailment by understanding the six root causes, assessing the extent to which they are affecting our

FIGURE 15.2
The Root Causes of Managerial Derailment and the Leader–Follower–Situation Model

Leader

Lack of self-awareness
Lack of situational awareness
Lack of intelligence
Lack of technical expertise
Lack of team know-how
Poor followership
Dark-side personality traits

Lack of Fit

Disgruntled employees
Criticizers
Slackers
Brown-nosers
Disruptive worker cliques

Competitive threats
Globalization
Government regulations
Natural disasters
Wars
Mergers
Bankruptcies
Reorganizations

Followers

Situation

Savvy managers figure out how to get things done, no matter what obstacles they face.

Mark Roellig, MassMutual

ability to build teams and get results through others, and then adopting some of the suggestions found in this section to minimize their effects.

As shown in Figure 15.2 and Table 15.2, there are six root causes of managerial derailment. Table 15.2 is not meant to be a comprehensive list of root causes—there are other reasons why taskmasters, figureheads, and cheerleaders occur so frequently. However, these six are likely to describe why many people are unable to build teams or get results. As an overview, certain situational and follower factors can make it difficult to build teams and get results. An example might include a commercial airline crew trying to deliver a planeload of international passengers to an airport that suddenly closes down due to a terrorist threat. The captain may have done a good job of getting the crew to work as a cohesive team to provide great passenger service but will not be able to achieve her on-time arrival goal because of the airport closure. Although situational and follower factors can sometimes play key roles, leader factors are much more likely to cause managerial incompetence and derailment. Some leaders cannot see how they impact others, some consistently exercise poor judgment, others do not value building teams or getting results, and others are such poor followers that they are fired from their leadership positions.

TABLE 15.2
Bad Leadership,
Managerial
Incompetence,
Managerial
Derailment, and
Root Causes

Leadership Type	Managerial Derailment Factors	Root Causes of Derailment
Destructive leadership	Failure to meet business objectives	Situational and follower factors
Competent managers	Inability to build and lead teams	Lack of organizational fit
Taskmasters	Inability to build relationships	Lack of situational or self-awareness
Cheerleaders	Inability to adapt	Lack of intelligence, technical expertise, or team-building know-how
Figureheads	Inadequate preparation for promotion	Poor followership; dark-side personality traits

Stuff Happens: Situational and Follower Factors in Managerial Derailment

The story in Highlight 15.6 concerns a scenario in where situational factors interfered with a person's ability to build teams and get results through others. Although most leaders will not encounter events on the scale of the Fukushima nuclear reactor disaster, situational changes frequently occur. Think about a person's ability to be a competent manager if he was a civic leader in Haiti immediately after the Port au Prince earthquake, a mid-level automobile parts manufacturing manager right after she was told her plant would be closing in the next six months, or a U.S. Army Reserve captain who was preparing his unit to be deployed to Afghanistan for the third time in seven years. It seems somewhat obvious, but situational and follower factors significantly affect a person's ability to build teams and get results.[12,50,55,56] Here are some of the situational factors that can interfere with a person's ability to be seen as a competent manager:

- New competitive threats, globalization, technology, changing customer preferences, unreliable suppliers, new governments or government regulations, unfavorable media coverage, natural disasters, and wars.
- Mergers, acquisitions, divestitures, bankruptcies, new strategies, reorganizations, major change initiatives, incidents of workplace violence, or environmental disasters.
- New bosses, peers, direct reports; disengaged or disgruntled employees; disruptive worker cliques; and strikes or dysfunctional turnover.
- New jobs, responsibilities, or projects.

Who the hell's in charge?
Naoto Kan, former Japanese Prime Minister

The Fukushima Daichi Nuclear Power Plant Disaster

HIGHLIGHT 15.6

On March 11, 2011, a magnitude 9.0 earthquake occurred off the northeast corner of Japan. This was the most powerful earthquake to ever hit Japan and caused a tsunami whose waves were estimated to be over 140 feet tall. The waves hit the island of Honshu with little warning and completely destroyed 130,000 buildings and damaged almost 1 million others. Approximately 20,000 people were either confirmed dead or missing and over 4 million homes lost power. This event has been called the biggest natural disaster in modern history.

The Fukushima Daichi nuclear power plant consists of six nuclear reactors near the Honshu coast. Although constructed to withstand natural disasters, the March 2011 earthquake and tsunami knocked the plant off the electrical grid and destroyed the backup generators for four reactors. With no power to run the water pumps needed to keep the reactors cool, hydrogen gas began building up to dangerous levels in some of the containment buildings. Being highly combustible, it was imperative that the plant operator, Tokyo Electric Power Company (TEPCO), cool the reactors using any means possible before a hydrogen gas explosion breached the containment walls and spread radioactivity across the region.

The plant was in major chaos after the tsunami: the power was out, all the buildings and equipment were damaged, and communication was down. Those on the ground made do with whatever they had to prevent a major nuclear disaster. One key decision was whether to use seawater to cool the reactors. The reactors normally used freshwater as a coolant because seawater would permanently destroy a multibillion dollar reactor. Those at the plant were not empowered to make this decision and those leading TEPCO dithered in making the call. As a result, the hydrogen gas in three of the reactors blew up and caused major radiation leaks that contaminated a 20-mile radius. Not only did TEPCO take too long to make the decision, the company withheld information about the extent of the damage, including how much radiation had been released, who was affected, and what was being done to repair the damage.

The government of Japan's response to this natural disaster was also far from stellar. It took 10 days before Japan released oil from its strategic reserves to generate the power needed for the affected areas. Trucks carrying medical supplies, food, and water were prevented from using the northern expressway because they were not designated as emergency vehicles, even though the route had no other traffic at the time.

How did the situation affect the Fukushima Daichi nuclear power plant manager and supervisors from building teams or getting results? How does the situation highlight managerial incompetence in TEPCO and the Japanese government?

Sources: "A Crisis of Leadership Too," *The Economist,* March 26, 2011, p. 14; N. Shirouzu, P Dvorak, Y. Hayashi, and A. Morse, "Bid to 'Protect Assets' Slowed Reactor Fight," *The Wall Street Journal,* March 19–20, 2011, pp. A1 and A8; M. Obe, "Fukushima Plant Hit by Power Outage," *The Wall Street Journal,* March 20, 2013, p. A10; News Services, "Japan Upgrades Severity of Crisis," *StarTribune,* March 19, 2011, pp. A1 and A11.

Figuring out how to build teams and get things done despite potentially disruptive situational and follower factors is part of any leadership role, but at times these external factors can be so overwhelming that there may be little a person can do to build teams or get results. What is interesting is how the four managerial types react when facing hopeless challenges. Competent managers take time to reflect on the situation, determine what they need to do differently, and then ensure that their decisions are executed. Competent managers often succeed where others fail because they investigate all the alternatives and then make the changes needed to maintain team cohesiveness and performance. Interestingly, one of these alternatives may include changing jobs or leaving the organization if the leader feels that others are better able to help the team cope with these challenges. Leaders may also believe that switching teams is a better option than remaining in the role and risk becoming cheerleaders, taskmasters, or figureheads.

Incompetent managers facing hopeless situations tend to act quite differently: they are likely to keep doing what they have always done but expect to achieve different results. For example, when faced with challenging followers or situations, taskmasters tend to focus more closely on goals, metrics, and bottom-line results and spend even less time with the people on their teams. Cheerleaders increase their team-building and relationship-building behaviors and try to keep teammates happy rather than making them more productive. And figureheads are even less likely to make decisions, take stands, lay out courses of action, or push team members to perform. All three types of incompetent managers try to leverage their strengths rather than change, which erodes their ability to build teams and get results.

Three additional points about these overwhelming situational and follower factors are worth noting. Although many situational and follower factors are beyond a manager's control, the manager can control his or her reactions to these events. A manager can step back, reflect upon the new situation, and determine what he or she needs to do differently; or the manager can continue to leverage his or her strengths and expect a different outcome. Reflection may be the key success factor when facing difficult situations, but too often people in positions of authority overreact, withhold information, and rush to judgment rather than explaining difficult facts and soliciting team members for ideas.

A second point concerns the concepts of episodic versus chronic incompetence. **Episodic managerial incompetence** occurs when people in positions of authority face extremely tough situational or follower events that temporarily interfere with their ability to build teams and get results. However, once they have reflected upon and taken action to cope with the event, they quickly regain their ability to successfully build teams and get results. **Chronic managerial incompetence** occurs when taxing situational or follower events permanently disrupt a person's ability to build teams or get results. All competent managers experience occasional episodic managerial incompetence; the trick is to limit the frequency and duration of these occurrences. But given their preferred ways of dealing with challenging events, cheerleaders, taskmasters, and figureheads seem to exemplify chronic managerial incompetence.

The definition of neurotic management is to continue to do the same things but expect different results.
Tom Peters, writer

Finally, when all is going smoothly most people assume competent managers run organizations; it may take some kind of emergency or crisis before an organization's chronic managerial incompetence becomes evident. To a large extent nobody thought about the leadership capabilities of FEMA, the Tokyo Electric Power Company (TEPCO), and BP until the Hurricane Katrina, Fukushima, and Gulf oil disasters, respectively. The high percentages of destructive leaders, figureheads, cheerleaders, and taskmasters became obvious only after these crises went public. Situational factors, social media, and the press can help to shine a bright light on the high levels of managerial incompetence existing in many organizations.

The Lack of Organizational Fit: Stranger in a Strange Land

The previous section described the role that situational and follower factors play in managerial competence and incompetence. Organizational culture also plays an important role in this matter. Chapter 12 defined organizational culture as a system of shared backgrounds, norms, values, or beliefs among members of a group. All organizations have cultures, but the content and strength of the beliefs underlying these cultures can vary dramatically. For example, the shared beliefs, norms, and values of the U.S. Marine Corps are quite different from those of PETA or Greenpeace.

Organizational culture is not one of those pervasive situational factors that doom managers to fail, but a person's fit with an organization's culture can cause him or her to be seen as incompetent. **Organizational fit** can be defined as the degree of agreement between personal and organizational values and beliefs.[13,50,56,57] If a person does not share the values or beliefs of the majority of members, then in all likelihood this person will be a poor fit with the organization. Many times people who do not fit with an organization's culture wield diminishing levels of influence, which interferes with their ability to build teams and get results. Highlight 15.7 describes a classic example of how the lack of organizational fit can cause someone to be perceived as an incompetent manager. In many ways Ann was precisely what the organization needed to turn things around. She had all the knowledge and skills necessary to succeed, but the senior staff felt their other responsibilities were more important than fund-raising. Thus Ann recognized that she was in a no-win situation and left the organization.

Organizations often realize that continuing to do things the same way will eventually result in failure, and one approach to fostering new ways of thinking is to hire people from the outside with different work experiences. New hires may have good ideas to remedy a situation, but whether they and their ideas are accepted will depend to a large extent on an organization's culture. The farther these ideas stray from the organization's prevailing values and beliefs, the more likely they are to be dismissed. Managers hired from the outside suffer the same fate as transplanted organs—those who are seen as a good fit are accepted, and those who are

Organizational Fit and Managerial Derailment

HIGHLIGHT 15.7

Ann had spent the past 30 years as a sales executive in the insurance industry. Savvy, sophisticated, and successful, over the years Ann had developed deep expertise in marketing, sales, contracting, invoicing, budgeting, and compensation. She also had over 20 years of sales leadership experience and had consistently built cohesive teams that exceeded their sales quotas. After a successful career of selling insurance, Ann was looking for a new challenge, and one of the local nonprofit organizations needed an executive to head up its fundraising function. The nonprofit had been around for over 50 years, employed over 300 people, and specialized in helping developmentally disabled adults live more independent lives. To achieve this mission the nonprofit provided lodging, skills training, transportation, and other services to its constituents. Ann was hired because the organization was running out of money—revenues were shrinking, expenses were rapidly rising, and donors were scaling back on their contributions. The main donor base was also growing old, and many major contributors were literally dying off.

Attracted to the mission and by the challenge of doing something new, Ann joined the organization and was told by the president to do whatever was needed to secure the existing funding base and find new sources of revenue. Ann started this effort by reviewing the donor database and soon discovered that the organization had done nothing more than send form thank-you letters to the major donors over the past five years. The organization had not visited or invited the donors to any functions or solicited funding from any new donors. She developed a strategic marketing plan that called for the senior staff to engage in a number of outreach activities with new and existing donors.

Ann was surprised by the organization's reaction to her strategic marketing plan. The president felt it was beneath her to engage in fund-raising activities and did not want the organization to be seen as having anything to do with fund solicitation. The president emphatically stated that the mission of the organization was to serve the developmentally disabled, not raise money. The rest of the senior staff wholeheartedly agreed with the president. Ann responded that the organization's costs were exceeding its revenues, and if the senior staff did not want to help generate more funding, then the alternative was to cut expenses. She reminded the staff that she had been told to do whatever was needed to raise cash, and now that her plan was put forward, it appeared that this was not really the case. The president said that money was not their concern and it was up to Ann, and Ann alone, to make things happen. Because of the organization's lack of urgency and genuine distaste for fundraising, Ann felt like a fish out of water. The things she cared about were of no interest to the senior leadership team, even though her plan would allow the organization to continue its mission. Because of this lack of fit, Ann left the organization less than a year later, and the organization laid off staff members to reduce expenses.

Source: G. J. Curphy, A. Baldrica, and R. T. Hogan, *Managerial Incompetence,* unpublished manuscript, 2009.

not are rejected. What is interesting about this phenomenon is that outsiders often possess exactly the knowledge and skills an organization needs to succeed, but because the solutions proposed are so antithetical to its culture, the ideas are attacked or discounted. The organizational fit phenomenon occurs not only when outsiders are brought in; it also happens when companies hire new CEOs or acquire other organizations. New CEOs often take steps to mold the organization's culture around their own personal values and beliefs, and some managers may no longer fit

Culture eats strategy for breakfast.

Peter Drucker, management writer

into the new culture. Likewise, managers from an acquired company can have considerable difficulty fitting into the other organization's culture. Because of this lack of fit, leaders from "old" culture or acquired companies can be perceived as incompetent even though they may have all the skills needed to build teams and get results through others. Acquiring organizations often act on these perceptions and limit the influences and resources provided to these managers, essentially setting them up for failure. As described earlier in this book, many mergers and organizational changes fail, and this is often due to cultural fit issues.[12,13,31,32]

What can leaders do to avoid being seen as organizational culture misfits? Perhaps the best thing to do is to minimize the risk of it happening at all. The first step in this process is to understand their own values, beliefs, and attitudes toward work. Some people go to work to make money, others are motivated by job security, and still others are driven to help others or make a difference. There are no right or wrong answers here, but it is important that people understand what they want out of a job. Once people clearly see what they want from work, the second step in the process is to determine the extent to which the cultures of potential employers are aligned with these beliefs. Determining an organization's culture may not be straightforward, however, because the underlying beliefs, norms, stories, and values are often unwritten. One way to determine an organization's culture is through informational interviews, in which employees are asked how things really get done, how employees treat each other, what is valued or punished, what the unwritten rules are, and so on. This information should help leaders determine the extent to which their personal values and beliefs are aligned with those of various employers. We realize there are times when people need to take jobs for the money and benefits, but they also need to realize that their level of satisfaction and ability to build teams and get results will be affected by the degree of fit between their personal values and the organization's culture. Those who do not fit run the risk of being seen as incompetent and may find that working elsewhere can help them be seen as competent managers.

More Clues for the Clueless: Lack of Situational and Self-Awareness

Most aircraft accidents are the result of pilot errors, and a lack of situational awareness is the leading cause of pilot errors.[58] **Situational awareness** refers to a pilot's ability to be cognizant of and accurately assess risks before, during, and after a flight.[59] In other words, pilots with good situational awareness know what their aircraft is doing, the weather, the positions of other aircraft in the area, the relationship of their aircraft to the ground, and the like. Like pilots, people in positions of authority must also have a high degree of situational awareness if they want to be seen as competent managers. This means competent managers must accurately read the situational and follower factors affecting their teams and remain

Situational and Self-Awareness and Managerial Incompetence

HIGHLIGHT 15.8

Dick was the chief of police in a medium-sized midwestern town. Because of a series of easily avoidable but high-profile blunders, the local newspaper and television stations were regularly running stories about department foul-ups. The city council began pressuring Dick to clean up the department's image, and he felt the best way to rectify the situation was to send a memo to the entire department. In the past Dick had relied on his executive assistant to write all his correspondence, but she was on vacation and he felt the memo could not wait until her return. He wrote the following memo and posted it at the department's main entrance:

Date: August 20, 2004

From: Dick Thompson, Chief of Police

Subject: Profesionalism

To: All Police Department Personal

It has come to my atention that the deparment lack profesionalism. I have seen several officers with dirty uniforms and untucked shirts and some of you need haircuts. We need to do a better job with our police reports—some have typological errors are not profesional. We need better in court too. Officers who can not meet these standards will be unpromotionable. if you have any questions see you Captain.

Less than a day later the posted memo looked like this:

Date: August 20, 2004

From: Dick Thompson, Chief of Police

Subject: Profesionalism   *[Spelling]*

To: All Police Department Personal   *[Spelling]*

It has come to my atention that the deparment lack *[Spelling]* profesionalism. I have seen several officers with *[Spelling]* dirty uniforms and untucked shirts and some of you need *also* haircuts. We need to do a better job with our police reports—some have typological *[typographical]* errors are not profesional. We need to be better in court too. *[Spelling]*

Officers who can not meet these standards will be unpromotionable. *[Is this a word?]* if you have any questions see you Captain.

Unfortunately for Dick, this memo was just the tip of the iceberg—he had a long history of misjudging events and making bad policy decisions, and as a result department morale was in the dumps. The city council finally came to its senses and asked the chief to leave. However, Dick was hired as the chief of police in another midwestern town, thus perpetuating incompetent management.

Source: G. J. Curphy, A. Baldrica, and R. T. Hogan, *Managerial Incompetence,* unpublished manuscript, 2009.

vigilant for changes. Competent managers not only have high levels of situational awareness—they also have high levels of **self-awareness.** As described in Chapter 2, individuals who are keenly aware of their own strengths and shortcomings often find ways to either manage or staff around their personal knowledge and skill gaps. In contrast, cheerleaders, figureheads, and taskmasters can have major situational and self-awareness blind spots (see Highlight 15.8). They either are unaware of or discount the impact of key situational or follower events and overestimate their ability to build teams and get results.[60]

644 Part Four *Focus on the Situation*

Research shows that in many cases incompetence is bliss, at least for the person demonstrating incompetence. Researchers Dunning and Kruger conducted a series of experiments that asked people to rate the funniness of 65 jokes. They then asked eight professional comedians to do the same and compared the differences between the experts' and test subjects' ratings. They found that some participants could not predict what others would find funny, yet they described themselves as excellent judges of humor. Similarly, Nilsen and Campbell reported that managers who consistently overrated their performance on 360-degree feedback instruments tended to overrate their performance on everything they did. Not only did these individuals believe they were good leaders, they also believed they were excellent drivers, mothers and fathers, athletes, dancers, judges of character, and so on, and they tended to overlook evidence that pointed to the contrary.[61,62]

There appear to be two reasons why some cheerleaders, taskmasters, and figureheads lack situational and self-awareness. One reason is that some incompetent managers are self-deluding, and the most incompetent managers may be those who are the most self-deluding.[63] Another reason why some incompetent managers lack situational and self-awareness is that they fail to heed direct report feedback. Cheerleaders and other incompetent leaders may spend considerably more time paying attention to and developing relationships with those who control their fate (that is, superiors) than with team members. They are also in a position where they can and often do ignore any feedback from their staff, even when this information would help them build teams and get results through others. And by regularly shooting the messenger, figureheads and taskmasters effectively dampen any additional feedback that would make them more effective and push self-starters over to the dark side of followership.

I wouldn't have been so mean to you over the past six months if I knew I was going to fire you.
Anonymous CEO

So what can people in positions of authority do to eliminate a lack of situational and self-awareness as an underlying cause of managerial derailment and incompetence? Given the research findings, it is imperative that people wanting to be competent managers get regular feedback on their performance, ideally in the form of 360-degree feedback. It is also imperative that people in positions of authority regularly ask team members for ideas on improving team performance and find ways to stay abreast of important situational and follower events. By building teams of self-starters, competent managers encourage team members to share ideas and solutions for improving team morale and performance, even if this means telling leaders what they personally need do differently in order to be more effective.

Lack of Intelligence, Subject Matter Expertise, and Team-Building Know-How: Real Men of Genius

People are put into positions of authority to make decisions. Each of these decisions is essentially a problem-solving exercise, and the history and

General Tommy Franks was strategically illiterate and refused to think seriously about what would happen after his forces attacked. . . . Franks fundamentally misconceived his war, leading to the deaths of thousands of Americans and an untold number of Iraqis."

**Thomas E. Ricks,
writer**

success of any organization are the cumulative sum of these problem-solving exercises. Organizations that do a better job of identifying the right problems to solve and developing effective solutions to these problems are often more successful than those that solve the wrong problems or develop ineffective solutions. The famous management consultant Peter Drucker has said that most businesses get into trouble because senior managers exercise bad judgment.[64] Business leaders are supposed to direct resources toward activities that increase profitability, but they often decide to spend time and money completing projects that do not matter.

As described in Chapter 6, intelligence can be defined as the ability to think clearly. Some significant components of thinking clearly involve learning new information quickly, making good assumptions and inferences, seeing connections between seemingly unrelated issues, accurately prioritizing issues, generating potential solutions, understanding the implications of various decision options, and being quick on one's feet. Although research has shown that people in positions of authority are generally brighter than others, the intelligence of managers varies greatly.[65,66]

Because a manager's intelligence is directly related to his or her ability to make decisions, intelligence also affects managers' ability to build cohesive teams and get results.[12,13,55,66,67] Smart managers tend to do a better job of recognizing problems, prioritizing issues, assigning team member roles, developing work processes, allocating workloads, hiring staff, and resolving problems, whereas less intelligent managers do more poorly on these issues. In other words, being smart improves the odds of being a competent manager; being less intelligent improves the odds of being a cheerleader or figurehead.

But intelligence alone does not equal good judgment. A shortfall in critical knowledge also decreases a person's ability to solve problems and make decisions and increases the odds of managerial incompetence. **Subject matter expertise** can be defined as the relevant knowledge or experience a person can leverage to solve a problem. People with high expertise have a lot of relevant knowledge and experience, whereas those with low expertise are unfamiliar with the task or problem at hand. For example, a marketing executive with 10 years of experience living overseas will have a lot more knowledge of how to effectively drive sales in Europe than will someone new to marketing who has never lived in another country. People with a lot of relevant expertise know what is to be done, how to get things done, and the interconnections between different processes and activities. They know which levers to pull to obtain a particular outcome and understand how decisions can affect activities three or four steps later in a procedure. Managers with relevant expertise have "street smarts"; they can use their knowledge of the what, how, and interconnections to help their teams set the right goals, adopt efficient work processes, and get superior results.

All positions of authority require some level of technical expertise. For example, manufacturing managers need to understand the ins and outs of the manufacturing process, suppliers, maintenance and operations procedures, safety, process control methods, budgets, and their interconnections. People run the risk of being seen as incompetent managers any time they move into jobs that are unrelated to their technical or functional expertise (see Highlight 15.9). Like intelligence, however, technical expertise is no guarantee that a person will be a competent manager. Too many people are promoted into positions of authority because of their technical expertise but fail as managers. Often the best programmers or accountants do a great job writing programs or reconciling the books but have difficulty getting teams of people to write great software or conduct effective audits. Even so, having relevant expertise increases the odds of being a competent manager, and lacking this expertise increases the likelihood of being perceived as a cheerleader, figurehead, or taskmaster.

Whereas subject matter expertise pertains to the knowledge and skills associated with a particular functional area or process, such as accounting or contracting, **team-building know-how** can be defined as the degree to which a leader knows the steps and processes needed to build high-performing teams.[8,55,67] As described earlier in this textbook, most people spend their careers working in groups but lack a fundamental understanding of what it takes to build cohesive, goal-oriented teams. Chances are good that most of these teams were led by cheerleaders, taskmasters, or figureheads and were more dysfunctional than effective. These experiences lead to a lack of team-building know-how, which contributes to the high base rate of managerial incompetence. Although most people readily acknowledge the importance of teamwork, most managers have no idea how to make teamwork happen.

What can leaders do to make up for a lack of intelligence, relevant subject matter expertise, or team-building know-how? Technology and staffing can make up for shortfalls in intelligence and subject matter expertise. Some companies, such as McDonald's, Target, UPS, and Best Buy, have sophisticated systems that give managers real-time information about revenues, costs, inventory turns, and the like to help them make better store staffing and stocking decisions. Generally speaking, the better the systems, the lower the intelligence needed to operate the systems. What is fascinating is that people with managerial aspirations and lower intelligence often gravitate to organizations with good systems. In other words, it is not unusual to find less intelligent but competent managers in organizations having good systems. These managers have learned how to leverage technology to make good judgments, which in turn helps them build teams and get results. Another way people with less intelligence and subject matter expertise can improve the odds of becoming competent managers is to surround themselves with smart, experienced people. People in positions

Relevant Expertise and Managerial Derailment

HIGHLIGHT 15.9

Debbie was a general manager at a management consulting firm. Debbie's job was to ensure her office met its revenue, profitability, and productivity numbers each year. Her track record against these three criteria was less than stellar, as she had consistently missed her targets since taking over as the office leader. But she managed to convince the firm's senior leaders that the office's financial woes were primarily a function of the local economy and everyone in her office was working really hard. In reality, Debbie ran the office like a social club and was constantly buying lunch for the office staff, setting up Friday night socials, and praising office staff for their performance (even though the office was not hitting its financial goals). Eventually everyone in the office came to believe that they were special and corporate would never understand the unique challenges they faced. Debbie often bragged that she had little financial savvy and even less interest in the performance of the office and truly believed her job was to improve staff morale.

One of Debbie's multibillion-dollar clients asked for help in hiring a new executive vice president of human resources. The previous head of human resources had been let go because he had been unable to resolve some major staffing, compensation, and HRIS issues that were hurting the company's bottom line. Debbie's firm specialized in the assessment of executive talent, and she led the effort to evaluate the top three candidates for the executive vice president position. Debbie determined that all three candidates had significant shortcomings and suggested that the client consider her as a candidate. Desperate to fill the position, the client decided to hire Debbie on the spot. Had the client followed the process used to evaluate the other candidates, it would have discovered that Debbie lacked any corporate, senior executive, board of director, compensation, or HRIS experience, was likely to run human resources like a social club, and would foster a we–they mentality between her department and the rest of the company.

Although she was offered executive coaching from a former head of human resources to help her transition into her new role, Debbie felt she already knew what she needed to know and did not capitalize on this resource. Less than a month after starting she made the first of what would be a series of fatal errors. Debbie looked somewhat frumpy and disheveled at her first board of directors meeting, and her presentation painted the CEO and several business unit leaders in an unflattering light. When the board raised questions about the costs and benefits of the strategic initiatives in her presentation, she stated that the company needed to do these things and costs were irrelevant. Board members were left scratching their heads and hoped that Debbie's performance would improve at subsequent meetings. The CEO then asked Debbie to provide more detailed cost and ROI estimates for her strategic initiatives at the next senior staff meeting. When pressed for details, it became apparent that Debbie had no idea how much these initiatives would cost and whether any benefits would drop to the bottom line. Over the next few months several major HRIS problems occurred, and the new compensation system devised by Debbie caused unprecedented levels of turnover among sales staff. To counter these problems Debbie added about 20 percent more staff and quickly began overspending her budget. The CFO kept reminding Debbie about the company's financial woes, but she countered that her people were the hardest working in the company and it would be some time before all their efforts paid off. As she had before, Debbie instituted regular lunches and happy hours and started pitting her staff against the rest of the organization. This went on for another six months before she was called into the CEO's office and let go. She got a nice six-figure severance package for her efforts, but it was clear that Debbie's lack of relevant expertise was one reason why she was eventually dismissed.

Source: G. J. Curphy, A. Baldrica, and R. T. Hogan, *Managerial Incompetence,* unpublished manuscript, 2009.

of authority can leverage the intelligence and experience of their staffs to identify and prioritize problems and develop solutions that help their teams succeed. A third way to improve the odds of becoming a competent manager is through hard work. There are many ways to succeed in any particular job, and people can sometimes compensate for their lower intelligence and expertise by putting in extra effort and working longer hours. Modeling a strong work ethic can also have a contagious effect on team members, which in turn can build team cohesiveness and drive team success. Attending training programs can also help leaders build relevant expertise and understand how to build high-performing teams. Along these lines, the Rocket Model© described earlier in this textbook gives managers a practical framework for understanding the critical components of and actions needed to improve team functioning and performance.

Poor Followership: Fire Me, Please

Chapter 1 introduced the concept of followership and how anyone in a position of authority has to play both leader and follower roles. Part 3 of this textbook provided a more detailed explanation of followership and introduced the Curphy and Roellig Followership Model. As a reminder, this model states that followers vary on two dimensions, which are critical thinking and engagement. Self-starters are followers who seek forgiveness rather than permission, offer solutions, and make things happen. Brown-nosers work hard but are loyal sycophants who never challenge their bosses; slackers do all they can to get out of work; and criticizers believe their purpose in life is to point out all the things their bosses and organizations are doing wrong. As described in Highlight 15.10, Joseph Lacher appeared to be someone who spent much of his career as a self-starter but became a criticizer after spending 20 months running Allstate's home and auto insurance business units. Although he was able to build a loyal staff, his ability to get results was severely limited once his criticisms became public. Angering one's boss through **poor followership** is not a particularly effective career advancement strategy, and Lacher paid the price for his subordination.

Highlight 15.10 illustrates how people in positions of authority who are criticizers often become incompetent managers. People in positions of authority who are brown-nosers and slackers are also likely to be seen as incompetent managers. With their eagerness to do whatever their superiors tell them to do and their inability to make independent decisions, brown-nosers are likely to be seen as cheerleaders or taskmasters. Slackers are so disconnected with the workplace that they are unlikely to build teams or get results, and they will be perceived as figureheads. Thus followership not only affects how one leads, it also determines whether one is seen as a competent or incompetent manager.[68]

So what can leaders do to avoid being seen as incompetent managers due to their followership types? The first thing they need to do is to realize

Want to Lose Your $3,200,000 Job? Call Your Boss a F-----g A-----e!

HIGHLIGHT 15.10

Joseph Lacher graduated Notre Dame with a degree in aerospace engineering before joining the insurance industry in the early 1990s. He spent the first 18 years of his career working at Travelers Insurance, where he was quickly promoted to director, vice president, senior vice president, executive vice president, chief financial officer, and chief executive officer at different divisions in Travelers. Because of his rapid career progression, Lacher was hired by Allstate, the largest publicly traded insurance company in the United States. As the president of Allstate Protection Company and executive vice president of Allstate Insurance Company, Lacher was responsible for generating 80 percent of the company's $30+ billion in annual revenues.

Thomas Wilson, the CEO of Allstate, felt the property and automobile insurance businesses at Allstate were lagging behind its competitors and brought in Lacher to turn things around. Lacher introduced a number of initiatives to improve his businesses but became increasingly frustrated with the magnitude and speed of the changes he was allowed to make. After 20 months as the head of property and automobile insurance there were few improvements to revenues and margins, and the CEO was becoming dissatisfied with Lacher's performance.

Allstate hosted an annual sales conference in 2011 that included more than 2,000 employees and agents. Lacher, one of the speakers at the conference, described initiatives to reduce the sales force and change compensation plans, initiatives that many in the audience did not like. Later that evening Lacher was at the bar speaking with some of the conference attendees who were disgruntled with his initiatives and said Tom Wilson was a "f-----g a-----e" if he didn't take responsibility for the home and automobile insurance business results. His comments permeated the conference the next day; eight weeks later Lacher resigned from his position. Apparently "you're not in good hands with Allstate" if you call your boss a "f-----g a-----e."

Was Joseph Lacher a competent manager, taskmaster, figurehead, or cheerleader at Travelers or Allstate Insurance? What kind of follower was Lacher when he worked in these two organizations? What information would you need to make these determinations?

Sources: E. Holm and J. S. Lublin, "Loose Lips Trip Up Good Hands," *The Wall Street Journal,* August 1, 2011, pp. C1 and C3; http://www.dailymail.co.uk/news/article-2021391/meet-insurance-executive-lost-3m-job-calling-boss-f---g---e-bar.html; http://investing.businessweek.com/research/stocks/people/person.asp?personId=1883277&ticker=ALL

As matters stand now, a private who loses his rifle suffers far greater consequences than a general who loses his part of the war.

Anonymous U.S. Army Colonel

---

that everything done at work (or even outside of work) counts. Day-to-day actions, work activities, Facebook entries, tweets, blogs, and e-mail all affect their perceived followership types. It may not be enough to just build cohesive teams and get results—competent managers also need to build good relationships with peers and superiors if they want to get resources and decision-making latitude. Second, leaders need to honestly assess their follower type. If they are criticizers, brown-nosers, or slackers, they need to figure out why they are these less effective follower types and what they need to do to become self-starters. As described in Part 3, a person's immediate boss is the leading cause of dysfunctional follower types. A leader may be working for a boss who is a cheerleader, taskmaster, or figurehead, in which case finding another boss may be a viable option (Also see Highlight 15.11.).

Do Personnel Policies Promote Managerial (In)competence?

HIGHLIGHT 15.11

Ninety-three percent of the 250 West Point graduates surveyed in 2010 indicate that the best and brightest leaders leave the service early rather pursue full military careers. The number-one reason why good leaders leave the U.S. Army is not frequent deployments (which ranks fifth), but frustration with the personnel system. Only 7 percent think the military personnel system does a good job retaining strong leaders, and 65 percent feel the system creates a less competent officer corps. The Army's loss is the private sector's gain, however, as having a military background improves the odds of becoming a corporate CEO three times more than any other life experience.

So what is it about the military personnel system that officers find so frustrating, and how does this system differ from those in the private sector? The U.S. military has a state-of-the-art personnel system from the 1960s: all job assignments are centrally planned; people with the same training are seen as functionally equivalent; officers must remain with the organization until their commitments are fulfilled; they must spend a certain time in grade before they are eligible for promotion; there are few meaningful metrics to measure results or team-building capabilities; innovation, risk taking, and failure are often career limiting; and everyone gets the same performance review ratings. All resemblance of entrepreneurship and meritocracy are driven out of the system, and those who do stay in and get promoted in the military tend to be loyal, dutiful, and eager to please micromanagers who keep their bosses happy and get along with everyone.

This is quite different from many private-sector companies, where managers must recruit, hire, and live with their staffing decisions; employees tend to be treated as individuals; people can choose to leave employers if they are unhappy; there are better results and team-building metrics to judge performance; risk taking and innovation are rewarded; and promotions and compensation are more likely to be awarded on merit, rather than time in grade.

At one time the military personnel system was very similar to what is found in the private sector. When George Marshall was appointed the chief of staff of the Army and Army Air Corps in 1939, he believed that the 190,000 troops under his command were not even a "third-rate military power." Over the next two years he eliminated more than 600 senior officers he felt were deadwood, and when World War II began, the generals serving below him had three to four months to lead troops in combat. Marshall rewarded innovation, risk taking, adaptability, and actual results. Dwight D. Eisenhower was a lieutenant colonel in 1939 and rose to become a five star general under the Marshall system. As much as Marshall rewarded good performance, he made equally quick decisions about those who were not successful. Marshall's system of reward and replacement fell by the wayside during the Korean War, however, as only a handful of military generals have since been removed from office by the military. Whereas corporate CEOs have a life expectancy of only three to four years, few generals are ever replaced for poor performance or incompetence.

Are the top military leaders in the United States that much better than their private-sector counterparts, or is something else going on? What information would you need to gather if you wanted to make comparisons between military generals and corporate CEOs in their abilities to achieve results and build teams? Why do you think that most retired generals move into civilian jobs that are much narrower in scope and responsibility than their military responsibilities?

Sources: A. Roberts, "A Few Good Leaders of Men," *The Wall Street Journal*, October 29, 2012, p. A19; T. E. Ricks, *Fiasco: The American Military Adventure in Iraq* (New York: Penguin Press, 2006); T. E. Ricks, *The Generals: American Military Command from World War II to Today* (New York: Penguin Press, 2012); http://www.usatoday.com/news/health/story/2012-08-05/apa-mean-bosses/56813062/1; http://news.yahoo.com/employees-reveal-why-hate-bosses-160226490.html; http://blogs.hbr.org/fronline-leadership/2010/11/bleeding-talent-the...urce=newsletter_daily_alert; http://www.theatlantic.com/magazine/print/2011/01/why-our-best-officers-are-leaving/8346/;

Dark-Side Personality Traits: Personality as a Method of Birth Control

Dark-side personality traits are irritating, counterproductive behavioral tendencies that interfere with a leader's ability to build cohesive teams and cause followers to exert less effort toward goal accomplishment.[12,13,40,43,46,56,69–74] A listing of 11 common dark-side traits can be found in Table 15.3. Any of these 11 tendencies, if exhibited regularly, will decrease the leader's ability to get results through others. And if you consider some of the worst bosses you have worked for, chances are these individuals possessed some of these 11 dark-side personality traits.

TABLE 15.3   **Dark-Side Personality Traits**

Excitable	Leaders with these tendencies have difficulties building teams because of their dramatic mood swings, emotional outbursts, and inability to persist on projects.
Skeptical	Leaders with this dark-side trait have an unhealthy mistrust of others, are constantly questioning the motives and challenging the integrity of their followers, and are vigilant for signs of disloyalty.
Cautious	Because these leaders are so fearful of making "dumb" mistakes, they alienate their staffs by not making decisions or taking action on issues.
Reserved	During times of stress these leaders become extremely withdrawn and are uncommunicative, difficult to find, and unconcerned about the welfare of their staffs.
Leisurely	These passive–aggressive leaders will exert effort only in the pursuit of their own agendas and will procrastinate on or not follow through with requests that are not in line with their agendas.
Bold	Because of their narcissistic tendencies, these leaders often get quite a bit done. But their feelings of entitlement, inability to share credit for success, tendency to blame their mistakes on others, and inability to learn from experience often result in trails of bruised followers.
Mischievous	These leaders tend to be quite charming but take pleasure in seeing if they can get away with breaking commitments, rules, policies, and laws. When caught, they also believe they can talk their way out of any problem.
Colorful	Leaders with this tendency believe they are "hot" and have an unhealthy need to be the center of attention. They are so preoccupied with being noticed that they are unable to share credit, maintain focus, or get much done.
Imaginative	Followers question the judgment of leaders with this tendency because these leaders think in eccentric ways, often change their minds, and make strange or odd decisions.
Diligent	Because of their perfectionist tendencies, these leaders frustrate and disempower their staffs through micromanagement, poor prioritization, and an inability to delegate.
Dutiful	These leaders deal with stress by showing ingratiating behavior to superiors. They lack spines, are unwilling to refuse unrealistic requests, won't stand up for their staffs, and burn them out as a result.

Source: Hogan Assessment Systems, *The Hogan Development Survey* (Tulsa, OK: 2002).

652 Part Four *Focus on the Situation*

FIGURE 15.3
Leadership Challenge Profile

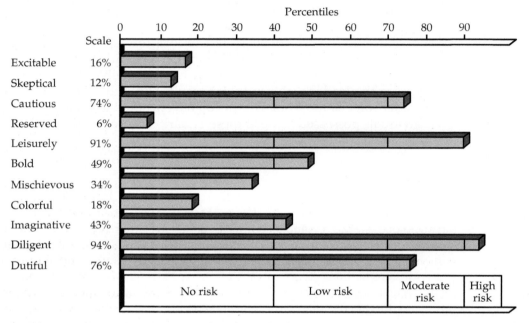

Source: Adapted with permission of Hogan Assessment Systems.

It is probably not an exaggeration to state that if individuals with significant narcissistic characteristics were stripped from the ranks of public figures, the ranks would be perilously thinned.

Jerrold M. Post, political psychologist

Several aspects of dark-side personality traits are worth noting. First, everyone has at least one dark-side personality trait. Figure 15.3 shows a graphic output from a typical dark-side personality measure, which shows that this individual has strong leisurely and diligent tendencies and moderate cautious and dutiful tendencies (scores above the 90th percentile indicate a high risk and within the 70th to 89th percentiles indicate a moderate risk of dark-side tendencies). The results in Figure 15.3 indicate that when in a crisis this leader will slow down the decision-making process, not follow though on commitments, tend to micromanage others, and not stand up for his or her followers and get them the resources they need. Second, dark-side traits usually emerge during crises or periods of high stress and are coping mechanisms for dealing with stress. People act differently when under stress, and the behaviors associated with dark-side traits help leaders deal with stress more effectively. The problem is that although these coping behaviors positively affect leaders' ability to deal with stress, these same behaviors negatively affect followers' motivation and performance. Although yelling and temper tantrums might help leaders blow off steam (excitable), such behavior makes followers feel like they are walking on eggshells and wonder if they are going to be the next target of their leader's tirades.

Third, dark-side traits have a bigger influence on performance for people in leadership versus followership roles. Individual contributors might have leisurely or cautious tendencies, but because they do not have to get work done through others these tendencies have less impact on their work units than if these same individuals were first-line supervisors or business unit leaders. These individual contributors may not be fun to work with, but their counterproductive tendencies will not be as debilitating as they would be if these people were leading teams. Fourth, dark-side traits are usually apparent only when leaders are not attending to their public image. In other words, people will not see the behaviors associated with dark-side traits when leaders are concerned with how they are coming across to others. These tendencies are much more likely to appear under times of stress, when leaders are multitasking or focusing on task accomplishment, during crises, or when leaders feel comfortable enough around others to "let their guard down."[12,13,43,56,74] And given the high levels of stress, challenge, and complexity associated with most leadership positions, the conditions are ripe for the appearance of dark-side traits.

Fifth, many dark-side traits covary with social skills and are difficult to detect in interviews or assessment centers or with bright-side personality inventories.[12,13,43,56,74] In other words, people who possess bold, mischievous, colorful, and imaginative dark-side traits often do well in interviews and get hired as a result. Only after these individuals have been on the job for some time do their dark-side tendencies begin to emerge. Sixth, the 11 dark-side personality traits are related to extreme FFM or OCEAN scores. For example, being diligent is often associated with extremely high conscientious scores, and being excitable is associated with extremely low neuroticism scores. However, just because a person has an extremely high or low OCEAN dimension score does not necessarily mean that he or she also possesses the corresponding dark-side personality trait. Seventh, the behaviors associated with dark-side personality traits can occur at any leadership level, and many times organizations tolerate these behaviors because a leader is smart or experienced or possesses unique skills (see Profiles in Leadership 15.1 to 15.5). Along these lines, people with bold tendencies are particularly adept at moving up in organizations. Nothing ever got launched without a healthy dose of narcissism, and leaders with bold tendencies are quick to volunteer for new assignments, take on seemingly impossible challenges, and consistently underestimate the amount of time, money, and effort it will take to get a job accomplished. In some cases these leaders pull off the seemingly impossible and get promoted because of their accomplishments. But when things go badly (which they often do), these same leaders are quick to blame the situation or others for their failures and as a result never learn from their mistakes.[12,13,43,56,72]

The final point to be made about dark-side tendencies is that they are probably the leading cause of managerial incompetence. Dark-side traits are prevalent (everybody has at least one), they are virtually impossible to detect using the most common selection techniques (interviews and résumés), and they tend to emerge during periods of stress (workloads, workplace stress, and burnout are at all-time highs these days). Competent

654   Part Four   *Focus on the Situation*

Rebekkah Brooks: The One-Time Queen of Fleet Street

PROFILES IN LEADERSHIP 15.5

The *News of the World* was once one of the top selling newspapers in the United Kingdom, having a circulation of nearly 3 million readers by the end of 2010. The newspaper boosted sales by running photos of topless models; salacious scoops about celebrities, sports figures, business executives, government officials, and the royal family; and investigative journalism articles. Although a tabloid, the paper won several major British Press awards and many of its competitors jealously tried to figure out how the *News of the World* reporters got their material.

Rebekkah Brooks was the editor of the *News of the World from* 2000 to 2011 and had joined the company in the late 1990s after completing some undergraduate courses in the United Kingdom and France. Starting as a secretary, Brooks developed a reputation for being bright, ambitious, and loyal, as she constantly peppered her bosses with ideas for stories rather than attending to administrative duties. Brooks was soon promoted to a Sunday magazine writer, where she developed a strong relationship with editor Piers Morgan. Brooks also caught the eye of Rupert Murdoch, the owner of the *News of the World* and one of the most powerful media moguls in the world. Murdoch admired Brooks's personal qualities and unswerving loyalty so much that she eventually became one of his closest advisors.

Upon becoming editor, Brooks emerged as a member of the British elite, developing friendships with Prime Ministers Blair, Brown, and Cameron and their families and rubbing shoulders with many of the most well-known politicians, business executives, sports figures, and celebrities in England. As a boss Brooks created an aggressive, pressure-cooker culture driven by bullying, lies, ruthlessness, and misogyny where reporters were told to do whatever was necessary to get a story. This included conducting overnight stakeouts, bribing corrupt police officers for inside information, dressing up reporters to entrap celebrities and other public figures, adding misinformation to stories to make them more outrageous, and hiring private investigators to hack the telephones of more than 7,000 citizens. Some of those whose phones were hacked included members of the royal family, relatives of British servicemen recently killed in action, and Milly Dowler, a young teen who had been reported missing and was later found murdered. A rival newspaper, *The Guardian*, broke the Milly Dowler phone-hacking story and brought many of these outrageous practices to light. Despite Rupert Murdoch's attempts to pressure the British government to downplay the *Guardian* stories, a formal inquiry discovered the full extent to which the *News of the World* had broken the law. Murdoch subsequently shut down the paper in July 2011.

What bright-side personality traits do you think contributed to Brooks's success? What dark-side traits do you think led to her downfall?

Sources: http://www.news.yahoo.com/brooks-arrested-tabloid-insiders-open-104104938.html: http://www.guardian.co.uk/media/2011/jul/07news-of-the-world-rupert-murdoch; http://www.bbc.co.uk/news/uk-1407033; http://guardian.co.uk/media/2011/jul/07news-of-the-world-history; http://abcnews.go.com/International/news-world-closed-telephone-hacking-scandal/story?id=14037284;

managers are those who have gained insight into their dark-side traits and have found ways to negate their debilitating effects on followers. Taskmasters are likely to exhibit excitable, reserved, bold, and diligent tendencies, and cheerleaders usually suffer from unchecked leisurely, mischievous, colorful, and dutiful tendencies. Figureheads often exhibit the behaviors associated with skeptical, cautious, and imaginative dark-side traits.

If virtually everyone has dark-side personality tendencies, what can individuals and organizations do about them? First and foremost, leaders

How the Mighty Fall

HIGHLIGHT 15.12

Chapter 14 included a highlight about Jim Collins's book *Good to Great*, which describes an alternative approach to organizational change. Collins and his research team investigated the performance of 1,400 publicly traded companies and determined that the top performers shared some common attributes. Several years later Collins and his team re-examined this database to determine if there were any common themes among once highly successful companies that subsequently failed. Some of these formerly high-flying companies included Zenith, Rubbermaid, Bear Sterns, Lehmann Brothers, Circuit City, Ames Department Stores, and AIG. Collins believed companies that stumble go through the following five-stage process:

- *Stage 1—hubris born of success:* Great businesses become insulated by success, and leaders with strong business results often become arrogant, adopt an entitlement mentality, and lose sight of what made their companies successful. They often get away with poor business and staffing decisions because their companies have such strong balance sheets.

- *Stage 2—undisciplined pursuit of more:* Because of the arrogance in stage 1, top leaders focus on growth, acclaim, and whatever those in charge deem as "success" and pursue ideas that are unrelated to the core business. Organizations that cannot fill all their key positions with internal talent because of their growth initiatives are probably in stage 2 decline.

- *Stage 3—denial of risk and peril:* As the warning signs from stage 2 begin to emerge, companies place the blame for their lack of success on external factors rather than on their own risky decisions to expand. In this stage vigorous, fact-based discussions disappear, and top leaders explain away or discount negative information.

- *Stage 4—grasping for salvation:* As the warning signs translate to actual business results and companies begin to drown in red ink, they often grasp at anything that will save them. This salvation sometimes comes from outside charismatic leaders, bold but untested strategies, hoped-for blockbuster products, or game-changing acquisitions. The initial results from these activities may appear positive but are often short-lived.

- *Stage 5—capitulation to irrelevance or death:* Accumulated setbacks and the continuous erosion of financial performance causes top leaders to lose hope and sell out; and the longer companies remain in stage 4, the more likely they will be declared bankrupt or be acquired by their competitors.

Collins believes most companies go through some of these stages, but the successful ones recognize when they are in stages 1 or 2 and then take steps to avoid moving into stages 3 or 4. The farther companies slide down the five-stage process, the harder it is for them to turn things around.

Although Collins does not write about managerial incompetence or derailment in this book, what role do you think these concepts play in his five-stage process? Where do the root causes of managerial incompetence and derailment come into play in this five-stage process?

Source: J. Collins, *How the Mighty Fall* (New York: HarperCollins, 2009).

and leaders-to-be need to identify their dark-side personality traits. This can be done by asking trusted others about how they act under pressure or what behaviors interfere with their ability to build teams, or by completing a dark-side personality assessment. Once these counterproductive tendencies are identified, leaders need to understand the situations or conditions in which these tendencies are likely to appear. Again, dark-side traits are most likely to appear under stress and heavy workloads, so finding ways to better manage stress and workloads will help reduce the impact of these dark-side tendencies. Just being aware of our dark-side tendencies and understanding the circumstances in which they appear will go a long way toward controlling the manifestation of counterproductive leadership behaviors. Exercise and other stress reduction techniques, and having trusted followers who can tell leaders when they are exhibiting dark-side traits, can also help control these tendencies. Finally, having lower scores on the OCEAN dimension of neuroticism also helps with some of these dimensions because these leaders seem to be better able to cope with stress than those with high scores.

Summary

As stated at the beginning of this chapter, leadership is arguably the most important concept in the world today. Who is in charge determines whom you can marry, where you work, how your kids will be educated, and whether you can travel freely or express your opinions. Although many in Western societies take these freedoms (and to some extent leadership) for granted, it is important to recognize that most people in the world today do not enjoy these privileges. Most people live under some form of dictatorship and have little say in what they do, whom they interact with, or who is in charge. Although the people in charge of dictatorships may find leadership to be relatively easy, those in positions of authority in more democratically oriented countries often find leadership to be a tremendously complex task. To succeed in these roles, leaders need to build teams and get results through others, but accomplishing these two ends is challenging. There are many ways for people in positions of authority to fail, and unfortunately most people are not particularly effective leaders.

This chapter began with a discussion of destructive leadership. Destructive leaders are those who can build teams but achieve results that are morally reprehensible or undermine organizational success. The current heads of North Korea, Belarus, Sudan, and Turkmenistan could be considered destructive leaders in that they have built loyal teams of followers but have done little to improve the lives of the vast majority of their citizens. Destructive leadership is not restricted to the world stage: many community and nonprofit leaders, first-line supervisors, midlevel managers, and executives who can build teams also get results that are misaligned with the needs of a majority of their constituents or their parent organizations. And exactly what constitutes good or destructive leadership may not be straightforward—initiatives initially deemed destructive might prove to be good in the long run.

Managerial incompetence describes people in positions of authority who have difficulties either in building teams or in getting results through others. There appear to be four managerial types: competent managers, cheerleaders, figureheads, and taskmasters. Research shows that the most people in positions of authority fall into one of these latter three types and are perceived as incompetent by many of their followers.

Managerial derailment is closely related to managerial incompetence and pertains to the reasons why competent managers can become cheerleaders, figureheads, or results-only managers. Some of the reasons why high-potential leaders become ineffective managers are because of their unpreparedness for promotion or inability to build teams, achieve business objectives, get along with others, or adapt to new situations. Although the managerial derailment research has been conducted on people who were once seen as high-potential candidates, it seems likely that these reasons for failure can apply to anyone in a position of authority.

The fact that most people know why leaders fail shows that simply knowing the common reasons for derailment is not enough to prevent it from happening. Something else must be occurring to cause a majority of persons in positions of authority to be seen as cheerleaders, figureheads, and taskmasters. Some not-so-obvious root causes for managerial incompetence and derailment include overwhelming situational and follower factors; a lack of organizational fit; a lack situational and self-awareness; a lack of intelligence, relevant subject matter expertise, and team-building know-how; poor followership; and dark-side personality traits. Unfortunately any one of these factors can cause people in positions of authority to fail, and many times a combination of these underlying causes may be at fault. The good news is that leaders and leaders-to-be can take steps to mitigate the impact of these factors on their ability to build teams and get results.

Key Terms

destructive leadership, *615*
managerial incompetence, *615*
managerial derailment, *615*
base rate of managerial incompetence, *620*
Dr. Gordy test, *622*
competent managers, *623*
taskmasters, *623*
programs for promotions initiatives, *623*
cheerleaders, *623*

figureheads, *624*
moronization of management, *627*
high-potential managers, *627*
failure to meet business objectives, *628*
inability to build and lead a team, *631*
inability to build relationships, *631*
inability to adapt, *633*
inadequate preparation for promotion, *633*

episodic managerial incompetence, *639*
chronic managerial incompetence, *639*
organizational fit, *640*
situational awareness, *642*
self-awareness, *643*
subject matter expertise, *645*
team-building know-how, *646*
poor followership, *648*
dark-side personality traits, *651*

Questions

1. The base rate of managerial incompetence is estimated to be 50 to 75 percent. This means that a majority of people in positions of authority have difficulties getting a group of people to work effectively together or get results. What do you think about this percentage of incompetent managers? For example, is it too high or low, and why?

2. Think about the ineffective leaders you have worked or played for. What dark-side traits did these leaders possess that caused them to be ineffective?

3. Do you know anyone who has derailed from a leadership position? What did the person do? Use the leader–follower–situation model and the six underlying causes of derailment to explain what happened.

4. What role would downsizing play in an organization's overall level of subject matter expertise?

5. Is Cristina Kirchner, the president of Argentina, a destructive leader? What data could you use to make this evaluation? Would your evaluation of Kirchner change if you lived in a slum or owned a large business in Argentina?

Activities

1. Count how many leaders for whom you have worked, played, or performed in the past. This number should include any position in which you were in a followership role. Once you have a total, count how many of these for whom leaders you would willingly work, play, or perform again. Then calculate the ratio of effective managers to total managers. Who were the worst and best leaders for whom you have worked, and what did they do that characterized them as effective or ineffective leaders?

2. Get into small groups and discuss whether the following people were good or destructive leaders. Provide the rationale and facts to support your positions.

   - Hugo Chavez
   - Evo Morales
   - Nancy Pelosi
   - Ron Paul
   - Xi Jinping
   - Vladimir Putin
   - Goodluck Jonathan
   - Mohammed Morsi
   - Benjamin Netanyahu
   - Nouri al-Maliki

3. Investigate and prepare short presentations about the underlying causes of derailment or incompetence for the following people:

   - David Petraeus
   - Stanley McChrystal
   - Jon Corzine
   - Paul Bremer
   - Rod Blagojevich
   - Omar al-Bashir
   - Silvio Berlusconi
   - Hamid Karzai
   - Asif Ali Zardari
   - Bashar al-Assad

Minicase

You Can't Make Stuff Like This Up

Steve once worked as a regional sales director for a large health insurance company called Blue Star Health. Blue Star Health was once quite successful but had become complacent over the past five years. Competitors gained market share using aggressive marketing and sales tactics, and Blue Star was selling antiquated products and using inefficient processes for settling claims. With falling revenues and margins, Blue Star became an acquisition target and was bought by Anthum, a Fortune 100 company. At the conclusion of the deal Anthum brought in an injection of cash, a reputation for operational excellence, and a new vice president of sales, Jim Blaylock. The CEO of Anthum described Jim as bright, experienced, successful, and "more energetic than the Energizer Bunny." Jim had joined the corporation immediately after college; because of his "potential" the company sent him to law school and rapidly promoted him into increasingly responsible positions. Senior management had tremendous confidence in Jim's leadership abilities and appointed him as the vice president of sales in Blue Star Health, even though he had no previous sales experience.

Steve was initially impressed with Jim's freshness and energy; he was constantly touting "Midwestern values" and the "work ethic of the Midwest." However, the sales management team soon became disenchanted with his views: Steve and his sales team were working 70 to 80 hours a week and becoming exhausted and frazzled. Moreover, Jim's interactions with internal and external clients were lessons in poor human relations. He seemed to seek confrontations, and as time passed, his behavior became steadily more extreme. Jim harangued people, ignored appointments and made no excuses for missing them, made promises he never kept, called sales directors at 6:00 a.m. with insignificant questions, and abused brokers. Those who questioned Jim's leadership were summarily dismissed.

One day Jim asked Steve to arrange a meeting with a broker at 9:00 p.m. The broker was from a large benefit house and was older, and the meeting time was late. However, he was a longtime personal friend of Steve's and as a courtesy agreed to the meeting. Jim did not show up for the appointment and would not answer Steve's calls to his cell phone. After an hour, Steve and the broker went home. When Steve asked Jim why he missed the appointment, he said he was drinking with a friend and did not think the meeting with the broker was important. Jim refused to apologize to the broker and was surprised when business with the broker's organization came to an end.

Jim loved working on high-visibility projects and landed an opportunity to convert the membership of another acquired company to Anthum.

This was an important project for Anthum, and shortly thereafter Jim set up an elaborate "war room" in which all sales planning and action would take place. He asked Steve to lead the conversion project, repeatedly announcing that the acquisition was to garner new contracts and to bring quality employees into the organization. At this point Steve had over 70 direct reports in five different locations across the state and some aggressive sales targets. It would be impossible for Steve to hit his revenue numbers and run the conversion project. But Jim cut Steve no slack, and the computer system intended to convert the contracts did not work. Jim spent no time with any of the newly acquired sales team members, and as a result they showed no interest in working for Anthum. Yet Jim made grandiose statements about the quality of the sales force at the acquired company, which implied the current sales employees were unsatisfactory and fostered a sense of mistrust in both sales organizations.

Because of Jim's shoddy treatment, the long hours, and poor sales and invoicing processes, the morale of the sales team began to plummet. Tantrums and tears occurred frequently, and Steve spent a lot of time smoothing feathers and telling team members that things would get better over time. But there was only so much Steve could do, and as team members began to quit, Jim blamed Steve for the decline in department morale. As the situation continued to deteriorate, Steve requested that Jim meet with the remaining staff to talk about their frustrations with Anthum. Jim opted to set up an all-employee breakfast at a local restaurant to address their concerns.

The night before the meeting a major snowstorm hit the city, and the streets were covered with a foot of snow. Some employees had to drive 40 miles to attend the meeting, but everyone made it to the restaurant. The only person missing was Jim, and Steve started calling him 10 minutes before the meeting start time to check on his status. Jim did not answer, so Steve began to call and leave messages every five minutes. Jim finally answered his phone 30 minutes after the meeting start time and told Steve that the reason he was not at the meeting was that he decided to go skiing and people would have to meet with him another day. He also asked Steve to quit bugging him by leaving messages every five minutes. Steve could do little to put a positive spin on this message, and the employees left the restaurant bitter and hurt. Of the 60 people who showed up for the meeting, only one was still with Anthum six months later. Jim never acknowledged his behavior and was "shocked" at the turnover in the sales group. Despite the turnover and declining sales revenues, Jim was still considered the company's darling, and it was commonly believed that the CEO tacitly condoned his behavior.

1. Was Jim Blaylock a destructive leader, a competent manager, taskmaster, figurehead, or a cheerleader? What data would you use to make this determination?

2. If Jim was an incompetent manager, what do you think were the underlying root causes of his incompetence?

3. Why do you think Jim was seen as a high-potential candidate? Why did the CEO still think he was a high performer?

4. What would you do if you were Jim's boss and heard about the information described here?

5. What would you do if you were Steve?

Source: G. J. Curphy, A. Baldrica, and R. T. Hogan, *Managerial Incompetence,* unpublished manuscript, 2009.

End Notes

1. J. M. Burns, *Leadership* (New York: Harper & Row, 1978).

2. S. Einarsen, M. Schanke Aasland, and A. Skogstad, "Destructive Leadership Behavior: A Definition and Conceptual Model," *The Leadership Quarterly* 18 (2007), pp. 207–16.

3. A. Padilla, R. T. Hogan, and R. B. Kaiser, "The Toxic Triangle: Destructive Leaders, Susceptible Followers, and Conducive Environments," *The Leadership Quarterly* 18 (2007), pp. 176–94.

4. J. Schaubroeck, F. O. Walumbwa, D. C. Ganster, and S. Kepes, "Destructive Leadership Traits and the Neutralizing Influence of an 'Enriched' Job," *The Leadership Quarterly* 18 (2007), pp. 235–51.

5. J. B. Shaw, A. Erickson, and M. Harvey, "A Method for Measuring Destructive Leadership and Identifying Destructive Leaders in Organizations," *The Leadership Quarterly* 22 (2011), pp. 575–90.

6. M. Schanke Aasland, A. Skogstad, G. Notelaers, M. Birkeland Nielsen, and S. Einarsen, "The Prevalence of Destructive Leadership Behaviour," *British Journal of Management* 21 (2010), pp. 438–52.

7. B. Kellerman, "Bad Leadership: What It Is, How It Happens, Why It Matters," *Leadership for the Common Good* (Boston, MA: Harvard Business School Press, 2004).

8. G. J. Curphy, "Investing in the Wrong Vehicle: The Neglect of Team Leadership," in *Why Is the Leadership Development Industry Failing?* R. B. Kaiser (chair). Symposium conducted at the 28th Annual Conference for the Society of Industrial and Organizational Psychology, Houston, April 2013.

9. J. Diamond, *Guns, Germs, and Steel: The Fates of Human Societies* (New York: W.W. Norton, 1999).

10. http://www.kellyocg.com/Knowledge/KellyOCG_Blog/The_Leadership_Disconnect/

11. B. Schyns and J. Schilling, "How Bad Are the Effects of Bad Leaders? A Meta-Analysis of Destructive Leadership and Its Outcomes," *The Leadership Quarterly* 24 (2013), pp. 138–58.

12. G. J. Curphy, A. Baldrica, and R. T. Hogan, *Managerial Incompetence,* unpublished manuscript, 2009.

13. R. T. Hogan, *Personality and the Fate of Organizations* (Mahwah, NJ: Lawrence Erlbaum, 2007).

14. R. Kaiser and G.J. Curphy, "Leadership Development: The Failures of an Industry and the Opportunities for Consulting Psychologists." Consulting Psychology Journal: Practice and Research, in press.

15. R. B. Kaiser, "The Disconnect between Development and the Evolutionary Laws of Leadership," in *Why Is the Leadership Development Industry Failing?* R. B. Kaiser, (chair). Symposium conducted at the 28th Annual Conference for the Society of Industrial and Organizational Psychology, Houston, April 2013.

16. G.J. Curphy, R. Kaiser, and RT. Hogan. Why is the Leadership Development Industry Failing? (and how to Fix it). (North Oaks, MN: Curphy Consulting Corporation, 2014).

17. B. Kellerman, "Things Change: Leadership, Followership, and the Indolence of an Industry," in *Why Is the Leadership Development Industry Failing?* R. B. Kaiser, (chair). Symposium conducted at the 28th Annual Conference for the Society of Industrial and Organizational Psychology, Houston, April 2013.

18. C. Lucier, P. Kocourek, and R. Habbel, "CEO Succession 2005: The Crest of the Wave," *Strategy + Business* 43 (2006), pp. 40–50.

19. "The Wheel of Fortune," *The Economist*, May 26, 2012, p. 70.

20. D. Jones, "Leadership Crisis Blamed for Some of the Nation's Problems," *USA Today*, November 5, 2008, p. 6B.

21. A. Ovans, "Morning Advantage: How Bosses Do Harm" http://blogs.hbr .org/morning-advantage/2012/09/morning-advantage-how-bosses-d.html

22. G. L. Neilson, B. A. Pasternack, and K. E. Van Nuys, "The Passive-Aggressive Organization," *Harvard Business Review,* October 2005, pp. 82–95.

23. M. Bardes Mawritz, D. M. Mayer, J. M. Hoobler, S. J. Wayne, and S. V. Marinova, "A Trickle-Down Model of Abusive Supervision," *Personnel Psychology* 62 (2012), pp. 325–57.

24. K. E. Klein, "What's Behind High Small-Biz Failure Rates," *Frontier Advice and Columns,* September 30, 1999, http://www.businessweek.com/smallbiz/ news/ coladvice/ask/sa990930.htm.

25. C. Denbow, "Small Business Failure," http://www.elib.org/articles/292/ small-business.

26. C. Tushabomwe-Kazooba, "Causes of Small Business Failure in Uganda: A Case Study from Bushenyi and Mbarara," *African Studies Quarterly* 8, no. 4 (2006), pp. 1–12.

27. S. Ward, "Part 4: Avoiding Business Failure," *Small Business: Canada,* 1997. http://sbinfrocanada.about.com/cs/startup/a/startownbiz.

28. G.J. Curphy. Why is the Leadership Development Industry Failing? (and How to Fix it) Presentation given to Metro, New York City, October, 2013.

29. C. Johnson, *Visualizing the Relationship between Human Error and Organizational Failure,* 1998, http://www.dcs.gla.ac.uk/~johnson/papers/fault_trees/ organizational_error.

30. The Standish Group, *Latest Standish Group CHAOS Report Shows Project Success Rates Have Improved 50%,* March 25, 2003, www.standishgroup.com/press/article.

31. J. A. Warden and L. A. Russell, *Winning in Fast Time* (Montgomery, AL: Venturist Publishing, 2002).

32. J. P. Kotter, *Leading Change* (Boston: Harvard Business School Press, 1996).

33. J. P. Steele. *Antecedents and Consequences of Toxic Leadership in the U.S. Army: A Two Year Review and Recommended Solutions* (Technical Report 2011-3) (Ft. Leavenworth, KS: Center for Army Leadership, 2011).

34. L. Cranshaw, "Coaching Abrasive Leaders: Using Action Research to Reduce Suffering and Increase Productivity in Organizations," *The International Journal of Coaching in Organizations* 29, no. 8, (2010), pp. 59–77.

35. M. Abrahams, "Random Promotion May Be Best, Research Suggests," *The Guardian*, November 1, 2010, http://www.guardian.co.uk/education/2010/nov/01/random-promotion-research.

36. M. A. Huselid, R. W. Beatty, and B. E. Becker, "'A Players' or 'A Positions'? The Strategic Logic of Workforce Management," *Harvard Business Review*, December 2005, pp. 110–21.

37. J. W. Boudreau and P. M. Ramstad, "Talentship and the New Paradigm for Human Resource Management: From Professional Practices to Strategic Talent Decision Science," *Human Resource Planning* 28, no. 2 (2005), pp. 17–26.

38. J. Dowdy, S. Dorgan, T. Rippen, J. Van Reenen, and N. Bloom, *Management Matters* (London: McKinsey & Company, 2005).

39. M. W. McCall Jr. and M. M. Lombardo, "Off the Track: Why and How Successful Executives Get Derailed," Technical Report No. 21 (Greensboro, NC: Center for Creative Leadership, 1983).

40. D. L. Dotlich and P. E. Cairo, *Why CEOs Fail: The 11 Behaviors That Can Derail Your Climb to the Top and How to Manage Them* (New York: Wiley, 2001).

41. J. F. Hazucha, *PDI Indicator: Competence, Potential, and Jeopardy. What Gets Managers Ahead May Not Keep Them out of Trouble* (Minneapolis, MN: Personnel Decisions, September 1992).

42. M. M. Lombardo, M. N. Ruderman, and C. D. McCauley, "Explorations of Success and Derailment in Upper-Level Management Positions," paper presented at meeting of the Academy of Management, New York, 1987.

43. J. C. Hogan, R. T. Hogan, and R. B. Kaiser, "Managerial Derailment," in *APA Handbook of Industrial and Organizational Psychology*, Vol. 3, ed. S. Zedeck (Washington, DC: American Psychological Association, 2011), pp. 555–76.

44. E. Van Velsor and J. B. Leslie, "Why Executives Derail: Perspectives across Time and Cultures," *Academy of Management Executive* 9, no. 4 (1995), pp. 62–71.

45. H. J. Foldes and D. S. Ones, "Wrongdoing among Senior Managers: Critical Incidents and their Co-Occurrence," in *Predicting Leadership: The Good, The Bad, the Indifferent, and the Unnecessary*, J. P. Campbell and M. J. Benson (chairs). Symposium conducted at the 22nd Annual Conference for the Society of Industrial and Organizational Psychology, New York, April 2007.

46. M. J. Benson and J. P. Campbell, "Derailing and Dark Side Personality: Incremental Prediction of Leadership (In)Effectiveness," in *Predicting Leadership: The Good, The Bad, the Indifferent, and the Unnecessary*, J. P. Campbell and M. J. Benson (chairs). Symposium conducted at the 22nd Annual Conference for the Society of Industrial and Organizational Psychology, New York, April 2007.

47. V. J. Bentz, "Research Findings from Personality Assessment of Executives," in *Personality Assessment in Organizations,* eds. J. H. Bernadin and D. A. Bownas (New York: Praeger, 1985), pp. 82–144.

48. A. M. Morrison, R. P. White, and E. Van Velsor, *Breaking the Glass Ceiling* (Reading, MA: Addison-Wesley, 1987).

49. R. Rasch, W. Shen, S. E. Davies, and J. Bono, *The Development of a Taxonomy of Ineffective Leadership Behaviors,* paper presented at the 23rd Annual Conference of the Society for Industrial and Organizational Psychology, San Francisco, CA, 2008.

50. G.J. Curphy, "The Dark Side of Leadership," Presentation given to the Vistage Group, Minneapolis, February 2013.

51. J. Martin and W.A. Gentry, "Derailment Signs across Generations," *The Psychologist-Manager Journal* 14 (2011), pp. 177–95.

52. http://blogs.hbr.org/cs/2012/08/are_you_sure_youre_not_a_bad_b.html?goback=%2Egde_110882_member_147568165.

53. R. Charan, S. Drotter, and J. Noel, *The Leadership Pipeline: How to Build the Leadership-Powered Company* (San Francisco: Jossey-Bass, 2001).

54. R. Charan and G. Colvin, "Why CEOs Fail," *Fortune,* June 21, 1999, pp. 69–82.

55. G. J. Curphy and R. Hogan, *The Rocket Model: Practical Advice for Building High Performing Teams* (Tulsa, OK: Hogan Press, 2012).

56. G. J. Curphy, "Why Leaders Fail," Presentation given to NYLife, Dallas, May 2012.

57. J. Hogan and R. T. Hogan, *Motives, Values and Preferences Inventory Manual* (Tulsa, OK: Hogan Assessment Systems, 1996).

58. P.A. Craig, *Controlling Pilot Error: Situational Awareness.* (New York, NY: McGraw-Hill, 2001).

59. P. A. Craig, *Controlling Pilot Error: Situational Awareness* (New York: McGraw-Hill, 2001).

60. P. D. Harms, S. M. Spain, and S. T. Hannah, "Leader Development and the Dark Side of Personality," *The Leadership Quarterly* 22 (2011), pp. 495–509.

61. J. Kruger and D. Dunning, "Unskilled and Unaware of It: How Difficulties in Recognizing One's Own Incompetence Lead to Inflated Self-Assessments," *Journal of Personality and Social Psychology* 77, no. 6 (1999), pp. 1121–34.

62. D. L. Nilsen, *Using Self and Observers' Ratings of Personality to Predict Leadership Performance,* unpublished doctoral dissertation, University of Minnesota, 1995.

63. R. I. Sutton, "Some Bosses Live in a Fool's Paradise," *Harvard Business Review Blog Network,* June 3, 2010, http://blogs.hbr.org/cs/2010/06/some_bosses_live_in_a_fools_pa.html?cm_mmc=npv.

64. P. F. Drucker, "The Theory of the Business," *Harvard Business Review,* September–October 1994.

65. R. T. Hogan and J. Hogan, *The Hogan Business Reasoning Inventory* (Tulsa, OK: Hogan Assessment Systems, 2007).

66. R. T. Hogan, *Intelligence and Good Judgment* (Tulsa, OK: Hogan Assessment Systems, 2008).

67. G. J. Curphy and R. T. Hogan, *A Guide to Building High Performing Teams* (North Oaks, MN: Curphy Consulting Corporation, 2010).

68. G. J. Curphy and R. M. Roellig, *Followership* (North Oaks, MN: Curphy Consulting Corporation, 2010).

69. M. J. Benson and J. P. Campbell, "To Be, or Not to Be, Linear: An Expanded Representation of Personality and Its Relationship to Leadership Performance," *International Journal of Selection and Assessment* 15 (2007), pp. 232–49.

70. G. J. Curphy and R. T. Hogan, *Managerial Incompetence: Is There a Dead Skunk on the Table?* working paper, 2004.

71. G. J. Curphy and R. T. Hogan, *What We Really Know about Leadership (but Seem Unwilling to Implement),* working paper, 2004.

72. R. T. Hogan and J. C. Hogan, "Assessing Leadership from the Dark Side," *International Journal of Selection and Assessment* 9, no. 1–2 (2001), pp. 40–51.

73. S. J. Peterson, B. M. Galvin, and D. Lange, "CEO Servant Leadership: Exploring Executive Characteristics and Firm Performance," *Personnel Psychology* 65 (2012), pp. 565–96.

74. S. B. Silverman, R. E. Johnson, N. McConnell, and A. Carr, "Arrogance: A Formula for Leadership Failure," *The Industrial-Organizational Psychologist* 50, no. 1 (2012), pp. 21–29.

Chapter

16

Skills for Optimizing Leadership as Situations Change

In this final chapter we offer some ideas about skills appropriate to the last element of the interactional framework. These skills include relatively advanced leadership skills useful in various specific situational challenges:

- Creating a compelling vision.
- Managing conflict.
- Negotiation.
- Diagnosing performance problems in individuals, groups, and organizations.
- Team building at the top.
- Punishment.

Creating a Compelling Vision

Suppose you are running the computer department at an electronics store. Overall the store has been having a good year: sales of cell phones, HDTVs and in-home theater equipment, and digital cameras have all been strong. But computer sales are lagging, and the store manager is exerting considerable pressure on you to increase sales. Your 11 sales associates are all relatively new to sales, and many do not have strong computer backgrounds. Your assistant department manager recently moved to the in-home theater department, and you have been screening candidates for this opening on your team. After failing to be impressed with the first four candidates interviewed, you notice that the next candidate, Colleen, has just moved to town and has a strong background in electronics sales. During the interview you become even more convinced that Colleen would be an ideal assistant department manager. Toward the end of the interview you ask Colleen if she has any questions about the position, and she states that she is considering several job offers and is asking all her prospective employers the same question, which is "Why should I work for you?"

What would you say if someone asked you this question? Would you be able to close the sale and make a strong case for getting someone to join your team? Believe it or not, many leaders cannot provide a compelling description of how they add value; as a result they have difficulty getting anyone excited to become part of their groups. And these struggles are not limited to new leaders—many seasoned leaders either do not have or cannot effectively articulate a clear and dynamic leadership vision. Yet many followers want to know where their team or group is going, how it intends to get there, and what they need to do to win. A leader's vision can answer these questions, explain why change is necessary, and keep team members motivated and focused. Because a leader's vision can have a pervasive effect on followers and teams, it is worth describing a process for building a compelling leadership vision.[1,2]

Before discussing the four components of leadership vision, it is worth noting that most people don't get particularly excited about a leader's vision by sitting through lengthy PowerPoint presentations or formal speeches. People tend to get more involved when leaders use stories, analogies, and personal experiences to paint compelling pictures of the future. As such, a leader's vision should be a personal statement that should help listeners answer the following questions:

- Where is the team going, and how will it get there?
- How does the team win, and how does it contribute to the broader organization's success?
- How does the speaker define leadership?
- What gets the speaker excited about being a leader?
- What are the speaker's key values? In other words, what are the leader's expectations for team members, and what will she or he not tolerate as a leader?

If you are currently in a leadership position, ask yourself how your direct reports would answer these questions. Would their answers to all five questions be the same, or would their answers differ? Alternatively, how would you answer these questions for your boss? If followers do not provide the same answers for these questions, leaders may need to create or better articulate their leadership vision. As shown in Figure 16.1, a leadership vision consists of four related components.

Ideas: The Future Picture

The idea component of a leader's vision begins with an honest assessment of the current situation facing the team.[3] Leaders need to clearly identify

FIGURE 16.1
The Four Components of a Leadership Vision

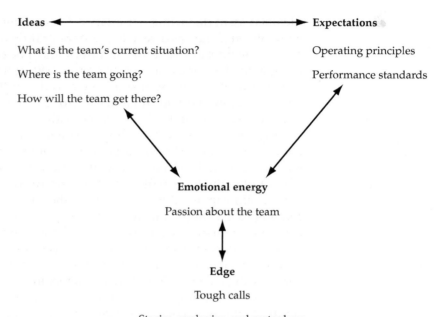

what the team is doing well, what it is not doing well, how it is performing compared to the competition, and what challenges it faces. Leaders should not pull any punches when assessing team performance because downplaying or overlooking team shortcomings will likely result in mediocrity. Once a leader has accurately assessed a team's strengths, weaknesses, and potential, he or she needs to clearly define where the team needs to be over the next 12–36 months. This future picture needs to describe the team's upcoming goals; the reputation it needs to have within the organization, among competitors, and with customers; and what strategies the team will pursue to achieve these outcomes. Ideas should also describe what changes the team must make to accomplish its major goals, explain why these changes are necessary, and give listeners hope for the future.[4]

Although leaders can complete the ideas component by themselves, they will often get considerably more commitment by working with their teams to assess the situation, set future team goals, and identify the changes needed for success. Whether the idea component is a solo or team effort, leaders will have successfully articulated their future pictures when everyone on their teams shares the same understanding of the situation and what they need to do to win.

Expectations: Values and Performance Standards

A leader's vision also needs to clearly describe her or his expectations for team member behavior. More specifically, what behaviors do leaders want team members to exhibit, and just as importantly, what behaviors will they not tolerate from team members? A leader's expectations for team members are highly related to his or her values. For example, if a leader believes winning is an important value, then he or she needs to say something about the levels of performance and commitment needed by team members. Or if leaders believe collaboration is an important value, they need to define how team members are supposed to work together. Because values and operating principles play such an important role in defining team member expectations, leaders should spend time identifying the team's core values and the positive and negative behaviors associated with these values. To improve understanding and buy-in, leaders can work with team members to jointly define a team's core values.

One important leadership role is to ensure that a team's core values are aligned with its future picture. For example, if the team has some aggressive performance goals, then its core values should include something about the performance and commitment expectations for individual team members. Team goals represent *what* a team must do to succeed; core values and operating principles represent *how* team members should behave if the team is to win. In addition, leaders should strive to implement a fairly limited (five to eight) set of core values. Team members often have difficulty recalling more than a half dozen core values, so the operating principles should be limited to only those values that are most directly related to team goals.

Leaders not only need to be role models for these core values—they also need to hold team members accountable for behaving in accordance with these operating principles. Nothing will erode a leader's credibility or team morale more quickly than leaders or team members not being held accountable for exhibiting behaviors that are misaligned with a team's operating principles. Leaders will have successfully conveyed their operating principles when everyone on the team understands and is behaving in accordance with the team's core values.

Emotional Energy: The Power and the Passion

The last two components of leadership vision, emotional energy and edge, are concerned more with delivery than content. Emotional energy is the level of enthusiasm leaders use to convey the future vision and the team's operating principles. Nothing kills follower enthusiasm and motivation for a leader's vision more quickly than a dull, monotone delivery. If leaders are not excited about where the team is going and how it will get there, it will be difficult to get others to join the effort. However, leaders who are excited about where their teams are going still need to make sure this enthusiasm is clear in the delivery of their vision. Emotional appeals make for compelling messages, and leaders should use a range of emotions when describing the future picture and operating principles. Leaders will have effectively mastered the emotional energy component when team members see that they are excited about where the team is going and being in a leadership role.

Edge: Stories, Analogies, and Metaphors

Perhaps the most difficult component to master when it comes to creating a leadership vision is edge. Edge pertains to lessons of leadership learned through personal experience that are related to the team's future picture and core values. Edge includes personal stories and examples that can help color a team's future picture. For example, edge might include stories about teams leaders have been on or have led in the past through similar situations. Edge would also include stories that illustrate why some of the team's core values are so important—examples of how team members did or did not act in accordance with a particular value and what happened as a result. Edge can also include slogans, analogies, and metaphors to help clarify and simplify where the team is going or what it stands for. In general, the more personal the examples and the simpler the stories, the more likely leaders will leave an impression on team members.

Leaders should not spend too much time worrying about edge until the team's future picture and core values are clearly defined. However, once these issues are clearly understood, leaders need to reflect on how their personal experiences can help team members understand where the team is going and why certain behaviors are important. They should also spend time brainstorming analogies, metaphors, and slogans that can distill team goals and behaviors into simple but memorable messages. As was described for the future picture and core values, these analogies and slogans do not have to be solo efforts; leaders can solicit team members' help in creating slogans that convey simple but compelling messages about the future direction for their teams.

Although ideas, expectations, emotional energy, and edge make up the four components of a leader's vision, several other leadership vision issues are worth noting. First, the delivery of a leader's vision improves with practice. The four components can help leaders define what they need to say and how they need to say it, but leaders should practice the delivery of their vision a number of times before going live with team members. Ideally they should use video recordings of some of these practice deliveries to ensure that key messages are being conveyed, the personal stories being used make sense and are easy to follow, and excitement and emotion are evident. Second, leaders need to remember that the most compelling leadership visions are relatively short and make sparing use of PowerPoint slides. Many of the best leadership visions are less than 10 minutes long and consist of no more than three to four slides. Third, leaders need to constantly tie team events back to their vision and core values. Reminding team members how delegated tasks relate to the team's vision, tying team member feedback to core values, and explaining how staff and strategy changes relate to team goals and operating principles are all effective ways to keep team members focused and motivated toward a leader's vision. And fourth, having a clear and compelling leadership vision should go a long way in answering the question posed at the beginning of this section, which was "Why should I work for you?"

Managing Conflict

We read or hear in the daily news about various types of negotiations. Nations often negotiate with each other over land or fishing rights, trade agreements, or diplomatic relations. Land developers often negotiate with city councils for variances of local zoning laws for their projects. Businesses often spend considerable time negotiating employee salaries and fringe benefits with labor unions. In a similar fashion, negotiations every day cover matters ranging from high school athletic schedules to where a new office copying machine will be located. In one sense, all these negotiations, big or small, are similar. In every case, representatives from different groups meet to resolve some sort of conflict. Conflict is an inevitable fact of life and an inevitable fact of leadership. Researchers have found that first-line supervisors and midlevel managers can spend more than 25 percent of their time dealing with conflict,[5] and resolving conflict has been found to be an important factor in leadership effectiveness.[6] In fact, successfully resolving conflicts is so important that it is a central theme in some of the literature about organizations.[7–9] Moreover, successfully resolving conflicts will become an increasingly important skill as leadership and management practice moves away from authoritarian directives and toward cooperative approaches emphasizing rational persuasion, collaboration, compromise, and solutions of mutual gain.

What Is Conflict?

Conflict occurs when opposing parties have interests or goals that appear to be incompatible.[10] There are a variety of sources of conflict in team, committee, work group, and organizational settings. For example, conflict can occur when group or team members (1) have strong differences in values, beliefs, or goals; (2) have high levels of task or lateral interdependence; (3) are competing for scarce resources or rewards; (4) are under high levels of stress; or (5) face uncertain or incompatible demands—that is, role ambiguity and role conflict.[11] Conflict can also occur when leaders act in a manner inconsistent with the vision and goals they have articulated for the organization.[12] Of these factors contributing to the level of conflict within or between groups, teams, or committees, probably the most important source of conflict is the lack of communication between parties.[13] Because many conflicts are the result of misunderstandings and communication breakdowns, leaders can minimize the level of conflict within and between groups by improving their communication and listening skills, as well as spending time networking with others.[14]

Before we review specific negotiation tips and conflict resolution strategies, it is necessary to describe several aspects of conflict that can have an impact on the resolution process. First, the size of an issue (bigger issues are more difficult to resolve), the extent to which parties define the problem egocentrically (how much they have personally invested in the problem), and the existence of hidden agendas (unstated but important concerns or objectives) can all affect the conflict resolution process. Second, seeing a conflict situation in win–lose or either–or terms restricts the perceived possible outcomes to either total satisfaction or total frustration. A similar but less extreme variant is to see a situation in zero-sum terms. A zero-sum situation is one in which intermediate degrees of satisfaction are possible, but increases in one party's satisfaction inherently decrease the other party's satisfaction, and vice versa. Still another variant can occur when parties perceive a conflict as unresolvable. In such cases neither party gains at the expense of the other, but each continues to perceive the other as an obstacle to satisfaction.[15]

Is Conflict Always Bad?

So far we have described conflict as an inherently negative aspect of any group, team, committee, or organization. This certainly was the prevailing view of conflict among researchers during the 1930s and 1940s, and it probably also represents the way many people are raised today (that is, most people have a strong value of minimizing or avoiding conflict). However, researchers studying group effectiveness today have come to a different conclusion. Some level of conflict may help bolster innovation and performance. Conflict that enhances group productivity is viewed as useful, and conflict that hinders group performance is viewed as counterproductive.[16] Various possible positive and negative effects of conflict are listed in Highlight 16.1.

Along these lines, researchers have found that conflict can cause a radical change in political power,[17,18] as well as dramatic changes in organizational structure and design, group cohesiveness, and group or organizational effectiveness.[19,20] Nevertheless, it is important to realize that this current conceptualization of conflict is still somewhat limited in scope. For example, increasing the level of conflict within a group or team may enhance immediate performance but may also have a disastrous effect on organizational climate and turnover. Leaders may be evaluated in terms of many criteria, however, only one of which is group performance. Thus leaders should probably use criteria such as turnover and absenteeism rates and followers' satisfaction or organizational climate ratings in addition to measures of group performance when trying to determine whether conflict is good or bad. Leaders are cautioned against using group performance alone because this may not reveal the overall effects of conflict on the group or team.

Possible Effects of Conflict

HIGHLIGHT 16.1

Possible Positive Effects of Conflict	Possible Negative Effects of Conflict
Increased effort.	Reduced productivity.
Feelings get aired.	Decreased communication.
Better understanding of others.	Negative feelings.
Impetus for change.	Stress.
Better decision making.	Poorer decision making.
Key issues surface.	Decreased cooperation.
Critical thinking stimulated.	Political backstabbing.

Conflict Resolution Strategies

In addition to spending time understanding and clarifying positions, separating people from the problem, and focusing on interests, leaders can use five strategies or approaches to resolve conflicts. Perhaps the best way to differentiate between these five strategies is to think of conflict resolution in terms of two independent dimensions: cooperativeness versus uncooperativeness and assertiveness versus unassertiveness (see Figure 16.2). Parties in conflict vary in their commitment to satisfy the other's concerns, but they also vary in the extent to which they assertively stand up for their own concerns.[21] Thus conflict resolution can be understood in terms of how cooperative or uncooperative the parties are and how assertive or unassertive they are.

Using this two-dimension scheme, Thomas[22] described five general approaches to managing conflict:

1. *Competition* reflects a desire to achieve one's own ends at the expense of someone else. This is domination, also known as a win–lose orientation.
2. *Accommodation* reflects a mirror image of competition—entirely giving in to someone else's concerns without making any effort to achieve one's own ends. This is a tactic of appeasement.
3. *Sharing* is an approach that represents a compromise between domination and appeasement. Both parties give up something, yet both parties get something. Both parties are moderately, but incompletely, satisfied.
4. *Collaboration* reflects an effort to fully satisfy both parties. This is a problem-solving approach that requires the integration of each party's concerns.
5. *Avoidance* involves indifference to the concerns of both parties. It reflects a withdrawal from or neglect of any party's interests.

FIGURE 16.2
Five Conflict-Handling Orientations, Plotted According to the Parties' Desire to Satisfy Own and Other's Concerns

Source: Modified and reproduced by special permission of the Publisher, CPP, Inc., Mountain View, CA 94043 from the Thomas-Kilmann Conflict Mode Instrument by Kenneth W. Thomas and Ralph H. Kilmann. Copyright 1974, 2002 by CPP, Inc. All rights reserved. Further reproduction is prohibited without the Publisher's written consent.

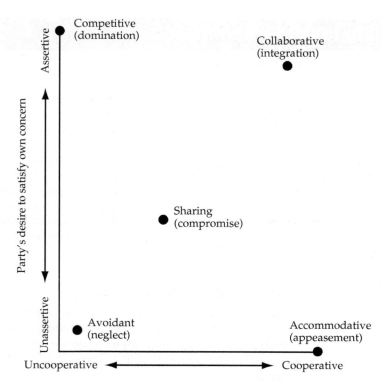

Does one of these approaches seem clearly better than the others to you? Each of them does, at least, reflect certain culturally valued modes of behavior.[23] For example, the esteem many people hold for athletic, business, and military heroes reflects our cultural valuation of competition. Valuation of a pragmatic approach to settling problems is reflected in the compromising approach. Cultural values of unselfishness, kindness, and generosity are reflected in accommodation, and even avoidance has roots in philosophies that emphasize caution, diplomacy, and turning away from worldly concerns. These cultural roots to each of the approaches to managing conflict suggest that no single one is likely to be right all the time. There probably are circumstances when each of the modes of conflict resolution can be appropriate. Rather than seeking a single best approach to managing conflict, it may be wisest to appreciate the relative advantages and disadvantages of all the approaches, as well as the circumstances when each may be most appropriate. A summary of experienced leaders' recommendations for when to use each strategy is presented in Highlight 16.2.

Finally, winning a negotiation at your counterpart's expense is likely to be only a short-term gain. Leaders should attempt to work out a resolution

Situations in Which to Use the Five Approaches to Conflict Management

HIGHLIGHT 16.2

COMPETING

1. When quick, decisive action is vital—such as emergencies.

2. On important issues where unpopular actions need implementing—cost cutting, enforcing unpopular rules, discipline.

3. On issues vital to company welfare when you know you're right.

4. Against people who take advantage of noncompetitive behavior.

COLLABORATING

1. To find an integrative solution when both sets of concerns are too important to be compromised.

2. When your objective is to learn.

3. To merge insights from people with different perspectives.

4. To gain commitment by incorporating concerns into a consensus.

5. To work through feelings that have interfered with a relationship.

COMPROMISING

1. When goals are important, but not worth the effort or potential disruption of more assertive modes.

2. When opponents with equal power are committed to mutually exclusive goals.

3. To achieve temporary settlements of complex issues.

4. To arrive at expedient solutions under time pressure.

5. As a backup when collaboration or competition is unsuccessful.

AVOIDING

1. When an issue is trivial or more important issues are pressing.

2. When you perceive no chance of satisfying your concerns.

3. When potential disruption outweighs the benefits of resolution.

4. To let people cool down and regain perspective.

5. When gathering information supersedes immediate decisions.

6. When others can resolve the conflict more effectively.

7. When issues seem tangential to or symptomatic of other issues.

ACCOMMODATING

1. When you find you are wrong—to allow a better position to be heard, to learn, and to show your reasonableness.

2. When issues are more important to others than yourself—to satisfy others and maintain cooperation.

3. To build social credits for later issues.

4. To minimize loss when you are outmatched and losing.

5. When harmony and stability are especially important.

6. To allow subordinates to develop by learning from mistakes.

Source: K. W. Thomas, "Toward Multidimensional Values in Teaching: The Example of Conflict Management," *Academy of Management Review* 2, no. 3 (1977), pp. 484–90. Copyright © 1977 Academy of Management, via Copyright Clearance Center.

How to Swim with Sharks

HIGHLIGHT 16.3

It is dangerous to swim with sharks, but not all sharks are found in the water. Some people may behave like sharks, and a best-selling book for executives written a few years ago took its title from that theme. However, an article appeared in the journal *Perspectives in Biology and Medicine* over three decades ago claiming to be a translated version of an essay written in France more than a century earlier for sponge divers. The essay notes that while no one wants to swim with sharks, it is an occupational hazard for certain people. For those who must swim with sharks, it can be essential to follow certain rules. See if you think the following rules for interacting with the sharks of the sea serve as useful analogies for interacting with the sharks of everyday life:

Rule 1: Assume any unidentified fish is a shark. Just because a fish may be acting in a docile manner does not mean it is not a shark. The real test is how it will act when blood is in the water.

Rule 2: Don't bleed. Bleeding will prompt even more aggressive behavior and the involvement of even more sharks. Of course, it is not easy to keep from bleeding when injured. Those who cannot do so are advised not to swim with sharks at all.

Rule 3: Confront aggression quickly. Sharks usually give warning before attacking a swimmer. Swimmers should watch for indications an attack is imminent and take prompt counteraction. A blow to the nose is often appropriate because it shows you understand the shark's intentions and will respond in kind. It is particularly dangerous to behave in an ingratiating manner toward sharks. People who once held this erroneous view often can be identified by a missing limb.

Rule 4: Get out of the water if anyone starts bleeding. Previously docile sharks may begin attacking if blood is in the water. Their behavior can become so irrational, even including attacking themselves, that it is safest to remove yourself entirely from the situation.

Rule 5: Create dissension among the attackers. Sharks are self-centered and rarely act in an organized fashion with other sharks. This significantly reduces the risk of swimming with sharks. Every now and then, however, sharks may launch a coordinated attack. The best strategy then is to create internal dissension among them because they already are quite prone to it; often sharks will fight among themselves over trivial or minor things. By the time their internal conflict is settled, sharks often have forgotten about their organized attack.

Rule 6: Never divert a shark attack toward another swimmer. Please observe this final item of swimming etiquette.

Source: V. Cousteau, "How to Swim with Sharks: A Primer," *Perspectives in Biology and Medicine,* Summer 1973, pp. 525–28. Copyright © 1973 University of Chicago Press. Reprinted with permission of The Johns Hopkins University Press.

by looking at long-term rather than short-term goals, and they should try to build a working relationship that will endure and be mutually trusting and beneficial beyond the present negotiation. Along these lines, leaders should always seek win–win outcomes that try to satisfy both sides' needs and continuing interests. It often takes creative problem solving to find new options that provide gains for both sides. Realistically, however, not all situations may be conducive to seeking win–win outcomes (see Highlight 16.3).

Negotiation

Negotiation is an approach that may help resolve some conflicts. The following negotiating tips, from Fisher and Ury,[24] include taking the time to prepare for a negotiating session; keeping the people and problems separate; and focusing on interests rather than on positions.

Prepare for the Negotiation

To successfully resolve conflicts, leaders may need to spend considerable time preparing for a negotiating session. Leaders should anticipate each side's key concerns and issues, attitudes, possible negotiating strategies, and goals.

Separate the People from the Problem

Fisher and Ury also advised negotiators to separate the people from the problem.[25] Because all negotiations involve substantive issues and relationships between negotiators, it is easy for these parts to become entangled. When that happens, parties may inadvertently treat the people and the problem as though they were the same. For example, a group of teachers angry that their salaries have not been raised for the fourth year in a row may direct their personal bitterness toward the school board president. However, reactions such as these are usually a mistake because the decision may be out of the other party's hands, and personally attacking the other party often makes the conflict even more difficult to resolve.

Leaders can do several things to separate the people from the problem. First, leaders should not let their fears color their perceptions of each side's intentions. It is easy to attribute negative qualities to others when we feel threatened. Similarly, it does no good to blame the other side for our own problems.[26] Even if this is justified, it is still usually counterproductive. Another thing leaders can do to separate the people from the problem is to communicate clearly. Earlier in this text we suggested techniques for active listening. Those guidelines are especially helpful in negotiating and resolving conflicts.

Focus on Interests, Not Positions

Another of Fisher and Ury's main points is to focus on interests, not positions. Focusing on interests depends on understanding the difference between interests and positions. Here is one example. Say Raoul has had the same reserved seats to the local symphony every season for several years, but he was just notified that he will no longer get his usual tickets. Feeling irate, he goes to the ticket office to complain. One approach he could take would be to demand the same seats he has always had; this would be his *position*. A different approach would be to find alternative seats that are just as satisfactory as his old seats were; this would be his *interest*. In negotiating, it is much more constructive to satisfy interests than to fight over positions. Furthermore, it is important to focus both on your counterpart's interests (not position) and on your own interests (not position).

Diagnosing Performance Problems in Individuals, Groups, and Organizations

In many ways leaders will be only as effective as the followers and teams they lead. Along these lines, one of the more difficult issues leaders must deal with is managing individuals or teams that are not performing up to expectations. What makes this issue even more difficult is that although the lack of performance may be obvious, the reasons for it may not. Leaders who correctly determine why a follower or team is exhibiting suboptimal performance are much more likely to implement an appropriate intervention to fix the problem. Unfortunately many leaders do not have a model or framework for diagnosing performance problems at work, and as a result many do a poor job of dealing with problem performers. The model in Figure 16.3 gives leaders a pragmatic framework for understanding why a follower or team may not be performing up to expectations and what the leader can do to improve the situation. This model maintains that performance is a function of expectations, capabilities, opportunities, and motivation and integrates concepts discussed in more detail earlier in this book.

The model is also a modification of earlier models developed by various experts.[27-29] Because it is a multiplicative rather than a compensatory model, a deficit in any component should result in a substantial decrement in performance that cannot be easily made up by increasing the other components. An example might help illuminate this point. Recently one of the authors was asked to help the manager of a nuclear power plant fix several safety and operational issues affecting the plant. Apparently many plant personnel did not feel they had to comply with governmental regulations regarding the proper use of safety equipment. An investigation into the problem revealed that the expectations for compliance were clear, everyone had been trained in the proper use of safety equipment, and the equipment was readily available. However, many personnel felt the equipment and procedures were a nuisance and unnecessary. The plant manager's initial attempt to rectify this problem was to run all plant personnel through a three-day nuclear safety training program. Much to the manager's surprise, the training program actually appeared to decrease safety compliance. This was due

FIGURE 16.3
A Model of Performance

Performance = f (Expectations $\times$ Capabilities $\times$ Opportunities $\times$ Motivation)

to the fact that the underlying issue was not expectations, capabilities, or opportunities but rather motivation. Even 30 days of training would not have helped motivation, which was the underlying barrier to performance. Because there were few if any positive or negative consequences for the staff's use or neglect of the equipment, the problem did not improve until the manager implemented a system of rewards and punishments for safety compliance. A more thorough explanation of the components of the model and what leaders can do to improve performance follows.

Expectations

Performance problems often occur because individuals or groups do not understand what they are supposed to do. In many instances talented, skilled groups accomplish the wrong objective because of miscommunication or sit idly while waiting for instructions that never arrive. It is the leader's responsibility to ensure that followers understand their roles, goals, performance standards, and the key metrics for determining success. More information about goal setting and clarifying team goals and roles can be found in the "Setting Goals" and "Building High-Performance Teams" sections of Chapter 11.

Capabilities

Just because followers understand what they are supposed to do does not necessarily mean they can do it. Sometimes followers and teams lack the capabilities needed to achieve a goal or perform above expectations. Abilities and skills are the two components that make up capabilities. Ability is really another name for raw talent, and includes such individual variables as athleticism, intelligence, creativity, and personality traits. As such, abilities are characteristics that are relatively difficult to change with training. Because abilities are relatively insensitive to training interventions, sending people who lack the required abilities to more training or motivating them to work harder will have relatively little impact on performance. Instead the best remedy for this situation is to select individuals with the abilities needed for performance.

Although followers may have the raw talent needed to perform a task, they still may lack the skills needed to perform at a high level. Such is the case with many athletic teams or musical groups at the beginning of the season or when a work group gets new equipment or responsibility for tasks it has no previous experience with. As discussed in the "Leadership Behavior" chapter (Chapter 7), skills consist of a well-defined body of knowledge and a set of related behaviors. Unlike abilities, skills are amenable to training, and leaders with high levels of relevant expertise may coach others in the development of skills, see that they are obtained in other ways on the job, or send their followers to training programs in order to improve their skill levels.

680   Part Four   *Focus on the Situation*

Opportunities

Performance can also be limited when followers lack the resources needed to get the job done. At other times followers may lack the opportunity to demonstrate acquired skills. Such is the case when passengers are hungry but flight attendants have no meals to pass out during the flight. In this situation the flight attendants could have high levels of customer service goals, capabilities, and motivation but will still not be able to satisfy customer needs. Leaders must ensure that followers and teams have the needed equipment, financial resources, and opportunities to exhibit their skills if they want to eliminate this constraint on performance.

Motivation

Many performance problems can be attributed to a lack of motivation. The critical issue here is whether followers or groups choose to perform or exhibit the level of effort necessary to accomplish a task. If this does not occur, the leader should first try to learn why people are unmotivated. Sometimes the task may involve risks the leader is not aware of. At other times individuals or groups may run out of steam to perform the task, or there may be few consequences for superior or unsatisfactory performance. Leaders have several options to resolve motivation problems in followers and teams. First, they can select followers who have higher levels of achievement or intrinsic motivation for the task. Second, they can set clear goals or do a better job of providing performance feedback. Third, they can reallocate work across the team or redesign the tasks to improve skill variety, task significance, and task identity. Fourth, they can restructure rewards and punishments so they are more closely linked to performance levels. See the "Motivation, Satisfaction, and Performance" chapter (Chapter 9) for more information about motivating followers.

Concluding Comments on the Diagnostic Model

In summary, this model provides an integrative framework for many of the topics affecting performance previously reviewed in this text. It reviews some of the factors that affect performance and suggests ideas for rectifying performance problems. However, this model addresses only follower, group, and organizational performance. Leaders need to remember that there are other desirable outcomes, too, such as organizational climate and job satisfaction, and that actions to increase performance (especially just in the short term) may adversely impact these other desirable outcomes.

Team Building at the Top

In certain ways, executive teams are similar to any other teams. For example, just about any group of senior executives that has faced a dire crisis and survived will note that teamwork was essential for its survival. In a nutshell, then, *when teamwork is critical,* all the lessons of the Chapter 11 section "Building High-Performance Teams" apply. More specifically, to really benefit from a team-building intervention, individual members must be comfortable with their own strengths and weaknesses and the strengths and weaknesses of their peers. But this raises a question: If all this is true, why do we include a separate section about team building for top teams? Because two important differences between most teams and "teams at the top" should be addressed.

Executive Teams Are Different

As opposed to other kinds of work teams, not all the work at the executive level requires all (or even any) of the team to be present. An example might help. In our research on teams we studied the air crews that fly the B-1 bomber. These are four-person teams comprising an aircraft commander, a copilot, an offensive systems officer, and a defensive systems officer. While each has individual responsibilities, in every bombing run we observed, it was essential that the team work together to accomplish the mission. They had all the components of a true team (complex and common goal, differentiated skills, interdependence), and no individual acting alone could have achieved success. But this is not always the case for executive teams.

As Katzenbach has observed,[30] many top leadership challenges do not require teamwork at all. Furthermore, many top leadership challenges that do constitute real team opportunities do not require or warrant full involvement by everyone who is officially on the team. In fact, an official "team at the top" rarely functions as a collective whole involving all the formal members. Thus the real trick for executive teams is to be able to apply both the technical individual skills that probably got the individuals to the team and the skills required for high-performance teamwork when a team situation presents itself.

Applying Individual Skills and Team Skills

There are two critical requirements if this is to work. First, leaders must have the diagnostic skills to discern whether a challenge involves an individual situation or a team situation. Then leaders must "stay the course" when a team situation is present. This means, for example, when pressure for results intensifies, not slipping back into the traditional modes of assigning work to an individual (such as one member of that top team), but rather allowing the team to complete the work *as a team.* Again, Katzenbach stated this clearly:

> Some leadership groups, of course, err in the opposite way, by attempting to forge a team around performance opportunities that do not call for a team approach. In fact, the increasing emphasis that team proponents place on "team-based organizations" creates real frustrations as top leadership groups try to rationalize good executive leadership instincts into

time-consuming team building that has no performance purpose. Catalyzing real team performances at the top does not mean replacing executive leadership with executive teams; it means being rigorous about the distinction between opportunities that require single-leader efforts and those that require team efforts—and applying the discipline that fits.[31]

To summarize this point, executives do not always need to perform as a team to be effective. But when they do need to perform as a team, the same lessons of team building discussed earlier can help enhance their team performance.

The second difference with executive teams is that they have an opportunity to enhance teamwork throughout their organization that few others have. It is our experience that *only the executive team can change organizational systems.* Recall that in Chapter 10 we described the Team Leadership Model and mentioned four systems issues critical to team performance. These systems were all located at the organizational level and consisted of reward systems, education systems, information systems, and control systems. The impact of these systems can be so pervasive across the entire organization that a small change in a system can have monumental impact in the organization. In a sense, then, the executive team has the power to do widespread team building in a manner different than we have discussed to this point. For example, consider the impact of changing a compensation system from an individual-based bonus plan to a team-based bonus plan.

Tripwire Lessons

Finally, our experience in working with executives has taught us that leaders at this level have important lessons to learn about team building at the top. Richard Hackman, in preparing the huge editorial task of having many people produce one coherent book (by his own admission, not necessarily the best of team tasks), assembled the various authors at a conference center. As one of the contributors, one of this text's authors (RCG) recalls the frustrating task of attempting to put together a simple checklist of steps to ensure that a team developed properly. As this arduous process dragged on and tempers flared, it became obvious that "Teamwork for Dummies" was never going to emerge. But something else did emerge. It became clear that *some behaviors leaders engaged in could virtually guarantee failure for their teams.* While not the intent, this experience yielded a worthwhile set of lessons. A condensed version of those lessons, labeled "trip wires" by Hackman, concludes our discussion of team building at the top.[32]

Trip Wire 1: Call the Performing Unit a Team but Really Manage Members as Individuals   One way to set up work is to assign specific responsibilities to specific individuals and then choreograph individuals' activities so their products coalesce into a team product. A contrasting strategy is to assign a team responsibility and accountability for an entire piece of work and let members decide among themselves how they will proceed to accomplish the work. Although either of these strategies can be effective, a choice must be made between them. A mixed model, in which people are told they are a team but are treated as individual performers with their own specific jobs to do, sends mixed signals to members, is likely to confuse everyone, and in the long run is probably untenable.

To reap the benefits of teamwork, a leader must actually build a team. Calling a set of people a team or exhorting them to work together is insufficient. Instead explicit action must be taken to establish the team's boundaries, to define the task as one for which members are collectively responsible and accountable, and to give members the authority to manage both their internal processes and the team's relations with external entities such as clients and co-workers. Once this is done, management behavior and organizational systems gradually can be changed as necessary to support teamwork.

Trip Wire 2: Create an Inappropriate Authority Balance   The exercise of authority creates anxiety, especially when a leader must balance between assigning a team authority for some parts of the work and withholding it for other parts. Because both managers and team members tend to be uncomfortable in such situations, they may collude to clarify them. Sometimes the result is the assignment of virtually all authority to the team—which can result in anarchy or a team that heads off in an inappropriate direction. At other times managers retain virtually all authority, dictating work procedures in detail to team members and, in the process, losing many of the advantages that can accrue from teamwork. In both cases the anxieties that accompany a mixed model are reduced, but at significant cost to team effectiveness.

Achieving a good balance of managerial and team authority is difficult. Moreover, merely deciding how much authority will be assigned to the group and how much will be retained by management is insufficient. Equally important are the domains of authority that are assigned and retained. Our findings suggest that managers should be unapologetic and insistent about exercising their authority over *direction*—the end states the team is to pursue—and over *outer-limit constraints on team behavior*—the things the team must always do or never do. At the same time managers should assign to the team full authority for the means by which it accomplishes its work—and then do whatever they can to ensure that team members understand and accept their responsibility and accountability for deciding how they will execute the work.

Few managerial behaviors are more consequential for the long-term existence of teams than those that address the partitioning of authority between managers and teams. It takes skill to accomplish this well, and this skill has emotional and behavioral as well as cognitive components. Just knowing the rules for partitioning authority is insufficient; leaders also need practice in applying those rules in situations where anxieties, including their own, are likely to be high. Especially challenging for managers are the early stages in the life of a team (when managers often are tempted to give away too much authority) and times when the going gets rough (when the temptation is to take authority back too soon). The management of authority relations with task-performing teams is much like walking on a balance beam, and our evidence suggests that it takes a good measure of knowledge, skill, and perseverance to keep from falling off.

Trip Wire 3: Assemble a Large Group of People, Tell Them in General Terms What Needs to Be Accomplished, and Let Them "Work Out the Details"   Traditionally, individually focused designs for work are plagued by constraining structures that have built up over the years to monitor and control employee behavior. When groups perform work, such structures tend to be viewed as unnecessary bureaucratic impediments to team functioning. Thus, just as managers sometimes (and mistakenly) attempt to empower teams by relinquishing all authority to them, so do some attempt to get rid of the dysfunctional features of existing organizational structures simply by taking down all the structures they can. Apparently the hope is that removing structures will release teams and enable members to work together creatively and effectively.

Managers who hold this view often wind up providing teams with less structure than they actually need. Tasks are defined only in vague, general terms. Group composition is unclear or fluid. The limits of the team's authority are kept deliberately fuzzy. The unstated assumption is that there is some magic in the group interaction process and that, by working together, members will evolve any structures the team needs.

This is a false hope; there is no such magic. Indeed, our findings suggest the opposite: groups that have appropriate structures tend to develop healthy internal processes, whereas groups with insufficient or inappropriate structures tend to have process problems. Worse, coaching and process consultation are unlikely to resolve these problems precisely because they are rooted in the team structure. For members to learn how to interact well within a flawed or underspecified structure is to swim upstream against a strong current.

Trip Wire 4: Specify Challenging Team Objectives, but Skimp on Organizational Supports   Even if a work team has clear, engaging direction and an enabling structure, its performance can go sour—or at least can fall below the group's potential—if the team is not well supported. Teams in high-commitment organizations fall victim to this trip wire when given "stretch" objectives but not the wherewithal to accomplish them; high initial enthusiasm soon changes into disillusionment.

It is no small undertaking to provide these supports to teams, especially in organizations designed to support work by individuals. Corporate compensation policy, for example, may make no provision for team bonuses and indeed may explicitly prohibit them. Human resource departments may be primed to identify individuals' training needs and provide first-rate courses to fill those needs, but training in team skills may be unavailable. Existing performance appraisal systems, which may be state-of-the-art for measuring individual contributions, are likely to be inappropriate for assessing and rewarding work done by teams. Information systems and control systems may give managers the data they need to monitor and control work processes, but they may be neither available nor appropriate for use by work teams. Finally, the material resources required for the work may have been prespecified by those who originally designed it, and there may be no procedure in place for a team to secure the special configuration of resources it needs to execute the particular performance strategy it has developed.

Aligning existing organizational systems with the needs of teams often requires managers to exercise power and influence upward and laterally in the organization. An organization set up to provide teams with full support for their work is noticeably different from one whose systems and policies are intended to support and control individual work, and many managers may find the prospect of changing to a group-oriented organization both unsettling and perhaps even vaguely revolutionary.

It is hard to provide good organizational support for task-performing teams, but generally it is worth the trouble. The potential of a well-directed, well-structured, well-supported team is tremendous. Moreover, stumbling over the organizational support trip wire is perhaps the saddest of all team failures. When a group is both excited about its work and all set up to execute it superbly, it is especially shattering to fail merely because the organizational supports required cannot be obtained. This is like being all dressed up and ready to go to the wedding only to have the car break down en route.

Trip Wire 5: Assume That Members Already Have All the Competence They Need to Work Well as a Team   Once a team is launched and operating under its own steam, managers sometimes assume their work is done. As we have seen, there are indeed some good reasons for giving a team ample room to go about its business in its own way; inappropriate or poorly timed managerial interventions have impaired the work of more than one group in our research. However, a strictly hands-off managerial stance also can limit a team's effectiveness, particularly when members are not already skilled and experienced in teamwork.

Punishment

In an ideal world, perhaps everyone would be dependable, achievement oriented, and committed to their organization's goals. However, leaders sometimes must deal with followers who are openly hostile or insubordinate, create conflicts among co-workers, do not work up to standards, or openly violate important rules or policies. In such cases leaders may need to administer punishment to change the followers' behavior.

Of all the different aspects of leadership, few are as controversial as punishment. Some of the primary reasons for this controversy stem from myths surrounding the use of punishment, as well as lack of knowledge of the effects of punishment on followers' motivation, satisfaction, and performance. This section is designed to shed light on the punishment controversy by (1) addressing several myths about the use of punishment, (2) reviewing research findings concerning the relationships between punishment and various organizational variables, and (3) giving leadership practitioners advice on how to properly administer punishment.

Myths Surrounding the Use of Punishment

We should begin by repeating the definition of punishment stated earlier in the book. Punishment is the administration of an aversive event or the withdrawal of a positive event or stimulus, which in turn decreases the likelihood that a particular behavior will be repeated.[33] Examples of punishment might include verbal reprimands, being moved to a less prestigious office, having pay docked, being fired, being made to run several laps around an athletic field, or losing eligibility for a sport entirely. We should note that, according to this definition, only those aversive events administered on a contingent basis are considered to be forms of punishment; aversive events administered on a noncontingent basis may constitute harsh and abusive treatment but are not punishment. Additionally, punishment appears to be in the eye of the beholder; aversive events that effectively change the direction, intensity, or persistence of one follower's behavior may have no effect on another's.[34] It is even possible that some followers may find the administration of a noxious event or the removal of a positive event to be reinforcing. For example, it is not uncommon for some children to misbehave if that increases the attention they receive from parents, even if the latter's behavior outwardly may seem punishing. (To the children, some parental attention of any kind may be preferable to no attention.) Similarly, some followers may see the verbal reprimands and notoriety they receive by being insubordinate or violating company policies as forms of attention. Because these followers enjoy being the center of attention, they may find this notoriety rewarding, and they may be even more likely to be insubordinate in the future.

We will examine some myths surrounding the use of punishment. Three of these myths were reviewed by Arvey and Ivancevich and include beliefs that the use of punishment results in undesirable emotional side effects on the part of the recipient, is unethical and inhumane, and rarely works anyway (that is, it seldom eliminates the undesirable behavior).[35]

B. F. Skinner's work in behavioral psychology lent support to the idea that punishment is ineffective and causes undesirable side effects. He based his conclusions on the unnatural behaviors manifested by rats and pigeons punished in various conditioning experiments.[36] Despite the dangers of generalizing from the behavior of rats to humans, many people accepted Skinner's contention that punishment is a futile and typically counterproductive tool for controlling human behavior. This was so despite the fact that considerable research regarding the emotional effects of punishment on humans did not support Skinner's claim.[37–39] Parke, for example, suggested that undesirable emotional side effects of punishment might occur only when punishment was administered indiscriminately or was particularly harsh.[40]

With respect to the myth that punishment is unethical or inhumane, it's been suggested that there is an ethical distinction between "future-oriented" and "past-oriented" punishment. Future-oriented punishment, intended to help improve behavior, may be effective in diminishing or eliminating undesirable behavior. Past-oriented punishment, or what we commonly think of as retribution, on the other hand, is simply a payback for past misdeeds. This sort of punishment may be more questionable ethically, especially when it is intended *only* as payback and not, say, as deterrent to others. Moreover, when considering the ethics of administering punishment, we must also consider the ethics of failing to administer punishment. The costs of failing to punish a potentially harmful behavior, such as unsafe workplace practices, may far outweigh those associated with the punishment itself.[41]

A third myth concerns the efficacy of punishment. Skinner[42] and others claimed that punishment did not result in permanent behavior change but instead only temporarily suppressed behavior.[43] Evidence to support this claim was found in one study in which incarcerated prisoners had a recidivism rate of 85 percent.[44] However, this high recidivism rate may be due to the fact that criminals may have received punishment primarily for retribution rather than for corrective purposes. Judicious administration of sanctions, combined with advice about how to avoid punishment in the future, may successfully eliminate undesirable behaviors on a more permanent basis.[45] Furthermore, it may be a moot point to argue (as Skinner did) that punishment only temporarily suppresses behavior; so long as sanctions for misdeeds remain in place, their impact on behavior should continue. In that regard, the "temporary" effects of punishment on behavior are no different from the "temporary" effects of reinforcement on behavior.

Punishment, Satisfaction, and Performance

It appears that properly administered punishment does not cause undesirable emotional side effects, is not unethical, and may effectively suppress undesirable behavior. However, we also should ask what effect punishment has on followers' satisfaction and performance. Most people probably would predict that leaders who use punishment frequently will have less satisfied and lower-performing followers. Interestingly, this does not appear to be the case—at least when punishment is used appropriately. Let us look more closely at this issue.

Several researchers have looked at whether leaders who administer punishment on a contingent basis also administered rewards on a contingent basis. Generally, researchers have found that there is a moderate positive relationship between leaders' contingent reward behaviors and contingent punishment behaviors.[46–48] There also are consistently strong negative correlations between leaders' contingent reward and noncontingent punishment behaviors. Thus leaders meting out rewards on a contingent basis are also more likely to administer punishment only when followers behave inappropriately or are not performing up to standards.

Keller and Szilagyi maintained that punishment can serve several constructive organizational purposes.[49,50] They said it can help clarify roles and expectations, as well as reduce role ambiguity. Several other authors have found that contingent punishment either is unrelated to followers' satisfaction with their supervisor or has a low positive relationship with it.[51,52] In other words, leaders who follow certain rules in administering punishment need not have dissatisfied subordinates. In fact, judicious and appropriate use of punishment by leaders may result in somewhat higher overall satisfaction of followers. These findings make sense when the entire work unit is considered; failing to use punishment when it seems called for in most followers' eyes may lead to perceptions of inequity, which may in turn reduce group cohesiveness and satisfaction.[53,54]

With respect to followers' work behaviors, Arvey and Jones reported that punishment has generally been found to reduce absenteeism and tardiness rates.[55] Nevertheless, the evidence about punishment's impact on performance appears mixed. Some authors report a strong positive relationship between punishment and performance,[56–59] whereas others found either no relationship between punishment and performance or a negative one.[60,61]

Despite such mixed findings, several points about the relationship between punishment and performance findings are worth noting. First, the levels of punishment as well as the manner in which it was administered across studies could have differed dramatically, and these factors could have affected the results. Second, of the studies reporting positive results, Schnake's experiment studying the vicarious effects of punishment is by far the most provocative. Schnake hired college students for a temporary job and, after several hours at work, publicly reduced the pay or threatened to reduce the pay of a confederate in the work group. As predicted, the more severe the punishment witnessed (either the threat of reduced pay or the reduction of pay), the higher the subsequent performance of other work group members.[62]

Although these findings demonstrated that merely witnessing rather than receiving punishment could increase performance, these results should be interpreted with caution. Because most of the individuals in the experiment did not know each other and had been working together only for several hours, there was probably not enough time for group cohesiveness or norms to develop. It is unclear whether members of cohesive groups or groups with strong norms would react in the same way if they observed another group member being punished. Third, one of the studies reporting less favorable punishment–performance results made an important point about the opportunities to punish. It examined the relationships between Little League coaches' behaviors and their teams' win–loss records. They found that coaches who punished more often had less successful teams. These coaches also, however, had less talented players and therefore had many more opportunities to use punishment. Coaches of successful teams had little if any reason to use punishment. Fourth, many behaviors that are punished may not have a direct link to job performance. For example, being insubordinate, violating company dress codes, and arriving late to meetings are all punishable behaviors that may not be directly linked to solving work-related problems or producing goods or services.[63]

Finally, almost all these studies implicitly assumed that punishment enhanced performance (by correcting problem behaviors), but Curphy and his associates were the only researchers who actually tested this assumption. They collected over 4,500 incidents of documented punishment and performance data from 40 identical organizations over a three-month period. (The punishment and performance data were collected monthly.) They found that low performance led to higher levels of punishment. Moreover, they found that inexperienced leaders administered almost twice as much punishment as experienced leaders. The authors hypothesized that inexperienced leaders used punishment (that is, relied on their coercive power) more frequently because, by being the newest arrivals to the organization, they lacked knowledge of the organizational norms, rules, and policies (expert power); had not yet established relationships with followers (referent power); and were severely limited in the rewards they could provide to followers (reward power).[64]

In summary, the research evidence shows that punishment can lead to positive organizational outcomes if administered properly. When administered on a contingent basis, it may help increase job satisfaction, may decrease role ambiguity and absenteeism rates, and, depending on the behaviors being punished, may improve performance. However, administering intense levels of punishment in a noncontingent or capricious manner can have a devastating effect on the work unit. Group cohesiveness may suffer, followers are likely to become more dissatisfied and less apt to come to work, and they may perform at a lower level in the long term. Thus learning how to properly administer punishment may be the key to maximizing the benefits associated with its use.

Administering Punishment

Usually leaders administer punishment to rectify some type of behavioral or performance problem at work. However, not every behavior or performance problem is punished, and leaders probably weigh several different factors before deciding whether to administer punishment. Green and Mitchell maintained that leaders' decisions concerning punishment depended on whether leaders made internal or external attributions about a subordinate's substandard performance. Leaders making internal attributions were more likely to administer punishment; leaders making external attributions were more likely to blame the substandard performance on situational factors beyond the follower's control.[65]

Attribution theory maintains that leaders weigh three factors when making internal or external attributions about a follower's substandard performance. Specifically, leaders would be more likely to make an internal attribution about a follower's substandard performance (and administer punishment) if the follower had previously completed the task before, if other followers had successfully completed the task, and if the follower had successfully completed other tasks in the past. Moreover, it was found that leaders were biased toward making internal attributions about followers' poor performance (the fundamental attribution error) and thus more likely to use punishment to modify a follower's behavior.[66,67]

Because leaders are biased toward making internal attributions about followers' substandard performance, leaders can administer punishment more effectively by being aware of this bias and getting as many facts as possible before deciding whether to administer punishment. Leaders also can improve the manner or skill with which they administer punishment by using certain tips, such as that punishment is administered most effectively when it focuses on the act, not the person.[68] Followers probably cannot change their personalities, values, or preferences, but they can change their behaviors. By focusing on specific behaviors, leaders minimize the threat to followers' self-concepts. Also, punishment needs to be consistent across both behaviors and leaders; the same actions need to have the same consequences across work groups, or feelings of inequity and favoritism will pervade the organization. One way to increase consistency of punishment is through the establishment of clearly specified organizational policies and procedures.

Administering punishment properly depends on effective two-way communication between the leader and follower. Leaders need to provide a clear rationale for punishment and indicate the consequences for unacceptable behavior in the future. Finally, leaders need to provide followers with guidance about how to improve. This guidance may entail role-modeling proper behaviors for followers, suggesting that followers take training courses, or giving followers accurate feedback about their behavior at work.[69]

Overall, it may be the manner in which punishment is administered, rather than the level of punishment, that has the greatest effect on followers' satisfaction and performance. Leaders need to realize that they may be biased toward administering punishment to rectify followers' substandard performance, and the best way to get around this bias is to collect as much information as possible before deciding whether to punish. By collecting the facts, leaders will be better able to focus on the act, not the person; be able to administer a punishment consistent with company policy; provide the rationale for the punishment; and give guidance to followers on how to improve.

A final caution that leaders need to be aware of concerns the reinforcing or rewarding nature of punishment. Behaviors that are rewarded are likely to be repeated. When leaders administer punishment and subsequently see improvement in a follower's behavior, the leaders will be rewarded and be more apt to use punishment in the future. Over time this may lead to an overreliance on punishment and an underemphasis on the other motivational strategies as means of correcting performance problems. Again, by collecting as much information as possible and by carefully considering the applicability of goal setting, job characteristics theory, and so on, to the problem, leaders may be able to successfully avoid having only one tool in their motivational toolkit.

End Notes

1. N. N. Tichy and N. Cardwell, *The Cycle of Leadership: How Great Companies Teach Their Leaders to Win* (New York: HarperBusiness, 2002).

2. G. J. Curphy, *The Role of the Supervisor Program for Andersen Corporation* (North Oaks, MN: Author, 2005).

3. J. Collins, *Good to Great* (New York: HarperCollins, 2001).

4. J. Krile, G. J. Curphy, and D. Lund. *The Community Leadership Handbook: Framing Ideas, Building Relationships, and Mobilizing Resources* (St. Paul, MN: Fieldstone Alliance, 2005).

5. K. W. Thomas and W. H. Schmidt, "A Survey of Managerial Interests with Respect to Conflict," *Academy of Management Journal* 19 (1976), pp. 315–18.

6. J. J. Morse and F. R. Wagner, "Measuring the Process of Managerial Effectiveness," *Academy of Management Journal* 21 (1978), pp. 23–35.

7. L. D. Brown, *Managing Conflict at Organizational Interfaces* (Reading, MA: Addison-Wesley, 1983).

8. W. G. Ouchi, *How American Business Can Meet the Japanese Challenge* (Reading, MA: Addison-Wesley, 1981).

9. T. J. Peters and R. H. Waterman, *In Search of Excellence* (New York: Harper & Row, 1982).

10. S. P. Robbins, *Organizational Behavior: Concepts, Controversies, and Applications* (Englewood Cliffs, NJ: Prentice Hall, 1986).

11. G. Yukl, *Leadership in Organizations*, 2nd ed. (Englewood Cliffs, NJ: Prentice Hall, 1989).

692 Part Four *Focus on the Situation*

12. M. F. R. Kets de Vries and D. Miller, "Managers Can Drive Their Subordinates Mad," in *The Irrational Executive: Psychoanalytic Explorations in Management,* ed. M. F. R. Kets de Vries (New York: International Universities Press, 1984).

13. Thomas and Schmidt, "A Survey of Managerial Interests with Respect to Conflict."

14. Yukl, *Leadership in Organizations.*

15. K. W. Thomas, "Conflict and Conflict Management," in *Handbook of Industrial and Organizational Psychology,* ed. M. D. Dunnette (Chicago: Rand McNally, 1976).

16. Robbins, *Organizational Behavior.*

17. B. M. Bass, *Leadership and Performance beyond Expectations* (New York: Free Press, 1985).

18. A. R. Willner, *The Spellbinders: Charismatic Political Leadership* (New Haven: Yale University Press, 1984).

19. N. C. Roberts and R. T. Bradley, "Limits of Charisma," in *Charismatic Leadership: The Elusive Factor in Organizational Effectiveness,* eds. J. A. Conger and R. N. Kanungo (San Francisco: Jossey-Bass, 1988), pp. 253–75.

20. R. M. Kanter, *The Change Masters* (New York: Simon & Schuster, 1983).

21. Thomas, "Conflict and Conflict Management."

22. Ibid.

23. K. W. Thomas, "Toward Multidimensional Values in Teaching: The Example of Conflict Management," *Academy of Management Review* 2, no. 3 (1977), pp. 484–90.

24. R. Fisher and W. Ury, *Getting to Yes* (Boston: Houghton Mifflin, 1981).

25. Ibid.

26. R. R. Blake, H. A. Shepard, and J. S. Mouton, *Managing Intergroup Conflict in Industry* (Houston, TX: Gulf, 1964).

27. J. P. Campbell, "The Cutting Edge of Leadership: An Overview," in *Leadership: The Cutting Edge,* eds. J. G. Hunt and L. L. Larson (Carbondale, IL: Southern Illinois University Press, 1977).

28. J. P. Campbell, R. A. McCloy, S. H. Oppler, and C. E. Sager, "A Theory of Performance," in *Frontiers in Industrial/Organizational Psychology and Personnel Selection,* eds. N. Schmitt and W. C. Borman (San Francisco: Jossey-Bass, 1993), pp. 35–70.

29. J. W. Boudreau and P. Ramstad, *Beyond HR: The New Science of Human Capital* (Boston, MA: Harvard Business School Press, 2007).

30. J. R. Katzenbach, *Teams at the Top* (Boston: Harvard Business School Press, 1998).

31. Ibid.

32. J. R. Hackman, *Groups That Work (and Those That Don't)* (San Francisco: Jossey-Bass, 1990).

33. R. D. Arvey and J. M. Ivancevich, "Punishment in Organizations: A Review, Propositions, and Research Suggestions," *Academy of Management Review* 5 (1980), pp. 123–32.

34. G. J. Curphy, F. W. Gibson, B. W. Asiu, C. P. McCown, and C. Brown, "A Field Study of the Causal Relationships between Organizational Performance, Punishment, and Justice," working paper, 1992.

35. R. D. Arvey and J. M. Ivancevich, "Punishment in Organizations: A Review, Propositions, and Research Suggestions," *Academy of Management Review* 5 (1980), pp. 123–32.

36. B. F. Skinner, *The Behavior of Organisms* (New York: Appleton-Century-Crofts, 1938).

37. A. E. Kazdin, *Behavior Modification in Applied Settings* (Homewood, IL: Dorsey, 1975).

38. J. M. Johnston, "Punishment of Human Behavior," *American Psychologist* 27 (1972), pp. 1033–54.

39. R. L. Solomon, "Punishment," *American Psychologist* 19 (1964), pp. 239–53.

40. R. D. Parke, "Some Effects of Punishment on Children's Behavior," in *The Young Child: Reviews of Research,* Vol. 2, ed. W. W. Hartup (Washington, DC: National Association for the Education of Young Children, 1972).

41. Arvey and Ivancevich, "Punishment in Organizations."

42. B. F. Skinner, *The Behavior of Organisms* (New York: Appleton-Century-Crofts, 1938).

43. F. Luthans, *Organizational Behavior,* 5th ed. (New York: McGraw-Hill, 1992).

44. J. Huberman, "Discipline without Punishment," *Harvard Business Review,* July–August 1964, p. 62.

45. Arvey and Ivancevich, "Punishment in Organizations."

46. R. D. Arvey, G. A. Davis, and S. M. Nelson, "Use of Discipline in an Organization: A Field Study," *Journal of Applied Psychology* 69 (1984), pp. 448–60.

47. P. M. Podsakoff and W. D. Todor, "Relationships between Leader Reward and Punishment Behavior and Group Process and Productivity," *Journal of Management* 11 (1985), pp. 55–73.

48. S. Strasser, R. C. Dailey, and T. S. Bateman, "Attitudinal Moderators and Effects of Leaders' Punitive Behavior," *Psychological Reports* 49 (1981), pp. 695–98.

49. R. T. Keller and A. D. Szilagyi, "Employee Reactions for Leader Reward Behavior," *Academy of Management Journal* 19 (1976), pp. 619–27.

50. R. T. Keller and A. D. Szilagyi, "A Longitudinal Study of Leader Reward Behavior, Subordinate Expectancies, and Satisfaction," *Personnel Psychology* 11 (1978), pp. 119–29.

51. Arvey et al. "Use of Discipline in an Organization."

52. P. M. Podsakoff, W. D. Todor, R. A. Grover, and V. L. Huber, "Situational Moderators of Leader Reward and Punishment Behaviors: Fact or Fiction?" *Organizational Behavior and Human Performance* 34 (1984), pp. 21–63.

53. G. J. Curphy, F. W. Gibson, B. W. Asiu, C. P. McCown, and C. Brown, "A Field Study of the Causal Relationships between Organizational Performance, Punishment, and Justice," working paper, 1992.

54. G. H. Dobbins and J. M. Russell, "The Biasing Effects of Subordinate Likeableness on Leaders' Responses to Poor Performance," *Personnel Psychology* 39 (1986), pp. 759–77.

55. R. D. Arvey and A. P. Jones, "The Use of Discipline in Organizational Settings: A Framework for Future Research," in *Research in Organizational Behavior,* Vol. 7, eds. L. L. Cummings and B. M. Staw (Greenwich, CT: JAI, 1985), pp. 367–408.

56. J. M. Beyer and H. M. Trice, "A Field Study in the Use and Perceived Effects of Discipline in Controlling Work Performance," *Academy of Management Journal* 27 (1984), pp. 743–64.

57. D. Katz, N. Maccoby, G. Gurin, and L. G. Floor, *Productivity, Supervision, and Morale among Railroad Workers* (Ann Arbor, MI: University of Michigan, Survey Research Center, Institute of Social Research, 1951).

58. Podsakoff and Todor, "Relationships between Leader Reward and Punishment Behavior and Group Process and Productivity."

59. M. E. Schnake, "Vicarious Punishment in a Work Setting," *Journal of Applied Psychology* 71 (1986), pp. 343–45.

60. Curphy, et al., "A Field Study of the Causal Relationships between Organizational Performance, Punishment, and Justice."

61. B. Curtis, R. E. Smith, and F. L. Smoll, "Scrutinizing the Skipper: A Study of Behaviors in the Dugout," *Journal of Applied Psychology* 64 (1979), pp. 391–400.

62. Schnake, "Vicarious Punishment in a Work Setting."

63. Curphy et al., "A Field Study of the Causal Relationships between Organizational Performance, Punishment, and Justice."

64. Ibid.

65. S. G. Green and T. R. Mitchell, "Attributional Processes of Leaders in Leader–Member Interactions," *Organizational Behavior and Human Performances* 23 (1979), pp. 429–58.

66. T. R. Mitchell, S. G. Green, and R. E. Wood, "An Attributional Model of Leadership and the Poor Performing Subordinate: Development and Validation," in *Research in Organizational Behavior,* eds. B. M. Staw and L. L. Cummings (Greenwich, CN: JAI, 1981), pp. 197–234.

67. T. R. Mitchell and R. E. Wood, "Supervisors' Responses to Subordinate Poor Performance: A Test of an Attributional Model," *Organizational Behavior and Human Performance* 25 (1980), pp. 123–38.

68. Arvey and Ivancevich, "Punishment in Organizations."

69. Ibid.

Name Index

Note: Page numbers followed by *n* indicate source notes and endnotes.

Aberman, R., 221, 224, 225, 239*n*108–109
Abraham, L. M., 390*n*137
Abrahams, M., 84*n*74
Acton, Lord, 116, 358
Adair, R., 320, 381*n*12
Adams, J., 611*n*150
Adams, S., 620
Agle, B., 184*n*70, 607*n*93, 609*n*132
Ahearne, M., 387*n*99
Alberti, R. E., 291, 314*n*18
Albrecht, K., 315*n*38
Alderfer, C. P., 438*n*34
Aldrich, H. E., 521*n*34
Alexander the Great, 617
Alkexander, C. S., 181*n*16, 181*n*19
Allen, D., 556*n*6
Allen, P., 601
Allen, T., 508
Allen, T. D., 84*n*71–72, 84*n*76–77
Allinger, G. M., 39*n*28, 233*n*4
Allport, G. W., 234*n*19
Amabile, T. M., 215–216, 238*n*83–84, 239*n*95–97, 345
Ambrose, M. L., 390*n*146
Amichai-Hamburger, Y., 610*n*135
Amin, I., 617, 620
Anchor, S., 389*n*135
Ancona, D., 253, 274*n*41
Anders, G., 380*n*1
Andersen, J. A., 183*n*63
Anderson, L. S., 386*n*83
Anderson, M. H., 610*n*146
Anderson, N., 236*n*58
Ang, S., 556*n*17
Antonakis, J., 197, 234*n*13, 609*n*124, 611*n*155
Antonioni, D., 275*n*65
Apotheker, L., 633
Argyris, C., 54–55, 81*n*20, 210
Aristotle, 187
Armenakis, A. A., 389*n*122
Armstrong, D. J., 431–432, 440*n*69

Armstrong, L., 159
Aron, D., 433, 440*n*73
Arthaud-Day, M. L., 382*n*14
Arthur, M. B., 583, 607*n*97, 608*n*109
Arthur, W., Jr., 83*n*49
Arvey, R. D., 236*n*46, 386*n*81, 387*n*94, 390*n*137, 686, 688, 692*n*33, 693*n*35, 693*n*41, 693*n*45–46, 693*n*51, 694*n*55, 694*n*68–69
Arvidson, D., 83*n*46
Aryee, S., 384*n*35
Ash, R. A., 274*n*38
Ashe, M. K., 346
Ashkanasy, N. M., 240*n*124
Asiu, B. W., 693*n*34, 693*n*53, 694*n*60, 694*n*63–64
Asplund, J., 205
Astin, A. W., 41*n*62
Atkins, P. W. B., 275*n*59
Atkinson, J. W., 343–344, 385*n*53
Attila the Hun, 617
Atwater, L. E., 276*n*78–79, 556*n*11
Avey, J. B., 82*n*35
Avolio, B. J., 70, 82*n*35, 112*n*23, 164, 166, 181*n*9, 183*n*45–46, 183*n*48, 183*n*51, 183*n*54, 183*n*56–59, 254, 583–584, 595, 597, 606*n*77, 606*n*81, 606*n*83, 607*n*98, 608*n*108, 608*n*110, 608*n*116, 609*n*119, 610*n*134, 611*n*155, 611*n*156
Azar, B., 237*n*66

Back, K. (Kate), 296
Back, K. (Ken), 296
Bacon, F., 58
Badin, I. J., 437*n*6
Baer, J., 237*n*74
Baker, S. D., 40*n*32–33
Baker, V. L., 181*n*1, 182*n*42
Baldrica, A., 7, 112*n*37, 338, 604*n*37, 625, 626, 641, 643, 647

Baldwin, B., 156
Baldwin, S., 4
Baldwin, T. T., 382*n*14
Balkundi, P., 609*n*133
Ballmer, S., 510
Baltzell, E. D., 40*n*30
Banaji, M. R., 182*n*25, 182*n*31–32, 182*n*34
Bandura, A., 162, 164, 182*n*40–41, 183*n*43–44, 440*n*61
Ban Ki-Moon, 249
Banks, W., 401, 438*n*26
Bardes Mawritz, M., 662*n*23
Barling, J., 597, 605*n*59, 611*n*160–161
Barlow, C. B., 40*n*45
Barnes, C. D., 182*n*38
Barnes, F., 147*n*29
Barnett, R. C., 273*n*27
Barney, M., 194
Barnum, D. F., 512, 522*n*70
Bar-On, R., 221, 222, 223, 224–225, 239*n*107, 240*n*118
Barrick, M. R., 234*n*22, 234*n*24, 385*n*55, 388*n*116
Bartol, K. M., 239*n*94, 387*n*97
Basadur, M., 238*n*89
Bass, B. M., 5, 39*n*12, 40*n*35, 111*n*21, 112*n*23, 146*n*7, 147*n*14, 273*n*20, 283, 313*n*4, 314*n*21, 437*n*10, 475*n*1, 475*n*9, 476*n*18, 476*n*30, 477*n*34, 477*n*36, 519*n*9, 520*n*21, 521*n*39, 521*n*41, 521*n*44, 521*n*46, 521*n*50, 583–584, 595–599, 602*n*1, 605*n*70, 606*n*75, 606*n*77–78, 606*n*83, 607*n*98, 608*n*116–117, 609*n*118, 609*n*121, 611*n*156, 692*n*17
Bateman, T. S., 693*n*48
Battista, M., 274*n*38
Batz, P. H., 273*n*27
Bauer, T. N., 556*n*15

Subject Index

Credits